Building a Liberal Europe: the ALDE Project

Graham Watson MEP

To Alice,

to say how pleased I am that you take an interest in the Liberal Democrats!

With liberal good wishes,

Graham Watson

Other books on the European Parliament:

The European Parliament, 7th edition

By *Richard Corbett, Francis Jacobs* and *Michael Shackleton*

Since 1990 this has been the standard textbook on the Parliament covering every aspect of how it is elected, organised and does its work. *"An indispensable guide... both an excellent primer for students and a reliable reference tool for practitioners"*, Hans-Gert Pöttering, President of the European Parliament in 2007-09. (2007, ISBN 978-0-9551144-7-2)

Six Battles that Shaped Europe's Parliament

By *Julian Priestley*

The former Secretary-General of the European Parliament describes six turning points in Parliament's struggle for power and recognition. *"One could hardly imagine a better commentator on the evolution of the European Parliament than Julian Priestley "*, Jean-Claude Juncker, Prime Minister of Luxembourg. (2008, ISBN 978-0-9556202-3-2)

Wreckers or Builders?: A History of Labour Members of the European Parliament 1979-1999

By *Anita Pollack*

"At last we have a history of Labour MEPs... a well-researched record – warts and all", Neil Kinnock, former Labour Party leader and European Commissioner (2009, ISBN 978-0-9556202-9-4)

For full details of these and other books, please visit

www.johnharperpublishing.co.uk

Building a Liberal Europe
The ALDE Project

Graham Watson MEP

JOHN HARPER
PUBLISHING

Building a Liberal Europe: the ALDE Project

Published by John Harper Publishing
27 Palace Gates Road
London N22 7BW, United Kingdom.

www.johnharperpublishing.co.uk

ISBN 978-0-9564508-1-4

Printed and Bound in Malta at Gutenberg Press.

To the Liberal Democrats of South West England and Gibraltar, who empowered me to play my part in this story

In memory of Russell Johnston (1932-2008)

TABLE OF CONTENTS

Preface

This book is not just the story of how the Liberal ranks in the European Parliament were more than doubled in number[1] within the space of five years. It is also about how the largest centre party in the European Parliament's history – the Alliance of Liberals and Democrats for Europe – used its power to shape the policies of the European Union[2] in the first decade of the new century.

I believe the achievements of the Alliance of Liberals and Democrats for Europe, an alliance which started in the European Parliament but was to be replicated on the EU's Committee of the Regions and on the Parliamentary Assembly of the Council of Europe, to be important. I have endeavoured in this book to provide an account of what I judge to be the main achievements at EU level, while also giving a flavour of the events and emotions of the period and the personalities involved. It is at least as much a personal memoir as a contribution to academic study, but I hope it may nonetheless assist the student of the European Union.

The ALDE is a substantially greater force than was its predecessor, the European Liberal Democrat and Reform group (ELDR). As I told delegates to the ELDR Party[3] congress in Budapest on 13 October 2006: 'We need no longer live like the hare in winter, turning white and vanishing against the snow[4]. Fellow Liberals, we can be proud of what we achieve. Share and shout about our successes. Live the life of Liberalism.'

The life of organised Liberalism in Europe had been in some doubt. It was dealt a serious blow by the First World War and the events of the second almost killed it stone dead. Yet the re-evaluation of Liberal ideas after the war – by the likes of Karl Popper and Isaiah Berlin, John Maynard Keynes and Ralf Dahrendorf, Luigi Einaudi and Raymond Aron and, from across the Atlantic, John Rawls and John Kenneth Galbraith – breathed into it a new life. Those ideas are still spreading. The potential for further growth of the European Liberal centre remains greater than at any point in the last 100 years.

As leader of a political group in the European Parliament I became aware of how my task was similar to that of the conductor of an orchestra. Very little of the music we played was new: the scores had been written by Liberal

---

1 From 50 MEPs (of a total of 626) in 2002 to 106 (of 732) in 2007.

2 There is an important legal distinction between the terms 'European Communities' and 'European Union'. In this book however, for ease of reading, I use 'European Union' (EU) to cover all aspects of co-operation within the framework established by the Treaty of Rome and its amending treaties.

3 The ELDR group in Parliament no longer exists. The ELDR party, however, continues. Its MEPs sit together in Parliament with the MEPs of the European Democratic Party (EDP) in the ALDE group.

4 Borrowed from Scottish poet Andrew Greig 'The Hare in Winter'.

philosophers down the ages. But it was my task to find new expressions of time honoured tunes, to accentuate some of the themes of our Liberal legacy and downplay others. I was fortunate to conduct some virtuoso players.

Though I was not finally to see through to the end my intention to run for the presidency of the European Parliament, since the outcome of the 2009 European election and the political alliances formed thereafter did not make it a realistic course to pursue, I have no doubt that our campaign was given credibility by the public perception of the strength of our Alliance; nor that our Alliance benefited from having a candidate to demonstrate and personify its new found influence. Journalists now invariably refer to ' the three big groups' when writing or speaking of the main political parties in Parliament; previously it was only ever of two.

Leading the Liberal Democrat group in the European Parliament was a great honour, normally a pleasure but occasionally a difficult and a thankless task. In the more difficult periods I was sustained by the friendship and support of many loyal colleagues and staff and by the sense of mission which makes politics more a vocation than a profession. I feel too that despite having doubled the size of the group we managed to retain a sense of belonging[5] which exceeds that in the other major political groups. I believe one of my most important and enduring contributions to have been in building a stronger sense of political family among the national political parties which form our alliance.

I am fortunate to have led the European Parliament's Liberal group in propitious conditions. The biggest political event of the last half-century, the fall of Europe's iron curtain, had rearranged the geopolitical map of our continent. Simultaneously, the challenges of a new global age – world population growth and migratory patterns, energy provision and climate change, cross-border violence and lawlessness – called for political thinking and responses which transcended the boundaries of the former century's nation states.

Europe's hour had come, and plenty of its politicians were found wanting. Conservatism and Christian Democracy were not well equipped to cope with the switch from traditional left-right linear politics to an axis whose hinge was the response to global pressures; if it was now a case of choosing to raise or lower the drawbridge of fortress Europe, many on the right sought solace in a new nationalism or an old religious orthodoxy. There were 'drawbridge up' politicians on the left too. Socialists not only lacked ideological maps for the new terrain; many believed arrogantly that experienced travellers needed no maps. Protectionism and other forms of opposition to 'globalisation' found many adherents on the left. Others sought an elusive 'third way' which looked increasingly like the international liberal capitalism of one hundred years before. Both left and right were deeply divided.

Liberals, by contrast – hitherto divided on the linear axis between economic Liberal and social Liberal approaches, splitting the centre between left and right – were now increasingly united. Committed to seek supranational solutions to supranational demands, they drew on the three traditional currents of their creed – classical Liberalism, economic Liberalism and social Liberalism – and their inspiration by the new environmental dimension of politics to influ-

---

5   This was perhaps most in evidence at the annual Christmas party and (latterly) the annual summer barbecue. The former was ably compered first by Dirk Sterckx MEP and later by Jorgo Chatzimarkakis MEP.

ence politics to an extent previously unimaginable in the fifty year history of the European project. All that was needed was to seize the moment.

In this account of fifteen years in the life of Liberals in the European Parliament I do not attempt to cover the work that we did in promoting Liberalism worldwide beyond the EU. That work is an area in which I participated enthusiastically and to which I committed a considerable proportion of my time, as did a number of my colleagues. Indeed I believe that without the work the European Parliament's Liberals did to promote Liberalism in Africa, Asia, Latin America and beyond, our ideology would be far less well represented today. We were not alone. We worked alongside Liberal MPs from national parliaments, our counterparts in the Council of Europe and bodies such as the Liberal International and the Friedrich Naumann Foundation. Nonetheless Liberal MEPs brought a unique and important element to the promotion of Liberalism worldwide. The work of Jules Maaten and Istvan Szent-Ivanyi in Asia deserves special mention, as does the work of Johan van Hecke in Africa, the work of Cecilia Malmstrom in Central America and that of Jan Kulakowski in South America. During the period 1994-2009 I paid over 20 visits to Asia, 11 to Africa, one to Central America and eight to North America. I believe that the Liberal networks established in Africa, Asia and Latin America benefited substantially from our attention. We certainly benefited from theirs and from the many deep friendships established, which endure.

This book spans a period which saw five major reviews of the EU treaties. If I spare the reader the details of each new treaty development in a way which some may consider excessively sketchy, it is because these have been exhaustively catalogued elsewhere[6]. And if I labour the descriptions of two events – the fall of the Santer Commission in 1999 and the composition of the Barroso Commission in 2004 – it is because they were truly extraordinary even by the standards of a Parliament which is itself extraordinary.

Little has been written about political parties and ideology at EU level. Why? Because the formation of EU-wide political parties, in any real sense, is so recent. Though transnational federations of parties in Europe's (and indeed latterly, the democratic world's) main political families existed for most of the twentieth century, these parties had little real function until the advent of direct elections to the European Parliament in the nine-country EU of 1979. And even after five sets of elections, in which the EU-wide parties each agreed a manifesto, the reality was that the European elections in 1999 still consisted essentially of different national campaigns in each of the fifteen member states. The right of EU citizens to vote and to stand as candidates in European elections in their country of residence (even if different from the country which issued their passport) was established during this period. Electors were invited to choose between candidates carrying national party labels from national, or in some cases sub-national, lists. At EU level the political families were increasingly well organised, their meetings increasingly regular and their parliamentary groups in the EP acting more and more as the driving force for cross-border ideological co-ordination in search of common positions for votes in Parliament. Yet it was not until December 2003 that a statute for EU-wide political parties was agreed, allowing each party a small taxpayer-funded sub-

6   In the works of my colleague Andrew Duff MEP and others.

sidy to maintain a European HQ[7]; and another four years elapsed before a fund was established in the EU budget to which each party could apply for political education work. Unlike Washington DC, in Brussels there was little private money chasing political parties in a quest for influence. Some argue that only the election of a percentage of MEPs on EU-wide electoral lists will bring the Brussels-based political parties fully into their own. Such a development is currently foreseen in discussion documents in the European Parliament but will not see the light of day before 2014 at the earliest.

I do not discuss in this book the question of voter participation in European elections. Many eminent academic studies have dealt with the public perception of European elections as 'second order' elections[8]. I agree with the remark of the European Commission's president-designate Barroso to the newly elected European Parliament in July 2004 that ' the biggest challenge we face is not the euro-scepticism of the few, but the euro-apathy of the many'. In my experience, however, if people in democracies are deeply discontented they vote in impressively large numbers.

Nonetheless, in the period covered by this study, Europe's political parties became better established. They gravitated around a European Parliament where (from 1994) considerable power was exercised. In Parliament during that time the mainstream right-wing MEPs were led by Belgian Wilfried Martens until 1999, German Hans-Gert Poettering until 2007 and then by Frenchman Joseph Daul; the Socialists were led by English MEP Pauline Green (1994-99), Spanish MEP Enrique Baron-Crespo (1999-2004) and then by Germany's Martin Schulz. I had the honour of succeeding Gijsbert de Vries (1994-98) and Patrick Cox (1998-2001) in leading the Liberal Democrat MEPs, first (2002-04) in the European Liberal Democrat and Reform Party and then (2004-09) in the new Alliance of Liberals and Democrats for Europe.

One challenge I have faced in writing this account is the absence of natural breaks or periods around which one can structure a history. For the parliamentarian like myself, the end of a five-year mandate and the start of a new mandate provides a natural break; and most parliamentary offices come up for re-election half way through the five-year cycle, including those of the political group leaders, thus dividing it into two halves. The rhythm of the EP's annual calendar – technically from January to December but for most purposes between our summer breaks, i.e. from late August to mid July – provides an unsatisfactory pattern but nonetheless one which influences MEPs' thinking. The presidency of the European Council (the chamber in which the member state governments are represented) has – for most of the period under review[9]

---

7 Hitherto their secretariats had been provided by and co-located with the parliamentary groups in the EP.

8 See, for example, the work by Yves Meny of the European University Institute and the work by Richard Sinnott of the University of Dublin.

9 This was not always the case. The European Council did not come into existence until 1974. It was not until 1986 that it was mentioned in a treaty. For many years it met only rarely, to hold informal exchanges of views. For the first four years of the period under review it met formally only twice a year, in June and December, adding a March 'economic policy' meeting from 1999 and increasingly regular formal autumn summits thereafter, bringing the norm up to four every year. From 2007 the number of European Council meetings grew to deal with the economic crisis. In February 2010 the first full time president of the Council, Herman van Rompuy, spoke of 'up to ten' meetings of the European Council every year. The Lisbon Treaty formally recognised the European Council as a Community institution.

– rotated every six months, with a new country taking the helm on 1 January and on 1 July each year, and this has an impact on our debates as each country tries to make its mark by highlighting particular concerns. Moreover, since Parliament receives statements from Council and Commission and debates both the preparation and the outcome of each European Council meeting these also serve to provide a chronological record of EU developments. The five-year mandate of the European Commission, which drafts our laws, does not coincide precisely with that of Parliament or Council, but nonetheless influences the work of both. Around all of these I have loosely structured this story.

My presidency of Parliament's Liberal group stretched from the half way point of the fifth legislature (January 2002) to the end of the sixth[10] (July 2009), the main period covered in this account. Nonetheless and for completeness I write also about the seven and a half years I served in Parliament prior to assuming the presidency of my group and briefly – and painfully incompletely, but by way of introduction – about the Liberal group in the fifteen years of the directly elected Parliament prior to my election.

Perhaps the most difficult aspect of writing a book about the achievements of many Liberals has been the growing awareness of how incomplete is my own perspective. For my first five years in parliament I served as a full member of the economic and monetary affairs committee, since the single market and the creation of a single currency struck me as the most interesting topics of that period, and as a substitute member of the budgets committee (on which I concentrated most of my energies in the first year, since I knew that to understand any level of government one needs to know how it raises and spends its money). In my second mandate, with the chance to chair a committee, I chose justice and home affairs since the Amsterdam Treaty had laid the basis for a massive expansion of European co-operation in that area. During my seven and a half years as leader of Parliament's Liberal group I did little, if any, committee work. And since then I have joined the foreign affairs committee because the Lisbon Treaty envisages a concentration of the Union's new development in foreign and security policy. Our Union is now so vast, however – geographically and politically – that one cannot hope to follow all developments.

I am aware that much more could be written about some aspects of Liberals' contribution to the EU's work. The work of colleagues on Parliament's budget committee has been particularly important and of course ideologically driven; of particular note have been the annual budgets steered through Parliament by Liberal MEPs Laurens Jan Brinkhorst in 1997, Jan Mulder in 2004 and Kyosti Virrankoski in 2008. Agriculture and fisheries policy have been central concerns of the European Union, though Parliament's role in policy formation has hitherto mainly been advisory. The work of colleagues in legal affairs and some other areas has been important and is insufficiently covered here. If I have perhaps over-indulged those who have worked on economic policy, on justice and home affairs, on transport and environment and on foreign policy it is because these have been the areas where Liberals have made the greatest ideological input to EU developments and the most obvious impact on the outcome of votes.

---

10 These legislatures are numbered since 1979. An indirectly elected assembly existed before this.

I fear, too, that some members may have been unfairly overlooked. To the 'ballast' members – those who see their role as providing stability and speak only when they have something important to say – a leader owes much. Colleagues such as Charles Goerens, Elena Vaz da Silva, Toomas Savi, Filiz Hyusmenova and Jean-Marie Beaupuy contributed greatly by the weight of their presence. Some others were as predictable as they were voluble.

European Liberals have been described as 'an important, albeit under-studied European political family' [11]. I hope that this work will go some way to reducing the size of this lacuna.

My primary source materials have been the official records of Parliament and the European Council; my personal diary, erratically kept and for some periods lost; and the weekly email newsletter I wrote to constituents throughout my time as leader of the EU's Liberal Democrat MEPs. I have also referred to a detailed appointments diary covering the whole period since 1996, thanks to having reverted to a Filofax after numerous electronic calendar breakdowns in the late 1990s. Moreover I have retained most of the set-piece speeches I have made beyond Parliament, some of them having been published alongside parliamentary interventions in two volumes of speeches covering the periods 1998 to 2003 and 2002 to 2006, which have served to augment this account.

I am not naturally gregarious and thus I have not spent much time quizzing colleagues about their experiences and developments in their chosen areas of policy, though many were kind enough to provide fulsome answers to a short questionnaire I sent them to assist me in my writing. In retrospect I am struck by how little time I spent even as leader of my political group in following the details of EU policy making; most of a leader's time, perhaps inevitably, is spent in representational activities.

Having a brain with sub-optimal database retrieval software I have relied also on the help of the recollections and notes of friends and colleagues. I am indebted to them, as I am to the staff of the ALDE group who served me ably throughout the period and were so kind as to assist me in retrieving information thereafter. Special thanks are due to Alexander Beels and to Niccolo Rinaldi, who served me as secretary general and deputy secretary general during my time as leader. Fausta Lucentini, who has catalogued the records of the Liberal group, has been a joy to work with; I am grateful too to the staff of the European Parliament's library. My private offices, both in Parliament and in my constituency, have been staffed by a series of talented and devoted people who have also helped in the writing of this book. Thanks are due to Frederica Findlater, Gauri Khandekar and Amy Busby, three stagiaires, who have assisted in my research.

Special thanks are also due to my wife and my children, who tolerated me with good grace during my long absences on parliamentary business and through the frustrations I displayed while collating this memoir.

Any errors in this book are mine and mine alone.

11   Lieven de Winter 'Liberalism and Liberal Parties in the EU', Ed.

Introduction: 1979 – 1994

A word of explanation

The European Union has two houses of parliament. The prime chamber in the legislature is the Council, in which each member state is represented by a government minister[12]. Citizens are also represented in the European Parliament, the second chamber, by members whom they elect directly from each member state in broad proportion to its population. The smallest member states have significantly more MEPs than their population alone would justify – to avoid a situation where on a strict per capita basis the smallest would scarcely be represented at all – and the largest have fewer. Until 2004, the four largest member states – France, Germany, Italy and the United Kingdom – each elected the same number of MEPs. Since then, Germany's quota has been increased in (delayed) recognition of the absorption of the population of East Germany at re-unification in 1990.

In the European Parliament, as in national parliaments, elected members sit with others with whom they share an ideological affinity. These political parties, or 'groups', reflect the federations of national parties which sprang up in response to the first direct elections[13] to the European Parliament. Prime among them are the European People's Party (EPP) group, composed of the representatives of national parties adhering to the European People's Party; the Socialist group (technically since 2009 the 'group of the Party of European Socialists and Democrats' but previously the group of the Party of European Socialists or PES) and the Liberal group (since 2004 the 'group of the Alliance of Liberals and Democrats for Europe', ALDE). For most of the directly elected Parliament's history there have also been a group representing Green parties and regional parties (though some regional parties are represented in other political groups), a group of the United European Left (mainly former Communists) and a group bringing together MEPs from Europe's far-right parties. In most parliaments there has also been at least one other political group on the right

---

12 The heads of state and government (one per country) meet in the European Council. There are also sectoral councils: the finance ministers meet in the Economic and Financial Council, the farm ministers in the Agriculture council and so on. Each member state has a number of votes proportionate to its population, though formal votes are rarely taken.

13 Informal political groups had existed from the very early days of the indirectly elected Assembly. The Liberal, Reformist and Democratic (LRD) group was first constituted on 20 June 1953. Indeed, it is since the Liberals decided to sit on that Assembly as a supranational group rather than in national delegations that other parties followed suit.

wing; currently there are two others[14]. MEPs adhering to no political group are represented through a technical group of non-aligned Members.

The political groups set Parliament's agenda. Their leaders, meeting in the 'conference of presidents of the political groups', propose Parliament's annual calendar, its order of business, the form and length of parliamentary debates, the invitations which Parliament sends to outside bodies and individuals and other matters[15]. While the plenary session of the full House can of course overturn their decisions, this rarely occurs.

Within the political groups, members enjoy preferment according primarily (but not exclusively) to the size of their national delegation under what is known as the d'Hondt system after the Belgian mathematician who invented it. Since member states are represented in proportion to their populations the largest national delegations – the Germans, the French, the British, the Italians and to a slightly lesser extent the Spanish and the Poles – tend to dominate, especially in the two largest political groups, in which these countries are all represented.

Liberal beginnings

Though the first leaders of the three main political groups in the 1979 Parliament were German, the Liberal group was dominated in its early years by its French contingent. From the first direct election in 1979 until 1994, over 25% of the Liberal group's members were provided by France. Germany and Italy were well represented too, but there were no UK members.[16] Indeed, France was to supply three of the group's first four leaders. The reason why it did not supply the first, in line with the prevailing assumption in all political groups that the leader of the largest national delegation led the group as a whole, was that Simone Veil, the leading Liberal, became the directly-elected European Parliament's first president.

Many had assumed that former Luxembourg prime minister Gaston Thorn, the most senior Liberal by rank, would lead the Liberal group in the first directly-elected European Parliament. The Luxemburger was to be outmanoeuvred, however, by the numerically superior German delegation, who struck an agreement[17] with the French to elect German MEP

---

14 The European Conservatives and Reformists group represents the UK Conservatives and their allies, mainly from Poland and the Czech Republic, who wish to halt the development of the EU; and the Europe of Freedom and Democracy group is composed of MEPs from the United Kingdom Independence Party and others who wish to withdraw their countries from the EU.

15 Some group leaders used the conference of presidents, which is attended also by 20-30 senior members of parliamentary and political group staff and a representative of Council and Commission, as a theatre in which to play-act a role. I made it my policy not to do so. Where I took major initiatives - such as to invite heads of state and government to address and debate with Parliament after the failure of the Constitutional Treaty or to establish a working group to review parliamentary procedures in the light of forthcoming treaty changes - they were related to the business of the House rather than the party-political point scoring which I found so depressing in these already lengthy meetings.

16 To make up for the lack of a UK presence the ELD group employed Richard Moore, a senior UK Liberal, whose influence in Parliament reached far beyond that of other members of staff of the political groups.

17 This agreement caused some bad blood since it was not communicated to others in advance. Indeed, FDP leader Hans Dietrich Genscher had promised his support to Thorn in Bangemann's presence.

and former economy minister Martin Bangemann as the ELD[18] group's leader.

Thorn, a forward-thinking Liberal, had enriched European debate with a modern Liberalism which stressed the need for the combination of a free market with social responsibility. By the time of his death in 2007 his ideas were to be almost fully integrated into the mainstream of the major western political ideologies. He was however to spend only two years in the European Parliament on this occasion[19]; in 1981 he became president of the European Commission.

The 45 year old Martin Bangemann was a rising star of Germany's Free Democratic (Liberal) party. A powerful speaker and a man of impressive energy, he was to become minister of economics in 1984 and a European commissioner in 1989, a post he was to hold for ten years.

Bangemann's election as the first leader of the group was not to be the only surprise in the sometimes Machiavellian workings of the Liberal group in the early elected parliaments. With the decision in December 1991 of the Liberal group's leader Valery Giscard d'Estaing to cross the floor of the House and join the European People's Party, the Liberal group was decapitated by its own head.

Giscard's election as president of France in 1974 had given a new lease of life to the centre in France, uniting its forces in a centre-right crusade to modernise the country. Combined with German Liberal strength (Walter Scheel was elected as president of Germany the same year) it had given Liberals a key role in the development of the EU. Giscard had despatched Simone Veil to lead his troops in the first direct elections to the European Parliament in 1979 in which they became the core of the Liberal group, with 17 MEPs out of a total of 43. It was through a combination of her own eminent qualifications for the job[20] and Giscard's considerable influence that Simone Veil became the directly-elected Parliament's first president.

Five years later, Veil was to succeed Bangemann as the leader of the Liberal group. It was on Veil's retirement in 1989 that Giscard – no longer president of France and now a man without a mission – decided to take a seat in Parliament and to assume the leadership of the group himself.[21]

Giscard's leadership of the ELD groupp was to be a short-lived affair, heavily influenced by French domestic politics. French Conservatives had never been happy supporting a government led from the centre and as Giscard's star waned they sought to re-group on the right. Giscard himself found his French contingent slightly less influential within the Liberal group after the 1989 elec-

18 The European Liberals and Democrats (ELD) were to become the European Liberals, Democrats and Reformers (ELDR) in the 1980s with the adhesion of Portugal's PSD since, for the Portuguese, the term Liberal was associated with the policies of the former dictator Salazar.

19 Thorn had been an MEP previously, from 1959 to 1969. He was to die in the summer of 2007.

20 Simone Veil was a survivor of the Nazi concentration camp at Auschwitz and had been France's minister of health (1974-79); she introduced the first law to permit abortion in France (1975).

21 It is rumoured that Giscard was advised by Michel Poniatowski, former minister of the interior and MEP and then member of the French Senate, that the group leadership (rather than a committee chair) would make him well-placed to become president of the European Parliament.

tions had returned them with just 13 of a total of 49 Liberal MEPs. Moreover, he found in leading a European parliamentary group that he lacked the carrots and sticks which assist party leaders to maintain discipline in national parliaments. He was perhaps unaccustomed to the lack of deference which is a hallmark of northern Liberals and dissatisfied with the lack of influence wielded by the Liberals within Parliament and by Parliament over the EU's executive; in any event he soon tired of the European Parliament's Liberal group and it of him. It is not necessary for Liberal troops to love their leader, provided there is respect; but it is necessary for a Liberal leader to love his troops[22]. When Giscard announced, at a press conference in Paris in December 1991, that 'the Liberal group [was] joining the European People's Party', the Liberal troops rioted. There had been no consultation of them and, unlike in French politics, for most there was a clear distinction between Liberals and the faith-based Christian Democrats which they were not prepared to blur by joining forces. In a famous scene in a Strasbourg committee room, Belgian MEP Jean Defraigne[23] summed up the mood of colleagues by hurling at Giscard the insult *'Crapule! Foutez le camp!'*[24], to great applause, leaving the Frenchman with little choice but to beat a hasty retreat with just three of his French followers, fewer no doubt than he expected[25].

Giscard's decision to join the EPP was in fact orchestrated by one of the main postwar architects of EU integration, German chancellor Helmut Kohl. Kohl's influence on the EU's development in the 1990s was greater even than that of Delors; his skill and tenacity in achieving his goal of a common European currency within the EU threw into sharp relief the pusillanimity of so many of his counterparts in the European Council in facing down the persistence of nationalism. But Kohl's achievements carried a party political price tag. His Konrad Adenauer Foundation ploughed millions of German marks into seducing political parties to join his neutrally-named European People's Party, which he regarded as the political avant-garde of European integration. To swell its ranks he had picked off most of the Liberals in Spain; now he had turned his attention to France. Portugal was soon to follow and then Hungary. Although former EPP leader Wilfried Martens denies that the EPP encouraged these moves, the growth of the EPP group in the EP was due in no small part to the financial clout of the CDU's generously state-funded political foundation[26].

One of the main influences on the directly-elected Parliament's first three terms was the gradual collapse of the governments of the central and eastern European countries in the Soviet bloc. The 'Helsinki process'[27] of

---

22 I owe this thought to former UK Liberal Democrat leader Paddy Ashdown.

23 Jean Defraigne had been the Liberal leader in the city of Liege, the speaker of the national parliament and Belgium's minister for public works.

24 'Scoundrel! Get out of here!'

25 Three MEPs left with him: Alain Lamassoure, Jeannou Lacaze and Robert Hersant.

26 Consistent with Germany's traditional role as a driving force of European unity, all its political foundations funded at that time most of the encounters between political parties of their persuasions. Each foundation received public funds in proportion to the level of popular support their party enjoyed at elections.

27 So called because the Conference on Security and Co-operation in Europe, a standing conference designed to facilitate dialogue and build trust between western and eastern European countries, first met in Helsinki.

engagement with these countries had borne fruit. The first direct impact on the European Parliament – and the event with the greatest impact on the subsequent fifteen years which are the main subject of this book – was the reunification of Germany on 3 October 1990. German foreign minister and leading European Liberal Hans-Dietrich Genscher had stood on the steps of the German embassy in Prague on 30 September 1989 and welcomed Germans who had fled the German Democratic Republic to board special trains to the Federal Republic of Germany. Parliament had established a committee in February 1990 to examine the impact of German unification on the European Community and had adopted a resolution on 12 July welcoming the prospect of such an historic development. In a further resolution on 24 October, following the reunification, it welcomed the entry into the European Community of 16 million citizens from the former German Democratic Republic and hoped that a unified Germany would serve as a bridge between the Community and the countries of eastern Europe.

In truth, many were a little afraid of the power a larger Germany would wield[28] and sought to tie down this new leviathan into a political, economic and monetary union through the Treaty of Maastricht. 'France throwing the grappling hooks around Germany', was how one commentator described it. The European Parliament was content to note 'the commitments given throughout this process by the German authorities that they consider German unification to be a contribution to the process of European unification', and urged rapid progress towards this latter goal. With Germany's decision a decade later at the intergovernmental conference preparing the Treaty of Nice to moderate its demand for voting strength in Council in favour of more seats in the European Parliament, however, it was to become a dominant force in the latter institution.

Giscard d'Estaing was succeeded as EP Liberal leader in December 1991 by Yves Galland[29], a member of France's Parti Radical Valoisien, the only party in France which really equated to the northern European Liberal tradition which now dominated the group intellectually. To choose another Frenchman was to cock a snook at the group's former leader but also to elevate to the chair a man seen to be competent and feisty. Galland's easy wit and Gallic charm fitted the bill perfectly. It was Galland who, during the UK presidency of the EU in 1992, arranged twelve Union Jacks on his desk during UK prime minister John Major's visit and explained – in his reply to Major's address – that these symbolised the MEPs his group was denied by the unfair European election voting system operated only in the UK.[30]

At the 1994 EP elections the Liberals were returned with 43 seats, including

28   Speaking in the House on 12 July 1990 Simone Veil MEP had said 'just imagine the problems that German unification would pose today if the Community did not exist, and if it did not constitute that pole of stability and security it has constructed over the last 40 years'.

29   Galland had been deputy mayor of Paris and a minister in the interior ministry.

30   The UK had become infamous not only for an anomalous voting system which - by exaggerating the strength of the Labour and Conservative contingents and denying represeantation to the Liberals - unbalanced the political forces in the EP; but also for the deal accepted by John Major at the Edinburgh summit in 1992 to insert into the EC treaties a requirement for the EP to meet at least twelve times a year in Strasbourg.

for the first time[31] two Liberal Democrats from the United Kingdom who had managed (due to growing Liberal strength in south west England and the extreme unpopularity of John Major's Conservative government) to break through the first-past-the-post system to secure election. Dutchman Gijs de Vries, the leader of the largest national component, was elected to lead the group, with Irish independent member Pat Cox as his deputy and your author as the group's whip[32].

31   UK MP Russell Johnston, a member of the unelected pre-1979 Assembly who had come close to winning Scotland's Highlands and Islands constituency in the 1979 direct elections, had been invited to attend ELD group meetings from 1979 despite not being a member. And Labour MEP Michael Gallagher had left the Labour Party in 1984 during his time as an MEP to join the SDP, though there is no record of him having joined the ELD group.

32   I knew De Vries, having been instrumental in securing his election as president of the Liberal Youth Movement of the European Communities some years before, and was honoured to serve as a lieutenant. In the interests of fairness, however, I was to relinquish the post to my UK colleague Robin Teverson MEP half way through the mandate.

Chapter 1:   1994 – 1999

The 1994-99 mandate saw the European Parliament's powers strengthened by the Maastricht Treaty, which gave MEPs powers of co-decision with national government ministers in the setting of single market legislation. During this period the Amsterdam Treaty was also negotiated, which was to extend the scope of measures decided under co-decision. The EU opened its doors to membership of Austria, Finland and Sweden and twelve EU member states were to lock together their currencies to lay the foundations for a single currency, the euro. Yet member state governments were also to be heavily occupied with the conflicts in the former Yugoslavia and the Union was to suffer from financial scandals caused by dishonesty and poor accounting practices which would bring about the downfall of the European Commission.

The presidency of the European Council during these years was held in turn by Germany (second half 1994), France and Spain (1995), Italy and Ireland (1996), the Netherlands and Luxembourg (1997), the UK and Austria (1998) and Germany again (1st half 1999).

Liberals make an early impact

The Treaty on European Union (the Maastricht Treaty) entered into force on 1 November 1993. The founder members of the EU saw it as an opportunity for rapid development of the Union. The UK and some other more recent adherents, however, sought to apply the brakes to developments beyond the field of economic co-operation. They wanted the EU to be a single market but nothing more.

Yet the EU was already moving beyond the purely commercial, as had been agreed (reluctantly by some) at Maastricht. The leaders of the EU's member states had adopted six months previously the Commission's white paper on growth, competitiveness and employment which they hoped would – together with the successful conclusion of the Uruguay round of world trade liberalisation measures – help to pull their continent out of economic recession. They had also established two new education and training programmes, Leonardo and Socrates; devoted one billion ecus[33] over five

---

33 ECU = European currency unit, the forerunner of the euro.

years to a Community initiative programme to help small and medium sized enterprises; agreed an ambitious five-year programme of scientific and technological research and resolved to establish Europol, a new European Police Office, to act in the fight against drug trafficking and other forms of organised crime. Liberals welcomed all these developments; indeed, Liberals had led the calls for many of them.[34]

Within the EU, the European Parliament elected in 1994 was to be more influential than any of its predecessors. The Maastricht Treaty was to give it new powers of co-decision. The development of the single market and co-ordination of member states' economic policies were to expand its sphere of activity. EU enlargement to three new member states and plans for further enlargement were to extend its reach.

The role of the Liberal group in the European Parliament in advancing a Liberal EU agenda was to be much assisted by the single mindedness and capacity for hard work of its new leader, Gijs de Vries. De Vries had served in the European Parliament since 1984 and had built a good reputation. He was a skilled linguist. His Protestant work ethic won him many admirers. He was perhaps helped by looking older and more distinguished than his 38 years. An able debater with a first class analytical brain, he was better at discomfiting Council and Commission representatives in debate than any of the other political group leaders.

De Vries was to lead the group for three and a half years, starting the process of reconstructing the centre after the collapse of a strong centrist voice in France and the defeat of Germany's FDP in the 1994 European elections. At the outset of the parliament's mandate, he decided to lead the Liberal MEPs in opposition to the nomination of Jacques Santer as Commission president;[35] in what way were Santer's views different from Dehaene's?, he asked; and why should Parliament be content with a man whose nomination represented a failure of the member states' governments to find any stronger candidate on whom they could all agree? It was a salutary shot across the bows of the major parties.

Santer was approved by Parliament in July 1994 – after last minute arm-twisting efforts by the German presidency of the EU – with the support of his right-wing party colleagues in the EPP and a large number of Socialists, by a margin of 22 votes; yet while the Socialists divided, the Liberals voted against[36]. Moreover, De Vries was to insist on and win Santer's agreement that member states' nominees for the college of commissioners would undergo parliamentary hearings and submit to parliamentary approval before taking office, an exercise never previously undertaken.

---

34 MEPs Mechthild von Alemann and Anne Andre had reported for Parliament on vocational training and Tove Nielsen MEP on SMEs, for example. The group now proposed a number of amendments to the EP report by Labour MEP Ken Coates in favour of a social model which combined social protection with flexibility.

35 The UK had vetoed Belgian candidate Jean-Luc Dehaene at the Corfu summit on the grounds of his avowedly federalist intent; an extraordinary European Council meeting in Brussels on 15 July had agreed that Luxemburger Jacques Santer should succeed Jacques Delors at the year's end.

36 There was one exception; the Liberal MEP from Luxembourg voted in favour of his fellow countryman. He had previously announced to colleagues his intention.

Though Santer was eventually to secure the support of the Liberal group in January 2005 for the investiture of his college of commissioners after the parliamentary hearings, it was not without guarantees that Irish nominee Padraig Flynn (social affairs) would lose sole oversight of the womens' rights portfolio or before Danish commissioner-designate Ritt Bjeregaard was obliged to apologise to Parliament for remarks she had made to journalists in Copenhagen about it being 'not a real parliament'. Moreover, Santer was obliged to concede to Parliament further guarantees, in the form of a written agreement between Commission and Parliament on relations between the two institutions, to recognise publicly (as provided for in Article 144 of the treaty) that the Commission was accountable to Parliament. Liberals believed that a Parliament newly equipped with powers of co-decision under the Maastricht Treaty should be prepared to exercise proper democratic control over the EU's executive arm and we played a crucial role in obtaining these concessions.

De Vries also led Liberal protests about the unfairness of the voting system employed in the UK to elect members to the European Parliament. Though the UK's Liberal Democrats had scored over 16% of the vote we had been rewarded with less than 2.5% of the UK's seats. Indeed, a further injustice had been perpetrated on the party: the intervention in Devon of a candidate running under the banner 'Literal Democrat' and securing over 10,000 votes while the Conservative candidate beat the Liberal Democrat into second place by a margin of just 700 had cost the party the third seat it had rightfully won in south west England[37]. Moreover, the disproportionate swings in UK representation caused by the UK's electoral system unbalanced the European Parliament's political groups. Though Labour had polled just over 40% of the votes cast it was rewarded with 62 of the UK's 87 seats, making it the largest delegation in the PES group. The Conservatives, by contrast, took just 18 seats (for 27% of the vote), unbalancing in similar fashion the representation of different national components within the EPP.

Within Parliament, Liberals were to elect one vice president and one committee chair. The former post was filled by Portuguese MEP Antonio Capucho, the latter by veteran Belgian Liberal Willy de Clercq, who continued to occupy the chair of the external economic relations committee which he had held throughout the previous mandate, though he was to switch to chairing the legal affairs committee in 1997.

Capucho had been a student leader in the Carnation Revolution and had risen quickly through the ranks of his Portuguese Social Democratic party. From 1980 to 1989 he had been a government minister and a close ally of Prime Minister Anibal Antonio Cavaco Silva. However his career had been essentially in the national domain and he was not well known among Liberals beyond. An MEP since Portuguese accession in 1986, a linguistic handicap and an abundance of other commitments prevented him from

---

37 Shockingly, the result of this contest was endorsed by the UK's electoral commission. Nonetheless, the UK Liberal MEPs were to keep up these protests throughout the Parliament through parliamentary initiatives and face to face meetings with national leaders, adding to the pressure which secured a proportional voting system for the UK for the 1999 European elections.

socialising much with his colleagues. The anglo-saxons dubbed him 'the prince of darkness' due to his tendency to endeavour to orchestrate developments from backstage. He was not much present in group meetings. Yet he was to fulfil his role as vice president of the House with some verve, chairing debates and voting sessions with the requisite gravitas.

De Clercq, by contrast, was the biggest beast in the European Liberal jungle. As a former party leader, deputy prime minister and European commissioner, Willy de Clercq was widely known and even more widely respected. At the age of 33 he had become the youngest Belgian ever to hold ministerial office, during a national parliamentary career which was to last 27 years. He had worked closely with Delors at the Commission as external trade commissioner between 1995 and 1999, the two having known each other previously as finance ministers from neighbouring countries. De Clercq had kicked off the Uruguay Round of world trade talks on behalf of the EU. His greatest triumph as commissioner had perhaps been to have threatened the USA with reprisals over their imposition of import duties and to have won. He had long been a passionate advocate of European federalism and was to serve a total of ten years as president of the ELD (later ELDR) party, from 1980 to 1985 and again from 1990 to 1995.

Using the powers of Maastricht

Liberals were concerned that many of the planks of the single market remained unlaid. How could the EU regain competitiveness and reach its full job-creating potential, Liberal MEPs asked, if it did not optimise the benefits of co-operation facilitated by the Single European Act, Delors' greatest achievement?

Prime Liberal movers on the economic and monetary affairs committee were Carles Gasoliba I Bohm and Pat Cox. Gasoliba spoke for Liberals on the economic policy co-ordination necessary to make the forthcoming economic and monetary union credible; Cox on monetary and tax harmonisation issues. As a freshman MEP I had joined the economic and monetary affairs committee and was fortunate to be able to learn the ropes by shadowing them. I was also fortunate to be appointed to report for Parliament on the functioning of the single market in 1994, which gave me an early insight into the core business of the EU[38].

As the EU started to emerge from recession towards the end of 1994, unemployment – particularly youth unemployment – remained dangerously high. The recovery was unlikely to be sufficient to resolve the problem of structural unemployment, which affected both the young and older workers. Liberals therefore agued for greater flexibility in the economy, reducing non-wage labour costs and promoting investment in new technologies in the hope of job creation. Liberalisation of the market in many kinds of services would, we maintained, dynamise Europe's economy.

---

38 I was fortunate too to have the expert advice of a friend, Dr Alan Butt-Philip of the University of Bath in assisting me with the report.

Most member states sought convergence of their economies to assist in the move towards economic and monetary union, which required strict observance of the criteria laid down in the Maastricht Treaty; Carles Gasoliba was to pilot through the House in 1997 a report on economic policy co-ordination which argued that a coherent and effective economic policy at EU level required the incorporation into the EU's annual economic review of a range of each member state's national government policies which had an impact on the economy.

Liberal action between Parliament and Commission was consistent, if not – in those days – concerted. Bangemann had been appointed commissioner for industrial affairs and information and telecommuications technologies. Part of his agenda within his brief was to liberalise the EU's telecommunications infrastructure by 1998, as had been proposed by Karel de Gucht MEP in the first directly elected parliament. Bangemann had chaired a group of leading figures in studying opportunities offered to the EU by the development of information technology under the buzzwords 'the information society'.

Similarly, Danish commissioner Henning Christophersen had chaired a high level group on the development of trans-European networks for transport, energy and environmental projects which had submitted to the June 1994 European Council an early proposal for priority to be given to eleven[39] major transport projects. The work of both had been commended by the European Council in Corfu[40] in June 1994 and the Commission invited by the Council to put their ideas into practice[41].

Liberal MEPs were also keen to support Commissioner Mario Monti, who had taken over the internal market brief which Bangemann had held (in addition to industry) in the Delors Commission, in his SLIM (Simpler Legislation for the Internal Market) initiative and the Better Regulation drive. Some were sceptical however of the headline goal of President Santer, who appeared to dance to the tune of some national capitals in arguing that the EU should 'do less, better'. The main problems with legislation lay more in delays in the implementation of EU directives by the member states, Liberals observed. In 2003 there were 134 single market directives which had not been implemented in at least one member state; and where they had been implemented, some governments had fallen for the temptation to 'gold plate'[42] the laws. In the protection of intellectual property, in public procurement policies and in insurance services very little progress had been made in bringing down barriers.

---

39 The list was subsequently lengthened to 14.

40 Indeed, Bangemann and Christophersen were the only commissioners cited by name in the presidency conclusions of the Corfu European Council of 1994.

41 One of these was the creation of the ".eu" top level domain name, to be steered through Parliament by Colette Flesch MEP in February 2002.

42 'Gold plating' was the requirement in national legislation of more than was required by the EU legislation being transposed. I was to join forces with other UK Conservative and Labour MEPs in raising this matter with UK deregulation minister Roger Freeman MP and two of his successors which led to the issuance of new guidelines to civil servants in the transposition of EU directives into UK law but not much practical progress. Yet when it came to pressing others to implement EU directives the UK was a champion. Its single market compliance unit does first class work in helping UK businesses overcome hurdles of non-implementation of EU law in other member states.

The EU enlarges

At the European Council in Corfu just after the 1994 elections a treaty of accession had been signed with four new member countries: Austria, Sweden, Finland and Norway, all of which were due to join the EU on 1 January 2005. The Austrian people had already given their assent: the Swedes and the Finns were soon to follow suit. Not so the Norwegians, however, who had been expected to join at the same time: they voted in a referendum on 28 November 1994 against joining the EU[43].

Liberals had welcomed the prospect of this enlargement, as of previous extensions of EU membership. In Finland, Sweden and Austria Liberals had campaigned fervently in favour, even if their Centre Party colleagues, who also swore allegiance to the Liberal family, were a little less enthusiastic. Only in Norway, where the Liberals had been divided, did the vote go against membership.

Cynics have speculated that this enlargement to relatively wealthy countries was a prerequisite to the subsequent and already envisaged expansion to take in the impoverished countries of the former Eastern bloc. Yet the main reasons why Liberals welcomed the new Baltic members lay in their commitment to transparency and open government and (for the more far-sighted) their determined efforts to promote environmental protection. Moreover, the Scandinavian countries had done more than most to combat the scourges of racism and xenophobia which were returning to haunt Europe.

France and Germany had proposed the establishment of a consultative commission involving justice and interior ministers to develop a strategy at EU level to combat acts of violence based on racial hatred and intolerance and to advise on the training of public officials. Liberals wanted to see urgent action and we had moved amendments to the EU budget in 1995 to provide half a million ECUs in financial assistance to allow NGOs working in this field to establish themselves in Brussels and another half a million for the preservation of concentration camps as historic monuments. In July 1998 Luxembourg Liberal Charles Goerens MEP was to be instrumental in defeating a parliamentary resolution on fundamentalism tabled by Dutch Calvinist Arie Oostlander MEP which singled out Muslim fundamentalism for condemnation. At the instigation of French Liberal Jean-Thomas Nordmann MEP there were to be two parliamentary enquiries into racism and xenophobia; and the Liberals' call for the setting up of an EU Monitoring Centre on Racism and Xenophobia was eventually to be taken up[44].

Liberals were impressed too by the Scandinavian countries' attachment to the primacy of the rule of law. Freed from the shackles of a French domination which, while centrist and republican, was not always Liberal in other

---

43   The result was close: 52.2% against, 47.8% in favour on a turnout of 88.6%.

44   The EUMC for Racism and Xenophobia, which Liberals had long called for, was established in Vienna in June 1998. In March 2007 its status was upgraded to an EU Agency for Fundamental Rights, again at the insistence of Liberal MEPs. ALDE continues to seek to expand its remit and powers.

senses[45], Liberals had resolved to campaign for the establishment in The Hague (which already hosted the International Court of Justice) of a permanent International Criminal Court to try those guilty of genocide and other crimes against humanity. Hitherto, only ad hoc tribunals had existed for these purposes, the latest being the tribunal for war crimes committed with horrific ferocity in Rwanda. Their Scandinavian sister parties were to bring more troops to assist in this campaign.

On 1 January 2005 the ELDR group gained eight new members: five from Finland, two from Sweden and one from Austria. But these were 'observer' MEPs, appointed from the ranks of national parliamentarians. By the time each country had organised a poll of its citizens for the purpose of electing MEPs the group was still to have eight members from the three countries, but some of the names and faces had changed.

For the European Commission, Finland and Sweden nominated Social Democrats and Austria a Christian Democrat. It would be almost ten years before Finland was to nominate a Liberal, to be joined by Sweden five years later.

The European Council in Cannes on 26 and 27 June 1995 was the first summit attended by 15 EU heads of state and government. France had also invited the heads of state and government of 11 countries associated with the EU. Six so-called 'Europe agreements' were already in force: in addition to those signed in 1994 with Hungary and Poland, the beginning of 1995 had witnessed the signing of agreements with Romania, Bulgaria, the Czech Republic and Slovakia. Association agreements had been signed on 12 June 1995 with the three Baltic States of Estonia, Latvia and Lithuania. Negotiations with Malta and Cyprus[46] were already quite advanced.

While much of the former Yugoslavia was at war, with Sarajevo under siege, and the EU itself still dogged by unemployment and by the aftershocks of currency turmoil, preparations were in full swing for the next enlargement and for the easing of the soon-to-be candidate countries into the economy of the single market.

Towards a community of values

With the new powers conferred on it by the Maastricht Treaty, the EU was to become far more than simply an economic union. The decision gradually to develop common policies in foreign and security matters and in justice and home affairs had given the EU's institutions a much wider brief. And the need for a common foreign policy and a common policy on asylum had been highlighted to an almost embarrassing extent by the conflict in the former Yugoslavia in the first half of the 1990s.

---

45   With the exception of representatives of the Parti Radical Valoisien and some MEPs from the west of France such as Jean-Pierre Raffarin, French members of the Liberal group often diverged in important respects from the views of other Liberals.

46   Association agreements had been signed with Malta in 1970 and Cyprus in 1972, boosting economic and commercial ties and envisaging eventual membership of the EU.

While other central and eastern European countries threw off the yoke of Communist oppression more or less peacefully, in Yugoslavia the reform was complicated by deep-rooted and unresolved ethnic hatreds. The voting down of Slovenian proposals for an end to the one-party system at the 14th (and final) conference of the Serbian-dominated Communist Party of Yugoslavia in January 1990 had led to the break up of the party and the state. Ethnic tensions broke into violent conflicts which were to involve ethnic cleansing and the use of rape as a weapon of war between Serbs and Croats, Bosniaks and Croats and Macedonians and Albanians. The European Union had proved powerless to bring a halt to the conflicts and had shown itself to be at sixes and sevens in dealing with the stream of refugees across its borders; even American intervention through NATO had barely been able to bring peace. While Slovenia had gained de facto independence after a limited ten day conflict in the summer of 1991, the Croatian war of independence involved serious war crimes such as the murder of soldiers taken prisoner. Though the January 1992 peace plan ended the worst of the fighting there, sporadic violence continued until 1995. Meanwhile the Bosnia conflict, which erupted in June 1992, pitted Bosniaks and Croats backed by Croatia against Serbs backed by Serbia and involved the full horrors of ethnic cleansing including the infamous scenes in Srebrenica and in the siege of Sarajevo. The first US brokered peace plan in 1994 and the second, the Dayton Agreement, in December 1995 finally stopped the fighting; but the social damage caused by the return of genocide to the continent and the economic damage inflicted by war would take years to overcome.

Half a million refugees from Yugoslavia had fled to EU countries seeking protection. Their reception had varied greatly from one member state to another. Jan-Kees Wiebenga MEP took action on Parliament's justice and home affairs committee, working with the European Commission to reach agreements on joint action to provide temporary protection in future in the case of mass influx of displaced persons[47]. Member states had vetoed the Commission's 1997 proposals for action on temporary protection of displaced persons; by setting a time limit of five years on the duration of the temporary protection regime, Wiebenga hoped to bring the European Council on board, but to no avail[48]. However a proposal for a Council directive on minimum standards for giving temporary protection in the event of a mass influx of displaced persons, adopted by the Commission in June 2000, was to enjoy more success. Wiebenga again became the rapporteur and was to see the measure adopted in Parliament on 13 March and by Council on 20 July 2001.

While what had been Yugoslavia needed peace before reconstruction could begin, other formerly Communist countries had needed urgent assistance with economic stability. This is what the Europe agreements were designed to provide. Liberals were active in supporting them, determined to see successful economies on the EU's borders with the goal of bringing these countries into the EU in due course. Within these countries too, Liberals were at the forefront of efforts for reform. Leszek Balcerowicz in Poland,

---

47 His report was adopted in October 1997.

48 The proposal was eventually withdrawn by the Commission on 24 March 2005

Lajos Bokros[49] in Hungary, Ivars Godmanis in Latvia and Janez Drnovsec in Slovenia were among the architects of economic reforms which allowed Europe agreements to be signed with the countries of the former Soviet bloc.

Using the EU to promote peace

Though much of the EU's attention was absorbed by developments to the east, the accession of Greece, Spain and Portugal in the 1980s had also made the EU more aware of the need to follow developments to the south. Across the Mediterranean, co-operation agreements were being forged with Israel, Morocco and Tunisia. The Oslo agreement appeared to offer the best hope in many years for lasting peace in the Middle East and unleashed a wave of optimism about prospects for economic development in the region. Since the Oslo peace agreements of 13 September 1993, Israel had reached an agreement with the PLO in Cairo on 4 May 1994 which foresaw the establishment of a Palestinian Authority in the Gaza Strip and Jericho and the creation of a Palestinian police force; and had more recently signed a peace agreement with Jordan. The EU perceived – in boosting its co-operation with Israel – a chance for the development of the Palestinian economy which would help underpin peace. As the largest financial donor to the Middle East peace process it sought more of a say in western policy and welcomed Spain's proposal to host a donor conference during its presidency of the EU in the second half of 1995. The hopes for a lasting peace expressed by external relations commissioner Hans van den Broek, however, were to be frustrated. By the summer of 1997 the situation had deteriorated considerably. In response to Palestinian terror attacks the Israeli government had tried to seal off the Palestinian territories and had frozen the payment to the Palestinian Authority of the tax revenue it collected on their behalf. The illegal building of new settlements continued. Speaking in a debate in Parliament on 17 September 1997, Jan-Willem Bertens MEP had called on Palestinian president Yassir Arafat to restrain Hamas but had also insisted that such over-reaction by Israel would only fuel extremism.

Liberals in the European Parliament were increasingly evenly divided about the rights and wrongs of the Middle East conflict. Under Simone Veil the group had been strongly pro-Israel. At the initiative of Charles Goerens MEP it had launched a campaign, 'the duty of memory', to facilitate visits of western European school children to Auschwitz. Indeed, when Belgian Liberal MEP Luc Beyer de Rijke had returned from a visit to Palestine and displayed to colleagues a suitcase full of spent munitions which the Israelis had fired at a school he had visited, he had been met with stony-faced silence from many who disliked being confronted with evidence of Israeli aggression. The entry into the group of Swedish Liberals, strongly pro-Israel, might have served to reinforce that school of thought. But the election of Liberals from the UK and the changing opinion of others had created a group in which opinion was more equally divided than before.

---

49 Though Bokros is considered a Liberal he was never a member of a Liberal party. He served as a Socialist MP, declared himself an independent finance minister and is now as a member of Hungary's MDF party, which is allied to the Liberal SZDSZ.

Concerned about the spread of extremist and Islamic fundamentalist forces in a number of North African countries[50], the EU sought to gain maximum influence; and while it would achieve little in its dealings with Syria, Libya or Algeria, at least Tunisia, Morocco and Jordan appeared to offer hopes for meaningful progress towards a wider peace. Involving Malta and Cyprus in negotiations for entry to the EU sent a signal to the southern Mediterranean countries, or so many thought, that – while interested in early eastern expansion – the EU was by no means blind to the needs of its southern neighbours.

The EU also still had unfinished business in the promotion of peace within its borders. The progress made in the early 1990s by John Major's government and its counterpart in Dublin in promoting peace in Northern Ireland had been impressive. When the European Council in Essen on 9 and 10 December 1994 agreed on the principle of a multiannual programme of financial support for Northern Ireland and the border counties in the south and the grant of a further ECU 300 millions to support the peace process, Liberals saw a belated recognition of the proposals made first by Liberal MEP Niels Haagerup in 1983, who had seen the opportunities offered by frequent contact in the wider EU context to bring UK and Irish policy-makers together. By the end of the European Parliament's 1994-99 mandate Northern Ireland's Protestant leader David Trimble and its Catholic leader John Hume MEP were jointly to have been awarded the Nobel peace prize in October 1998 and – at the suggestion of Northern Ireland's Alliance Party leader John Alderdice, who had played an important role in the peace process – Trimble was to have brought the entire Northern Ireland Assembly (parliament) to Brussels to discuss the use of EU funding for reconstruction in the province.

The European Union had the promotion of peace in its DNA. Turning swords into ploughshares united the vast majority of MEPs from across the political spectrum. Netherlands' Liberal Jan Willem Bertens had done much work towards banning the production and export of land mines, for example. French president Chirac's decision to test a nuclear weapon under the Pacific atoll of Mururoa during his country's 1995 EU presidency, after having announced a suspension of testing on the atoll in 1992, led to strong protests in the European Parliament. While stopping short of the tactic employed by the Greens of dressing up in costume in order to gain publicity, Liberals took seriously this issue. Addressing the House on 19 December 1995, De Vries spoke of the hypocrisy of French politicians 'who on Sunday were all in favour of a common defence policy, but on Monday insisted on keeping their own sovereign defence policy'. Countries sharing a single currency and a single market can no longer refuse a single foreign and security policy, he added.

France's EU presidency had been marked by a change of horses in midstream. President Francois Mitterand, suffering from poor health and leading a difficult co-habitation with a right-wing majority in the Assemblee Nationale, had been succeeded as president on 17 May 1995 by Gaullist Jacques Chirac. In carrying out the nuclear test, Chirac had ignored Articles

---

50   A fatwa on the life of author Salman Rushdie and an attempt to assassinate Egyptian president Mubarak were to draw particular attention to this. Meanwhile Islamic fundamentalists in Algeria had gained substantial political support.

34 and 35 of the Euratom Treaty under which the European Commission and the European Parliament should have been given a chance to have their say.

Changing perceptions of the EU

In June 1994 the heads of state and government decided to establish a reflection group to prepare the 1996 intergovernmental conference, which in its turn should reform the EU treaties in preparation for a further enlargement to the east and the south, involving former Communist countries[51] plus Malta and Cyprus. The group was to begin its work the following year. The European Council had agreed to Parliament's suggestion that the reflection group should have among its members, for the first time, two representatives of the European Parliament. EPP and PES groups combined to divide the spoils and deny Liberal MEPs representation. Liberals were to be represented, however, through the presence of Werner Hoyer, EU affairs minister of Germany; Hoyer was to report regularly and diligently to the Parliament's Liberal group on progress in the reflection group's deliberations.

The reflection group, which started its work in Messina on 2 June 1995, had been urged to look at foreign and security policy, justice and home affairs and the workings of democracy within the Union. Successive presidencies of Germany, France, Spain and Italy – from July 1994 to June 1996 – were driving forward EU integration. The Union's political weight was not commensurate with its economic strength, their leaders reasoned, and this had to be rectified.

Liberals perceived another change, underlying much thinking in the EU in the mid-1990s but not regularly identified. This was a change in the way Europeans were interpreting events in the world around them. The 'peace dividend' promise of the fall of the Berlin Wall and Francis Fukuyama's prediction of 'the end of history' had both proven illusory. If anything, the world was now less predictable than during the era of the USSR-USA standoff. Globalisation of the economy and its consequences for jobs and competitiveness; terrorism, the drugs trade and other forms of internationally organised crime; world population growth and migratory pressures and the challenge of dealing with environmental degradation – all these had combined to create a vast global challenge to which European nation states seemed too small to respond. This had been recognised for some years by the smaller of them; now it was dawning not only on the Germans and the Italians, who had long since forgotten their dreams of empire, but even on the more far-sighted among the French and the British.

Economic and monetary union

The third and final stage of preparation for economic and monetary union was due to begin on 1 January 1999, when the currencies of the participating member states would be locked together in the creation of a 'hard ecu' in advance of the issuance of a single currency. The European Council in Madrid in December 1995 had confirmed that the timetable remained in

---

51   Hungary and Poland had already applied for membership, on 31 April and 4 March 1994 respectively.

place; the European Monetary Institute (forerunner of the European Central Bank) and the Commission now had to redouble their efforts to establish a new voluntary exchange rate mechanism and prepare the legal framework for a single currency. By the end of 1996 the legal framework had been agreed, the structure of the new exchange rate mechanism approved and the principles of a Stability and Growth Pact delineated to ensure the necessary budgetary discipline, with a framework for effective multilateral surveillance and an 'excessive deficit procedure' to sanction countries which failed to respect the pact. Agreement had even been reached on the design of the euro notes and coins. The Finnish markka had entered the ERM on 12 October 1996 and the Italian lira had re-entered five weeks later[52]. Baron Alexandre Lamfalussy, president of the European Monetary Institute, was to be succeeded in July 1997 by Dutchman Wim Duisenberg, who was expected subsequently to be confirmed as the first president of the ECB.

Speaking in a parliamentary debate on 10 June 1997 Cox had warned that unless wider economic reforms were undertaken there was a danger of a weak euro leading to high inflation and high interest rates. I had argued for the setting up of an independent body to look in detail at fiscal union, which surely had to be the next step.

Yet for all the progress towards monetary union, the completion of economic union remained elusive. Despite two years of work by industry commissioner Bangemann, the European Council meeting in Dublin on 13 and 14 December 1996 was unable to break the deadlock between member states which had strangled the development of an internal market in postal services proposed by the Commission four years previously. Though Council was to reach agreement and the European Parliament was to vote on the matter at second reading in September 1997, the liberalisation was only partial. It would have to be revisited, Liberals insisted, in the next mandate. Little progress was made on proposals to harmonise working time regulations. However much Europe's leaders willed the ends, willing the means in the jungle of political controversy was sometimes beyond them.

Justice and home affairs

As the drive towards a single market appeared to stall and unemployment remained high, so support for the European project threatened to wane. France's president Jacques Chirac and German chancellor Helmut Kohl chose October 1996 to write an open letter to their fellow heads of state and government about the failure of the intergovernmental conference to agree hitherto on a revision of the EU treaties. They were determined that this work should be completed by June of the following year, in time for the European Council meeting in Amsterdam. In particular they wanted to see a greater capacity for the EU to act in the field of justice and home affairs – the mass influx of refugees from the former Yugoslavia of the early 1990s and the increasing porosity of borders to organised criminal gangs were a

52   Denmark had voted in a referendum on 28 September 1993 by 53% to 47% against joining the new single currency.

cause for alarm, particularly to the east of the Rhine; and in developing a common foreign and security policy.

The drive for greater EU coherence now also had backers across the Atlantic. Under pressure from the USA[53], where President Clinton was leading a messianic drive for a better world, Europe was working hard to improve its efficiency in the fight against narcotic drug abuse. Member states needed to get their police forces, customs services and judicial authorities working together. Approximation of laws and practices was a further requirement. Action against the money laundering efforts of the drug traffickers was needed too. Yet common action was by diplomatic convention, a long-winded approach with outcomes difficult to enforce. Liberals believed these matters had to be brought into the mainstream of EU competences, where decisions could be made by majority voting and where the European Court of Justice could be called on to ensure their enforcement. Moreover, evidence was emerging of drug traffickers expanding their cooperation in to the area of the trafficking of people, for the purposes of slave labour or, worse, sexual exploitation, often of minors.

Of course, such new policy development did not come without a cost to the taxpayer. The EP's budget rapporteur in 1996 (for the 1997 budget), former Dutch state secretary for European affairs and European Commission official Laurens-Jan Brinkhorst MEP, fought successfully to obtain a budget for refugees and another to establish an embryo EU foreign service.

Beyond the EU

The first and second of March 1996 saw the first ever formal summit between the EU and Asian countries, as recommended by Belgian Liberal MEP Jean Gol in a report adopted by Parliament on 12 April 1995. While the USA had enjoyed relations with Asian countries for many years through the Association of South East Asian Nations (ASEAN), which it had helped to form, the Asia-Europe Meeting (ASEM) in Bangkok was a fledgling new arrival. EU leaders agreed to regular summits of this nature with their Asian counterparts, aware that dialogue with the fast growing nations of the region would be essential to Europe's economic prosperity and that successful trading relations would benefit from a firm cultural underpinning[54].

Gol and his Liberal colleagues, however, had sought a more ambitious formula to promote enhanced co-operation between the two continents. To enhance economic relations, Jan Willem Bertens MEP called[55] on the Council to draw up an action plan for the promotion of investment in each other's economies. As for wider strategic goals, part of the thinking behind Liberal support for the process was that if EU member states negotiated as one they

---

53 With which the EU had pledged in December 1995 to work more closely under a 'new transatlantic agenda' and had adopted in this regard a joint EU-US action plan.

54 I was among those privileged to participate in a number of the early ASEM projects including exchanges of young politicians from EU and Asian countries and to make many friendships which were later developed through the work of the Council of Asian Liberals and Democrats.

55 Speaking in a debate in Parliament on the preparations for the second ASEM summit in London in 1998.

would have far more clout, particularly when standing up to a powerful authoritarian country like China. Member states were reluctant, however, to do this: China was increasing its diplomatic pressure in line with its economic power and five years later not one of them was bold enough to table a motion critical of China's human rights record at the annual UN human rights conference in Geneva in March.

Closer to the east there were also interesting developments. A presidential election in Russia held out the promise of democratic reform there. The EU had signed with Russia a partnership and co-operation agreement which it wished to see ratified to provide the basis for a close relationship and a substantial partnership. It saw the accession of Russia to the Council of Europe on 28 February 1996 as a further step in this direction. This was a move that was welcomed at the time by Liberal members of the Parliamentary Assembly of the Council of Europe but greeted with some scepticism on the Liberal benches in the European Parliament. Russia was making a contribution to IFOR[56]; the EU sought to engage Moscow more widely in the development of 'a comprehensive European security architecture'. Paavo Vayrynen MEP, Liberal group spokesman on relations with Russia, argued for an approach based on concentric circles, consisting on the one hand of flexible differentiation within the Union and, on the other, of the creation of functional circles of cooperation around it. There would be an inner sphere including candidate countries; a wider Europe including those countries which remained outside the EU; and a European neighbourhood in which different forms of co-operation with Russia would be possible. This, he argued, would facilitate a solution to the conflict between the Union's consolidation and its expansion; but his enthusiasm for the concept was not widely shared, even among his fellow Liberals.

Liberals were concerned to see progress in relations with lesser developed countries too. The EU's relations with the former colonies of its member states in Africa, the Caribbean and the Pacific Ocean – organised through the Lome Convention – came up for review in 1997. Italian Liberal MEP Raimondo Fassa spearheaded action to fulfil Liberal hopes to see the policy of development succeed, so that all the ACP countries could abide by WTO rules and play a full role in the world trading arrangements. A WTO ruling in September 1997 declared the EU's arrangements for the import of bananas from the Caribbean to be incompatible with its WTO obligations since it discriminated against banana exporters from other Latin American countries; though the matter was not to be resolved for over ten years, the wind of change was blowing – imperial preferences could not continue indefinitely. Fassa recognised that change could not happen overnight; he steered through the House in July 1998 a report calling for greater EU support for fair trade arrangements with these countries.

Across the world in Hong Kong the UK government was in the process of returning five million people to rule from Beijing. Though certain safeguards were to be put in place to safeguard the territory's 'way of life' after the transfer of sovereignty in 1997, Hong Kong's democrats were naturally worried. Having lived and worked in Hong Kong, I took up the cudgels in the

---

56 A NATO-led multinational peacekeeping force in Bosnia and Herzegovina established in 1995.

European Parliament on behalf of the maintenance of democratic freedoms there and was pleased to be joined by MEPs of different nationalities and political groups in a series of visits to the island. We raised the issue in debate and sought assurances from external relations commissioner Leon Brittan about the future for democracy and the rule of law. From now on, Liberals argued, it would be up to the EU as a whole to take an interest in Hong Kong's future.[57]

Liberals squeezed

Counted on the basis of MEPs whose parties adhered to the European Liberal Democrat and Reform Party, the Liberals in 1994 had commanded the loyalty of just 43 MEPs. The 1995 enlargement had brought another eight MEPs. De Vries was under pressure from within to seek to attract others to the Liberal ranks. Belgian Liberal MEPs, under Jean Gol, sought an alliance with the right. UK Liberal MEPs and others pressed for an opening to the left. De Vries therefore engaged in discussions in 1995 and 1996 with both a right-wing splinter group, based on the French Gaullists and known as the Union for Europe (UFE) group, led by MEPs Jean-Claude Pasty and Giancarlo Ligabue and a left-wing splinter group called the European Radical Alliance (ERA), led by Frenchwoman Catherine Lalumiere. He knew that size in politics is important. But, as he suspected from the outset, the talks came to nought. Even had the opportunity arisen to form such an alliance, it is unclear whether the Liberals would all have consented to join forces with either one or the other. The division between those of an economic and those of a social Liberal hue was still considerable and the gap between right and left beyond the Liberal family still too large.

The existence of the UFE and ERA groups, however, proved a challenge for Liberals. De Vries had welcomed into Liberal ranks in 1994 the MEPs of the recently-formed Lega Nord from Italy, on the recommendation of Italian Republican colleague Giorgio La Malfa who described them to colleagues as 'regionalists capable of developing into a Liberal force'.[58] With the notable exceptions of former Varese Mayor Raimondo Fassa, an intellectual in the Liberal tradition, and charming folk-singer Gipo Farrassino, the Lega Nord MEPs never really settled. The increasingly strident populist tones of their leader Umberto Bossi, himself an MEP, started to jar with Liberal MEPs. The Lega Nord's campaigns to keep 'foreigners' out of 'Padania' (the land of the valley of the River Po) began to sound dangerously right wing. Difficulties were sometimes as much cultural as ideological. Bossi showed little interest in the European Parliament[59] and De Vries little interest in Italy. Empathy and sociability, so important to political leadership, were never among De Vries'

---

57 I was pleased to have my work on behalf of Hong Kong's people recognised publicly in his approval hearing by Commissioner Patten, Brittan's successor, who had been Governor of Hong Kong at the time.

58 The Lega Nord MEPs under Umberto Bossi were admitted with the votes of all members bar two. One colleague abstained; I voted against, knowing something of Italian politics through marriage and convinced that the Lega Nord was anything but Liberal.

59 Other than trying, together with former Milan mayor Marco Formentini MEP, to get EU financial aid for Milan's Malpensa airport.

greatest strengths. To southern Europeans in particular he came across as cold and distant, with little of the bonhomie endemic in their political cultures and too often unwilling to compromise in order to provide for their comfort.

In July 1996 the Lega Nord MEPs[60] left the ELDR group to join the new Union for Europe group, within just hours of a vote which would have delivered a clear majority in favour of their expulsion. The loss of seven Lega Nord MEPs was soon to be followed by the departure[61] of the eight Portuguese Social Democrats to swell the ranks of the EPP, bought and sold for German gold.

Thus in November 1996 the Liberals lost their position as the third party to a newly formed Union for Europe (UFE) group on the right wing. For Gijs de Vries, now called to speak only fourth in the major debates, this was a significant blow. For it to occur on the eve of a Dutch presidency of the EU was more galling still. Liberal prestige had taken a hit.

The Amsterdam Treaty

The Netherlands presidency, albeit noteworthy for little else, concluded successfully with the intergovernmental conference in Amsterdam at the European Council meeting of 16 and 17 June. Though less progress had been made in new treaty provisions for greater co-operation in justice and home affairs and common foreign and security policy than many had hoped, due to the intransigence of the UK and others, the new Amsterdam Treaty was deemed to involve sufficient reform of the EU's decision-making procedures to allow the EU to proceed towards enlargement to its south and east. With member state economies having pulled out of recession, progress was also deemed still to be on track for the EU's planned economic and monetary union.

Bringing into the EU some one hundred million eastern and southern neighbours, however, would be expensive. True, they would represent only 20% of the EU's population after the twelve new countries had joined, but the implications for agricultural support for farmers and the EU's structural funds to help poorer regions were significant. The European Commission therefore started a debate with Council and Parliament under the title 'Agenda 2000', with a view to building a consensus for reforms which would allow for the opening of accession negotiations in 1998. The content of their proposals, however, was as unimaginative as the title: 'adequate rather than visionary' was Cox's judgement on behalf of the Liberals.

Addressing the European Parliament on 16 July 1997, Commission president Santer had proposed an ECU 75bn plan to help the candidate countries of central and eastern Europe prepare for membership of the EU. Current EU member states would see a reduction in structural fund support, for example in regional aid, and cuts in the prices guaranteed to farmers for beef, cereals and milk. Liberals argued that the EU's budget should be increased; but since the Commission had been obliged to work with a total EU budget limited by

---

60 With the exception of Fassa, who stayed.

61 In a move orchestrated by Jose Manuel Barroso and despite a last minute appeal by De Vries in the form of an article in the Portuguese newspaper *Espresso* entitled 'Is the PSD for sale?'

the member states to just 1.27% of GDP, we backed the proposals. As our leader Gijs de Vries said in the debate, the economic and political advantages of enlargement outweighed any budgetary disadvantages.

UK Conservatives succeeded by Labour

Amsterdam had also witnessed an important change in the UK. The Conservative Party had lost the UK general election in June 1997, to be replaced by 'New' Labour under Tony Blair. Former Prime Minister Major's failure to control[62] the anti-Europeans who were increasingly active within his party and who had almost sabotaged the UK's ratification of the Maastricht Treaty had worried many of his continental counterparts; the treaty had secured approval in the House of Commons due only to Liberal support.[63] Moreover, Major's 'period of non co-operation with Europe'[64] in the aftermath of a ban on British beef exports to the continent had embarrassed the UK. While the Labour Party's election manifesto had been ingeniously unspecific and nobody knew much about Blair's view of the EU, he offered at least a fresh start.

An early welcome development was the UK's decision soon after the election[65] to move to a system of proportional representation for the 1999 European elections, in line with the recommendations from the European Parliament in the Giovanni Report[66]; though the Conservatives (under new leader William Hague) were to frustrate this legislation five times in the House of Lords and it was to be adopted only after a showdown between Lords and Commons[67], justice was finally to prevail. Another was its move at the EU's intergovernmental conference in Amsterdam to sign the Agreement on Social Policy annexed to protocol 14 to the TEU, thereby acceding to the social policy provisions of the new treaty. A campaign by the UK's popular press against 'Europe's social charter' had spread the belief that the EU sought a return to the corporate politics of the 1970s; social policy was to be foisted on the EU 'through the back door'[68], it was alleged. For a short while it even looked as if the UK might join the euro[69]. In fact the

---

62 On 22 June 1995 Major was to resign from his position as leader of the Conservative MPs and seek re-election in order to re-assert his authority, challenging his detractors to 'put up, or shut up'. It had little impact on the behaviour of the rebels.

63 German chancellor Helmut Kohl recognised this when he invited the UK Liberals' EU affairs spokesperson Charles Kennedy, their leader on the Parliamentary Assembly of the Council of Europe, Russell Johnston, and their leader in the European Parliament, Graham Watson, to a meeting in his office in Bonn in March 1996. No similar invitation was extended to the UK's Conservatives.

64 A decision by the EU standing veterinary committee to maintain a ban on UK exports of gelatine, semen and tallow after the lifting of the ban on beef meat was used by the UK government to justify a policy whereby the UK veto would be invoked to stop any EU decision requiring unanimity.

65 Clear by the end of June 1997 when the review of European Constituency electoral boundaries was halted, though not announced formally until some months later.

66 And earlier in a series of reports by Belgian Liberal Karel de Gucht MEP and others.

67 The agreement reached with the House of Lords to allow a change in the voting system led a furious William Hague to sack the leader of the Conservative peers, Lord Cranborne.

68 Or 'through the back Delors' as one headline writer put it.

69 Hague's stance against joining the euro had led Tory MEP James Moorhouse and former Tory MEP Paul Marshall to leave the Conservative party in October 1998 and join the Liberal Democrats. Moorhouse thus left the EPP group and joined ELDR.

UK government's change of approach was to prove more cosmetic than real; but at least the mood music from London sounded more cheerful.

Climate change

The 1997 Netherlands' presidency of the EU, with strong Liberal input from foreign minister Hans van Mierlo (D66) and solid support from EU affairs minister Michiel Patijn (VVD), had also been concerned that the EU should recognise the growing danger of human-induced climate change. American scientists had been warning for almost 20 years of the adverse impact of human activity on the planet's eco-system. The European Union took up these concerns and had been a sponsor of the Earth Summit on environment and development in Rio de Janeiro in 1991; Liberals now called for the Rio process to be accelerated to ensure sustainable global development through a change in production and consumption patterns. Legally binding commitments to reduce greenhouse gases had been sought; Netherlands' Liberal MEP Doeke Eisma[70] had worked hard to ensure a European offer in the UN Framework Convention on Climate Change (UNFCCC) to cut emissions of greenhouse gases by 15% below 1990 levels, in the hope that other parties to the convention would make similar commitments. Across the Atlantic, vice president-designate Al Gore was pursuing similar moves. Eisma, who had worked with Gore in the pressure group Parliamentarians for Global Action, redoubled his efforts to persuade his party colleagues in government in The Hague to push these matters firmly onto the EU's agenda. Lone Dybkjaer MEP was successfully to amend the EU's fifth environmental action programme in July 1998 to include the integration of environmental considerations into agricultural policy-making and to integrate the 'polluter pays' principle more widely into EU law-making. She secured agreement that taxation could be used to achieve environmental objectives.

Juncker emerges

The impact of globalisation of the economy on Europe's society was influencing thinking too. In the mid-1990s Europe was still grappling with the aftermath of recession. The Essen summit of December 1994, dubbed the 'jobs summit', had agreed an ambitious investment programme for cross border transport projects, now fourteen in total, to be financed with the help of the European Investment Bank to the tune of ECU 500 million. These were intended to help create jobs and lay the basis for future wealth-creation. In 1996 the Commission published a paper entitled *Action for employment in Europe; a confidence pact*; France published a memorandum on a 'European social model'. Both drew on the ideas contained in Delors' 1994 white paper on growth, competitiveness and employment. Yet creating a macro-economic framework favourable to employment and exploiting the full potential of the European single market were easier said than done. If there was much emphasis on the role of small and medium sized enter-

---

70   Eisma's report on monitoring greenhouse gases was to be adopted in September 1997.

prises, cynics sneered, it was partly because the larger ones were vanishing like snow off a dyke.

The European Parliament, in which the PES still formed the largest group, took the initiative in presenting to Commission and Council a resolution on boosting employment. Parliament's president was now a Christian Democrat – Jose Maria Gil Robles Gil Delgado having succeeded German Socialist Klaus Haensch at the halfway stage of the parliamentary mandate – and the Christian Democrats were keen to show they were at least as concerned as the Socialists about full employment. The impressively sharp and energetic Luxembourg Christian Democrat Jean-Claude Juncker, who had succeeded the valetudinarian Jacques Santer as prime minister, decided to convene an extraordinary European Council meeting on employment during the Luxembourg presidency of the Union in November 1997. He had asked Parliament to find ECU 150 million in the EU budget for employment initiatives[71]; and from now on, the Council resolved, member states' employment policies would form part of the multilateral surveillance of economic policy and 'employment guidelines' would be drawn up. Community institutions, the social partners and government at national and sub-national level were exhorted to join a determined approach across the EU to increase job opportunities for citizens. 'Good practices' were to be identified and disseminated.

Juncker was increasingly to take personal charge of the preparations for economic and monetary union. The process had been kept on track by German chancellor Helmut Kohl at the Amsterdam conference in mid-year, though Kohl had needed to sacrifice many of his other ambitions for Europe in so doing. Many hoped that the UK, under a new government, would decide to join, but their hopes were dashed in mid-October when UK chancellor of the exchequer Gordon Brown, in an interview with one of Rupert Murdoch's newspapers, had ruled out UK participation during Labour's first term of office.[72] Despite much talk about the need to make the single market function properly, Britain had failed to put its money where its mouth was.

Increasingly, however, definition of 'good practice' was to divide Socialists. Delors' model, embraced by French prime minister Alain Juppe and UK prime minister Tony Blair, still struck many Socialists as over-reliant on the market forces admired by Liberals since the teachings of Adam Smith over 300 years earlier. Hillary Clinton invited Europe's Socialist leaders to a conference on 'The Third Way' in New York in early September 1998 and Tony Blair was to tell a European Socialist conference in Italy in March 1999 that revision of left-wing economic policies was essential. Yet their views were rejected by many on the European left, encouraged by the likes of German Socialist firebrand Oskar Lafontaine MdB, who figured that if SDP leader Schroeder could beat Kohl in Germany's general election in September 1998 then little could be wrong. This division was to

71 As budget rapporteur for the economic and monetary affairs committee in 1997, it had fallen partly to me to do so. I persuaded the House to back me in a number of amendments to the budget including halting the publication of public contracts in the Official Journal in printed form; instead they would be available electronically.

72 Even the UK's Liberal Democrats, flushed with electoral success (46 MPs) and desperate for an accommodation with Labour, moved at their autumn conference to tone down their policy commitment to UK euro entry (despite the active opposition of your author).

weaken Europe's Socialist parties increasingly over the ensuing 15 years and to lead to a right-wing majority in the EU's institutions of government. It was to be exploited by Liberals, whose ideas were resurgent and who had found a new champion in single market commissioner Mario Monti to work alongside industry commissioner and long-time Liberal Martin Bangemann.

Paving the way for greater cohesion...

The 1997 Luxembourg presidency had also continued work on the transition to the single currency and established the ECOFIN Council as the co-ordinating body for member states' economic policies. Commissioner Monti had created a 'scoreboard' on which countries' progress in implementing single market laws would be measured and displayed. The work of making the EU a single economic entity was to be progressed through the triumvirate of the Luxembourg, UK and Austrian presidencies. Thus on 3 May 1998, under the UK presidency of the Union, it was announced that eleven member states met the conditions for joining the single currency and on 1 June the European Central Bank was formally established. The rate of exchange at which each participating country would join the euro had been agreed the previous autumn and though their currencies would continue in use for a further three years, from 1 January 1999 they would no longer be independent entities.

Not only was the economy picking up; Europe was getting its economic policy act together. The broad guidelines of economic policy, including structural reform, plus matters of budgetary discipline, were now to be agreed in common among the participating member states. On 9 June 1998 Carles Gasoliba MEP piloted through the House a series of recommendations for member states' economic policies: he stressed that investment was an important factor in fostering economic growth which would increase European competitiveness and that remaining obstacles to the single market needed to be swept away. Unemployment not only cost society directly, he pointed out: it represented a wasted growth potential. By June 1998 all 15 member states had submitted employment action plans as agreed the previous year. During 1998 some 1.7 million new jobs were to be created and unemployment across the EU was to fall below 10% for the first time since 1992.

... and for EU enlargement

Since the revolution in central and eastern Europe a number of former Soviet-bloc countries and two Mediterranean islands had been aiming for EU membership. The Luxembourg presidency of the EU in the second half of 1997 started to prepare the Union to accommodate them. It was agreed that each of the applicant states would proceed at its own pace, that a European conference would be set up (in London in March 1998) as a forum for political consultation with the countries seeking accession and that financial assistance to those countries would be increased substantially to help them reinforce their administrative and judicial capacity and to improve their economic infrastructure. However the talk was now only of ten former Soviet bloc countries plus Cyprus; the victory of the Labour Party in Malta's general election in October 1996 had changed that country's policy and it was not until the end of 1998 that the Maltese were again to express their desire to join the EU. Unlike in most European countries, with just two political parties represented in the Maltese capital Valetta[73] there was no Liberal centre to swing the balance in favour of EU integration.

The European Council meeting in Luxembourg on 12 and 13 December 1997 defined the basic conditions for those wishing to join. They had to share 'a common commitment to peace, security and good neighbourliness, respect for other countries' sovereignty, the principles on which the EU is founded, the integrity and inviolability of external borders and the principles of international law and a commitment to the settlement of territorial disputes by peaceful means, in particular through the jurisdiction of the International Court of Justice in the Hague.' Having witnessed the carnage in the former Yugoslavia, the EU member countries sought to lay down firm ground rules.

How enlargement of the EU was to be paid for remained a matter of contention. There was broad agreement that a new 'financial perspective' (pluri-annual budget) would be needed; it was agreed in 1998 that this should be of seven years duration. Yet there were already difficulties in finding the money pledged for the trans-European networks deemed essential to competitiveness; and member states were arguing about the size of their respective contributions to the EU's budget. Though negotiations for EU accession were opened with six countries on 31 March 1998 it was not until a year later, at an ad hoc meeting of the European Council in Berlin, that agreement was to be reached on budgetary matters.

Slovenia had largely escaped Yugoslavia's civil war and was now offered a bilateral intergovernmental conference to begin accession negotiations along with Hungary, Poland, the Czech Republic, Estonia and Cyprus. Liberals[74] were in government there, under Prime Minister Janez Drnovsec.

Turkish membership of the EU was also still on the agenda. In 1995 the Union had agreed to a customs union with Turkey; this had operated well; it had encouraged economic reform and helped to balance trade, but had not led to progress in political reforms. In March 1998 the Commission published a paper on helping Turkey to prepare for EU membership. Liberals supported this from the beginning. In a parliamentary debate on 16 September 1998 ELDR MEPs Jan Willem Bertens and Hans Lindqvist stressed the need for the Turkish government to comply with the Copenhagen criteria on respect for democracy and human rights which had to be observed by all applicant states. For Liberals, this had been and was to remain a sine qua non for the opening of accession negotiations.

Kosovo

In countries where no EU membership perspective could credibly be offered, Liberals argued for EU action to promote stability. Relations

---

73 The electoral system used in Malta was similar to that of the UK.

74 They were Liberals of strange heritage. The former League of Young Communists in Slovenia had effectively taken over the running of the country and now called itself Liberal Democrats of Slovenia. They had joined the European Liberal Democrat and Reform Party and behaved just like classical Liberals. They were to play – together with Hungary's FIDESZ youth movement – an important role in Liberal co-operation in central and eastern Europe.

between the EU and the Western European Union (WEU) were being consolidated; the EU was playing an active role in NATO's operations in Bosnia
and Herzegovina and in Kosovo. Yet police 'anti-terrorist' operations by
Milosevic's forces in Kosovo early in 1998 had left 80 people dead, including women, children and elderly people. While the European Parliament
had warned of impending violence and while the Americans had a special
envoy in place, the EU had failed to act. Milosevic's refusal to negotiate with
Kosovo's ethnic Albanian leader Ibrahim Rugova had created a quarter of a
million refugees unable to return to their homes. As the year progressed it
became clear that the Kosovo conflict threatened the EU with another mass
influx of refugees for which it was ill prepared. On 18 November 1998
Parliament was to adopt another report by Jan-Kees Wiebenga calling for
temporary protection for displaced persons; it was irresponsible that the EU
had no proper arrangements, he argued, calling for rules on burden sharing
to ensure a balanced distribution of refugees in the event of mass influx.

Speaking in a debate in the House on 11 March 1998 De Vries was unchar-
acteristically blunt, condemning the EU's response to the violence as 'shame-
ful and hypocritical' and calling for military intervention. Cox was to repeat
the call in September. Brinkhorst was active on the EP's budget committee in
making financial provisions for an EU defence policy. By September the
Commission had taken up the Liberals' call for military intervention, if
backed by an EU or UN Security Council resolution. Cox said in the House
that the lessons of Bosnia showed that a strong stance was needed. The EU
decided to contribute 1,000 men to a 2,000 man unarmed observer force (the
Kosovo verification mission); and it turned down Milosevic's proposal that
he should run EU-funded food centres for Kosovan refugees which Liberal
commissioner Emma Bonino, in charge of humanitarian affairs, had
described as 'like letting Dracula run a blood bank'.

By the time of the European election campaign in 1999 the most immediate challenge facing the Union was to be the raging civil war in Kosovo.
Serbia had shown at the Chateau Rambouillet talks in early March that it
was in no mood for peace. NATO countries were not prepared to send in
ground troops to protect the Kosovan Albanians but were ready to conduct
an aerial bombing campaign, Operation Allied Force, against Serb targets.
From the end of March until early June 1999 this was to dominate news coverage, almost eclipsing any other issues in the European election campaign.

Citizens' concerns

Yet for all the moves to make the EU's response to supranational challenges
more coherent, Europe's citizens remained unconvinced. They wanted the EU
to help resolve the problems they encountered in their daily lives. Through
Parliament's petitions committee and other channels, MEPs sought to assist.
For example, MEPs[75] had complained to the Commission early in 1998 that

---

75 36 MEPs took the case to court, led by Belgian Socialist Philippe de Coene and your author; the latter was to
receive an award from the UK Football Supporters Association for his efforts.

France was contravening EU competition law in its plans for the distribution of tickets for the football World Cup to be held in France that year. This had been organised in such way that few if any tickets were to be made available on the free market, resulting in a black market where extortionate prices were demanded. Commissioner Van Miert looked into the matter, clearly irritating France. In June 1998, preparing for the European Council meeting in Cardiff under the UK presidency, Kohl and Chirac sent a letter to other heads of state and government arguing for greater 'subsidiarity'. They wanted Brussels off their backs. Chirac was to take Commission president Jacques Santer to one side at the Cardiff meeting and tell him that the Commission should cease meddling in the preparations of the organising committee for the World Cup. I was one of 36 MEPs who decided to take the matter to court in Paris. Our case was dismissed on a technicality (the court ruled that since we had not attempted to purchase tickets ourselves, we did not qualify as litigants), and the Commission was to levy only a paltry fine of around 5,000 French francs (less than 1,000 euros in today's terms). Nonetheless the Court recognised the strength of our case; an extra 6,000 tickets were made available as a result of our action and the Commission was to make sure that ticket distribution in future sporting tournaments, such as the Euro 2000 championship in Belgium and the Netherlands, complied with EU law.

Nor were Liberal MEPs to shirk from criticism of their own member states. During the UK presidency in 1998, a UK Liberal MEP was to raise concerns about the lack of enfranchisement of Gibraltar's citizens in European elections; and a Belgian Liberal MEP led Parliament's call in July 1998 for the Belgian government to transpose into national law a 1994 directive giving citizens from other EU countries resident in Belgium the right to vote in municipal elections.

Liberal MEPs had been active in securing the appointment of an EU ombudsman in 1995. Though the post had been provided for in the Maastricht Treaty of 1992 it had not been filled. Elisabeth Rehn had led a campaign to have the first ombudsman appointed and her successor Astrid Thors was to lead a campaign in 1998 in support of Ombudsman Jakob Soederman's calls for greater public access to documents held by the EU institutions.

Concerned too about the cultural side of EU integration, Liberal MEPs sought to advance where possible the promotion of a common European culture and access to culture. Thus Philippe Monfils of Belgium's Mouvement Reformateur was to work on the proposal for an annual European capital of culture and Finnish MEP Mirja Ryynanen was to lead calls for the modernisation of libraries and their linking together across frontiers. Where we differed from neo-Liberals was that we were not market fundamentalists. Markets, while useful, were not to be worshipped. The social nature of human beings, their capacity for charity and reciprocity and their ability to express their values through literature, music and the arts was important to us.

Fisheries

Among the environmental concerns felt strongly by Liberals was the EU's common fisheries policy (CFP). The world had witnessed the collapse of cod stocks on the Grand Banks of Newfoundland in 1992. Scientists were warning that the same phenomenon could appear in the North Sea, the EU's main fishing ground. Subsidies to fishermen under the CFP were encouraging over-fishing and depletion of fish stocks; moreover, the EU was paying developing countries like Senegal and Mauritius to allow EU boats to fish in their waters for pelagic stocks and MEPs were concerned about the sustainability of this practice. We started to vote against partnership and co-operation agreements with developing countries unless we were satisfied with the sustainability of the fisheries component. The European People's Party favoured treating fisheries as simply another sector of economic activity[76]. Concerned about this approach, Commissioner Emma Bonino set up in 1997 a task force on the future of the CFP, to report to the Commission by the end of 2002.

Fisheries inspections were the responsibility of the EU member states, however, with the Commission's inspectors occupying only a secondary role. Bonino proposed reforms which would allow EU inspectors to make spot checks and demand instant access to documents. Robin Teverson MEP called on the Commission to go further to stop illegal fishing, which was rife, and led Parliament's call in October 1998 for tougher controls than those proposed by the Commission: in particular he wanted controls extended throughout the supply chain with criminal sanctions on those caught handling 'illegal' fish. Moreover, penalties for infringements should be comparable across the EU.

The Commission's downfall

De Vries' VVD party had entered government as a coalition partner in 1994 and a reshuffle of ministerial portfolios in the Netherlands at the end of July 1998 saw Gijs de Vries called to The Hague as a government minister. Although a convinced European federalist, De Vries was now less enamoured of prospects in Brussels and was tempted home[77]. With just nine months to go until the 1999 elections he was succeeded by his deputy Pat Cox[78] as Liberal leader. Though neither Cox nor De Vries could have known it, a rare political opportunity was soon to fall into the Liberal leader's hands.

In the autumn of 1997 the European Court of Auditors, reporting on the Union's 1996 accounts, declined to give a statement of global assurance with regard to the legality and regularity of payments made by the European Commission. This was not in itself surprising: 80% of all payments made from the EU budget were in fact made by national governments and the EU treaties did not give the ECA the right to inspect member state accounts in all spending areas. The Union's accounts were desperately complicated and its accounting systems obtuse, compounded by the fact that shortage of staff in the

---

76 See, for example, the motion for a parliamentary resolution by Carmen Fraga MEP, 6 November 1997.77 De Vries had been offered a similar ministerial post earlier in the government but had turned it down; he did not wish to say No a second time, though the proposed to him were on neither occasion a generous offer to a man of his talents. Indeed he had given an interview to a newspaper announcing that he would not seek re-election to the EP in 1999 and that if he could not find a role in national politics he would look for opportunities in the private sector.

77 De Vries had been offered a similar ministerial post earlier in the government but had turned it down; he did not wish to say No a second time, though the roles proposed to him were on neither occasion a generous offer to a man of his talents. Indeed he had given an interview to a newspaper announcing that he would not seek re-election to the EP in 1999 and that if he could not find a role in national politics he would look for opportunities in the private sector.

78 Cox was elected unopposed at an ELDR group meeting in Venice early in September 1998.

European Commission had led to increasing reliance on outside agencies known as Technical Assistance Offices, often responsible for the spending of considerable amounts of taxpayers' money. Problems had been identified and highlighted by the EP's budgetary control committee, chaired by formidable German Conservative Diemut Theato, which had made countless recommendations for improvements. But as the decade progressed, the level of journalistic interest in public accounts – and the development of a new breed of journalists who sought to sniff out and expose corruption in government – had grown rapidly, particularly in Italy, France and the UK. A number of newspaper proprietors were enamoured of the opportunity to expose financial misdeeds in the EU and what has been described as 'a little cottage industry of sleaze busting' was developing in Brussels. Inevitably this industry would attract a few MEPs keen to make a name for themselves as champions of the public financial interest and to enjoy a level of media attention which rarely accrued to those choosing a political career in Brussels.

Liberal members of the EP's budgetary control committee had been pursuing allegations of fraud for some time. Danish Liberal MEP Eva Kjer-Hansen had raised the case of fraudulent claims for travel expenses made by members of the Economic and Social Committee. Italian Liberal Stefano de Luca had carried out an enquiry into fraud against the tourism budget.

By the end of March 1998 Parliament's budgetary control committee had responded to the auditors' report by proposing to postpone the granting of discharge for 1996 until the Commission had answered a number of questions, particularly about its failure to act on earlier parliamentary recommendations. MEPs felt a growing concern about the arrogance of certain commissioners and their officials towards a Parliament to which they were theoretically accountable but which in practice they often ignored and, at times, treated with contempt. They were concerned too that by the middle of 1998 member states had not yet ratified the Convention on the Protection of the European Communities' Financial Interests, which sought to enlist member state authorities to help in the fight against fraud. The Commission was given until mid-September 1998 to come up with its explanations. However a series of developments carrying the whiff of scandal intervened, and by the autumn the mood among even ardently federalist MEPs who would normally defend the Commission against all criticism was one of disquiet. Prime amongst the allegations of wrongdoing was the payment of monies to one Rene Berthelot, formally a technical adviser to the Commission but in reality a dentist by profession and Edith Cresson's personal astrologer (and rumoured in the French press to have been her lover). The Commission's failure to deliver to Parliament's satisfaction by 15 September 1998 the information MEPs had sought, a series of further revelations during the autumn months of corruption or financial mismanagement and an ECA report on the 1997 accounts which suggested continuing difficulties – plus, crucially, the failure of the college of commissioners to read the political danger signals – combined to create a perfect and rapidly gathering political storm.

As is often the case, the reaction of the officials to the frustration and scepticism of MEPs contributed to making matters worse. In replies to parliamentary debates in Brussels in November and in Strasbourg on 2 December 1998 Commission president Santer failed to convince MEPs that he took their concerns seriously; on the latter occasion he lost his temper and challenged Parliament to bring on a motion of censure against his Commission. This 'nuclear option' had not been considered or proposed by Parliament, which was debating the much milder sanction of refusal to discharge the Commission for its handling of one year's accounts (which, though serious, is not linked in the powers conferred on Parliament by the EU treaties to a motion of censure).

Parliamentary opinion was deeply divided. The Socialist MEPs had no wish to cause a crisis in their relations with a college of commissioners composed mainly of fellow Socialists. The Christian Democrats did not wish to bring down one of their own, Commission president Jacques Santer. Leading members of the budgetary control committee understood, however – perhaps more than their group leaders – the seriousness of the situation. When the committee voted on 10 December 1998 – by a margin of just one vote – to grant discharge while adopting a report which suggested refusal, it was due to pressure from the leaders of the two major groups on their committee members. Rapporteur James Elles and committee chair Diemut Theato were outvoted.

The European Council meeting in Vienna on 11 and 12 December 1998 maintained a stony silence about these developments. In an abdication of leadership which was to be repeated in another Commission crisis six years later, the heads of state and government left Parliament and Commission to sort out difficulties which threatened to paralyse the Union. While the member state leaders discussed improvements to the functioning of the EU's institutions including working procedures of the Council, ratification of the Amsterdam Treaty and reform of the Commission they said little[79] about the EU's current difficulty other than urging action to fight fraud wherever it occurred and welcoming the Commission's proposal to establish an independent office to investigate fraud.

Five days later, on 15 December 1998, the committee's report – which accused the European Commission of doing 'serious harm' to the EU – came to the floor of the House. Worried that, on the basis of the report, the House might refuse to grant discharge, budget commissioner Erkki Likkanen and Socialist group leader Pauline Green MEP hatched a plan whereby if discharge were refused a motion of no confidence in the Commission would be tabled, sure that MEPs would baulk at such a move and that the Commission's authority would thus be restored. Opinion among the Liberals and the Greens, however, had hardened, partly because a Commission official called Paul van Buitenen had started passing confidential information to the Greens and sharing it with fellow Dutchman and former Commission colleague Jan Mulder MEP, who spoke for the Liberals on budgetary issues. While the parliamentary debate on 15 December was inconclusive, Santer scored a second own goal the following day by announcing his intention to seek a vote of confidence should Parliament reject discharge in the vote the next day[80]. On 17 December 1998, before the

---

79 The matter was deemed to merit just one paragraph (paragraph 82) in almost 125 paragraphs of presidency conclusions from the summit.

80 Under the European Parliament's somewhat arcane procedures a vote is sometimes postponed until two days after the debate.

vote, a sour exchange of views took place on the floor of the House between fatigued group leaders united only in their view that the Commission had handled the whole affair badly. By 270 votes to 225 with 23 abstentions the House refused to approve the Commission's handling of the EU's finances. While most speakers insisted this was not a vote of censure, it was clearly the beginning of the end for Jacques Santer, now fatally wounded. Though Liberal leader Pat Cox had voted for discharge, most of his colleagues had not; even EPP leader Wilfried Martens abstained, unable to bring himself to do more to save his Benelux EPP colleague Santer.

A motion to censure the Commission was duly tabled by Socialist leader Pauline Green, who insisted that her group would vote against the motion to allow the Commission to continue in office. Under Parliament's rules, however, the motion could not be debated until three days had elapsed; and since the House rose on 18 December this meant that when Parliament returned in January the matter was still the House's primary concern. The media was thus treated to a banquet of headlines crying 'scandal' just six months before the European elections.

By January, the Socialists had decided to try to get themselves off the hook of their own making by calling for an independent review to investigate how allegations of wrongdoing against individual commissioners are dealt with. The Liberals and the EPP, however – not wishing to see the whole Commission sacrificed – favoured narrowing the matter down by calling for the heads of Commissioners Cresson and Marin.

In the debate on censure on 11 January 1999, EPP leader Wilfried Martens had to pull his punches to avoid wounding Santer too much. Liberal leader Pat Cox found his moment. Speaking of the principle of collective responsibility, while reminding his audience that in national governments ministers are also held individually responsible for their departments, he pointed out that making everyone responsible effectively meant that no-one is responsible. 'The rot ... will never stop if every commissioner can constantly rely on the shield of collegiality and avoid personal responsibility', he stated to widespread applause. Santer's reply to the debate was better than his previous efforts; but the agreement by Commissioners Cresson and Marin, sitting with their colleagues alongside their president, to take the floor to defend themselves towards the end of the debate sealed the Commission's fate. Edith Cresson's refusal to stand to address the House was even worse than the attitude she displayed in her intervention. While Marin, the more substantial and experienced politician, ate humble pie, Commissioner Cresson treated her audience with thinly disguised contempt.

Liberals sought to bring closure to the affair as quickly as possible, anxious that it should not hang over the European election campaign. Yet an agreement between left and right ensured that the motion of censure was withdrawn before the vote three days later, in favour of a motion to establish a committee of independent experts to examine the way in which the Commission detects and deals with fraud, mismanagement and nepotism. The process would now be dragged out almost to the point at which Parliament dissolved for the election. And the college of commissioners was a row of sitting ducks for any amateur marksman.

On 15 March 1999 the independent experts published their 142-page report, which was particularly severe in its criticism of Commissioner Cresson and mismanagement by her department of the Leonardo programme, and thorough and damning in many of its conclusions. The phrase 'It is becoming difficult to find anyone [in the Commission] who has even the slightest sense of responsibility', inserted late in the day, was the straw which broke the camel's back. By ten o'clock that evening the Commission had resigned collectively.

The EU's German presidency used the subsequent spring European Council on 24 and 25 March 1999 to sort out the messy aftermath. The heads of state and government 'noted with respect' the resignation of the Commission and thanked it for the work it had done. They decided to nominate former Italian prime minister Romano Prodi to form a new Commission to take office that autumn while the current administration continued purely on a 'caretaker' basis.

If Jacques Santer had been seen by some governments in 1994 as a Commission president whom they could more easily control after the roller coaster days of Jacques Delors (and the UK's veto of the more heavyweight Franco-German candidate Jean-Luc Dehaene), the European Parliament was often still viewed by national leaders as a pubescent gathering to be treated more with tolerance than respect. Yet with its actions at the time of the investiture of the Santer Commission and again at the time of its dismissal, Parliament had shown that it had arrived.

On 25 May 1999 the new European anti-fraud office was established. Thanks to close and constructive co-operation between Parliament, Council and Commission it began its work on 1 June. One of its key tasks was to be an investigation of all offices and agencies established by the EU, to root out any further problems. Combined with the far reaching reforms Prodi had undertaken to carry out in the Commission, the Augean Stables were expected to sparkle.

To the astonishment of Liberals, Santer was subsequently and successfully to stand for election to the European Parliament where, in addition to his generous pension from the European Commission, he could be seen signing the register every day to claim his allowances while apparently doing little, if any, work.

Amsterdam enters into force

When the European Council met on 3 and 4 June 1999 under the German presidency it appointed former Spanish minister Javier Solana[81] as its secretary general and high representative for foreign and security policy, a post which had been created in the Amsterdam Treaty. Solana was to speak and act for Europe's governments on foreign affairs matters. Yet if the creation of the euro meant the EU could play a global role commensurate with its economic weight, no similar locking together of foreign policies was to occur. And though limited progress was to be made in coaxing and cajoling EU member states to act together, when Solana left office ten years later it was to be without the EU having had any significant impact in promoting

---

81 A grandson of Don Salvador de Madariaga, one of the founders of the Liberal International; but Javier Solana wore Socialist colours and had been a minister in Socialist governments.

peace in the Middle East, on which Solana chose to concentrate most of his efforts, and after the Union had been shown to be hopelessly divided over the American-led invasion of Iraq.

As the spring progressed, Liberal prospects looked good. The ELDR Party met in Berlin at the beginning of May in good spirits. In Finland, Centre Party leader and former prime minister Esko Aho[82] had taken his party to 22.4% of the vote in the general election in March, close on the heels of the Socialists. In Scotland and Wales Liberal Democrats had entered government in May in the new devolved assemblies. On 7 June, the same day as the European election, the Democratic Party of Luxembourg replaced the Socialist Party as the junior government coalition partner and a week later the Liberals were to triumph over the Christian Democrats in Belgium.

The European elections of 4-7 June 1999 brought an important political change. The Party of European Socialists, the largest group in every previous mandate, was overtaken by the right-wing European People's Party. With 233 MEPs to the Socialists' 180, the EPP was triumphant.

Liberals returned from the election once more as Parliament's third largest force and in slightly greater numbers. Ten MEPs were elected from the UK, changing considerably the internal balance in the group; the Netherlands, Denmark, Finland and Belgium were also still strongly represented, as was Italy.

I sought to boost our numbers further by bringing over the Italian Radical Party MEPs, of whom there were seven; but Italian centre leader Francesco Rutelli was not keen, nor Cox.[83] The Radicals were not traditional Liberals, though they had formed as a breakaway from a Liberal party: they acted more like campaigners from a pressure group, over a wide variety of subjects, and were ready to use civil disobedience and hunger strikes to advance their causes. The Radicals – fired by a mission against the Catholic church on issues of society and morality in particular – would take up issues long before there was any evident public support for change and seek to build it. The hesitation about a joining of our forces was not only on the Liberal side, however; Radical Party leader Pannella and leading light Emma Bonino were not convinced they could feel comfortable in a group together with Rutelli and his followers.

Part of the reason for Cox's reluctance, perhaps, was that having so many Italians would alter substantially the internal balance within the ELDR group. The D'Hondt system which has traditionally ordered affairs in the European Parliament dictates that the leader of the largest delegation in each political group has first choice of the positions of authority available. There might be a danger that the Italians would seek the group's leadership.

For Cox, this danger existed theoretically with the UK delegation too. As a result of the election I was now the head of the largest national delegation

---

82   Esko Aho had become, at 36, the youngest prime minister in Finnish history when he led a centre-right coalition from 1991 to 1995. His clever diplomacy had won over the doubters in his Keskusta party and steered Finland into the EU. In 2000 his bid for the presidency of Finland was to fail and he was to retire from active politics.

83   I had talks with Rutelli on 20 June 1999 and with Pannella (and separately with independent MEP Vittorio Sgarbi) the following day. I finally persuaded Cox to speak directly to Emma Bonino on 7 July.

within the European Liberal Democrat and Reform group. I was aware, however, that my new colleagues from the UK brought an intriguing mix of character and skills which would require time to 'bed in', and also that I had only five years' experience of the House and none in a position of great responsibility. Although some colleagues urged me to assume the leadership of the group, I believed an alternative solution might be both possible and preferable.

I knew that many EPP MEPs, including their new leader Hans-Gert Poettering, had been annoyed by their own group's unwillingness to rock the boat over the Commission's financial mismanagement; they had been impressed in contrast by Cox's bold action, believing that public confidence in the EU required a European Parliament ready to take up the cudgels when circumstances required. They recognised that the 1999 Parliament had much to do to earn its laurels and perceived the Liberals as possible partners in this process. Moreover, they had become for the first time ever the largest group in the House and might be tempted to underline their new found position of strength by offering a power-sharing agreement to the Liberals rather than the Socialists. If they could be persuaded to assist me in obtaining my first choice of committee chair, thus affording me a prominent parliamentary committee and a chance to gain experience of the higher echelons of the House, I would be persuaded to back Cox to continue as ELDR group leader for the first half of the parliamentary mandate.

Naturally the ELDR group spoke to both sides, each of which was prepared to offer similar terms in a power-sharing arrangement. But the majority of Liberals favoured an alliance with the EPP, this coalition being also numerically stronger. On 8 July 1999 negotiators from the two parties met[84]. And although the ELDR negotiators held further formal meetings with each party on Tuesday of the following week, the die had effectively been cast.

As had become the norm for PES-EPP coalitions, the EPP-ELDR pact took the form of an agreement whereby, in exchange for Liberal support for EPP candidate Nicole Fontaine as president of Parliament for the first half of the mandate, the EPP would lend its support to the election of Liberal leader Pat Cox as speaker from January 2002 to July 2004.

Moreover, since the agreement involved jam today in exchange for jam tomorrow, the EPP also agreed to assist the Liberals with their first choice of committee for the one committee chairman's post to which our numbers entitled us.

I therefore decided to support Cox to continue for two and a half years while I took up a position as chairman of the committee on citizens' rights and freedoms, justice and home affairs. It was broadly understood by colleagues that I was the leader-in-waiting, expected to take over when Cox was elevated to the post of speaker. I had helped secure for the ELDR group a position we had not held since 1979, the presidency of our House. For my part, I knew I had also built a golden bridge over which Cox could withdraw gracefully.

84   For the EPP Poettering, Martens, and Galeote; for the ELDR Cox, Haarder and Watson, accompanied by the secretary general of each group, over supper at Chez Marius en Provence in Brussels.

Chapter 2:   1999 – 2001

The EU embarked on a programme of policy harmonisation in justice and home affairs, as foreseen in the Maastricht and Amsterdam treaties; this was to be given added saliency by the Al Qaida attacks on New York and Washington on 11 September 2001. Member states were to attempt to agree on further reforms needed to the EU to accommodate new member states from central and eastern Europe and the Mediterranean: the French presidency was unable to secure agreement but a new attempt was made under the Belgian presidency, with its Laeken Declaration establishing a convention to elaborate a new treaty. Euro notes and coins were printed by the end of 2001 for entry into circulation on 1 January 2002. Meanwhile political parties of the far right enjoyed a growth in public support.

Council presidencies during this period were assumed by Finland (2nd half 1999), Portugal and France (2000), and Sweden and Belgium (2001).

The European Parliament which assembled in July 1999 was an institution strengthened not only by its predecessor's dismissal of Jacques Santer's Commission, but also by the acquisition of new powers under the Amsterdam Treaty which gave MEPs powers of co-decision with the Council of Ministers over many new areas of policy.

Pat Cox, who had succeeded Gijs de Vries just nine months prior to the elections, was re-elected unopposed as ELDR group leader. The group secured the election of Jan Kees Wiebenga as a vice president of Parliament, though he was appointed Queen's counsel in the Netherlands before the mid-term of the mandate and was to be succeeded on 23 October 2001 by Elly Plooij. Similarly, I was elected to chair the committee on citizens' rights and freedoms, justice and home affairs but was destined to step down at the mid-term, at which point Italian Liberal Luciano Caveri was elected to chair the committee on regional policy, transport and tourism.

The composition of the Liberal group differed substantially from that of the Christian Democrat or Socialist groups. The introduction of proportional representation for European elections in the UK had re-balanced the representation of the largest member states within the major political groups. This was particularly important since, across the 15 member state Parliament, the four largest member states provided almost 60% of the MEPs. In the ELDR group, however, this figure was barely 30%. The introduction of a fair voting system in the UK had given me nine new Liberal Democrat compatriots and Italian Liberal representation had swollen with the arrival of six MEPs from the Democratic Party, under Francesco Rutelli. However Liberals in Germany had been unable since 1989 to overcome the hurdle of 5% of the popular vote to secure election to Strasbourg[85]; and in France no recognisably Liberal party any longer existed. This gave the smaller national delegations comparatively more sway than in the two big groups. Although Austria, Greece and Portugal returned no Liberal MEP, the Netherlands, Belgium, Denmark and Finland were all strongly represented.

As leader of the UK Liberal Democrat MEPs I worked hard to ensure that the talented intake of nine new UK members was well represented in the distribution within our group of committee co-ordinator posts; while none enjoyed the previous experience in the European Parliament which would qualify them well for greater responsibilities initially[86], all were capable of learning fast and prepared to work hard.

In this new parliament, though only 50 of 626 MEPs at the outset, Liberals found themselves able to make a difference to voters' everyday lives: since neither the Christian Democrats (233 Members) nor the Socialists (180) alone could form a majority[87], Liberal votes frequently determined the winning coalition[88].

The link to new Commission president Romano Prodi through the Italian Democrats not only gave the Liberal group substantial representation from Italy, but also an inside track to the very top of the new European Commission. Numerical representation of Liberals in the early colleges of commissioners had not been strong. It had risen to four in the Delors colleges[89], but fallen back to two under Santer, in Martin Bangemann from Germany, re-appointed for a second term, and Italian commissioner Emma Bonino. In the current Commission, besides Prodi, the other European commissioner to whom Liberals had privileged access through party political affiliation was the Netherlands' Frits Bolkestein, responsible for the internal market. Bolkestein was well known in Liberal circles beyond the Netherlands, having served as leader of his party, the VVD, and as president of the Liberal International from June 1996 to March 1999.

---

85   German MP Werner Hoyer was to share with MEPs Mulder and Watson, during their visit to Berlin on 3-4 December, his frustration with his party's performance. If they failed to do well in next spring's elections in Schleswig Holstein and Rheinland Pfalz it would be not just their embattled leader Wolfgang Gerhardt who would be finished 'but the party itself'. One of the party's Young Turks, Jorgo Chatzimarkakis, was already calling for a change of strategy towards an alliance with Germany's Green party.

86   One cruel irony of the introduction of proportional representation was that it cost the UK Liberals the second MEP who had been elected in 1994, Robin Teverson, who narrowly failed to secure re-election. I was in fact able to secure for Baroness Nicholson, an experienced UK parliamentarian, the first vice chair of the foreign affairs committee. And parliamentary experience in the UK Liberal ranks was to be boosted in November 2000 when UK Conservative MEP Bill Newton-Dunn, a long serving MEP increasingly frustrated with his own party's anti-Europeanism, crossed the floor of the House to join us.

87   There were 48 Greens and Regionalists in the G-EFA group, 42 former Communists in the EUL group and 73 others in smaller groups or non-attached.

88   For example, we were able to achieve a more integrated single market and defend the principles of a sound economy by forming a centre-right majority; and to advance environmental sustainability or protect civil liberties by siding with the left.

89   By rotation Martin Bangemann, Willy de Clercq, Henning Christophersen, Cristiane Scrivener, Antonio Cardoso e Cunha.

Though Prodi and Bolkestein, both in their 60s, were the oldest members of the college of commissioners, their energy was impressive. Prodi was to oversee the introduction of the euro notes and coins and the enlargement of the EU from 15 to 25 member states while simultaneously managing to inspire and guide the opposition in Italy to the government of Silvio Berlusconi, in office since May 1994. Bolkestein was to secure significant legislative advances during his five year term of office and was to cap his achievements in the provocative style of politics which he so much enjoyed by lobbing at his successors a political hand grenade in the form of a draft directive on the liberalisation of the internal market in services.

Liberal strength in the European Council, though weak compared to the days of Giscard's presidency of France and Genscher's time at the German foreign ministry, was also once more on the rise. Belgian prime minister Guy Verhofstadt, who had won election on 13 June 1999, was to be joined by Denmark's Anders Fogh Rasmussen in November 2001 and Finland's Matti Vanhanen in June 2003. The terrain seemed increasingly favourable for European Liberal forces again to play a bigger role in the management of their continent's affairs.

Freedom, security and justice

Fundamental to Liberals is the defence of citizens' rights. Having sought and obtained the chair of the justice and home affairs committee for the first half of Parliament's mandate we sought to make best use of the political opportunities it could bring. We were assisted in this task by Socialist commissioner Antonio Vitorino of Portugal, a man whose sharp intellect and liberal convictions were to contribute importantly to the development of the EU. In one of the most challenging roles in Prodi's Commission, Vitorino inherited a secretariat of just 20 people under Commission official Adrian Fortescue with the task of building it into a directorate general for a policy area which – with the growing pressures of migration and increasingly sophisticated international criminal activity and the new powers conferred on the EU by the Treaty of Amsterdam – had suddenly assumed a new importance.

Having already built a single market and an economic and monetary union, which they considered the main planks of a shared area of peace and prosperity, EU leaders now sought to ensure that their citizens could enjoy freedom in conditions of security and justice available to all. The freedoms generated by the single market had thrown into sharp relief the lack of a single legal area, which had been highlighted in a parliamentary report by Dutch Liberal Jan Kees Wiebenga in April 1999, shortly before the House rose for elections. It was Europe's failure to build common policies in justice and home affairs that the heads of state and government now sought to rectify.

Liberals had promoted back in 1989 a celebration by the European Parliament of the bi-centenary of the French Revolution and the adoption of a 'Declaration of Fundamental Rights and Freedoms'. Ten years later, after the heads of state and government agreed at the Cologne European Council in June 1999 that the time had come for the EU to draw up a Charter of Fundamental Rights – to catalogue in one document the civil, political, economic and social rights of EU citizens – Liberals were again in the vanguard. At an extraordinary meeting under the Finnish presidency in Tampere on 15

and 16 October 1999 the European Council set out to create 'an area of freedom, security and justice' within the European Union. Though we were to
complain that there was too much emphasis on security, not enough on freedom and far too little on justice, we supported the Council's decision to 'place
and maintain this objective at the very top of the political agenda': and its
resolve to establish a body to draw up a draft Charter of Fundamental Rights
for the EU[90], to be composed of one representative of each member state, one
representative of the European Commission and sixteen representatives of the
European Parliament. Whereas Liberal MEPs had failed to secure representation on previous such bodies, this time we were to be successful.[91]

The convention to draft the charter was presided over by the former president of Germany, Roman Herzog and opened in December that year. Among
its members were prominent Liberal and former Italian prime minister
Lamberto Dini. Parliament's joint rapporteurs were Liberal MEP Andrew Duff
and Green MEP Johannes Voggenhuber. Duff presented to the House in March
2000 a draft of Parliament's priorities for the convention, designed to update
the 1953 European Convention on Human Rights of the Council of Europe.
MEPs were to play an important role in the proceedings of the convention and
the charter was adopted by the convention on 2 October 2000, approved by the
informal European Council meting in Biarritz on 13 October and by Parliament
on 14 November and formally proclaimed by the Nice European Council on 7
December 2000. Liberals were angry however that it was not formally incorporated into the Treaty of Nice and made legally binding; for this it would
have to await the Treaty of Lisbon, ten years later.

Moreover the Council agreed in Tampere to mobilise the police and judicial
resources of the member states in a common fight against crime. They agreed
to move towards a system of 'common definitions, incriminations and sanctions' for offences such as money laundering, the trafficking of drugs and
people, sexual exploitation of children, technology-based crime and environmental crime. To complement the work of Europol[92] they agreed to establish
two new bodies: a European Police College for the training of law enforcement
officials and a body called Eurojust to bring together prosecutors in the fight
against cross-border crime. Better access to justice, mutual recognition of judicial decisions and greater convergence in civil law were also to be worked on.

Some governments were keen to to harmonise offences and penalties in
the fight against crime: an ambitious project, especially in view of the difficulties which had been encountered in harmonising economic measures to
create the single market. Liberals felt that mutual recognition of judicial
standards would be a more practical approach, at least initially, to allow the
EU to operate as if there were no legal boundaries. The key concept had to
be full confidence in each others' legal systems. We sought common minimum standards and safeguards in, for example, the treatment of suspects in

---

90   In 1989 the European Parliament had adopted a declaration of fundamental rights and freedoms, based on
work done by Karel de Gucht MEP earlier in the 1984-89 EP mandate.

91   Of the 16 EP representatives there were two ELDR MEPs: Andrew Duff and Lone Dybkjaer.

92   The European Police Office was established by convention in July 1995. The convention was ratified early in
1998.

custody, and some were attracted by the proposal for a system of 'euro bail'[93], where suspects could be granted bail while they awaited trial and serve the period of bail in their home state.

The EU also decided to continue the work of its high-level working group on asylum and immigration and to work to integrate better into the EU third country nationals currently residing there[94], approximating their legal status to that of the member states' nationals.

The political challenge in asylum and immigration policy lay in striking a balance between the need to safeguard asylum as an individual right and thus ensure the proper protection of refugees, and the desire to limit economic migration. The EU needed a common policy on asylum, Liberals argued, or at least minimum common standards based on the 1951 Geneva Convention and on the UNHCR guidelines. We were concerned about the danger of a lowest common denominator approach which could lead to a downward spiral in the level of protection. We feared the temptation to create a 'fortress Europe', terrified of infection from without, and sought to retain the commitment of member states to remain a refuge for the persecuted and the dispossessed. Asylum had to remain a human right rather than becoming a matter of political discretion for the government of the day.

At the Tampere summit, member state governments reaffirmed their commitment to the Geneva Convention and agreed to elaborate a common EU policy on asylum and immigration, though they stopped short of agreeing the single asylum system which Liberals sought. Agreement was also reached to set up a European Refugee Fund, a form of burden-sharing which stopped short of quotas.

If Finland was to kick off this work, however, its ministers seemed hardly up to the task[95]. A nervous debutante Finnish presidency needed MEPs' assistance as it tiptoed through the minefields of controversy which littered the ground demarcated by the heads of state and government in Tampere. It was an agenda in which Liberals were to play an active role, taking through the House legislation to combat racism, to improve the status of third country nationals in the EU and to set minimum standards for temporary protection of migrants in the event of a mass influx of refugees such as that some member states had encountered during the Balkan wars of the 1990s.

The 'Tampere agenda' of creating a single European legal area was the main subject of discussion at the COSAC[96] meeting hosted by the Finnish Parliament in Helsinki on 12 October 1999. Although representatives of the European Parliament were famously unwelcome at COSAC meetings, which national

---

93 This concept was designed by Stephen Jakobi of the London-based NGO Fair Trials Abroad.

94 'It would be in contradiction with Europe's traditions to deny ... freedom to those whose circumstances lead them justifiably to seek access to our territory', the Council meeting declared grandly.

95 At a meeting hosted by Finland's permanent representative, Antti Satuli, for his country's ministers of justice and home affairs to meet Parliament's JHA committee chair, they had little to say for themselves. Their appearance before the committee on two occasions was to make this clear to MEPs; when asked questions about their presentations, which they read from government briefings, they simply re-read the relevant paragraphs.

96 The Conference of European Affairs Committees of parliaments within the EU, an inter-parliamentary body which brought together representatives of national parliaments who specialised in EU affairs.   .

parliamentarians jealously preserved as their own, I was invited and was surprised to find that no caucus meeting of Liberal parliamentarians was scheduled. I took it on myself to invite to breakfast the Liberals in attendance, to discuss from a Liberal perspective the challenges to the Union in justice and home affairs. Unless national parliamentarians were prepared to work together on grounds of ideological affinity, I reasoned, the European Union would never realise its full potential. Liberals were currently fewer in number than the EPP or the PES political families, certainly; but we too could benefit from the solidarity which came from such ideological affinity and hope to carry public support for a European area of freedom, security and justice.

Transparency and openness

The European Council in Tampere had also welcomed the Commission's intention to table in January 2000 a proposal on the principles governing the right of access to European Parliament, Council and Commission documents. This measure, foreseen in Article 255 of the consolidated EU treaties since the entry into force of the Treaty of Nice and published on 26 January 2000, was to become known as the 'access to documents' regulation. As chairman of Parliament's justice and home affairs committee I worked with co-rapporteurs British Labour MEP Michael Cashman and Netherlands Christian Democrat MEP Hanja Maij-Weggen to agree, under the Swedish presidency in 2001, a law on freedom of information which opened substantially the institutions of EU government to public scrutiny. The measure established a public register of the documents held by each institution of government at EU level, an agreement that all documents would be available unless contrary to the public interest and a commitment obliging each institution to publish an annual report on openness specifying the number of documents to which a request for access had been refused. A provision was made for the oversight of documents with a security classification by designated MEPs, though agreeing the modalities of the latter was to require substantially more time. The measure was voted through committee on 25 April 2001 and through the House on 16 May. However, when Parliament came to review the matter in December 2001 it found that while the provisions of the law had been put in place in the European Parliament, this was not the case for the Council of Ministers. Defending the Council's view that government officials, even those not holding elected political office, should be able to decide which sensitive documents could be made public, Belgium's EU affairs minister Annemie Neyts confronted MEPs who had insisted in a parliamentary debate that such decisions needed political accountability. 'I do not understand the distinction some of you are making', Neyts told the House: 'this is not my philosophy. It may be yours, but I do not share it.'

A new idealism?

At the European Council meeting in Helsinki on 10 and 11 December 1999 the heads of state and government also returned to the challenges posed by the hoped-for enlargement of the EU. The Union should be in a position to welcome new member states from the end of 2000, they decided, which meant agreeing a set of institutional reforms[97] by December 2000, just one year away; building a competitive, job-generating, sustainable economy and helping the candidate countries prepare for EU membership.

As 1999 drew to a close the EU's leaders decided to adopt a declaration to mark the millennium. The Millennium Declaration was to recognise the progress made during 50 years of EU integration, to reassert the EU's roots in democracy and the rule of law, to delineate the challenges ahead and to call for a rejuvenation of the idea of a Europe for all. The dawn of the new millennium – combined with a special ceremony to reflect on the horrors of 20th century Europe – had reignited the global humanitarian vision in the minds of Europe's leaders which was often smothered by the pressure of day to day management of their countries.

The Millennium Declaration's principles were to be tested far sooner than most expected. On 4 February 2000 the main right-wing Austrian People's Party (ÖVP), which had been overtaken in the general election of 3 October 1999[98] by the far-right Freedom Party of Austria (FPO) led by Nazi sympathiser Joerg Haider – and which was either unwilling or unable to form a coalition with the largest party, the Socialists – agreed a governing coalition with the Freedom Party. The European Council's new president-in-office, Antonio Gutierrez, from a Portugal liberated from fascism only in the final quarter of the century, called for sanctions against Austria.

Liberals were divided. Some, like Baronesses Nicholson and Ludford, supported the calls for sanctions; others, like me, believed that a party should be judged by what it did in office rather than what it said from the opposition benches. A heated debate ensued in Parliament and Council and a directive on measures to combat racism was hurriedly put into law[99]: other than that, however, nothing happened, and six months later the matter was quietly buried; Austria had disturbed but not completely reawakened the ghosts of its recent past.

A harsh and anti-immigrant tone was also creeping into politics in Germany, the EU's most powerful member state, however. In regional elections in North Rhine Westphalia the CDU had run a campaign with racist undertones under the slogan 'Kinder statt Inder' (Children before Indians). The FDP, under flamboyant regional leader Juergen Moelleman, polled 9.8% in North Rhine Westphalia as moderate Christian Democrat voters defected to them. Moelleman sought to use this success to challenge lacklustre FDP leader Wolfgang Gerhardt, by arguing that the roles of party leader and prime ministerial candidate should be separated; predictably, he saw himself in the latter. At the party's conference in Nuremberg on 15 and 16 June 2000 the challenge came to a head. The experienced former minister

---

97   Including the size and composition of the college of European commissioners, the number of votes allocated to each member state in Council by virtue of its population and the possible extension of decision-making in Council by qualified majority voting.

98   In this election the ten MPs of the Liberal Forum had all lost their seats, leaving it unrepresented in parliament.

99   In a piece of political skulduggery involving the president of the EP, France tried to delay the introduction of the measure until its own EU presidency. When Parliament came to vote on the matter it was discovered that no version was available in French. Your author, as chairman of the committee responsible, persuaded the House to proceed to a vote nonetheless.

– who had worked with Genscher to form an alliance in 1982 with Kohl's CDU in which Moelleman had served in three ministries and as vice chancellor – stole the show; and unlike the party leader he received a public handshake afterwards on the conference platform from Genscher. But many of the party members did not trust Moelleman, and within a year they had elected FDP general secretary Guido Westerwelle to the leadership of the party to succeed Gerhardt. It was Westerwelle who was to rebuild the party and take it back into government in 2009.[100]

Haunting memories of the impact of extremist ideologies spurred Europe's leaders on to lock their countries together in a Union founded on democratic principles. The European Parliament found itself more and more involved in this process. The chairmen of Parliament's education and justice and home affairs committees were invited early by the Portuguese presidency and subsequently by the French presidency to participate in informal meetings of the pertinent Council configurations in a recognition of Parliament's role in legislation in these areas through its new co-decision powers.[101]

Foreign policy

By 1999 the EU's leaders could no longer easily justify to their electorates the Union's dire incapacity to act in matters foreign. Not only were the Americans continuing to dominate policy in the Middle East, considered by many Europeans to be 'Uncle Jacques' back yard' rather than Uncle Sam's; but it seemed Europe was incapable of policing its own continent. In Northern Ireland the peace process had been chaired by US senator George Mitchell: in the Balkans the major peace initiatives had been led by the Americans at Wye River and in Dayton and at Chateau Rambouillet, while European countries had squabbled over which should provide shelter to refugees; and even in Greek-influenced Cyprus, peace talks were to be held in New York, under UN auspices. True, in the Balkans the EU was supporting Montenegro's policies of ethnic tolerance and Kosovo's plans for free and fair municipal elections in the face of extreme pressure from Belgrade. The European Commission, meanwhile, held out to the countries of the western Balkans the hope of EU membership. This 'soft power' – regime change using a carrot rather than a stick – was the EU's only effective weapon. Addressing Parliament on 14 September 2000 Prodi spoke of 'a shared identity; a new European soul'.

By mid-2000, accession negotiations had been opened with Malta, Latvia, Lithuania, Slovakia, Romania and Bulgaria. Discussions with Turkey were also proceeding well. Europe wanted peace and prosperity on its borders and at the Nice European Council in December 2001 agreed funding for its Mediterranean partners and its west Balkan neighbours of almost EUR 1 billion a year for each bloc. One year later, at the Laeken European Council in December 2002, the heads of state and government noted that 10 candidate

---

100   Moelleman subsequently resigned from the FDP to form his own party. In June 2003 he died in a parachuting accident.

101   At the latter, which involved me, only the Luxembourg delegation protested to the Portuguese presidency about the invitation to the EP committee chair; and this was doubtless stimulated by the representative of the Council Secretariat, who was a Luxembourger.

countries were on course to complete accession negotiations by the end of 2002, that two would need a little more time and that the prospects for opening accession talks with Turkey had advanced further.

With the new powers conferred on the Union in foreign and security policy by the Treaty of Amsterdam, heads of state and government were determined to begin to develop an autonomous capacity to take decisions and, where NATO as a whole was not engaged, to launch and conduct EU-led military operations in response to international crises. It was still a case of slowly, slowly: to avoid trespassing on UK, Irish and Danish sensitivities particularly, the Helsinki European Council in December 1999 spelled out that this did 'not imply the creation of a European army'. Nonetheless the Council agreed that by 2003 member states should be able 'to deploy within 60 days and sustain for at least one year' military forces of between fifty and sixty thousand persons capable of the full range of Petersberg[102] tasks. They foresaw new political and military bodies within the Council secretariat, reporting to the high representative, to allow this.

Under the Portuguese presidency of the EU in 2000, further progress was made towards a common foreign and security policy. Recognising that military capability remained central to the credibility of such a policy it had agreed to a capabilities commitment conference in the second half of 2000, under the French presidency. Turkey, Norway, Poland and the Czech Republic had all pledged support for EU-led military operations, although they were not members of the EU, and a committee for civilian aspects of crisis management had already received commitments to making 5,000 police officers available for EU missions across the range of conflict prevention and crisis management tasks. Permanent political and military structures were not yet in place, but it was expected that they would be within a year.

Monetary and economic policy

Since 1994, most economic policy formation had been through a process of co-decision which gave Parliament a say equal to that of the Council of Ministers. Even in areas where no formal co-decision existed, the new relationship between Parliament and Council had allowed Parliament to enlarge considerably its field of influence.

European monetary union had been advanced through the locking together of the currencies of twelve of the fifteen member states on 1 January 1999, as the EU once again confounded sceptics in the UK and elsewhere. To facilitate this, the European Monetary Institute had been designated as the precursor to the European Central Bank which would take over some currency management functions from national central banks.

It had perhaps not been anticipated by member state governments that the European Parliament would wish to vet appointments to the governing board of the European Central Bank, but nor did the treaties exclude it; and that is what Parliament had proceeded to do. Moreover, German committee chair

---

102   Defined in June 1992 at the Hotel Petersberg near Bonn at a meeting of the Council of the Western European Union (WEU), these are military tasks of a humanitarian, crisis management, peacekeeping and peacemaking nature which, under the Amsterdam Treaty, the EU is empowered to do.

and long-serving Social Democrat MEP Christa Randzio-Plath insisted Parliament should be kept informed of policy considerations and was to continue her predecessor's policy of ensuring that MEPs paid frequent visits to the Bank's HQ in Frankfurt.[103]

Such visits were to become a feature of parliamentary oversight of the ECB, as were appearances of its senior officials at parliamentary committee meetings and other hearings. Liberal MEPs, mindful of the treaties' requirement that the European Parliament be responsible for monitoring the ECB's work, consistently fought for greater transparency within the Bank. It fell to an ELDR MEP, Chris Huhne, to draw up Parliament's first annual report on the ECB in October 1999. His report called for six measures to increase transparency: ECB hearings after each significant policy action; six-monthly forecasts for economic development within the euro area; regular overall reports for economic developments in each euro-area country, to facilitate comparisons of best practice and enable early warnings; the publication of summary minutes outlining the arguments made for and against monetary policy actions; publication of the names of Council members voting for and against monetary action; and publication of any econometric model for the euro area. Liberals believed that in order to hold the ECB to account for the management of monetary policy, MEPs and the public needed to know how the Bank reached its conclusions and on what facts it based them. We sought a level of transparency equivalent to that of the US Federal Reserve. All of the proposals were backed by Parliament with the exception of the publication of voting records, which it was decided should be recorded on an anonymous basis. The ECB now implements almost all the report's demands.

Euro notes and coins were to be introduced smoothly on 1 January 2002 across the eurozone; and those countries which had legislated for dual pricing for a reasonable period both before and after introduction avoided the consequences of the temptation by some retailers artificially to inflate their prices.

The arguments about joining continued to rage, however, in the countries which stayed outside: I was to advocate UK membership at nearly 100 different meetings in my constituency, to write many articles, to receive many business people concerned about the impact of the UK's hesitation and to hear warnings from senior industrialists, UK and Japanese, that failure to join would impact negatively on investment in the UK, as indeed it has[104]. My opponents were to be equally active, however; the Conservative and UKIP MEPs in my region outnumbered me heavily.

Since 1999 Europe's economic recovery had gathered momentum. Investment conditions were favourable, public finances had improved and inflation remained low. Unemployment, while still high, was declining and

---

103   There they had been received on one early occasion (19 Oct 1998) by Governor Wim Duisenberg and his deputy (and antithesis) Christian Noyer who appeared surprised to find themselves accountable to parliamentarians; the only question they ducked was an indelicate one from a young Liberal MEP enquiring how much the Bank expected to profit from seigneurage income. My diary records that my question found Duisenberg 'looking like a bewildered rhinoceros'. I was aware that one estimate had put the answer to my question at ten billion euros.

104   Today, after 2008's 25% devaluation of sterling against the euro, my constituency mailbag contains many tales of woe from retired UK citizens who spend part of each year living in the eurozone while their income is in pounds sterling.

the Broad Economic Guidelines provided a framework for defining common economic policies. Nonetheless many European manufacturers were still less competitive than their opposite numbers in North America or the Far East and were losing world market share. Thus the Portuguese presidency of the Union, which took office in January 2000, decided to convene in Lisbon on 23 and 24 March an extraordinary meeting of heads of state and government to examine the policies needed for the creation of a successful knowledge-based economy.

At Lisbon the heads of state and government elaborated a new goal: to make the EU 'the most competitive and dynamic knowledge-based economy in the world, capable of sustainable economic growth with more and better jobs and greater social cohesion'. They gave themselves a decade to achieve this. They pledged to hold an 'economic summit' annually in the spring to oversee progress towards 'a digital, knowledge-based economy' and to use a new, open method of policy co-ordination[105] to achieve it. Much of the legislation needed for this was already in the pipeline, though often moving at snail's pace; the Council called for action 'as rapidly as possible' on pending legislation such as electronic commerce, copyright and financial services; they also wanted fully integrated and liberalised telecommunications markets and high speed interconnections for internet access. Markets in gas, electricity, postal services and transport were to be liberalised and efficient and transparent financial markets created. 'Benchmarking against the best in the world' was one of the new catch-phrases.

Though recognising that markets do not always work as they should, Liberal MEPs were decisive in securing backing for the EU's 'Lisbon' competitiveness strategy. Liberals secured approval in Parliament for Carles Gasoliba MEP to draw up a report on the impact of economic liberalisation on economic growth, as part of the European Parliament's preparations for the Stockholm Council in 2001. The report, which advocated ways of achieving sustainable growth based on higher standards through greater liberalisation of transport, telecoms and energy markets, pointed out that the EU countries with the greatest degree of deregulation and labour market flexibility were also the ones which saw the greatest falls in unemployment and the greatest increases in economic growth, though Liberals also supported measures in Parliament to ensure that market liberalisation went hand in hand with appropriate policies to promote environmental sustainability and consumer choice. Luciano Caveri succeeded in gaining support in the regional policy committee on 21 February 2002 for a two-stage liberalisation of postal services over a five year period. Nick Clegg, barely into his second year of elected office[106], took through Parliament a groundbreaking new EU regulation on 'unbundling the local loop', a law to oblige telecoms operators

---

105 The open method of co-ordination relied on encouraging reform through benchmarking and the common study of best practice. It implied a recognition that the member states did not wish to be told what to do by the European Commission but might gradually be coaxed and cajoled into action.

106 Clegg came to Parliament with a good understanding of how the EU worked, having served previously in the European Commission, where his talent had been recognised. While there, he had been a member of an informal advisory group I set up called the Bagehot Club, at which I was pleased to be instrumental in persuading him to join the UK Liberal Democrats and to seek election to Parliament.

to allow their competitors to provide services to customers (especially internet services), over the existing 'last mile' of copper wire telephone infrastructure, providing a boost to the take-up of high speed internet services at
reasonable cost. Swedish Liberal MEP Olle Schmidt piloted through the
House the Commission's proposal to extend the markets in investments,
combining a liberal approach to investment markets with adequate protection for consumers in the so-called UCITS[107] directive. Dirk Sterckx made
proposals for a single European airspace with a unified air traffic management capability and a common air traffic liberalisation agreement with the
USA. And Diana Wallis was active in promoting e-commerce through
ensuring that disgruntled customers could have greater access to justice
across borders or in cyberspace in disputes with suppliers.

Liberals supported consistently throughout the Parliament the steady
reduction of state aid to industry, moves towards a single market for public
procurement and a genuine single market for financial services. We pressed
successfully for a range of safeguards (in the form of transparency rules and
the use of sunset clauses) in debate on the Lamfalussy approach[108] to financial services regulation.

But Liberals were not always able to carry the day. Liberal strength and
influence were commensurate only to the ELDR group's size. The EPP and
PES groups, with 233 and 180 MEPs respectively and the lions' share of the
17 committee chairs, picked the plum dossiers for their members and, when
their major national delegations were in agreement, almost invariably
secured a majority. A central plank of the Lisbon strategy, for example, was
a draft directive on takeover bids, which sought to apply common rules to
takeover bids in all EU countries and to prevent member states disallowing
takeovers by companies headquartered in another member state. This had
completed most of the stages of consideration in Council and Parliament
and would probably have secured adoption had it not been for a highly-
leveraged bid for German steel manufacturer Mannesmann AG by the UK
mobile telephone service provider Vodafone. This sent shock waves
through continental Europe about the import of 'anglo-saxon' business
practices and contributed to the directive's rejection in a dramatic tied vote
(273 votes to 273, with 22 abstentions) on 4th July 2001.[109] The ELDR group
was the only group in Parliament unanimously to back the proposal. Fifteen
months later, in October 2002, the Commission was to propose a new
takeover bids directive, which was welcomed warmly by Liberals and
adopted before the end of Parliament's mandate.

In October 2000 the ELDR Party congress was held in Tenerife in the
Canary Islands, immediately following a meeting of the ELDR parliamentary group hosted by local MEP Isidoro Sanchez. The conference welcomed

---

107   Undertakings for Collective Investments in Transferable Securities.

108   Baron Alexandre Lamfalussy had chaired a 'committee of wise men' which had developed an approach to
convergence in supervision and regulation of financial services allowing regulation to keep pace with market
developments.

109   Two years later a new Commission proposal was to be approved by Parliament, the Germans having been
brought on board.

the proposed EU Lisbon strategy and committed Liberals to supporting it. Moreover it elected Werner Hoyer of Germany to succeed Uffe Elleman-Jensen of Denmark as party president[110]. Hoyer was an economist and a European federalist from North Rhine Westphalia who had enjoyed success within his party and his country. His economic Liberalism had become clear when, as secretary general of the FDP in 1993 and 1994, he had promoted the aspirational election slogan *Die Partei der Besserverdienende* (the party for higher earners). A member of the German Bundestag since 1987, he had served from 1984 to 1988 as EU affairs minister.

The Union was determined to accelerate the pace of economic reform. At its first annual spring meeting on economic policy, a year after the adoption of the Lisbon strategy, it recognised the demographic challenge facing a union with an ageing population and the pressure this would put on social security systems, in particular pensions, health care and care for the elderly. Since developments in the world economy were less favourable it sought to move faster in exploiting the potential of Europe's domestic market through faster transposition into national law of market-opening measures and liberalisation of the gas, electricity, air and rail travel markets. It sought to widen internet access and the use of electronic commerce. The focus of the Swedish presidency in the fist half of 2001, however, was to be on environmental sustainability; an environmental agenda adopted at the Gothenburg Council in June 2001 was designed to complement the social (Cardiff) and economic (Lisbon) objectives of the Union.

Not only was sustainable development seen as important for the quality of life and preservation of the planet's ecosystems, it also had the potential to unleash a wave of technological innovation. From now on, the EU would seek to ensure that all major policy proposals included an environmental sustainability assessment. Moreover the EU sought to promote the sustainability agenda in bilateral relations with third countries and in international fora: since pollution paid no respect to national borders it was illusory to believe that the EU or any of its member states possessed 'sovereignty' in such matters.

Heads of state and government therefore committed themselves to making a success of the conference of the parties to the UN's Kyoto Protocol, scheduled for mid-July 2001 in Bonn, reaffirming their commitment to meet the Kyoto targets and to generate 20% of all EU electricity needs by 2010 from renewable sources of energy. New US president George W. Bush, visiting Gothenburg for a meeting with EU leaders on 14 June, told them he was not prepared to ratify the Kyoto agreement; but growing concerns about man-made climate change persuaded the EU to go ahead nonetheless.

Environment and public health

The ratification of the Kyoto Protocol, signed on 11 December 1997, was a priority for the European Union. If the EU was to lead the way in turning growing global concern about climate change in to policy action it had to lead by example. Liberal MEPs played an active role in passing laws on

---

110   Hoyer defeated Karel de Gucht of Belgium, a former Liberal MEP.

national emissions ceilings, emissions trading, vehicle exhaust emissions and other Kyoto-related issues. Of great sensitivity to Germany, the largest economy in the EU, was the health of its car industry which still produced heavy, expensive and inefficient vehicles. The work of Mimi Kestelijn-Sierens in the previous mandate was built on so as to strengthen Council proposals to improve fuel economy labelling for cars. Chris Davies legislated to limit CO_2 emissions from new passenger cars. And Dirk Sterckx was active in the adoption of laws to ensure that manufacturers covered the cost of recycling cars at the end of their useful lives.

Liberals were active too on issues of food safety. Food safety had been a matter of concern to citizens for some years as a result of a series of minor health scares[111] but had risen rapidly up the political agenda with the impact of the BSE[112] crisis of 1996-98. This crisis broke on 19 March 1996 when the UK health secretary announced that his government's medical advisers could no longer rule out a link between the disease BSE in cattle and Creutzfeld Jakobs Disease in human beings. The UK government had known of the problem for some time but had not advised its trading partners or (until ten minutes before making the announcement) the European Commission. Indeed it made the announcement only after learning that the report had leaked to a national newspaper. The effect on the consumption of beef across the continent, especially in Germany, was major; and since continental countries predictably closed their markets to the import of UK beef, the impact on UK producers was severe.[113] These market closures and the failure of 'Brussels' to prevent them had led to vigorous protests in the UK, though many countries worldwide had also banned imports. EU solidarity with the UK was not lacking, however. At the European Council meeting in Florence on 21 and 22 June 1996 the heads of state and government agreed to spend ECU 850 million to support livestock farmers hit by the crisis. The UK government took action, striking 'an uneasy compromise between the scientifically necessary and the politically deliverable'[114]; and as the disease was gradually eliminated, so the export bans were lifted in the EU. By November 1998, UK beef was back on continental markets, though not on those of the UK's traditional allies elsewhere in the world. Yet concern for the safety of meat remained. In the autumn the European Parliament established a committee of inquiry into the Commission's handling of the crisis caused by the disease, on which the ELDR group was represented by the aptly-named Danish Liberal Niels Kofoed[115] MEP; and Finnish Liberal MEP Sirka-Liisa Anttila was to take through the House in

111   In particular the listeria virus in pate and the salmonella virus in eggs.

112   Bovine Spongiform Encepalopathy, commonly dubbed Mad Cow Disease, is a brain disease in cattle which is transmissible to human beings in the form of brain disorder Creutzfeld Jakobs Disease (CJD) through meat consumption.

113   At a meeting I hosted for farmers in my constituency on 30 March, 160 people came. A further 200 attended another meeting on 30 May.

114   I owe the phrase to Sir Stephen Wall, UK permanent representative to the EU 1995-2000, and quote it from his book 'A stranger in Europe'.

115   Niels' surname, he delighted in telling his colleagues, derives from the Danish for 'cow food'.

1997 a report on the export and import of veal and beef, calling for a strengthening of welfare provisions and veterinary controls.

In June 1999, following a dioxin scare in chicken, eggs and pork in Belgium we secured an emergency joint meeting of Parliament's agriculture and environment committees and argued that food safety policy must apply to the entire animal and human food chain. We sought an EU food safety agency with the power to withdraw suspect products from the food chain, as proposed by President Prodi. The Commission had produced a white paper on food safety which argued for an independent European food safety agency to be established to complement preventive surveillance by the national authorities. Liberals pressed the Commission to come forward with a legislative proposal by September 2000 and helped to expedite its passage through Parliament. The resultant European Food Safety Authority was eventually to be located in Parma, in Italy, despite a diplomatic gaffe by Prodi's successor Berlusconi[116].

The ELDR group's Nordic MEPs led on the issue. Thus Finland's Mikko Pesala was active in ensuring appropriate action to combat and limit the impact of transmissible spongiform encephalopathies and Sweden's Karl Erik Olsson[117] piloted through the House a measure to extend the ban on the use of growth hormones in cattle-rearing in the light of scientific evidence of carcinogenic effects. His compatriot Marit Paulsen framed legislation to improve animal nutrition and to ensure safe handling of animal by-products[118] and Denmark's Niels Busk was Parliament's rapporteur on improved welfare standards for intensively-reared pigs.

Belgian Frederique Ries sought to ensure stricter controls in food distribution, while Liz Lynne was active in the promotion of higher standards in the light of the BSE outbreak which had affected UK farmers. Liz was also to enjoy being the scourge of the French government, protesting colourfully against the situation in which, a year after the ban was lifted by other EU countries, it was still maintained by France. She and I were successfully to press the Commission to take legal action against France in defence of British farmers.

In another area of consumer protection the ELDR also scored a success when Jules Maaten's law on the manufacture and presentation of tobacco products saw off a hugely well-financed tobacco industry lobby to cut maximum levels for tar, nicotine and carbon monoxide and secured larger and more explicit health warnings on cigarette packs[119].

116 When Finland bid to host the agency, Berlusconi dismissed the bid insultingly with the words 'they've never even heard of prosciutto'. On winning the battle he was to claim that his 'latin lover' charm had won over Finland's president, Tarja Halonen, a claim which led to a diplomatic protest by Finland.

117 In May 2002, reporting to Parliament retrospectively on the monitoring of the BSE crisis and the measures taken, Olsson was to recommend that monitoring for animal diseases be extended to sheep.

118 Marit Paulsen's legislation was to ban the practice of animal remains being fed to animals of the same species, which was believed to have caused animal diseases such as BSE.

119 The tobacco industry was to challenge in court the legality of this directive. In December 2002 the ECJ ruled in favour of the EU institutions.

Budgetary control

In the wake of the Cresson affair described in Chapter 1, parliamentarians were naturally concerned to improve controls on EU spending. The ELDR group had led in exposing the fault lines in budgetary control in the previous Commission. We argued that effective parliamentary scrutiny had to be ensured and the Commission held to account in a fair and robust manner. Nonetheless we admired Commissioner Kinnock's dedication to resolving the problems and argued that Parliament also had a duty to defend due process and resist the temptation to fight fraud in the media spotlight.

Thus Liberals worked with the Commission and the Court of Auditors to provide a clearer breakdown of financial management by sector to help identify where the problem areas lay. Liberal MEP Jan Mulder drafted on Parliament's behalf a paper proposing new rules to govern the complex discharge procedure. It called for specific statements of assurance for individual directorates general within the Commission rather than a single, blanket statement, in order better to identify areas of success and failure in managing the accounts.

Problems continued, however. In December 1999[120] the Court of Auditors refused to sign off the EU's accounts for 1998 although, as ECA president Jan Karlsson told MEPs: 'the errors not only reflected on the Commission but also on the member states who are responsible for executing some 80 per cent of the budget. There were still problems with the administration and control of programmes'. Only one member state had ratified the relevant conventions and protocols on protecting the European Community's financial interests, he added. Liberals nonetheless led a campaign to postpone discharge of the Commission for its 1998 accounts, delaying the granting of discharge from April 2000 to July 2000 until we were satisfied that the Commission had put essential safeguards in place. Liberals welcomed the establishment of OLAF[121], the EU's new independent anti-fraud office, but sought also the appointment of a European public prosecutor to defend the taxpayer against fraud at EU level.

Liberals also set about putting Parliament's own house in order, piloting through the House the highly sensitive and traditionally controversial discharge report on Parliament's own budget for the year 2000. As Lousewies van der Laan MEP insisted correctly, Parliament had itself to be above suspicion.

The social agenda

In 2001 and 2002 a European social agenda was elaborated, largely at the insistence of France. The first priority was to create jobs. By 2002, economic growth had reached 3.5%, unemployment was down below 9% and still falling and the rate of employment had increased to over 62%, though 70% was the Union's goal. Anne Jensen piloted through Parliament a measure to put in place EU-level incentives for employment and did battle with Council to increase the

---

120 The Auditors report should have been presented two months previously; but MEPs, furious that the report's contents had been leaked to the press before they were made available to Parliament, delayed their deliberations.

121 The acronym OLAF derives from the French 'Office pour la Lutte Anti-Fraude'.

budget for them from EUR 50m to EUR 65m. The second priority was worker involvement in decision-making: the French wanted to secure worker involvement in economic decisions by all employers in Europe, whatever their jurisdiction of origin, similar to that for French national companies. A draft directive on the information and consultation of employees was doing the rounds. The third priority was provision of essential services. The French presidency was to secure recognition that services of general interest (such as energy, telecoms, public transport, schools, health and social services, etc) should not be subject to the same economic disciplines as those not universally needed. Europe's leaders were to agree a set of objectives to combat poverty and social exclusion and foresee the drawing up of national action plans in these areas by each member state. And Astrid Thors MEP was key to an agreement whereby public authorities could take into account social and environmental criteria in the award of public contracts, provided the criteria were announced in advance and applied in a non-discriminatory way. A more caring Europe, many believed, would be more likely to earn the respect and support of its citizens.

The French had the satisfaction of the formal declaration, under their presidency, of the Charter of Fundamental Rights of EU citizens. Success in closing dossiers on other matters of justice and home affairs largely eluded them however, not least because a government re-shuffle during the presidency changed the ministers responsible.

If a fair measure of agreement could be reached among member states on how to use the EU's existing powers, however, there was little unanimity on extension of the EU's competences. The French presidency ended with a European Council meeting which failed to agree internal reforms recommended by the intergovernmental conference established in February 2000. After three days and nights of talks, 15 weary heads of state and government emerged from the conference centre with an agreement that was barely satisfactory. Many despaired at the working methods of a Union which had assumed new dimensions. To add insult to injury, Chirac was to describe Prodi at the conference as a 'petty bureaucrat', which earned the former a reception of stony silence and the latter a round of spontaneous applause when they appeared before Parliament to present the results of the IGC.

Some federalists favoured voting in Parliament to reject the Nice Treaty, which they argued was unsatisfactory. In the ELDR group Andrew Duff made this case. But wise counsel prevailed; half a loaf was better than no bread. In any event, the treaty was to be rejected – albeit for very different reasons – by Ireland's voters in a referendum on 7 June 2001, which would delay its entry into force until after a second referendum on the Emerald Isle on 21 October 2002[122].

122   The Nice Treaty was put to a second referendum in Ireland in the autumn on 2002 after a declaration on Ireland's military neutrality had been approved by the European Council meeting in Seville in June 2002 and appended to the treaty. This proviso satisfied the Irish electorate.

Liberals move up a gear

As 2001 opened, Cox moved to prepare his campaign for presidency of the European Parliament. Over supper in Strasbourg with close colleagues he prepared for a discussion with the bureau members of his group. Flying back to Brussels from a visit of Liberals to Zagreb on 30 January I discussed the matter with him. Though our relations had never been warm and were to endure a few ups and downs over the course of the year, we recognised a common interest for Liberals in his election as president of Parliament and a smooth succession. The previously tacit assumption that I should succeed him was now being talked about openly among colleagues, though it was not unchallenged. Bertel Haarder was to tell me a fortnight later that – should his party not be in government by then, in which case he hoped to become a minister – he also harboured ambitions to succeed Cox. Jan Mulder was to tell me on 26 September 2001 that he might run for the group leadership; and Liz Lynne was to suggest in December that Colette Flesch[123] might be a candidate. I had worked hard over two years, however, to build support among colleagues: and none of my potential challengers had put in the same amount of focussed effort. I took the view that since the balance of opinion appeared to favour my chances no change in my strategy was necessary. Whether we liked it or not, Cox and I were zipped together as if in a pantomime horse and it was in our interests to move in convoy rather than to pull apart.

I was already actively involved in trying to build up the strength of our group and was enjoying unexpected success as a recruiting sergeant. I believed the UK Conservative Party offered fertile ground for converts. In February 1999, former Conservative MEPs John Stevens and Brendan Donnelly had left the Conservative Party and formed the 'Pro-Euro Conservative Party' to contest the June 1999 EP elections. They hoped to persuade leading Conservative luminaries Ken Clarke, Michael Heseltine and Chris Patten to mount an SDP-style breakaway from the Conservatives, to work in combination with the Liberal Democrats. At the same time James Moorhouse MEP and Conservative Party vice chairman Emma Nicholson MP had decided to move straight over and join the Liberal Democrats: I had welcomed the former into our ranks towards the end of the 1994-99 mandate; the latter had joined us at Westminster and had subsequently been elected to the European Parliament under Liberal colours. The failure of others to rally to the Pro-Euro Conservative Party's standard, however, and the victory of Iain Duncan-Smith MP over Clarke in the Conservative Party leadership contest in September 2001 led to its disbandment later that year. Stevens and Donnelly both joined the Liberal Democrats. I hoped we might gain more and I actively solicited converts. Thus Bill Newton-Dunn MEP was to join us from the Conservatives on 21 November 2001. Other Conservative MEPs such as Christopher Beazley came close to joining, such was the distaste in which they held developments in their own party.

---

123   Colette Flesch MEP was a Luxembourg Liberal with a proud record of European commitment. She had served in the European Commission as director general for youth and culture and had provided inter alia GBP 6 million to help convert The Beatles' former school into the Liverpool Institute for Performing Arts. She had also been ELD party president 1985-90, mayor of Luxembourg and foreign minister.

My prospecting for converts was not limited to UK MEPs, however. On 5 December 2001 my prospecting among Italian MEPs paid off partially, as Claudio Martelli left his seat with the non-attached Members to join ELDR. But Franceso Rutelli again blocked the group's recruitment of the Italian Radical Party's MEPs, who would by now have joined if invited; their re-integration into the Liberal family would have to wait until 2004. My efforts to bring French members over to the group were to meet with partial success too. Though Thierry Cornillet and Michele Scarbonchi were to fail to demonstrate the courage of convictions professed over many months, Herve Novelli did join the ELDR group.

My profile was growing both beyond and within the European Parliament. The outbreak of foot and mouth disease which spread across the UK in the spring was to provide a platform for me in Parliament and beyond. As a member for south west England, the UK's most important dairying region, I could not allow the matter to escape my attention; and since the UK's Conservative Party was in a worse state than the Labour Party had been in 1983[124] it provided me an opportunity to appeal to the mainly Conservative farming vote. At the 25th anniversary congress of the ELDR Party, held at the European Parliament in Brussels on 7 June 2001, I was given a valuable speaking slot to talk about my work as chair of the committee on justice and home affairs, which was giving me ample opportunity to shine in the House. The Italian police response to the protesters at the G8 summit in Genova in July also gave me further exposure, since the EP reacted strongly in its criticism. And the events of September 11 were to give me more prominence in the autumn of 2001 than almost any other MEP.

In November 2000 I had been given permission to draw up, on behalf of Parliament, a recommendation on action needed by the EU to protect itself against the persistent phenomenon of terrorism. For all the talk of police and judicial co-operation, too little was happening in practice. On 6 September 2001 my report – calling for a series of anti-terrorist measures based on a common definition of terrorism, action to combat money laundering by serious criminals and a European arrest warrant – was adopted by Parliament by 497 votes to 14, with 27 abstentions. It was frequently the case that such decisions, expressing Parliament's wishes but having no legal force, would be placed on a shelf to gather dust. The events of five days later in New York, however, were to give a saliency to the report which was to see many of its recommendation made law in record-breaking time.

By the time of the ELDR Party conference in Ljubljana in September 2001, the succession within the parliamentary group's leadership seemed clear. On 4 October at a restaurant in Strasbourg appropriately named *Le Dauphin* I secured the support of my UK Liberal Democrat colleagues and on 7 November, at a meeting of the ELDR group's bureau, the formal support of the other delegations within the group.

---

124 Their leader William Hague MP was to resign in June 2001 after a poor showing in a UK general election in which the Liberals gained six seats.

September 11

The events of 11 September 2001 were world-changing.[125] As reports of the events came in I summarily suspended the committee meeting I was chairing so that members could turn on their televisions to watch the news. Parliament assembled in special session on 12 September 2001 to debate the attacks. Cox, speaking on behalf of the Liberals, described them as 'war, without a declaration of war'. On 19 September Parliament met in extraordinary session with Prodi and Solana. I pointed out to the House that the Americans must shake their heads in disbelief at the multitude of bilateral extradition agreements that they needed to employ to seek the arrest of people on European soil who might be responsible; and I challenged ministers who – in the secrecy of the Council chamber – were blocking reform, to explain publicly their actions. The EU's heads of state and government met in extraordinary session on 21 September 2001 to analyse the situation and agreed to co-operate with the USA in bringing to justice and punishing the perpetrators, their sponsors and accomplices. They called for the broadest possible global coalition against terrorism and agreed to adopt urgently the measures I had proposed, including a European arrest warrant, to combat it.

The main recommendations of my report from the committee on citizens' rights and freedoms, justice and home affairs had been for member states to adopt a common definition of terrorism, to establish common minimum laws and penalties to counter terrorist acts, to abolish formal extradition procedures for those suspected or convicted of terrorist crimes and to establish a European search and arrest warrant procedure whereby the issue of a warrant in any member state for the arrest of a person suspected of serious criminal behaviour would automatically require the authorities of other member states to assist in the capture and return of the suspect. It was a major development in criminal law, making extradition essentially an administrative rather than a judicial procedure[126]. Such was the pressure for action in the aftermath of the New York atrocities, however, that the Belgian presidency of the EU, ably guided by Belgium's Liberal interior minister Antoine Duquesne and working closely with Commissioner Vitorino, ensured the measure was made law within four months. Osama bin Laden, I quipped to a journalist, had done more for EU integration than anybody since Jacques Delors.

The EU also reviewed, at an extraordinary European Council meeting in Brussels on 21 September 2001, its judicial co-operation with the USA. Liberals insisted on four key requirements for any extradition agreement. They were: full respect for the European Convention on Human Rights; no extradition of persons likely to face military tribunals; no extradition if the accused risked facing the death penalty; and that any measures affecting

125 A collection of essays by Liberal MEPs and other leading Liberal figures entitled '2020 vision : Liberalism and Globalisation' which I published in August 2001 soon looked very dated as the world around us changed. I collated and edited a second series of essays in 2006 with colleagues from the subsequent parliament entitled 'Liberal Democracy and Globalisation'.

126 Though with judicial safeguards, of course.

data protection should be proportionate, effective and time-limited. For this we gained the support of the House, but governments were in a mood to move fast to assist the USA and some were tempted to play fast and loose with democratic safeguards. Within two years the member state governments had concluded two EU-level extradition agreements with the USA without democratic consultation with the European Parliament or even, in at least one case, with their national parliament[127]. These 'Article 24' agreements caused outrage in the European Parliament which had a right, under the treaties[128], to be consulted on 'the main aspects and the basic choices' in all areas of foreign policy.

In the week of 12 November Parliament adopted four reports which I had piloted through the House. But disagreements in Council were to hamper the adoption of a proposal by the Commission on 2 October 2001 for a Council regulation to freeze the assets of terrorist groups. At times like this the EU needed to act fast, but found it could not. As I was to point out to Parliament, the clumsy decision making mechanisms of the third pillar left terrorists laughing all the way to the cash machine.

As so often in situations of crisis, moreover, important Liberal ideas were overlooked. Liberals in the EP had insisted that the European arrest warrant be accompanied by a directive setting out minimum judicial standards in criminal legal proceedings, to ensure that civil liberties were respected; despite the best efforts of Belgian justice minister Marc Verwilghen and a commitment from the Commission to advance rapidly and press for such a measure, and despite continuous reminders from Sarah Ludford MEP and me, the matter remains (at the time of writing, nine years later) firmly stuck in the in-tray of the Council of Ministers.

Liberals were concerned too about some of the reactions to the terrorist attacks. George W. Bush had written to the president-in-office of the Council proposing 40 measures the EU should take to improve its capacity to fight terrorism, including things the USA did not require in its own laws. The US sought extradition of suspects to the USA for trial. Yet the proposed American Military Tribunals Order – an executive order from the Oval Office – provided for trials in which the defendant had no access to legal advice, in which the prosecution could withhold evidence from the defendant, and for the passing of a sentence, including the death sentence, by a majority of two-thirds of the jurors[129]. Moreover, while we supported the bombing early in October of Afghanistan, which was believed to harbour Al Qaida, we were opposed to talk of an 'axis of evil' and an attack on Iraq. Nor were we supportive of the language being used by Europe's right wing; Italy's prime minister was to assert that Christianity was 'superior to Islam'.

---

127 In France, the Conseil d"Etat refused the Assemblee Nationale the right to approve the agreements.

128 TEU Article 21. Article 24 covered the right of the EU to agree such treaties.

129 The law finally adopted required unanimity for the passing of a death sentence and a presumption in favour of openness of trial proceedings. I had expressed EU reservations to Congressman James Sensenbrenner and Senator Patrick Leahy, chairmen of the judiciary committees in House and Senate respectively.

Laeken

2001's Belgian presidency of the EU, under the country's Liberal-led government[130], was to leave an important legacy in the form of a declaration
adopted at the European Council in Laeken on 14 and 15 December 2001.
The Laeken Declaration described the Union's success in bringing peace and
prosperity to its peoples but stated that the EU now faced twin challenges,
that of being more open and responsive to its citizens through better democratic scrutiny of decision-making and that of upholding and promoting its
values across the world, shouldering its responsibilities in the governance of
globalisation[131].

The establishment of a large Convention on the Future of Europe to draw
up a constitution for the EU was intended to secure a wide input of ideas.
The heads of state and government agreed that it should be chaired by
Valery Giscard d'Estaing[132] and that its membership should be drawn
widely from national parliaments, the European Parliament and representatives of the heads of state and government. With the world in some turmoil after the 9-11 attacks, with the process of EU treaty making by heads of
state and government meeting behind closed doors having so evidently
reached its limits and with the euro notes and coins, a potent symbol of integration, about to replace national currencies of 12 member states[133] as legal
tender, Verhofstadt had seized his moment.

---

130   Among the unsung heroes of EU presidencies are often the country's permanent representative to the EU.
Frans van Daele of Belgium was one such.

131   On 12 December 2001 the House adopted a set of recommendations I proposed to deal with security at EU
summits and similar international gatherings. It recommended improving dialogue with civil society on the right
to peaceful protest and a firm but proportionate response to criminal behaviour by demonstrators. Verhofstadt
had taken on the anti-globalisation protesters who had massed at European Councils and other world leaders'
summits, such as Gothenburg and Genoa, as they gathered in Brussels; descending into the street he had argued
with them about the importance of the EU to its citizens. His Irish counterparts had not.

132   With Giuliano Amato of Italy and Jean-Luc Dehaene of Belgium as vice chairmen.

133   Greece had been a late joiner, though it was later (2009) to admit that it had cooked its books to give the
impression that it met the criteria for joining.

Chapter 3:   January 2002 – June 2004

The latter half of the 1999-2004 Parliament was dominated by the invasion of Iraq, which divided EU member states and fuelled tensions between Muslims, Jews and Christians, and other aspects of the aftermath of 11 September 2001. The EU was also increasingly occupied with the growing global challenges of migration and climate change. Preparations for enlargement of the EU to ten new member states absorbed much energy. In the case of Cyprus, no agreement was reached on reunification of the island prior to its EU entry. The Italian presidency of 2003 was to prove controversial with the European Parliament. Issues of financial reform – of Parliament and the European Commission – also continued to attract media interest.

The Council was presided over during this period by Spain and Denmark (2002), Greece and Italy (2003) and Ireland (1st half 2004).

A second Liberal presidency of Parliament

The election of Irish MEP Pat Cox to the presidency of the European Parliament in 2002 was a moment for Liberals to savour. Though he scraped home after three rounds of voting by a margin of just 61 votes on 15 January 2002, Cox was to prove one of Parliament's better presidents[134]. He was to broker a consensus around which important reforms of Parliament could later be carried out; and he was to act with vigour to ensure a successful welcome for the ten new member states due to join the EU in 2004.

Pat Cox's most evident strengths were his easy bonhomie and his instinct for good political drama. As a former university lecturer in economics and later a television presenter, he possessed good communication skills which he devoted to the service of an increasingly important body in a Union desperately lacking in openness, transparency and citizen-friendliness. His energy, even after late night socialising, became legendary. His ability to concentrate on the big picture and pick the right words for every occasion, in a language of inclusiveness, won him many friends.

Nor was Cox lacking in courage or imagination. A Liberal initiative to bring Chen Shui-bian, the new Liberal president of international pariah Taiwan to Parliament to receive the Prize for Freedom by Liberal International won his backing; and though the move was ultimately thwarted by the cowardice of the French and Belgian governments[135], neither of which would accord the

---

134   Cox was to be assisted as president by ELDR staff Bo Manderup Jensen, Mia Asenius, Alison Suttie, Elisabetta Faraggi, Edel Crosse, Anne Marie Janssen and Ibrahim Thiam.

135   Belgium at least discussed the matter in Cabinet, on 20 February 2003.

European Parliament the neutral territorial status which the USA gives the General Assembly of the United Nations and which would have allowed President Chen to visit, Cox was prepared to receive the president's wife and the speaker of Taiwan's Legislative Yuan (parliament)[136]. Cox moved too to secure the first ever address to Parliament by an African head of state, inviting Senegal's president Abdoulaye Wade[137] to Strasbourg.

Cox was to have less freedom of manoeuvre, however, in seeing through his commitment to reform the EP's rules on the payment of expenses and allowances to members. The legal position and the terms and conditions of MEPs were governed by a statute which had not been amended since 1965, though Liberal MEPs had sought reform since 1979. The so-called 'members' statute', intended to be agreed between Parliament and Council and to enter into force with the EU's constitution, was however to prove a matter of fierce contention.

Under new management

Early in December 2001 the ELDR group's bureau had confirmed me and Alexander Beels as leader and secretary general-designate and tasked us with finding a consensus on the 'package' of posts to be filled. Yet organising the succession to Cox was to be no easy task. I recruited the assistance of a small number of colleagues with whom I saw eye to eye on the challenges faced by Liberals: first Jules Maaten MEP, with whom I had worked at EU level in my Young Liberal days, who had joined me as a colleague in 1999 and who was an imaginative thinker[138]; then Cecilia Malmstrom MEP, newly elected from Sweden and full of reformist vigour; my UK colleague Diana Wallis, one of the best of the British bunch, whose election to succeed me as UK delegation leader I had assisted, and the flamboyant and fun-loving Karin Riis MEP from Denmark. I also sought the assistance of Alexander Beels, the group's deputy secretary general and my choice to become head of staff if elected, and of Niccolo Rinaldi, who I wanted as my deputy secretary general. I knew they would provide a reliable sounding board, offer good advice, come up with good ideas and defend me when I needed it. I had wined and dined other colleagues intensively (and, inevitably in Brussels, expensively) and ensured that – while I could not win over everybody – I would make no enemies through neglect. Two new colleagues, Ole B. Sorensen MEP and Herman Vermeer MEP, were the target of my prandial petitioning in January 2002, with only days left to run.

Perhaps unsurprisingly, Cox and ELDR group general secretary Bo Manderup Jensen did little to pave the way for a smooth succession. Cox was worried that it would look presumptuous to organise it formally prior to his election as speaker and that if he failed to be elected he would find himself in

---

136   Liberals were also to succeed in inviting Taiwan's vice president Annette Lu to the Liberal International conference in Budapest in 2003.

137   Wade's party, the Parti Democratique Senegalais, was a member of the Liberal International.

138   Maaten was to produce in 2008 a spoof James Bond film about the ALDE group, which was shown to great amusement at the annual Christmas party.

any case displaced as group leader. Manderup Jensen felt the same hot breath of Alexander Beels on the back of his neck. Neither dampened the ambitions of Netherlands MEP Jan Mulder to challenge for the office, though Mulder's challenge[139] fizzled out as he withdrew on the day of the vote.

On 15 January 2002 I was elected unopposed as leader of the ELDR group, with Karin Riis as my deputy and Belgian MEP Dirk Sterckx as our Whip. We put up Bertel Haarder as a candidate for vice president of Parliament and were pleased to secure his election. The ELDR committee chair passed to Luciano Caveri of the Valle d'Aosta in northern Italy, though it was to pass again to his colleague Paolo Costa within a year, since Caveri was to be elected to his regional council and became an 'assessore'[140].

I told my colleagues that afternoon that I sought to grow our group; to concentrate on issues where Parliament had legal powers in order to show our electors how Liberal MEPs made the difference, and to communicate our work in Parliament to 'every member of every member party'.

Having set out formally my manifesto and secured the backing of my colleagues for it, I set straight to work to communicate better with Liberals in member states, building a sense of political family at EU level; to reflect in the group's staff recruitment policies the diversity of the society we represented; and to lift the gaze of members beyond the confines (however much broader the 2004 enlargement was to make them) of the European Union, in order to develop supranational responses to the increasingly supranational challenges of the new century.

On 16 January 2002 Spain's prime minister, Jose Maria Aznar, came to present his country's plans for the EU Council presidency, laid out in a document entitled 'More Europe', with a speech to Parliament in Strasbourg. He had seized on the opportunities offered by the 'war on terror' to launch a new offensive against Basque separatists, for which he sought the EU's blessing. In my maiden speech as leader of the ELDR group I told him that this was no conventional war and would not be won with conventional weapons: military solutions risked causing collateral damage, which could be offset only by the deployment of emotional intelligence. Aware of the tensions in highly centralised Spain and keen to attract regionalist parties to the Liberal standard, I regretted that there appeared to be no recognition of Europe's different regions and cultures in his 'rather Castilian' programme.

I had frequently been critical of Aznar's heavy-handed approach to tackling terrorism while I chaired Parliament's justice and home affairs committee, so he knew I was not a political ally. But over the lunch in the president's dining room which followed the debate he did little to hide his anger at my remarks,

---

139 Mulder's ambitions had become apparent to colleagues some months earlier at a clumsily handled social evening at his home, but he told me of them formally only seven days before the vote. Nonetheless I was subsequently to ask Mulder to draw up a position paper for the ELDR group for the committee of inquiry which Parliament had decided to establish to investigate foot and mouth disease, in order to make use of his expertise and also to bring him firmly back on board.

140 Prodi had made known to me through Giovanni Procacci MEP in July 2001 that he sought a parliamentary committee chair for his delegation and that Caveri was his choice. It was a position to which their numbers would entitle them. Caveri was subsequently to host a meeting of the Liberal group in his constituency which included a visit to a casino at which the presence of scantily clad dancing girls tested the diplomacy of his guests.

I learned immediately that the major debates with representatives of the Council presidency – normally the head of state or government but occasionally the foreign or other minister – were a useful forum for scoring political points; and I was able two years later to bring the Basque national party – with whose leading light Josu Jon Imaz MEP I had struck up a good relationship in the previous parliament (1994-1999) – into our ALDE ranks.

Promoting a wider Liberal vision

On 28 January 2002 I met Belgian prime minister Guy Verhofstadt.[141] He had been in office since 1999 and was Europe's most senior Liberal holding public office. I had procured an invitation to him to address the UK Liberal Democrats' annual conference in September 2000 and hit it off well with him. I imagine he preferred my social Liberal attitude to the more economic Liberal approach of Cox. He agreed with alacrity to my suggestion that, since most European Council meetings would henceforth be held in Brussels, he should host regular lunch meetings for summit participants and other leading Liberals from across the EU on these occasions at his official residence[142]. He also agreed to assist in my strategy of expanding the group.

In late November 2001 Danish Liberal leader Anders Fogh Rasmussen had led his party to victory at the polls. He was to form a right-wing governing coalition while the Radikale Venstre party, the social Liberals, went into opposition. I had chatted at length to Fogh Rasmussen at the ELDR Party conference in Ljubljana in September 2001 and had appreciated his intellect, but had not warmed to him as I had to his predecessor as party leader, Uffe Elleman-Jensen. Nonetheless I was to come to like him and to respect and value his strong commitment to the Liberal political family. One consequence of his victory at the polls was that the ELDR group was to lose a senior MEP and former vice president of the EP in the form of Bertel Haarder, called back to Denmark as EU affairs minister with just a few months to prepare for Denmark's forthcoming EU presidency.

I felt it important to be as inclusive as possible in building Liberal co-operation at European level. In addition to seeking good relations with the Liberal commissioners, prime ministers and leaders of the national parties which sent MEPs to my group, I set out to cultivate Liberals elsewhere in Europe's institutions. While some of my colleagues paid precious little attention to the EU's nascent Committee of the Regions, on which representatives of local and regional government were represented, it was in my view important to involve people at all levels of society in EU decision-making and to reach into the member states beyond national capitals. Moreover, while Liberals were sometimes absent from national government we were frequently in office at regional or local level. Thus it was that I paid an early visit, just a fortnight after my election, to address the ELDR group on the Committee of the Regions

---

141   He was accompanied by his foreign minister Karel de Gucht and Flanders minister (and soon to become national interior minister) Patrick Dewael. I took with me Alexander Beels.

142   It has been alleged (see Eppink's 'Life of a European Mandarin') that Verhofstadt was to exclude Bolkestein from these meetings. I can find no evidence that this is true.

under its new and sound Swedish Centre Party leader Kent Johannsen. I was to pay a similar visit to ELDR colleagues on the Parliamentary Assembly of the Council of Europe, led by Matyas Eorsi[143] but still under the tutelage of my distinguished mentor and friend Lord Russell Johnston, president of the Parliamentary Assembly of the Council of Europe 1999-2002. The more I could share my ideas and seek the advice of a wide range of Liberals, the better informed I knew my actions would be.

On 6 February 2002 Valery Giscard d'Estaing came before the political group leaders to share with us his plans[144] for the grandly-named Convention on the Future of Europe, which he had been asked to lead following the Belgian presidency's initiative at the European Council in Laeken the previous December. The constitution was to be many months in the making; though the main parts of the document were published on 13 June 2003, Giscard was not to return to present his final draft until 3 September 2003.

I had been pleased to be able to put onto the Convention on the Future of Europe Andrew Duff MEP, whom I asked to co-ordinate the work of the Liberal participants, and Lone Dybkjaer MEP as his substitute. I knew the Liberal family was also to have strong representation of pragmatists through the representatives of governments and national parliaments[145]. In an address to Liberal members of the Convention at the supper I hosted for them on the day of its opening I spoke of the opportunity offered by the Convention to reconnect the EU to its citizens by enhancing democracy and placing our common European values at the centre of a new constitutional settlement. But I warned against trying to convince our citizens that treaty changes were the main focus of our work. A similar approach was adopted by Werner Hoyer MP, former EU affairs minister of Germany and a participant in intergovernmental conferences and now president of the ELDR Party. He told the ELDR Party bureau meeting in Amsterdam that while the Convention was important to a necessary reform of the EU treaties we should not overlook the rather greater and more immediate importance of the Lisbon agenda of economic reform or the preparations for enlargement of the EU to the east. Both Werner and I understood from our experience of national politics that constitutional reform is rarely a matter which inspires voters. The message to Liberals under our leadership was going to be 'engage by all means in the intellectual debates; but campaign on the bread-and-butter issues'.

Moreover, it was time for Liberals to recognise that while the EU was essential to the peace, prosperity and liberal democracy which we advocated, it was no longer sufficient. Global challenges had become so evident and so pressing that an excessive euro-centrism would be self-defeating. A

---

143   Matyas Eorsi was elected leader in January 2002 when his predecessor Kristina Ojuland became foreign minister of Estonia. Kristina was to bring her wide experience to the European Parliament in 2009.

144   I was pleased to greet him warmly as a predecessor of mine but to make clear my satisfaction that in Sir John Kerr, secretary general to the Convention, he would have wise and sure-footed counsel.

145   Liberals on the Convention were to include prominent figures such as Henning Christophersen, Lamberto Dini, Hans van Mierlo and Louis Michel.

rare occasion[146] to set out my stall presented itself in Parliament just eight weeks after my election as leader. The commissioner for economic and monetary affairs, Pedro Solbes, had presented to Parliament a Commission paper entitled 'Response to the challenges of globalisation'. Both the World Economic Forum and the World Social Forum had met, in New York and Puerto Alegre respectively, and had provided very different diagnoses of the world's ills and most effective cures. I found the Commission's paper rather one-sided and set out a Liberal alternative: the establishment of effective instruments of supra-national governance, based on the model of the EU, involving the African Union, Mercosur and the South Asian Area of Regional Co-operation, to provide global solutions to global challenges.

EU expansion was also more likely to inspire Europeans' enthusiasm than discourse about constitutions, however important these were. Parliament was to debate enlargement on 13 March 2002. While Commissioner Verheugen outlined the major challenges and the costs of expansion, the president-in-office of the Council, Spanish minister Josep Pique, spoke far-sightedly of the problems and likely costs of not seizing the opportunity of such an historic enlargement to the east.

I had discussed EU enlargement with Romano Prodi on 25 February 2002.[147] Prodi had not been one of the architects of enlargement, other than in his role as a member of the European Council from May 1996 to October 1998. But as a free-thinking federalist he had grasped, ahead of many of his compatriots and many on the right wing, the historic imperative of the venture. In alliance with the Liberals leading Parliament and Council he was to drive through the Union's policy-making processes a series of measures which were to make enlargement a success. While he was moving the agenda forward in the Commission, we agreed, Liberals in Parliament would establish a 'Re-uniting Europe' campaign involving regular visits and exchanges and would invite 'virtual MEPs' from our sister parties in central and eastern Europe to attend events at which enlargement was discussed. Thus it was that on 12 June 2002 I used my reply to Council and Commission in a parliamentary debate on enlargement to welcome parliamentarians from 12 applicant countries who were following the debate from the visitors' gallery and for whom a programme of conferences and meetings had been arranged. However, aware of the opposition to enlargement which was creeping into debate in other political groups – in which MEPs were abusing the enlargement process to re-open old wounds, as with the debate about the Benes decrees in the Czech Republic[148] – I reminded MEPs that not everything in member states was perfect; and that what really mattered to the health of a country was the direction in which its face was set.

146 Parliament was not to debate the matter again by name until 15 November 2007, on a motion entitled 'The European interest: succeeding in the age of globalisation' on which Margarita Starkeviciute MEP was a rapporteur.

147 At my first private supper with Prodi at *Le Pou Qui Tousse*, a small Sardinian restaurant of his choice in Brussels.

148 The Benes decrees were enacted by Czechoslovakia after World War II and legitimised the confiscation of lands formerly belonging to Sudeten Germans and Hungarians. Czech prime minister Zeman and Commissioner Verheugen were to say on 11 April 2002 that they were not part of the EU accession negotiations 'and should have no bearing on them'.

A pact with Prodi

Prodi came from a Christian Democratic but not a conservative background. In his home city of Bologna the Christian Democrats had enjoyed a close working relationship with Socialist and Communist parties since the years in which they had fought together in the Italian resistance. The Bolognese Christian Democrats belonged mainly to the left of the party and were adherents to social Christian doctrine. Romano Prodi himself, the eighth of nine children, was a genial, hardworking and socially committed person. Within the course of a decade he was to move his troops from the right wing to the left wing of the political spectrum with hardly a blink of self doubt. My relationship with him was to prove crucial to my success in ensuring – in line with Louis XIV's doctrine *'se servir des conjonctures'* – that they sojourned with the Liberals en route.

An invitation to address the annual conference of the La Margherita party in Rome in June 2002 offered an opportunity to deepen relations. This party was the product of a merger between Prodi's Democrats and the followers of Francesco Rutelli. While Prodi had kept some of his party's MEPs in the EP's EPP group, his relations with the EPP were strained by the presence in their ranks of MEPs from Forza Italia, the party of his arch enemy Silvio Berlusconi. Liberals were interested in having all Prodi's MEPs, but after our error in the previous mandate in admitting the Lega Nord I felt it essential that we first got to know what kind of party La Margherita would turn out to be.

It was important too that they did not raise objections to the presence in the ELDR group of any other Italians. While the old Italian Liberal Party had died by this point, with those of its members who had joined us after being elected on the Forza Italia list in 1994[149] having paid the price of de-selection, the Republicans still clung to existence and contributed to our ranks the fire-brand Luciana Sbarbati, who will be long remembered for her temper after she told a very diplomatic interpreter *'Macche "a little upset"! Digli che sono incazzata nera!!'*[150]. Assisted by an Italian Liberal lawyer called Giuseppe Benedetto I had also brought into the group Claudio Martelli, a former disciple of Bettino Craxi, who was trying to create a space for what he called a liberal-socialist movement on the centre left. I had a number of discussions with Mario Segni MEP, a fierce opponent of Berlusconi's who shared my view that we needed EU competition policy to prevent monopolies in media ownership as in other areas; but our joint activities in pressing the Commission to act on the matter did not suffice to bring him over. The fish I was trying hardest to catch was the Italian Radical Party, which continued to play an important role in Italian politics; but the Radical MEPs sat in the technical group of non-aligned MEPs and relations between their leader Marco Pannella and Margherita leader Franceso Rutelli were jaundiced by a shared history[151].

---

149   MEPs Luigi Caligaris and Stefano de Luca

150   'What do you mean "a little upset"?! Tell them I'm absolutely furious!'

151   Rutelli had been one of the many promising young men in the Radical Party who eventually left out of frustration with the domineering leadership style of Pannella.

Prodi agreed to my suggestion that he attend the Liberal prime ministers' and EU leaders' meeting in Seville in advance of the EU summit in June 2004, where he consented even to join the Liberal family photocall.

Prodi did not always endear himself to Liberals, however. After the steep decline of the world's economy the previous year, Liberals were keen to ensure that co-ordination of member states' fiscal policies was maintained, the long-term sustainability of public finances being to us the basis of sound management of the economy. We had been angry when, in February 2002, the Commission had not issued early warnings to Germany and Portugal about the state of their public accounts, despite having imposed sanctions on Ireland the previous year for a lesser offence. The entry into force of the balanced budget provision of the EU's Stability and Growth Pact had already been delayed for two years in recognition of the difficulties Germany and France were facing due to the economic recession. Meeting in Bath, in my constituency in the south west of England, in October of 2002, Liberals had insisted on member states balancing their budgets over the economic cycle. Francesco Rutelli MEP was to tell congress delegates: 'The modern liberal democratic and reform culture is the only way to manage the current economic crisis. That is why I say "no" to withdrawing from the stability and growth pact and "yes" to financial stability and fiscal discipline'. Yet on 18 October 2002 Prodi was to call the discipline of the stability pact 'stupid'[152] in an interview with French newspaper *Le Monde*.

I had met Prodi earlier in the month over breakfast[153] and defended him from attack by EPP leader Hans-Gert Poettering seven days later when the leak of the Commission's report on the preparedness for accession of the ten new member states upset MEPs. My colleagues would have been most dissatisfied however, had I not joined the chorus of condemnation of Prodi's newspaper interview during a parliamentary debate on the ECB on 21 October 2002. Liberals were at the forefront of moves to keep public deficits under control and wanted a new target for reducing structural deficits to be included in the Stability and Growth Pact; any suggestion that this was not important would naturally occasion concern in our ranks.

At the European Council on 24 October 2002 the heads of the three main EU institutions – Council, Parliament and Commission – were all adherents to the Liberal family[154]. Though Prodi was not always keen to defend this allegiance in public[155], half of his EP troops were already in the Liberal

---

152   Prodi was subsequently to point out that he had said 'stupid, like all decisions that are rigid'. But Commissioner Lamy had described the pact as 'mediaeval' and French finance minister Francis Mer had given such a warm welcome to both remarks that Liberals feared France would now feel empowered to flout the rules.

153   At the Commission's Breydel building. Prodi was accompanied, as usual, by assistants Lucio Gussetti and Stefano Manservisi, I by Alexander Beels. He promised me a favourable Commission response to my Oral Question on media concentration, calling for action to prevent monopoly media ownership, but this did not materialise.

154   This was not quite a first. In the summer of 1981 both Parliament and Commission had been presided over by Liberals while Netherlands foreign minister Christoph van der Klaauw had – to all intents and purposes – assumed the presidency of the Council though Christian Democrat Dries van Agt was prime minister.

155   On one occasion, when challenged by Socialist group leader Martin Schulz, he said '*Je suis un président multicolore*', professing allegiance to more than two parties.

group and the other half to join within 21 months. The EU's historic enlargement, it seemed, would coincide with a Liberal dawn.

As 2002 had drawn to a close the ELDR group numbered 53 members. Stealing an idea from a UK Liberal MP I decided to produce a commemorative pack of playing cards, with 52 cards carrying the photographs of members as different players and a joker bearing the photo of our trump card, Pat Cox. Apart from Cox and me, cast – at the urging of my assistant Sarah Kent – as the King of Hearts, each MEP was assigned a card at random. The dangers of such ideas were brought home to me when a deeply distraught Finnish colleague – a person for whom I had great respect and would not have wished to offend – sought me out to complain bitterly at having been cast as the ace of spades.

Single market elusive

Liberals believed that the benefits of the single currency could be fully realised only if the benefits of the internal market were optimised. Yet ten years on from the 'bonfire of regulations' of 1992, only seven of the 15 member states had achieved the Union's goal of implementing 98.5% of all internal market legislation. At the spring European Council in Barcelona in March 2002 the heads of state and government had reached agreement on liberalising energy markets, but only for industrial users; Joe Public would have to wait. The goal of full employment remained elusive; barriers to the participation of women and older workers presented challenges, and tax burdens on low paid workers meant that working did not always pay. Skills did not match opportunities available and labour unions often sought wage increases for their members unrelated to levels of productivity in the company or industry concerned. In Council there was still no 'common position' (consensus) on a draft pension funds directive which had been approved by Parliament at first reading in July the previous year. And the Commission had been moved to take to the Court of Justice a dispute with the Council over powers to police state aids to industry[156]. Within Liberal ranks, criticism of the economic failures of the EU under Prodi had therefore started to grow. When one of my colleagues asked Frits Bolkestein at a Liberal networking meeting in October whether it was true that Prodi might stay on for a second term, Bolkestein voiced no reply. Yet he both answered the question and expressed his opinion on the prospect with a judicious movement of his eyebrows.

Migration

Under Spain's presidency in the first half of 2002 the emphasis was on controlling migration. The geographical position of Spain and the Canary Islands made them vulnerable to illegal immigration from Africa which they found hard to control. Moreover, fear of migration was rising quickly

---

156 This centred on the Council's decision to overrule Commission findings in 1999 and 2000 banning Portuguese government aid to pig farmers.

up the list of voters' concerns in Spain and elsewhere. In the French presidential election of 2002 French far-right politician Jean Marie Le Pen had defeated socialist candidate Lionel Jospin in the first round, taking 18% of the vote, and was a candidate in the run off against incumbent Jacques Chirac. In elections in the Netherlands the same year an anti-immigration party led by Pim Fortuyn had polled 17% of the vote. Though public opinion in Spain was more tolerant, Aznar's Partido Popular had pledged to crack down on immigration and he used the EU summit in Seville, in southern Spain, on 21 and 22 June 2002 to highlight his policy[157]. Some governments again argued that the 1951 Geneva Convention on refugees gave too great an opportunity to economic migrants to claim protection as refugees and wished to restrict this. Under Spanish pressure the Council was to describe asylum and immigration as 'separate, but closely related'; while compliance with the Geneva Convention was stipulated by the heads of state and government, as in Tampere in 1999, they now sought to 'balance' it with resolute action to combat illegal immigration and trafficking in human beings. For the first time they spoke publicly about 'absorption capacity' – stating 'the legitimate aspiration to a better life must be reconcilable with the reception capacity of the Union and its Member states' – and of the need to return quickly to their countries of origin refugees whose applications for asylum had failed.

Liberals believed there was both a moral and an economic case for managed immigration. Inspired by the experience of Canada's Liberal government, which had opened the front door to legal migration in order to close more effectively the back door used by the people-traffickers, and committed to an active policy of citizenship promotion, most of us shared the view of J.K. Galbraith that migration was the oldest form of action against poverty and joined him in posing the question: 'What is the perversity in the human soul that causes people to resist so obvious a good?' Speaking in the parliamentary debate ahead of the European Council meeting in Seville, Sarah Ludford found distressing the proposal by Prime Ministers Aznar, Berlusconi and Blair to deny development aid to countries of origin of illegal migrants to the EU, pointing out that it would only make them worse off and encourage further illegal migration. And speaking on behalf of the Liberal group in the debate on the outcome of the summit I criticised the decision by the Spanish government to close its borders in advance of the summit, fearful of the anti-globalisation protesters who had become a feature of these events, in contravention of EU laws on freedom of movement.

Six months after the Spanish presidency, in January 2003, Greece took over the presidency of the European Council. Like Spain, Greece found itself

---

157   Fortuyn was murdered on 6 May 2002, during the election campaign, but the election went ahead although campaigning was suspended. Liberals were relieved that there was not a swing to anti-immigrant parties everywhere. In the German region of Sachsen Anhalt the FDP increased its share of the vote by 10% against extremists. And in Hungary the Free Democrats and their soon-to-be allies the Socialists had seen off a strong challenge from Viktor Orban's right-wing Fidesz party. Liberals in the European Parliament called on all democratic political parties to re-commit themselves to the Charter of political parties for a non-racist society, first proclaimed by 100 political parties at Utrecht in February 1998.

the first port of call for many of those migrating into Europe. Though the government of Costas Simitis was to be more liberal in its approach than that of Aznar, the debate on immigration during their trick at the helm was to reach new peaks of controversy, with UK home secretary David Blunkett proposing the establishment of refugee camps in the north African desert to house those who had left their homes to seek a better life in Europe and some of his counterparts making similar proposals.[158] Discussing progress towards the Lisbon agenda at the European Council in Brussels on 20 and 21 March 2003, heads of state and government for the first time made an explicit connection between immigration and employment[159], welcoming the Commission's intention to report on how skill shortages and demographic change might be compensated for by the creation of routes for legal migration into the Union and better integration of migrants. To calm the 'noises off' from populist politicians in various national capitals, the Commission therefore published on 3 June 2003 a 'Communication on Immigration, Integration and Employment' pointing out the importance of migrants to the EU's labour market in the context of an ageing EU workforce. A courageous Commissioner Diamantopoulou stressed: 'Zero immigration is not an option … properly managed immigration will be necessary to meet the future needs of the labour market'.

Despite the entry into force of the Amsterdam Treaty, progress in developing common policies in the field of justice and home affairs was painfully slow; partly because Amsterdam obliged the Union to consider initiatives proposed by each individual member state or a group of states acting together, which had the effect of clogging up the EU's policy-making system with proposals reflecting the whim of every hyperactive minister, however unlikely they would command a consensus of opinion. Indeed the decision in the Amsterdam Treaty to give the members of the Council a right of initiative alongside that of the Commission added to Europe's incapacity rather than improving its capacity to take decisions. The Nice Treaty was not to change fundamentally this state of affairs; indeed it was not until the Lisbon Treaty entered into force in December 2009 that the EU would see a streamlining of policy making in this area through the 'Stockholm programme' developed by Sweden's Conservative-Liberal government.

Nonetheless some progress was being made, with Liberals active in achieving it. Agreement had been reached under the Danish presidency at the European Council on 24 and 25 October 2002 on transit arrangements through Lithuania from Russian port enclave Kaliningrad to the rest of Russia. And on 23 December the House approved the EU's first readmission agreement[160], whereby a third country would agree to take back any citizen

---

158   A letter from the UK to its EU partners proposing new approaches to asylum had raised eyebrows in Council. The Commission was invited by the spring European Council in March to 'explore the ideas further, in particular with UNHCR'.

159   At the same time, recognising that their goal of 70% employment could not be met without far-reaching structural reform and unsuccessful in coaxing their countries towards it, they appointed former Netherlands prime minister Wim Kok to head a European Employment Task Force.

160   The rapporteur was your author.

who had migrated illegally into the EU (and vice versa). Though related to Hong Kong, which posed few difficulties in this regard, it was to be the first of many such agreements.

Under the Greek presidency, political agreement was reached on the rights of long-term residents from third countries, with Sarah Ludford having secured parliamentary consent for the proposals. But on asylum, agreement still eluded the Union. A proposed directive on the status of third country nationals and another on minimum standards for granting and withdrawing refugee status were held up not only by fundamental disagreement among member states but also by concerns in Parliament that the directive would deal only with refugee status (leaving subsidiary protection to be determined at a later date) and that the definition of a family was insufficiently broad. Ole Sorensen MEP had spoken of the need for a system in which 'Illegal immigration and people smuggling must be combated, but genuine refugees must be helped'[161]; but the right wing claimed that there was an attempt to expand the definition of 'refugee' beyond what was contained in the Geneva Convention.

The Greek presidency concluded with a commitment by the EU's heads of state and government to speed up the implementation of all aspects of the Tampere programme which now included, they specified, exploring legal migration channels. They foresaw a common EU border force, a union-wide policy on the use of biometric identifiers and policies for the return of illegal migrants.

Parliamentary reform

MEPs' pay and allowances had increasingly become a matter of public concern, verging on scandal. MEPs were paid by their national governments and earned the same salary as that earned by members of their national parliaments. To German and Italian MEPs this was very generous; to the Spanish and Portuguese much less so. To overcome the problems faced by some, a generous system of allowances had been devised, mainly in reimbursement of the travel undertaken on a weekly basis to Brussels or Strasbourg and back. This and the allowance received for staffing their offices were, however, subject to very few auditing controls. The extent of abuse of the system by some MEPs, and the increasing criticism this was generating in the press and broadcast media, convinced many MEPs that reform had to come. It was resisted by some of those whom the arrangements treated most favourably.

German and Austrian MEPs, in particular, strongly resisted Cox's plans for reform of Parliament's system of pay and allowances. And since the German MEPs carried so much weight in the House they were formidable opponents. Socialist MEP Willi Rothley, an experienced parliamentarian and rapporteur for the reform dossier in the legal affairs committee, was to fight Cox tooth and nail. He was able to frustrate the wishes of Parliament's president time and time again.

---

161 Debate in the House, 21 October 2002.

Cox was not to be deterred. He raised the matter on every possible occasion with national governments, needing their support for any agreement, and worked closely with members of Parliament's legal affairs committee.

Liberals had been at the forefront of the campaign for reform, but we did not want reform at any cost. Rothley's first formal proposal was to pay MEPs 50% of the basic salary of a judge at the European Court of Justice, considerably higher than the salary proposed by a group of independent experts[162], and to continue to refund travel allowances on the existing basis, an amount per kilometre travelled which left some MEPs with a substantial profit on each journey. It was to be voted on the floor of the House on 5 December 2002. Though Cox had written to every MEP urging them to support the proposal as a basis for negotiations with Council, it was unacceptable to most of the Liberal group, who believed not only that the salary was unwisely generous but that travel expenses should be reimbursed at cost. An alternative motion by Liberals, Greens and the United European Left was rejected as the majority of PES and EPP MEPs supported Rothley. Bertel Haarder, president-in-office of the Council, opined that the proposal did not fulfil the Council's conditions for agreement. Cox sought to buy time by hailing it as 'a mandate for negotiation' with the Council and established a contact group for discussions.

By 2 June 2003 the contact group had brought a slightly revised proposal to the House. But again German MEPs Willi Rothley for the Socialists and Klaus-Heiner Lehne for the EPP were determined to avoid a system where travel expenses were reimbursed at cost; and though a paragraph in the draft agreement called on Parliament's bureau to decide new rules for reimbursement of travel costs they were to ensure its removal. Moreover, they had hardened their stance on taxation and were now insisting that MEPs should pay only the same tax as civil servants of the European Communities, thus removing the opportunity for member states to decide to tax MEPs at the same rate as other citizens. Cox, however, desperately wanted an agreement and decided to support the text to be voted on 4 June 2003 by Parliament. At a tense meeting of the Liberal group, on the eve of the vote, the group's legal affairs co-ordinator Diana Wallis and Cox had a showdown. Neither won outright and the group decided to abstain in the vote, convinced of the principle but opposing the content of the proposal. Yet Cox decided to leave the speaker's chair the following day, resume his seat on the Liberal benches and intervene to tell the House that he had voted in favour. Though Liberals had rejected his call and either abstained or voted against, the serried ranks of the EPP and PES groups had voted to support Rothley's proposal. The press the following day screamed outrage that MEPs had voted themselves a 17% pay rise, most newspapers failing to explain to their readers the fact that MEPs have never had the power to determine their own salaries. Indeed, those who could make the decision – the national governments – were to reject Parliament's proposal at their European Council meeting in Thessaloniki on 19 June 2003. Just one year before the

---

162   Composed of three former MEPs and three former senior figures from the other EU institutions, including former Liberal MEP Elisabeth Rehn and former Commission secretary general (and Liberal) David (now Lord) Williamson.

European elections such attention was most unwelcome. Work was therefore accelerated and a new proposal put to the House on 17 December 2003. It was taken up by the incoming Irish Council presidency in January 2004 but was to fall when Germany[163], France and Sweden formed a blocking minority. It was not until 18 July 2005, during Josep Borrell's presidency of Parliament and the UK presidency of the Council that agreement was finally to be reached.

Liberals sought other reforms of Parliament too. Lousewies van der Laan, who had been elected in 1999, recruited other young MEPs in the running of an impressive campaign to abolish the requirement – in the EU treaties since 1992 – for the EP to meet twelve times a year in Strasbourg. Through an online petition they collected over one million signatures and although ultimately unsuccessful, they laid the basis for similar campaigns in subsequent parliaments to settle the vexatious issue of the cost and disruption of maintaining two meeting places. Cecilia Malmstrom acted to secure greater involvement in Parliament in the preparation and oversight of the Union's annual legislative programme; and Ole Andreasen took through Parliament recommendations on how to improve the EU's communication with citizens.

These reforms reflected a growing consensus in Brussels, across the EU institutions, that with the new century had come the time for the EU to raise its game. Thus a series of reforms were also agreed to the workings of the European Council and the Council of Ministers. Henceforth nine sectoral Council formations would meet; the European Council itself would meet four times a year (twice in each six-month presidency); its meetings would be prepared normally by EU affairs ministers, meeting in the renamed General Affairs and External Relations Council; and – in a very limited concession to the Liberal campaign for transparency – meetings would be broadcast to the public at certain points of the policy making process when the dossiers under discussion were matters where decision-making was done jointly with the European Parliament.

Internal reforms were important in the Commission, too. Where Prodi could not be faulted was in the seriousness with which he took this issue. An accountant named Marta Andreasen had been engaged to help the Commission sort out its finances, having previously been employed at the Organisation for Economic Co-operation and Development for a similar purpose, but had found the task beyond her. She then chose to present herself to the press as a 'whistleblower' on corruption, much as Paul van Buitenen had done a few years previously.[164] The 'scandals' on which she 'blew the whistle' were already well known to MEPs, who had raised many of these issues through parliamentary channels, but Rupert Murdoch and others took up her claims and gave her the reputation in sections of public opinion of being a 'wronged' woman. It was only the strong support which Prodi gave to Commissioners Neil Kinnock and Michele Schreyer which brought matters back under some control. Andreasen herself went on to become treasurer of

---

163   The German SPD MEPs had secretly persuaded their Cabinet colleagues in Gerhard Schroeder's government at home to reject it, such was their resistance to change.

164   Ironically, it was budget commissioner Michele Schreyer who had insisted on the appointment of Marta Andreasen against the Commission's normal rules, unaware that Andreasen had been suspended from her job at the OECD amid similar controversy.

UKIP in 2007 and was elected as a UKIP MEP in June 2009, shortly after her party leader became embroiled in controversy over his own use of public funds.

Israel and Palestine

The 2001 Al Qaida attacks on New York and Washington and the American reaction had heightened tensions between Christians, Jews and Muslims right across the world. Nowhere was this more keenly felt than in Palestine, where the tectonic plates of the Abrahamic religions collide. One issue which was to divide Liberals increasingly was worsening relations between Israelis and Palestinians.

Israel's prime minister Ariel Sharon had met Palestinian leaders early in 2002 for the first time since taking office a year earlier, just prior to a visit to Washington. Yet Israel's refusal to show any real commitment to peace and its continued victimisation of migrant workers were to the minds of some Liberals short-sighted and self-defeating. My criticism of Israel in a parliamentary debate on 5 February 2002 was not particularly strident[165]. I called for a pull-back of Israeli troops from the occupied territories and welcomed the news that some Israeli reservists were refusing to serve outside the country's pre-June 1967 frontiers[166]. The power of the Zionist lobby, however, is as strong in Europe's capital as anywhere else; and my approach involved a change of tone from that employed by my predecessor. At the first meeting of our group after the debate a number of colleagues took issue with me. I heard what they said, but I was clear in my own mind that I had no intention of trimming my views or of having somebody more malleable speak on behalf of my group on such issues.

Moreover, my concerns and those of many other MEPs were shared by ministers in Council. Though their discussions in February and March 2002 were held informally over lunch and therefore not minuted (an administrative ploy), by April they were expressing open concern and by May – with the escalating violence centred on the Church of the Nativity in Bethlehem and the EU offering sanctuary to 13 Palestinians who had sought refuge there – they recognised that the actions of the Israeli government were becoming indefensible. Israel had prevented a delegation of visiting MEPs from meeting Palestinian leader Yassir Arafat. It had again violated the human rights provisions of its association agreement with the EU. And its forces had destroyed projects in Palestine funded by the EU taxpayer.

The EU's heads of state and government, meeting in Barcelona on 15 and 16 March 2002, had called on Israel 'immediately to withdraw its military forces from areas placed under the control of the Palestinian Authority, stop extrajudicial executions, lift the closures and restrictions, freeze settlements and respect international law'. And speaking in a debate in Parliament on 25 April 2002 my deputy leader, Karin Riis-Jorgensen was to say: 'The Israeli

---

165 I was to make a far more strident intervention in a debate on 9 April 2002 when, as reports came in of a massacre of Palestinians by Israeli soldiers in Jenin, I suggested that Ariel Sharon might be among the first of those tried for crimes against humanity by the International Criminal Court in The Hague.

166 Similar pressure from reservists had led to Israel's withdrawal of forces from the Lebanon.

government must accept that criticism from its candid friends is not an act of enmity and certainly not an act of anti-Semitism'.

Europe's objective remained two-fold: the creation of a democratic, viable and independent State of Palestine, bringing to an end the occupation of 1967; and the right of Israel to live within safe and secure boundaries guaranteed by the international community.

By June the situation was even worse. The Seville European Council in June 2002 warned of 'a dramatic turning point' and asserted that further escalation would render the situation uncontrollable. It called for the early convening of an international conference to bring together two sides which, on their own, could not find a solution. By their Copenhagen meeting at the year's end the heads of state and government were calling on Israel to stop 'making life increasingly intolerable for ordinary Palestinians and fuelling extremism' and to put an end to 'excessive use of force and extra-judicial killings'.

The systematic discrimination practised by the Israeli government against the people they had callously displaced was illiberal in the extreme. In saying so openly I was to upset some of my colleagues on a number of occasions subsequently – though Colette Flesch MEP[167], who recommended increased aid for education, health and social services in Palestine, was helpful latterly in bringing many around to my point of view.

Islam and Christianity

One of the difficulties involved in Europe's switch from being a continent of net emigration to one of net immigration was the fact that many immigrants were of the Islamic faith whereas most EU citizens described themselves as Christian. This was to lead to a debate in the Convention on the Future of Europe about whether to accept a proposal from Vatican representative Jean Louis Tauran to include a reference to the EU's 'Christian heritage' in the preamble to the constitution being prepared. Liberals opposed such a move. While the EU's cultural heritage was undoubtedly predominantly Christian, there was also an important Islamic heritage (from the Islamic caliphates in Constantinople and Cordoba, for example) and a Jewish and a secular heritage too. To define heritage in terms of only one faith would be divisive.

Anti-clericalism remained an important strand of the Liberal approach, though not exclusive; the theme we chose for our New Year's policy seminar (an initiative I had introduced) in 2003 was Liberalism under Christianity and Islam. As one speaker was to say, the EU's relations with Turkey 'are a testing ground for many of the other more abstract and worthy concepts which we claim to support. If you cannot treat with the willing, how can you begin to deal with the unwilling?'

Two days earlier the EPP group had voted against Turkey becoming a member of the EU. Since Turkey's governing Justice and Development Party (the AKP) is almost the mirror image of the German CDU after the war,

---

167   Colette Flesch was Parliament's rapporteur for EU funding to the UN Relief and Works Agency for Palestinian refugees. Her report, adopted in September 2002, saw a very substantial increase in the aid budget and its extension for a further four years.

Liberals perceived the EPP's opposition to be rooted in religious prejudice and therefore unprincipled.

The same theme was taken up by the Liberal International at its executive committee meeting in Casablanca in March 2003, where a discussion took place on the basis of papers prepared by Otto Graf Lambsdorff and Abdoulaye Wade and again at its congress in Dakar in October of that year, both locations having been chosen to facilitate dialogue. Liberals sought to unite those of independent mind from all sides. The issue, we agreed, was not the division between Islam and the West, but between secular government and its enemies: Christians were not natural democrats, nor Muslims inherent authoritarians; all could be Liberals. The political liberalism of Locke and Milton had stressed that to guarantee the individual's freedom of conscience, religion should be kept out of the marketplace and the rooms of government. Yet the Old Testament sensibilities of the US administration and the definition of Jewish hopes by biblical prophecy rather than the practicalities of co-existence were encouraging delusions of martyrdom.

Britain's Chief Rabbi Jonathan Sacks had been shouted down by his conservative peers when he had said that religious conviction was essentially an opinion, albeit a deeply held opinion. Yet most Liberals agreed and redoubled their search for non-confessional politics.

Iraq

Liberals had generally welcomed President Clinton's approach to global affairs. A new age had appeared to be dawning with a fresh commitment to the promotion of democracy. Indeed, a rapid development of democracy, in part under American patronage, had seen the number of countries practicing democracy rise considerably by the turn of the century. The influence of Liberal ideas on the Clinton presidency, while not universal, was something European Liberals had not expected; and George W. Bush's disputed victory in Florida over Al Gore was a setback the gravity of which became increasingly rapidly clear as the influence of the religious right and the oil lobby on US politics grew and the US commitment to promoting democracy and the rule of law at home and abroad declined. Disagreement about civil liberties in the wake of 9-11 added to the tensions between the EU and the USA, where many Liberals hoped ardently for the return of a Democratic administration; but by early 2003 the opinion polls suggested that war-president Bush had already created the circumstances for his victory over the Democrats the following year and would be elected for a second four-year term of office.

Iraq was increasingly a matter of concern for the EU. Baroness Nicholson steered through Parliament in May 2002 a report calling for the setting up of an inquiry office to investigate human rights violations in a country where the government had used chemical weaponry against its own people. Since the end of the Gulf War provoked ten years previously by the Iraqi military incursion into Kuwait, economic and social conditions had deteriorated considerably. Child mortality had doubled and Iraq was suspected of seeking to develop nuclear weapons. On 14 May 2002 UN resolution 1409 had modernised the 'Food for Oil' programme under which the western countries provided food rather than money which might be misused by a corrupt government. The EU was a major donor of humanitarian aid, having allocated EUR 270 million in assistance. Yet it appeared to have little influence in a country in which there seemed a risk of a grave new crisis emerging. US Defence Secretary Donald Rumsfeld had argued for an invasion of Iraq, comparing the case for it to the case made by Churchill for entering the Second World War. EU leaders had met at the European Council in Elsinore to discuss the situation, but there was no consensus among them for participation in any US led invasion; and summit host Anders Fogh Rasmussen had called for the early establishment of a Palestinian State in the Middle East as the best way of defusing tension in the area.

EU member states were divided in their reactions to any invasion of Iraq. On 31 January 2003 seven EU prime ministers, co-ordinated by Tony Blair, published a joint letter in major European newspapers urging military action against 'the Iraqi regime and its weapons of mass destruction' although, as UN Chief Weapons Inspector Hans Blix (also a member of Sweden's Liberal Party) was to tell MEPs by videoconference from Washington DC on 28th January 2003, there was no conclusive proof of the existence of such weapons. But whereas in December the European Council had noted 'Iraq's acceptance of Resolution 1441 and that it has, as required, submitted a declaration on its programmes to develop weapons of mass destruction', at a special summit in Brussels called by the Greek presidency on 17 February 2003 to discuss the possible invasion they noted that inspections could not 'continue indefinitely in the absence of full Iraqi co-operation' and that the EU remained committed to working with its partners, 'especially the United States, for the disarmament of Iraq'. The extraordinary summit tried to paper over the divisions between the member states by re-affirming that the EU's objective for Iraq remained full and effective disarmament in accordance with the relevant UNSC resolutions, in particular resolution 1441. But it was clear that the full weight of American diplomacy had been brought to bear in EU member states' capitals.

In the UK, the Liberal Democrats were the only party to vote in the House of Commons (on 18 March 2003) against the war; indeed, the party's spring conference in Torquay just three days previously had been dominated by debates and fringe meetings[168] about the issue. But some Liberal parties, such as Denmark's governing Venstre party and the Dutch VVD, decided to join the 'coalition of the willing'. This issue was to divide Liberals[169] as it divided other political parties: and since Belgium's Liberal prime minister opposed the war his Danish counterpart felt it wise not to attend the Liberal prime ministers' pre-summit meeting on 20 March 2003[170].

The people's directly elected representatives in the European Parliament debated the situation almost every time they met in formal session in the early months of 2003. On 29 January, High Representative Javier Solana told the

---

168   In which I played an active part.

169   The Netherlands D66, for example, left the government in protest.

170   Anders Fogh Rasmussen had a well developed sense of political family and it was probably the only such meeting he missed in his time as prime minister.

House that although important differences between EU member states remained, they agreed on the goal of disarmament of Iraq's weapons of mass destruction and on the primacy of the UNSC in maintaining international peace and security. Parliament adopted a resolution, however, stating that the breach of UNSCR 1441 identified by the inspectors did not justify military action and that a pre-emptive strike would contravene international law. It called for Saddam Hussein to be brought before the International Criminal Court on charges of genocide against the marsh Arabs. But the House was divided and the resolution was adopted by 287 against 209 with 26 abstentions; the ELDR group was not the only one to split three ways in the vote[171]. On 12 February, two days before the weapons inspectors reported again to the UNSC, there was a further debate. In view of the differences between national capitals, Greece had called an extraordinary meeting of the EU's leaders for 17 February. Speaking in the House, Commissioner Poul Nielson said the EU was now 'weaker than ever' due to the divergence of opinion between member states. Even Parliament proved unable to find consensus on a common position in another vote three days later.

On 12 March 2003 Greek foreign minister George Papandreou, speaking for the Council, told Parliament that the Iraq crisis had acutely increased the tension between the US and the EU. Commissioner Patten took EU member states to task for public squabbling and lamented a European foreign policy of the lowest common denominator which had 'never been more evident than over the last few miserable weeks'. The following day UN Secretary General Kofi Annan[172] told Parliament's group leaders of his deep concern about the illegitimacy of the invasion and the way in which the UN had been swept aside.

Portugal hosted a summit meeting in the Azores on 16 March 2003 involving the USA, the UK, Portugal and Spain, probably the biggest happening there since Columbus was arrested on his way back from the new world, in which the three European countries committed themselves to support for America in the coming hostilities. It was perhaps the decisive moment in the division of EU member states between those supporting the invasion of Iraq and those opposed to it. The battle at the UN Security Council was a struggle about the exercise of American power. Europe's troubled tribalism meant that Washington would win against the concept of world order laid down in the UN Charter.

Though Hans Blix was to report that 'no evidence of proscribed activities' had been found, the USA led a 'coalition of the willing' in launching an invasion of Iraq on 20 March 2003. At an extraordinary plenary session of the EP that day, President Cox spoke of 'the vulnerability of innocent Iraqi citizens whose humanitarian situation already was precarious before a shot was fired' and spoke of Europe as 'a House divided against itself'. Few in

---

171 Two of our members voted against the motion for a resolution and four abstained, with the majority voting in favour.

172 Annan had made himself available for private meetings with EP group leaders in Brussels in mid-February 2003. I had found him haunted by the memory of Kosovo, where war was waged without explicit UN backing but the UN had been expected to help create peace afterwards.

Europe had wanted war or believed that it was justified at this point. Across Europe's cities, people hung from their windows flags calling for peace.

On 28 March 2003 there was a major clash between London and Paris. With the invasion going badly at the start of April, Verhofstadt called a conference on EU security. The Union was riven by disagreement over the legality and advisability of the US-led invasion of Iraq.

The Americans, fearful that they were losing the propaganda war in Europe, sent Secretary of State Colin Powell to help garner support. With the fall of Baghdad on 9 April 2003 the tension eased a little, but the rights and wrongs of the invasion of Iraq still divided Liberal MEPs and had led to a fissiparous debate six days earlier.

Whether they were for or against the invasion of Iraq, there was a broad consensus among Liberal MEPs that the war was being fought in unacceptable ways. Speaking for the group on the invasion of Iraq I was highly critical of the USA, both for their use of white phosphorus weapons in the initial 'shock and awe' attack and for their treatment of prisoners of war (to whom they denied such status, categorising them merely as 'enemy combatants') at the Guantanamo Bay detention camp. This was unworthy of a country with America's proud history of civil liberties. On 25 October 2003 I was to engage in an act of political theatre more often associated with fringe groups than with Liberals and to risk the ire of Parliament's authorities by bringing into the debating chamber in Strasbourg 26 candles, one for each of the EU citizens illegally held at Guantanamo. I ensured that Parliament filed an amicus brief to the US Supreme Court on behalf of the detainees. On 13 December 2003 at the conference of presidents we moved to secure a Council statement on Guantanamo. And when Parliament adopted the following week the EU's budget for 2004, ELDR MEP and EP rapporteur Jan Mulder was to have obliged the member states to use the flexibility instrument[173] to provide one third of the money they sought.

The EU learns from defeat; develops defence policy

One impact of the division in the EU over the invasion of Iraq was to bring to boiling point the simmering feeling that the Union needed its own defence and security policy, independent of the American-sponsored NATO shield. European dismay at the foreign policy of the Bush administration was to spur calls for action. Liberals had long advocated greater EU co-operation in defence. Moreover, during an inquiry established by Parliament in 2000 into the ECHELON military surveillance system many of us had come to the conclusion that the EU also needed to establish its own similar military intelligence operation.

Some of the work done for the Liberals on this agenda by former Italian general Luigi Caligaris MEP had been taken on in the 2004-09 parliament by Claudio Martelli MEP, who was to summarise his ideas in a pamphlet called

---

173   This meant providing extra funds from the EU's budget rather than re-allocating spending already agreed. Member states were traditionally unwilling to do this, since it reduced their end-of-year rebate of any unspent EU monies.

A sword for Europe[174], launched in October 2002 at a public hearing in Parliament in the presence of Prodi and Cox.

The Seville summit in 2002 had agreed to the EU's first police mission, to take over from the UN operation in Bosnia with effect from January 2003; and its first military mission was foreseen with the expression of the Union's willingness to take over from NATO in the Former Yugoslav Republic of Macedonia when the NATO mission's mandate came to an end. In fact, the EU's first military mission was launched in April 2003. Liberal MEPs gave their support to EPP MEP and former French army general Philippe Morillon's report advocating inter alia a collective defence clause in the Constitutional Treaty and the establishment of an EU armaments and research agency[175].

On 9 April 2003 the Council of Ministers made a statement to Parliament about defence policy in reply to proposals for an EU defence policy elaborated by Morillon[176], who had drawn attention to the deficiencies of Europe's joint defence capabilities and set out priorities to rectify them. The situation in Iraq gave them a new saliency. The EU had a single trade policy, a common development aid policy and an embryonic EU diplomatic corps in the Commission's offices around the world. These were powerful instruments and would be all the more so if combined under the umbrella of a common foreign policy. Yet with combined defence spending less than half that of the USA and with only one tenth of the number of 'bangs per buck', urgent action was necessary. The Liberal group therefore supported the establishment of armaments and research agencies[177]; and there was sufficient support among my colleagues for a collective defence commitment in the draft Constitutional Treaty, similar to that under the WEU Treaty, for me to call in the House for such a clause[178].

Denmark's Liberal-led presidency did much to develop the foreign and security policy capacity of the EU. It brokered an EU agreement on the involvement of member states which were not members of NATO in operations involving NATO assets and the sharing of NATO-held intelligence information, for example. Agreement was thus reached for the EU to take over from NATO the policing mission in Macedonia from December 2002 and plans laid for the EU to take over from SFOR in Bosnia.

On 19 June the European Parliament's group leaders met EU High Representative for Common Foreign and Security Policy Javier Solana. On the occasion of the December 2002 Congress on European Defence, organised annually by Karl von Wogau MEP in the German capital I argued for a

---

174   In his pamphlet, Martelli examined the failures of the EU in dealing with conflict in the former Yugoslavia, analysed new threats facing the Union and called for the development of common armed forces to assist the Union in projecting its values.

175   Representing a constituency with a considerable presence of land, sea and air forces and substantial economic interests in the production of weapons systems I knew I would please many of my voters with the stance I took.

176   Morillon, elected in 1999 on the list of France's UDF party, sat with the EPP. He was to join the Liberals in 2004.

177   In a vote on 10 April 2003.

178   Debate on the Morillon Report, 9 April 2003.

common European defence policy with an integrated command capability 'as we have for example in monetary policy within the euro-zone'. We had to close Europe's 'security deficit'; and this would mean an increase in defence expenditure and a rationalisation of defence efforts, especially in procurement and in research and development.

Vital to any discussion of military policy was keeping in touch with developments in Washington DC. I had met NATO Secretary General George Robertson on 7 October 2002. We discussed the question mark over the future of NATO. Though, for the first time ever, Article 5 of the North Atlantic Treaty[179] had been invoked after 9-11, the USA had subsequently shunned NATO in favour of an ad hoc coalition of nations in its Afghanistan campaign. If the Americans perceived NATO to be too weighed down by bureaucracy and cumbersome decision-making procedures to respond quickly and effectively to the threat of Al Qaida, surely NATO needed reform. And if the EU could play an active part in reforming NATO, as well as enlarging NATO, perhaps we could prevent a further unilateral drift in US policy. I saw Robertson again in August the following year and in October 2003 I visited the US House and Senate. Few there seemed any longer to value NATO; and the divergences from EU opinion seemed to me to be wider than ever. With the Patriot Act and the Military Tribunals Order, for example, the US seemed to be riding roughshod over civil liberties in its quest for revenge for the 9-11 bombings.

On my return I hosted a conference on defence in the European Parliament with two defence ministers and speakers from NATO and put the issue of defence policy on the agenda of the Liberal prime ministers' meeting on 16 October 2003. While previously US and EU policies had been anchored in the postwar settlement of 1945, Europe's were now defined by the fall of the Berlin Wall and America's by 9-11.

Liberals were concerned too about the threat of a new superpower arms race. We expressed concern when the EU invited China to join its putative Galileo satellite navigation system, worried that we would be giving the People's Republic of China a valuable military tool. On 20 November 2003, speaking on behalf of my group at a conference in Strasbourg on the growing militarisation of the world, I said: 'We will not hurry the arrival of democracy in China by selling arms to those who would repress it'. On 30 October 2003 the Council had asked the EU's foreign ministers to review the issue of arms sales to China, governed by the embargo put in place after Chinese troops opened fire on their own citizens in Beijing's Tiananmen Square on 4 June 1989. I resisted this strongly, sponsoring a motion in Parliament which was adopted on 18 December 2003 by 373 votes to 32. Europe's arms manufacturers were 'itching' to supply China's modernising military forces and tired of watching their Russian counterparts take advantage of Europe's reticence, I said. 'But the guiding logic of the ban is ethical. It is a statement of revulsion. The pressure to lift it is purely and simply commercial'.

---

179   Which states that an attack on one member of the alliance is an attack on the alliance as a whole.

Ward Beysen

In March 2002, Belgian Liberal MEP Ward Beysen decided to leave the Belgian VLD and establish another party, Liberaal Appel. Though I sought to maximise the size of the Liberal group my view was that Beysen should be expelled. He had in any case long been something of a maverick and had recently taken positions that were quite right-wing; and I believed that colleagues could be persuaded after due consideration to support a move to expel him for campaigning against his party. What I had not anticipated was a phone call from Guy Verhofstadt threatening me with withdrawal of his party's troops were Beysen not to be expelled. It was an empty threat, since there was no other political group the Belgian Liberal MEPs could credibly have joined. While such tactics may work in national politics, where a leader has carrots and sticks, they sit uneasily with the laborious consensus-building needed in a multinational assembly. Nor was it constructive in achieving its declared goal. Had I mentioned the phone call to my colleagues they might well have dug in their heels and refused to eject the hapless Beysen. As I had anticipated, however, Liberals voted by an overwhelming majority on 12 February 2003 to expel Beysen. Such procedures are never pleasant, but they are useful to preserve group and party discipline and keep faith with our principles.

The UK and 'Europe'

Towards the end of 2002 the attention of the UK Liberal MEPs, including mine, was to some extent drawn homewards by the decision of my party to establish the lists of candidates for the 2004 European elections some 18 months hence. It was not an easy time to argue for Europe in the UK. The newspapers were more interested in scandal and scorn than in serious matters. In January 2003 the newspapers ran headlines about how a new EU law on animal welfare would require farmers to give toys to their pigs. Indeed the headline 'Pigs need playthings' probably sold more newspapers than the more serious news that the prime minister had decided to abandon the idea of a referendum on entry into the euro. I noted in my diary on 18 May my horror at the falsehoods and innuendo contained in articles in *The Daily Telegraph* about the Convention on the Future of Europe and the euro; and when I addressed the Institution of Civil Engineers in London on 27 May 2003 about progress towards a European constitution it was against a backdrop of a headline in a major newspaper screaming 'End of 1,000 years of British history'.

The official reaction to all of this was silence. For all his professed European conviction, and with a favourable wind behind him in the Labour party, Tony Blair probably achieved less for the UK in Europe than his Europe-embattled predecessor John Major, though his superior sense of diplomacy prevented him from embarking on anything quite as humiliating as Major's 'period of non-co-operation with Europe'.

This was the background against which UK MEPs had to campaign for re-selection. Thus I spent a weekend early in February with five long-suffering women supporters, telephone-canvassing party members in my constituency to test the level of support for my re-selection. While 64% of respondents said I would enjoy their first preference vote, the support was not evenly spread, and I found myself over some twelve weeks haring from continental commitments involving presidents and prime ministers to constituency events, such as the occasion when I cut short a visit to the conference of the ruling (Liberal) party in Slovenia to attend a coffee morning in Cornwall. In the event I was voted No.1 on my party's list in south west England with a substantial lead over my competitors, but my schedule was such I had no time to attend the counting of the votes on 8 March 2003.

Enlargement

Parliament had prepared the way for enlargement of the EU in a series of reports in the first half of 2002. On 13 June MEPs had adopted by 396 votes to 16 a resolution describing enlargement of the EU as an 'historical necessity' to ensure lasting peace, stability and prosperity. Though Liberal MEPs were concerned about issues such as nuclear safety and the possible impact on farm spending and the state of the natural environment – and were also dissatisfied with the spending of pre-accession assistance, especially the Special Accession Programme for Agriculture and Rural Development (SAPARD) – enlargement was generally welcomed as a sign of the EU's success. Swedish Liberal MEP Karl Erik Olsson had been tasked with making recommendations on the integration of the new member states into the Common Agricultural Policy and favoured a phasing in of agricultural subsidies over a ten year period to avoiding upsetting the balance between farm and non-farm income in rural areas. And Olle Schmidt MEP had conducted an appraisal of lending to the candidate countries by the European Investment Bank.

Liberals were to make a defining impact on the enlargement policy of the EU in the latter half of 2002. With a Council presidency led by Prime Minister Anders Fogh Rasmussen, ably assisted in the EU affairs portfolio by former Liberal MEP Bertel Haarder, the presidency worked to advance Liberal ideas wherever possible. The 'yes' vote in Ireland's second referendum on the Nice Treaty, for which Pat Cox had spent so much time campaigning, despite the pressure of his other duties as EP president, would allow the treaty to enter into force early the next year. It therefore paved the way to an agreement among member states to present negotiating positions to the candidate states with a view to concluding enlargement negotiations with ten countries at the European Council in Copenhagen in December 2002. The Commission had reported to Council and Parliament that these countries fulfilled the political criteria for membership and were expected to fulfil the economic criteria and thus be able to assume the obligations of membership at the beginning of 2004. The accession treaties were expected to be signed in Athens, under the EU's Greek presidency, in April 2003. In addition to reaching agreement to the accession of ten new member states in May 2004, they also secured an understanding that Romania and Bulgaria would join the Union in January 2007. While the United Kingdom wanted to finance enlargement through reform of the CAP and France through the abolition of the UK's rebate, Liberals on Parliament's budget committee worked to ensure an increase in pre-accession assistance was foreseen through shifting money from one budget heading to another: less headline-grabbing, but with greater chances of success.

It was noted too that Turkey had made significant strides which had brought forward the date at which accession negotiations could be opened. In a rousing declaration adopted at the European Council meeting in Copenhagen in December 2002 entitled 'One Europe', enlargement was described as 'continuous, inclusive and irreversible' and the development of closer relations with the western Balkans, Ukraine, Moldova, Belarus and the countries of the southern Mediterranean aspired to.

Council and Parliament were to agree, however, to a proposal from the Commission for two specific safeguard clauses to be inserted into the accession treaties: one governing the operation of the single market, the other in the area of justice and home affairs. In view of potential problems in the latter particularly, a special transition facility for institution-building was to be established. Ceilings were agreed for farm support spending and for structural and cohesion funds for the new joiners for the period 2004-06, though with the proviso that if any of the new member states became a net contributor to the Union's budget a compensatory payment would be made.

Some had sought to increase the EU's budget in order to finance enlargement. They resisted the idea of cutting subsidies to western European farmers or reducing the so-called 'cohesion' funds which ensure a small annual fiscal transfer from the EU's wealthier regions to the poorer. Indeed, when Commissioner Fischler published his proposals for CAP reform in January 2003, France and Germany were to mount a ferocious lobby against and eventually to agree in June on a joint plan to try to water them down.[180] Liberals argued that the existing budget was sufficient to accommodate the costs of new members, not only for reasons of fiscal rectitude but also to avoid scaremongering about the costs of an enlargement which – though it involved ten countries – was smaller in proportion than the accession of the UK, Ireland and Denmark in 1973. However, in advance of a special meeting of the European Council in October to discuss the financing, Netherlands' finance minister Gerrit Zalm stepped out of line[181], appearing to oppose enlargement in an attempt to win back the voters his VVD party was losing to the populist LPF[182], thus joining what the *Frankfurter Allgemeine Zeitung* was to call 'an unholy alliance of egoists and cowards'.

Severe flooding in the Czech Republic and Germany over the summer of 2002 had demonstrated yet again how much the two halves of Europe needed to work together in managing cross-border challenges. As Liberal MEPs sat down on 26 November 2002 to supper in Warsaw with Adam Michnik, Bronislaw Geremek, Wladislaw Frasyniuk and other freedom fighters, in the restaurant whose cellars had hosted the cells in which Polish Liberals had been tortured by the secret police, we were reminded of the importance of democratic reforms and the reconstruction of civil society; and though the launch in Parliament the following week of a book warning of the dangers posed by a new generation of right-wing extremists in

---

180 It is hardly surprising that the Convention on the Future of Europe was to recommend that decisions on farm spending be made in future under the co-decision procedure.

181 The Netherlands' EU affairs minister Atzo Nicolai had his ears boxed by the other participants at the Liberal leaders' pre-summit lunch meeting about the remarks of his party's leader.

182 'List Pim Fortuyn', the anti-immigrant party named after its former leader.

Europe brought protests from the EPP, some of whose leading figures were cited as examples, Liberals continued to insist that society must be ever vigilant of creeds which preach intolerance or cut legal corners or both.

In my first year as leader I had invested heavily in getting to know the central and eastern European countries which were expected to join the Union in 2004 and 2007. Through my involvement with the European Youth Centre and European Youth Foundation in the late seventies and early 1980s, as vice president and then secretary general of the International Federation of Liberal and Radical Youth, I had developed a good knowledge of western European countries which gave my subsequent career as a MEP a flying start. Through the 'Helsinki process', set in train by the Conference on Security and Co-operation in Europe, I had enjoyed some travel in Soviet bloc countries and had some contact with their politicians. Yet despite this and a period of study at the Karl Marx University in Leipzig in 1978 I did not know the countries of central and eastern Europe well. As the Berlin Wall came down, tempted as I was to re-visit a city which I found exciting even under normal circumstances, my focus had been more on the Far East[183] than on the eastern half of our continent. Thus I had to work hard to get to know the candidate countries of the Union, paying visits in 2002 to Poland, Hungary, the Czech Republic, Bulgaria, Lithuania, Latvia and Estonia, and seizing every opportunity to invite representatives of the Liberal family there to Brussels and Strasbourg. The representatives of these countries (many of which had Liberals in government) needed reassurance of the EU's genuine intention to bring them into membership as soon as possible; they were fighting a difficult battle to throw off the vestiges and attitudes of Communism and modernise their countries and needed encouragement. While MEPs from other parties were getting cold feet about enlarging the EU, Liberals again hosted in Strasbourg in October 2002 (to coincide with a report to Parliament on progress towards enlargement) a conference to which we brought representatives of the applicant countries to meet Prodi and Cox.

Liberal MEPs devoted time to campaigning in the countries due to join the EU, each of which had to secure public support in a popular referendum for so doing. In the early autumn of 2002 I had visited Latvia to meet Liberal prime minister Andris Berzins and his colleagues. I addressed Lithuanian MPs visiting Parliament at my invitation in February 2003, campaigned with Liberals in Slovakia in their referendum campaign in March and paid subsequent visits in each of April and May, arranged for my group to visit Budapest in March and returned again alone the following month to campaign with the dynamic young chairman of their Parliament's foreign affairs committee, Istvan Szent-Ivanyi. I visited Poland twice to campaign in mid-May and the Czech Republic ten days before voters went to the polls in June. MEPs Nick Clegg, Anne Jensen, Herman Vermeer and Ole Andreasen were also to make major contributions to the campaigns in central and eastern Europe. Altogether, ALDE MEPs were to be involved in over 20 visits to assist in the referendum campaigns of the would-be joiners.

---

183 I was an employee of the Hongkong and Shanghai Banking Corporation at the time and travelled widely in the Far East.

In all of these countries there were Liberal forces to be encountered, aspects of EU membership to explain and young people eager to become European citizens. It was in stark contrast to the local election campaigning I did in the UK in April 2003 where, after thirty years of EU membership, understanding of the EU was pitiful and acceptance of UK membership was still at best begrudging.

When the European Parliament voted to approve the accession treaties with each candidate country on 9 April 2003, the Liberal group was the only group to vote 100% in favour. On 1 May, at the Liberals' initiative, Parliament welcomed 162 'observer' MEPs from the prospective new member states. In the Liberal group, uniquely, the thirteen observer MEPs were given full speaking and voting rights.

As 2003 advanced, the candidate countries voted one by one in favour of membership. Following advice from the powerful Liberal triumvirate of Cox, Rasmussen and Prodi, the referendum dates had been staggered to ensure the best chance of a virtuous crescendo of approval. Thus Malta and Slovenia, probably the most advanced, voted on 8 March and 23 March respectively; Hungary on 12 April, Cyprus on 16 April and Lithuania on 11 May. In Slovakia, popular support was not assured. A 50% turnout was necessary for the referendum to be valid. In the event 52.15% of the population went to the polls on 17 May and 93.7% voted yes[184]. Poland voted on 7 June and the Czech Republic on 15 June, Estonia and Latvia on 13 and 20 September respectively.

As the EU sailed full steam ahead with the integration of ten new countries, two countries presented considerable difficulties. Romania – due to join in 2007 – continued to cause concern among MEPs. In July 2003 I was to pay a two day visit when I was taken by Liberal leader Calin Tariceanu to meet Prime Minister Nastase. My Liberal Democrat colleague Emma Nicholson, Parliament's rapporteur for Romania, had taken a very tough line on the issue of the treatment of children in orphanages; she and others were threatening to suspend negotiations on Romania's accession unless progress could be made faster and had tabled a motion to this effect in the foreign affairs committee to underline their threat. The Romanian government pulled out all the stops to save the day, including the sending of opposition party members to Brussels to lobby in their country's interests. When Parliament debated Emma's report on the accession of Romania on 10 March 2004 MEPs heard stern warnings to Bucharest that negotiations would be suspended if they could not overcome problems of corruption among public officials, improve public administration and stop corrupt practices regarding international adoption of children.

The referendum question

While referenda on accession to the EU, first used by Norway in 1972, had become the norm Western European countries, by and large, did not hold referenda on subsequent European treaties. Ireland, which deemed that its con-

---

184   I campaigned in Slovakia more than any other country in support of the Yes campaign led by Pavel Rusko's ANO party and fronted by energetic young Liberal Katarina Gloncakova.

stitution required them, had needed two referenda to secure popular approval for the Treaty of Nice in 2001 and 2002. Yet opponents of the EU, who had found a platform for their propaganda in the referendum campaigns in the accession states, now sought to profit from the referendum mechanism and to demand referenda on individual decisions related to EU membership and on the draft Constitutional Treaty expected to emerge from the Convention.

On 10 June 2003 UK chancellor Gordon Brown conceded to pressure for a debate in the UK on euro entry with a statement which committed the UK to a referendum. 'I have always said we can win a referendum if we have got the economics right', he argued[185]. As the Liberal prime ministers gathered in Thessaloniki for their pre-summit meeting with Presidents Cox and Prodi the mood was sombre; might the next concession be a UK referendum on the Constitutional Treaty? Our prescience was to be proven justified within a year.

Liberals were divided in their response to such demands. Liberal Democrats in the UK, who had encountered popular hostility when the party had on one occasion rescued John Major's government by voting to support the ratification of the Treaty of Maastricht – and had voted under Blair to ratify Nice – now added their voices to calls for a referendum. In Germany the FDP, out of power for some years, was tempted similarly to populism, which was to become increasingly a draw for Netherlands' Liberals in the VVD, who had traditionally been opposed to referenda. MEPs and the other members of each party's foreign policy elite had to seek increasingly to staff the fire engines to save their colleagues at home from the folly of folk-heroism, but they were not always successful, and some found themselves obliged to defend party policies with which they disagreed.

Berlusconi runs amok

The Italian presidency in the second half of 2003 was to descend rapidly into political slap-stick comedy. Italy's right-wing Christian Democrats, who had dominated the country's politics since World War II, had disintegrated after the tangentopoli scandals and had been to a large extent displaced by other right-wing forces. The country's government (June 2001 to July 2004) was now a coalition of three parties: the formerly fascist Allianza Nazionale which had been steered adroitly towards acceptable positions by its new leader and foreign minister Gianfranco Fini; the Lega Nord under Umberto Bossi (see chapter 1) and Silvio Berlusconi's Forza Italia. This coalition had swept all before it in the general election of June 2001. Romano Prodi, leading the Commission, must have had many sleepless nights deciding how to handle a presidency of the Council run by the man who had ousted him from the prime minister's office. And indeed Berlusconi's government was controversial not only because, to the left, their policies were red rags to a bull, but also because to the right they were an unknown quantity and sat uneasily with Christian Democrats from other countries. On a wing and a prayer the Brussels establishment hoped that Italy's diplomatic service would be able to smooth over any frictions and keep EU business under control. It was not to be.

---

185   This led to a blazing row between me and Neil Kinnock after a radio programme on which we were interviewed together. It is the only occasion I can recall on which we disagreed fundamentally.

The stage was set for a showdown with the European Parliament before the presidency took office. MEPs had been particularly critical of many of Berlusconi's actions. Not only did he combine political and media power in an unhealthy way; he had ridden roughshod over EU laws on freedom of movement of citizens and treatment of detainees at the G8 summit in Genoa in July 2001 and had sought to cut legal corners to promote his own business interests. Italy was to be the last EU country to ratify the European arrest warrant proposal, for example, which Berlusconi feared might be used to target some of his business associates charged with illegal activities.

When Berlusconi invited the European Parliament's group leaders to meet him and his ministers in Rome on 27 June tension was already high. I had made a speech in Frascati that morning at a conference of one of the opposition parties, critical of the Italian government, press reports of which must have been drawn to the government's attention before the meeting. Dany Cohn-Bendit and Monica Frassoni, co-leaders of the EP's Green group, had given interviews to the media revealing views even more scathing than mine. But the most wildly outspoken critic of Berlusconi was without doubt the Socialist group's new leader, Martin Schulz.

Berlusconi's presentation to the political group leaders of his presidency's priorities passed off without incident, though he surprised us over supper afterwards at Cesare Borgia's Villa Madama by departing almost immediately from his script and regaling us for two hours with a series of jokes of particularly bad taste.[186]

When Berlusconi addressed Parliament in Strasbourg on 2 July his speech, though challenging, was not beyond the bounds of decency for the occasion. It was greeted by EPP group leader Poettering with words of welcome, received by me on behalf of the ELDR group with expressions of disagreement and doubt but lambasted by Schulz. Now it was Schulz who dangled the red rag at which Berlusconi charged. In his reply to the debate the Italian PM dismissed MEPs as 'the tourists of democracy' and proposed that Schulz would be well cast as the concentration camp 'kapo' in a film currently being shot. Offered the opportunity repeatedly by Speaker Cox to withdraw the latter remark, which was clearly particularly offensive to a German, Berlusconi refused. His subsequent press conference and the next day's headlines all over Europe showed what a disastrous start the presidency had made.[187]

The six-month Italian presidency never really recovered from that moment. Berlusconi was to go on to upset the French a week later by telling them to 'shut up' about his decision not to meet Palestinian leaders while on a visit to Israel as EU Council president[188], please authoritarian China by

---

186 To add do our discomfort, as we left we were each presented with a beautiful and clearly expensive coffee-table book about Italy, funded by the Italian taxpayer and not coincidentally published by Mondadori, a company belonging to the prime minister.

187 Ironically, the German newspaper *Frankfurter Rundschau* had run an article just a few days previously under the title *Wer kennt Martin Schulz?* (Who knows Martin Schulz?), pointing out that this German MEP was important in Strasbourg but almost unheard of at home. Berlusconi made Schulz famous overnight.

188 French foreign minister Dominique de Villepin said that Berlusconi 'had not satisfied the European position' since he had met only Israeli officials. Berlusconi's reply echoed the words of French president Chirac when he criticised eastern European leaders earlier that year for backing the American invasion of Iraq.

endeavouring to lift the EU arms embargo, condone Russia's increasingly anti-democratic moves with ill-considered comments about Chechnya and the arrest and detention of Mikhail Khodorkovsky (which also contravened the EU's stated position) and upset fellow democracies India and Canada by cancelling at short notice the bilateral summits which were scheduled with the EU. Liberals took the view that the EU's positions had been badly compromised by the man charged with representing the Union. On 21 November he and Prodi were to clash publicly when Prodi – neck and neck with Berlusconi in opinion polls to be the next prime minister of Italy – said that Berlusconi's government had caused anguish to Italy through its handling of the EU presidency.

Crucially, and despite having boasted for weeks in advance that he would produce solutions on the basis of a piece of paper he was keeping in his pocket, Berlusconi failed at December's summit either to bring EU countries to an agreement about how to proceed with the Constitutional Treaty or to advance significantly the Lisbon agenda. I achieved spontaneous applause in the chamber when I declared in December's debate to close the presidency: 'The piece of paper in Mr Berlusconi's pocket turned out to be a gelato-stained[189] napkin with a few bad jokes scribbled on it'.

Berlusconi's presidency did make progress in EU-Mediterranean relations. Through a series of meetings in Palermo, Venice, Rome and Naples co-operation with southern Mediterranean countries had been advanced; and the Union now had more effective instruments for its development such as a Euro-Med Parliamentary Assembly, a Foundation of the Dialogue of Cultures and a reinforced facility for investment in the development of the southern Mediterranean countries' infrastructure. Ambassador Vattani sought to run a tight ship and progress was made on some dossiers, for example the agreement on the 'single European sky', steered through the House by Dutch Liberal Marieke Sanders, which was the first move towards improved air traffic management in the EU. Moreover, in the field of fighting crime, Europol had been given new powers and agreements reached in tackling drug trafficking and abuse. Wim Kok's task force on creating jobs had repeated the platitudes which had been iterated and reiterated at each spring European Council and were chanted again at an extraordinary summit on growth and employment held on the eve of the December European Council,[190] but its effort helped to keep on board the governments which still had difficulty swallowing monetarist economic medicine; and more government money was agreed for trans-European transport networks, probably the Union's most effective job-creating tool.

But there were persistent problems in other areas. The European Court of Auditors had declined, for the ninth consecutive year, to sign off the accounts for the 80% of EU expenditure which was managed by the member states: there were errors in half of all claims in farm subsidies (and 90% of all claims in Luxembourg!). Liberal MEPs proposed that the Commission withhold funds from member states which failed to apply proper controls.

---

189 The Italians had served ice-cream to the heads of state and government at the European Council meeting.

190 Kok was to be invited by the subsequent European Council meeting in March 2004 to lead a further group in an independent review of the delivery of the Lisbon agenda targets.

The Eurostat affair

The image of the EU as a badly run body, now frequently portrayed in the popular press in northern Europe, was heightened by allegations in June 2003 of fraud in Eurostat, the EU's statistical office. Its director, Yves Franchet, was under investigation on charges of having siphoned money into undeclared accounts. It could not have come at a worse time for a Commission in the process of cleaning up its finances. Commissioners Kinnock (vice president of the Commission), Schreyer (budget commissioner) and Solbes (economic and financial affairs commissioner) appeared before Parliament's budgetary control committee on 17 June, shortly before the EU summit in Thessaloniki, to give evidence on the matter. Kinnock and Solbes were to appear again on 9 July before the EP's conference of presidents to explain that the problems were deeper than initially thought; indeed, such was the gravity of the situation that the conference of presidents authorised the budgetary control committee to meet during the 2003 summer recess to deal with it. Just as the Convention on the Future of Europe was putting the finishing touches to the Union's new draft constitution, the stink of scandal had returned to pollute the air. When the Liberal group met at the end of August for the first time after the summer recess there was a strong feeling among its MEPs that heads should roll. My colleagues wanted at least the resignation of Commissioner Solbes if the Commission's investigation were to confirm malpractice on his part in failing adequately to supervise the financial affairs of the statisticians. I had seen Romano Prodi during August[191] and had warned him of possible trouble in my ranks.

I met a deeply worried Pedro Solbes on 11 September and the following day breakfasted with Prodi. Liberal calls for Solbes' head were being echoed elsewhere. On 25 September 2003 the Commission's taskforce investigating Eurostat reported its findings. Some 400 contracts awarded by Eurostat had been investigated and the internal audit service recommended strict separation in future of the tasks of management, supervision and auditing. I had been given a copy of the report late the previous evening. In my view the report contained no direct incrimination of Pedro Solbes; indeed, in some respects he was the victim of a system under which civil servants could feather their own nests with relative impunity. But to me the political responsibility of commissioners for activities within their departments was clear; and the principle of individual accountability of commissioners, reflected in the commitment which each commissioner had given to Prodi before taking office, was one on which Liberals had insisted. When Prodi met Parliament's political group leaders the following day to defend the Commission's findings this view was shared by others. In the end I was able to satisfy my colleagues that the matter should be pursued by the budgetary control committee; and when Parliament voted to give the Commission discharge for 2001's accounts in January 2004 a Liberal amendment regretting that Solbes 'did not act sooner on the growing evidence of irregular financial management between 2000 and 2003 nor accept political

---

191   On a private visit with my wife to Romano and Flavia at their family home in the mountains above Bologna.

responsibility as soon as the scale of the problems in his department came to light, in summer 2003' was adopted. Parliament recognised that the Commission was taking action to prevent this kind of situation from recurring and would in future ensure a structural change in relations between commissioners and their directors general and the creation of an outside body to which whistleblowers could turn. Liberals would continue rightly to make the case, however, for more accountability of commissioners for what happened on their watches.

Growing the Liberal family

By the autumn of 2003 the Liberal group's efforts to swell its ranks with new members were going well. As a result, in part, of our campaigning in central and eastern Europe, the ELDR group included 13 observer MEPs and looked set to do well from the enlargement in January 2004 which would see the observers succeeded by fully fledged MEPs. We welcomed the news[192] that Prodi was now considering bringing all his troops to the ELDR group. Enrique Monsonis Domingo, a Spanish Regionalist from the Castellon region – who had succeeded Canary Islands deputy Isidoro Sanchez under a mandate-sharing agreement reached when their joint list had been established – was highly active in trying to establish a list of candidates across Spain in which those in favour of greater regional autonomy would have a chance of securing election even under Spain's national list system which favours parties with a state-wide presence. In close liaison with ELDR Party president Werner Hoyer, meetings were organised in September and October with Liberal counterparts on the Committee of the Regions and the Parliamentary Assembly of the Council of Europe in an attempt to recruit all leading Liberals to the task of expansion of our family.

Liberal MEPs were also concerned to do whatever we could to help ensure the return of German Liberals to the European Parliament. Under its new leader Guido Westerwelle, elected in 2001, there was a fresh wind blowing in the Free Democratic Party. I travelled to Wiesbaden on 21 January to address the leaders of their groups in the different Landtage (regional parliaments) and to Berlin in late February to speak to their MPs in the Bundestag. I had regular meetings with Silvana Koch-Mehrin, a Brussels-based FDP member slated to head their list in the 2004 European elections, kept in close touch with ELDR president and German MP Werner Hoyer and welcomed Westerwelle to Brussels on 2 June. I ensured that other German-speaking MEPs maintained similar contacts. I was satisfied that preparations were in hand for the European election the following summer[193] and that the prospects for the FDP's return to Brussels after a ten year absence appeared to have improved.

On 26 November 2003 I journeyed to Paris to meet French centrist leader Francois Bayrou at a lunch arranged by ELDR MEP and long-time French Liberal Jean-Thomas Nordmann, who had quit the EPP on 16 December 2002

---

192   My conversation with Francesco Rutelli, 25 September.
193   In a conversation with FDP general secretary Cornelia Pieper.

to rejoin the Liberal group (of which he had been a member from April 1982 to July 1994 and from May 1995 to July 1999). That meeting was to lead to Bayrou bringing his troops out of the EPP the following year and over to the Liberal benches.

In Ireland, Bertie Ahern's Fianna Fail government was about to assume the presidency of the EU without access to the privileged network of any of the established political families. Though efforts to bring their MEPs to the Liberal benches were not finally to succeed until five years later, contacts with Foreign Minister Brian Cowen and Ireland's commissioner David Byrne at that time were to be central to Cowen's decision, as party leader and prime minister a few years hence, to make the move.

With an eye very much to the future the Liberal family was cultivating relations with Liberals in Turkey's broadly-based AKP. On 20 May 2003 I paid my first visit to Ankara to meet newly-elected prime minister Erdogan. Our overtures were reciprocated, and I accepted his invitation to address 30,000 party members gathered at their biennial congress on 12 October in and beyond a sports stadium on the outskirts of Ankara. The tragic bomb attacks on Istanbul on 15 and 20 November were to show that if some Europeans harboured doubts about whether Turkey was a 'western' country, Islamic extremists gathered under the Al Qaida banner had no such doubts. Our subsequent friendly relations led to Defence Minister Vecdi Gonul agreeing to speak at a conference the ELDR group hosted on defence policy on 15 October 2003, the day on which NATO announced – in reaction to recent EU developments – that it would establish its own rapid reaction force; and to Prime Minister Erdogan joining the Liberal leaders at their pre-summit lunch meeting on 11 December 2003, the first of a number of such meetings he would attend[194].

Party groups in the European Parliament are by necessity more diverse and at times less ideologically coherent than their equivalents in national parliaments. One of Liberalism's strengths is that – unlike Marxism – it is a formula rather than a blueprint; and though the formula remains x its application to country y may produce quite a different result than its application to country z. Thus Liberals in countries with high taxation and well developed welfare states might argue for tax cuts while Liberals in low tax, low spend regimes might call for tax rises. This is not always understood, however, and opposition to the strategy of building the Liberal group through bringing in parties with policies which occasionally diverged from the norm began to emerge within our own party family. I had taken the precaution of holding a meeting of the bureau of my group in Luxembourg early in November 2003 to secure agreement for a possible expansion. At the ELDR Party conference in Amsterdam ten days later there may have been grumblings, but not in public. Yet as 2003 drew to a close my plan to gather a larger and perhaps slightly more diverse group of MEPs in July 2004 had run into heavy weather.

When Europe's leading Liberals gathered at the Lambermont Palace in Brussels to prepare December 2003's European Council meeting we had for

---

194   The wing of the AK party favouring relations with the EPP rather than ELDR was almost certainly the stronger; but internal divisions within the EPP family over possible Turkish membership of the EU prevented EPP-AKP relations bearing fruit.

the first time six prime ministers present, more than the Socialists could muster at their meeting. The prime ministers of Belgium, Denmark, and Finland had been joined at my initiative by their counterparts from Slovenia, Bulgaria and Turkey. Yet there was opposition from ELDR Party president Werner Hoyer – reflecting, no doubt, the views of some national party leaders – to the idea of a substantial expansion of the party's EP troops. It may be that Hoyer had become aware of MEPs' readiness to change the name of the parliamentary group if necessary to reflect a wider alliance[195].

Parliamentary success

One feature of the ELDR group in the latter half of the 1999-2004 Parliament was our success in being Parliament's most effective environmentalists. On the transport committee the work of Luciano Caveri to ensure the safety of chemical compounds on ships and that of Dirk Sterckx on the safety of rail transport and on protecting the marine environment after the *Prestige* disaster[196] were to gain recognition, while Paolo Costa revised legislation on lorry transit and on vehicle speed limitation devices and Florus Wijsenbeek did work on urban transport and the bicycle as a means of transport which was subsequently taken up by the European Commission: on the fisheries committee the work of Niels Busk on illegal fishing and that of Elspeth Attwooll on protection of the marine environment were also impressive. Marit Paulsen pioneered new measures to deal with zoonotic diseases, to control salmonella and to set maximum safety levels for food additives; on legal affairs Toine Manders was Parliament's rapporteur on stricter environmental liability rules and was to establish a Europe-wide legal basis to make polluters pay. Frederique Ries was to steer through the environment committee new laws on toxic chemicals used as fire retardants. While MEPs of the Green group worked hard to advance an environmental agenda the fundamentalism of many was to frustrate their chances of success: Liberals showed the way forward.

Liberals were among the EU's most effective federalists too. The Convention on the Future of Europe published in June 2003 the first parts of

---

195   Just as UK Liberal leader David Steel had discovered some twenty years previously, the idea of creating a separate vehicle to accommodate those who wish to journey with you but not under your colours and hitching the two together to travel in convoy is not always easily understood; and a name change encounters even more opposition.

196   In November 2002 the oil tanker *Prestige* was involved in an accident off the north west coast of Spain which led to a major oil spill. Following the spill from the *Erika* off the coast of France in December 1999, action to improve maritime safety had been taken: indeed in April 2002 Dirk Sterckx secured the support of the House at second reading for a package of measures (dubbed the Erika II package) relating to ship safety, the bunkering of oil at sea and the role of ports in helping vessels in distress. Sterckx was backed up in this by new French prime minister Jean-Pierre Raffarin, a senator from the Democratie Liberale movement and former ELDR MEP. Liberals were concerned that it could be many months before these measures were transposed into national law in the member states. Installation of vessel traffic monitoring and information systems, designation of ports of refuge and better controls in ports had all been agreed by Council and Parliament. Moreover, we had long called for a measure to prevent the carriage of oil in single-hulled tankers and for the introduction of criminal sanctions for pollution offences. These should now be top priority, Liberal MEPs insisted.

a draft treaty establishing a European Constitution. Described by the UK government as 'a tidying-up exercise', to Liberals it was far more. The innovative nature of a 105-person convention, meeting in public, had closed the book on the secretive, unaccountable and elitist approach of intergovernmental conferences of the past. National governments could be obliged to make their cases in public and to justify their stances. The draft constitution would give national parliaments a stronger role in holding their ministers to account by debating legislative proposals at an early stage, before ministers committed themselves. It would give the European Parliament greater legislative powers and ensure that any scrutiny lost at national level was reinstated at European level. It would also make the European Commission more accountable to Parliament.

We had not won all of our battles on the Convention, but we had won many. Liberals opposed but failed to stop the proposal for a full time president of the European Council, arguing that this would undermine the position of the president of the European Commission and the principle of equality between member states; we argued for an integrated presidency of the EU, with the Commission president chairing European Council meetings. We sought, with partial success, the merger of the three pillars of the Maastricht Treaty, expanding substantially the realm of qualified majority voting in Council and co-decision with the European Parliament. We also argued successfully for a secession clause to allow a member state a mechanism for orderly and legal withdrawal from the EU if it so chose.

Had the draft Constitutional Treaty remained as presented in June 2003, it might have become law. But the European Council was to ask the Convention to work over the summer to propose mechanisms for policy formulation to a level of detail which – arguably – had no place in a Constitutional Treaty. These were adopted by the subsequent intergovernmental conference[197] into the draft treaty and were to be a contributory factor to its downfall.

The election approaches

2003 ended with allied forces in Afghanistan losing ground due to insufficiency of troops and equipment but with the capture of Iraq's Saddam Hussein giving the US and its allies a fillip. The latter served at least to take the media spotlight away from the failure of Italy's EU presidency to make any progress on agreeing the new constitution[198]. As Parliament's political group leaders met Ireland's cabinet in Dublin to discuss the forthcoming Irish presidency we heaved a collective sigh of relief that the Irish appeared far better prepared than the Italians.

2004 was to be a year for elections to the European Parliament and the appointment of a new European Commission. The parliamentary year opened with the Irish presidency presenting plans for their six months in

---

197   On this intergovernmental conference, once again, Parliament was to be granted only two representatives. They were to be one EPP and one Socialist MEP.

198   Saddam Hussein was discovered hidden away in a fox hole. This allowed me to quip 'While the US was pulling Saddam Hussein out of a hole in Iraq, the EU was digging itself into one in Brussels'.

office and coming immediately under fire, from the leader of the EPP MEPs, for a comment their prime minister made about the next president of the Commission. Bertie Ahern said that the heads of state and government would choose the best person for the job, irrespective of party affiliation. Poettering, who perhaps feared that Prodi (who had moved away from the EPP) would be given a second term of office or that the Irish government would manoeuvre to put Cox in the job, insisted that the next Commission president should come from the ranks of the largest party in the European Parliament. MEPs knew that by May the House would rise for the election campaign.

Economic policy dominated the year's start; and the policy was Liberal. Commissioner Solbes pressed the Commission to take legal action against the Council for its decision to exempt France and Germany from the rules of the EU's Growth and Stability Pact. The Commission published on 13 January 2004 a draft directive on services, long in the making in the services of Commissioner Frits Bolkestein, which was to become a centre-piece of the election campaign. As the EU prepared for its spring European Council meeting on economic competitiveness the Socialists were spoiling for a fight against what they depicted to be a free-wheeling casino-capitalist EU government.

Liberals were able to exploit this atmosphere to call for legislation to tackle media concentration in Europe. I had been working throughout the parliament to try to persuade Bolkestein and Prodi to act against unhealthy concentration of media ownership in Italy, Germany, Slovakia and the UK. While the internet was increasing public access to alternative sources of information for the internet-using generation, television, radio and print media were falling into fewer and fewer hands. In Italy the case was particularly severe: not only did the prime minister own a television media empire but as prime minister he also had an unhealthy influence on public broadcasting. I had worked with Socialist and Green MEPs on this dossier and was pleased to see the adoption by Parliament, by a large majority despite a campaign against it by the EPP, of a report by my colleague Johanna Boogerd on 22 April 2004 calling for a directive on action needed to promote and safeguard media pluralism.

Liberals were also able, despite the growing attacks on economic Liberalism, to steer through the EU an agreement on the 'second railways package'. Having led moves to liberalise air transport more than a decade earlier, we now secured Parliament's backing for the development of a common European safety system for railways (and the prevention of new national safety rules as a back-door form of protectionism) and the extension of laws on interoperability to cover the entire rail network of all member states. International rail freight services were to be open to competition from 2006 and domestic rail freight the following year. A European railway agency was to be established to oversee these procedures. The EU's transport ministers had not wished to move quite so far or so fast, but Dirk Sterckx had shunted them into position.

Liberals started the year by bringing together in Brussels the campaign managers from their member parties, determined to impress upon them the merits of singing from the same hymn sheet during the campaign and able to offer support during the campaign with information on developments in Parliament.

Keen to consolidate growing Liberal influence in the Commission too,

Parliament's Liberal group hosted a meeting for commissioners-designate on 16 April 2004. Of nine commissioners nominated by candidate countries, four – Siim Kallas, Janez Potocnik, Markos Kyprianou and Pavel Telicka – attended and were ready to be paraded as representatives of Europe's Liberal family.

The expansion of the Liberal group continued apace. Belgian Liberals assisted with the recruitment of MEPs Johan van Hecke and Gerard Deprez, both hitherto with the EPP. Van Hecke was to join immediately, Deprez after the European election. In Italy, Antonio di Pietro MEP's party Italia dei Valori had fought the 1999 European election on a common list with Romano Prodi's followers in a movement called Democratici dell' Asinello which Prodi led for two months before being chosen to head the European Commission. Yet the movement broke up in April 2000 over the nomination of Giulio Amato as prime minister. Italia dei Valori had been re-formed and had joined the ELDR Party on 28 September 2000. It was to fight the 2004 election on a common list with left-wing dinosaur Achille Occhetto and appeared to have good prospects for success. The Italian newspaper *Il Corriere della Sera* ran a story reporting that Romano Prodi would indeed form a new party in the EP 'with the British Liberals'; three weeks later I was invited to a conference of his party to meet Lapo Pistelli MEP and his colleagues then sitting with the EPP. On 5 February 2004 I received a visit from Czech deputy prime minister Petr Mares who expressed interest in bringing his small centre-right party into our ranks.

The plan hitherto had been to bring into the ELDR group as many new parties as possible. However we had not excluded the formula used in realigning UK politics – that of setting up another party with which Liberals could ally – if there were sufficient numbers to make it feasible and if there was continued reluctance in Liberal ranks to accept them or in their own ranks to adopt the Liberal colours. The possibility of such a development was discussed at the Margherita conference in Rome on 21 February 2004. By early March the ELDR group had given me the go-ahead to enter negotiations for a new centre party in Parliament.

On 3 March 2004 I used a conference on EU-USA relations, to which I had invited Romano Prodi and Francois Bayrou as speakers, as the occasion on which to agree with them a ten point plan which would form the basis of the new Alliance of Liberals and Democrats for Europe, a union of the parliamentary representatives of the ELDR Party and those of the soon-to-be-formed European Democratic Party. We met after the conference in Prodi's office at the Commission; apart from a few points Bayrou wished to amend regarding the Common Agricultural Policy, my proposed document was agreed as a policy basis for our alliance. Later that afternoon I met ELDR Party president Werner Hoyer to brief him on the talks. The following day I hosted a press lunch to brief journalists on our agreement to create a new group in Parliament.

While in Brussels I was launching a new group to challenge the established parties in Parliament, in my constituency I was engaged in what felt like trench warfare against factions within my own party. Party leader Charles Kennedy kept up at national level an honest, pro-European position in line with the traditions of the Liberal Democrats and their predecessor parties. His aide Richard Grayson, as director of policy, produced an excellent manifesto for the European elections which was approved by the party's federal policy committee on 8 March. Yet the party's chief executive, Chris Rennard, appeared to be sounding a different (and, to me, repugnant) trumpet note at party HQ. His network of regional agents was instructed to fight a campaign which talked as little as possible about the EU. And among the party's Westminster MPs, particularly some of those in the euro-sceptic south west of England, lack of knowledge of the EU combined with fear to foster opposition to showing our European colours. In a direct challenge to Kennedy's leadership, shadow Chancellor Vince Cable MP was to tell an interviewer on BBC Radio Four on 1 June 2004 that the Liberal Democrats were 'becoming a euro-sceptic party'.

These factors inevitably affected our campaign. Despite continued enthusiasm among party members in the regional constituencies for the building of a truly united EU, the campaign was presented through a Westminster prism. In south west England the organisation by the party centrally of the election campaign was shambolic; so much so that I was to publish[199] with others who felt the same way a counterblast in a pamphlet entitled *Liberalism: something to shout about*.

Cyprus

Meanwhile Cyprus, due to join the EU on 1 May 2004, held parallel referenda of its Turkish and Greek communities on the peace plan sponsored by UN Secretary General Kofi Annan. On 24 April 2004, the Turkish Cypriots voted by a convincing majority, with 64.9% in favour, for re-unification under the terms of the Annan Plan. Commissioner Verheugen, responsible for EU enlargement, had reported to Parliament on 26 March 2004 that the peace plan was proceeding well. Just two weeks later, however, UN special representative Alvaro de Soto reported that the Greek Cypriots looked likely to reject the plan.

The European Council had consistently expressed its 'preference' for the accession to the EU of a united Cyprus, but since the Copenhagen Council in December 2002 had added that: 'in the absence of a settlement, the application of the acquis to the northern [i.e. Turkish] part of the island shall be suspended, until the Council decided unanimously otherwise'. This was a mistake, since it gave the Greek Cypriots carte blanche to vote against the Annan Plan knowing that they would in any case be able to join the EU.

On 21 April the EP debated the matter. President Cox opened the debate by regretting the unfair presentation of the Annan Plan on Greek Cypriot television and the exclusion from the debate of foreigners, including Commissioner Verheugen. Speaking on behalf of my group I stated that the Cypriots were at a historic junction where possible reconciliation involoved important concessions for both sides. I saluted Cypriot leaders who called for a 'yes' vote, arguing that a 'no' vote would be based on sectarian values and could put back the chance of reunification by a generation. 'What Cyprus needs is a modus vivendi', I argued, 'some way of living that looks forwards rather than backwards'. Indeed, at a press conference later I

---

199 In September 2006.

argued for a postponement of Cyprus' entry into the EU in the event of a 'no'.

On 24 April 2004, while Turkish Cypriots voted Yes, Greek Cypriots voted by 76% to 24% to reject the Plan. They had found fire in old ashes. Cyprus would join the EU as a divided island.

At the opening of the first sitting of the enlarged European Parliament on 3 May 2004 Pat Cox paid tribute to Commissioner Verheugen and all the others who had worked to see a successful enlargement, quoting Seamus Heaney: 'on a day when newcomers appear, let it be a homecoming'. I decided to cede my place in the debate to one of the newcomers, Hungarian MEP Matyas Eorsi who, as leader of our troops on the Parliamentary Assembly of the Council of Europe, I deemed to be the most senior of our new members. Thus the leaders of the EPP and PES groups were followed by the first of the new MEPs to speak in the chamber. Matyas spoke for us all when he said he was 'delighted to see the legacy of Yalta consigned to the dustbin of history'.

Terrorism and civil liberties

On 5 January 2004 three MEPs received letter bombs through the post. The first was sent to the parliamentary office of EPP group leader Hans-Gert Poettering, the second to the constituency office of the leader of the UK Labour MEPs, Gary Titley, and the third to Spanish Popular Party MEP Jose Ignacio Salafranca. Though this was a minor incident in which fortunately nobody was killed or seriously injured, it drew attention to the pitiful absence of adequate security controls. Very much more seriously, on 11 March a major Al Qaida attack on Madrid's rail network left 191 dead and 2050 injured. As in London and in Istanbul, Islamist terrorists had shown their ability to inflict grievous loss of life in the heart of major European cities. When the Liberal Democrat prime ministers gathered on 25 March 2004 they called for a more intelligent approach to combating the threat of terror. The European Council of 25 and 26 March, in addition to its normal economic competitiveness concerns, called for a long term strategy to combat terrorism, involving greater co-operation between member states in border control.

In an 18-page declaration on combating terrorism, it considered acts of terrorism to be attacks against the values on which the Union is founded. Member states pledged themselves to solidarity and collective action in defeating terrorism and asked the high representative to bring forward proposals for action. Noting that not all member states had carried out the recommendations of the action plan drawn up after the 9-11 attacks, it called for more effective judicial co-operation on a series of strategic objectives. In particular, it called on member states to improve co-operation between police, security and intelligence services.

Unlike the USA, however, the old continent reacted with grim stoicism to the challenge of terrorism. Though worrying, it was not a new feature in European politics. The re-organisation of American government in response to 9-11 had brought many changes, taking America in a different direction from the more diffident Europeans.

The new US Department for Homeland Security had introduced fingerprinting of all visitors to the country, though US tourists to Brazil were up in arms when Brazil returned the compliment by fingerprinting US nationals entering their country. Airline security had become a major focus of American concern, creating tensions over data protection concerns between the EU and the USA.

The issue of passenger name recognition (PNR) data had become totemic for MEPs, especially for Liberals. Netherlands Liberal MEP Johanna Boogerd-Quaak, the rapporteur in charge of the matter in committee, was leading a crusade against giving the Americans information about EU citizens without adequate protection against abuse. Liberals argued that more information was being sought than was strictly necessary; that information could be held for too long with no right for the individual to correct it; that there was no legal redress against abuse of data by the state, and no right to compensation for people denied boarding of aircraft.

As I was to say in the House on 29 March 2004: 'it is possible to be both tough on terrorism and true to the treaties we have signed on civil liberties. We bow to nobody in our determination to fight terrorism … but let us do so intelligently, with a response that is measured and proportionate, and not sacrifice our freedoms in our determination to fight those who threaten them'.

On 31 March 2004 Johanna Boogerd took through Parliament a resolution on behalf of the committee on justice and home affairs, calling on the Commission to withdraw the so called 'adequacy finding' under which the Commission deemed its draft agreement for the transfer of data about airline passengers to the US government to be in conformity with EU law. The resolution stipulated what the agreement would need to contain in order – in the view of MEPs – to ensure conformity.

On 6 April I took the initiative in the conference of presidents to refer the issue to the European Court of Justice, against opposition from Cox[200]. I believed that the European Commission largely shared Parliament's frustration at the unwillingness of the US government to accommodate the EU's legitimate privacy and data protection concerns[201]. And in a further debate on 20 April 2004 Commissioner Patten told the House that data transfers remained a matter of concern for the Commission. Yet the amendment proposed by the Commission to the data transfer agreement did not satisfy Parliament. The following day, by 276 votes to 260, Parliament decided to refer the matter to the European Court of Justice.

The Council of Ministers was determined to secure an agreement with the USA on the matter, however, and used a procedural device to oblige Parliament to vote again at its very last sitting before rising for the elections, believing that the influx of MEPs from the new member states might this time swing the majority in their favour. At the ELDR election rally on 29 April 2004, Liberals castigated the Council's action.

In the first week of May 2004 Parliament gathered in Strasbourg for its final formal sitting before the election. Our ranks had been swelled by the arrival of 162 new MEPs from ten new member countries. We approved the

---

200   Cox was to try to delay or frustrate the action agreed by the House. He did not succeed.

201   I received phone calls one weekend from Bolkestein and Vitorino about these difficulties.

appointment of a commissioner from each of the new member states (and the approval of replacement commissioners for some who had left)[202]. And to the eternal credit of those who had recently emerged from the shadow of totalitarian regimes (encouraged by a letter from me setting out the Liberal case), Parliament voted to reject the Council's proposal on PNR by 343 votes to 301.[203] The ECJ was due to hear Parliament's case on 6 June.

Of the 162 new MEPs, more than 25% joined the ELDR group. 44 new members swelled our ranks. On 29-30 April 2004 the ELDR Party held a congress in Brussels and endorsed by acclamation new statutes reflecting the new legal status of European political parties. Party president Werner Hoyer spoke of the 'coming of age' of a party established in 1976. As the party adopted its manifesto for the forthcoming elections, Slovenian prime minister Anton Rop said: 'We have the programme, we have the vision and we have fresh ideas.' On 5 May 2004 four of the ten new commissioners (Kallas, Kyprianou, Potocnik and Telicka) joined leading ELDR MEPs at a regular lunch which had previously attracted only Commissioner Bolkestein. Taking on the anti-immigration fearmongers in the other parties, we noted studies which predicted that just 1% of the population of the new member states intended to move to the EU 15 and that those were predominantly young and well educated people without dependants. Europe needed more mobility, we agreed, not the restrictions sought by left and right.

Our group had performed well in the 1999-2004 mandate. It had the strongest record on reform. It had the strongest record on green issues of any major group. It had the best record of group cohesion and the best attendance rates at votes. Liberals went into the 2004 election campaign in high spirits.

---

202 Anna Diamantopoulou was succeeded by Stavros Dimas, Pedro Solbes by Joaquin Almunia and Michel Barnier by Jacques Barrot.

203 Technically it was a vote not to put the matter on the agenda. I had written to every individual MEP, however, explaining for the benefit of those new to Parliament the implications of the vote.

Chapter 4:   July 2004 – December 2006

The European Union's sixth legislature saw the formation of the new political group the Alliance of Liberals and Democrats for Europe. At its peak it was to number 106 members. It made its mark early in the approval of a new Commission president, Jose Manuel Durao Barroso, and in the rejection of Italy's first nominee for the college of commissioners.

The first half of Parliament's mandate was much influenced by developments to the east, as Bulgaria and Romania prepared for EU membership and Ukraine enjoyed a democratic revolution. Developments to the south, including the war in Lebanon, also impinged on the EU's work.

The defeat of the EU's Constitutional Treaty in referenda in two of the founder members of the Union and the failure of the Union to make its economy significantly more competitive were accompanied by a row over the future financing of the EU and deepening transatlantic tensions. Only in agreeing on the need for new policies to combat climate change and develop a common energy policy did the Union make significant progress.

The Council presidencies of this period were held by the Netherlands (2nd half 2004), Luxembourg and the UK (2005) and Austria and Finland (2006).

Largest third party ever

The European election results on 13 June 2004 produced a parliament in which Liberals were stronger than ever before. The European Liberal Democrat and Reform Party returned 67 MEPs[204], including a healthy number from the ten member states which had joined the EU in January of that year. We welcomed the German FDP back to Brussels after a ten year absence. UK representation had risen from 10 to 12 MEPs and our Polish Unia Wolnosci colleagues had elected four members.

Our new allies had performed well too. Prodi now brought over to our ranks all of his MEPs, some seven in total. Seven French members had been elected on the UDF list. Shortly to join the French and Italians in the formation of the new European Democratic Party were five MEPs from the Lithuanian Labour Party, Gerard Deprez of Belgium and Jose Ortuondo of the Basque National Party. Together we would count 88 of a total of 732 MEPs, convincingly holding the balance of power and with all the large member states represented in our ranks.

Shortly after the election I met Francois Bayrou and spoke to Romano Prodi. Both reaffirmed their backing for the alliance between the EDP and

---

204   Up from 8% to over 9% of the total.

the ELDR parliamentary groups. A supper with ELDR Party chairman Werner Hoyer on Wednesday 16 June, the night before the European Council (and, more importantly, before the ELDR leaders' meeting and lunch for our prime ministers which preceded the European Council) ironed out the few remaining difficulties, though I was aware that some doubters remained[205]. The ELDR prime ministers and party leaders duly gave me their backing on 17 June.

I could proceed to meet EPP-ED group leader Hans-Gert Poettering and then the Socialist duo of Martin Schulz, their parliamentary leader-elect (elected on 5 July 2004) and party president Poul Nyrup Rasmussen[206]. Liberals would have welcomed the chance of a coalition with the EPP, as per the previous mandate, and most would not have rejected out of hand any similar proposal from the Socialists. But it soon became clear that a grand coalition between the two had been cooked up in Berlin some seven or eight months previously and that we Liberals would find ourselves once again in our familiar opposition role.

On 17 and 18 June 2004 the European Council, thanks to the quiet diplomacy of the Irish presidency, agreed the broad outlines of the new Constitutional Treaty as proposed by the intergovernmental conference, which had received the draft the previous year from the Convention on the Future of Europe. It was to be signed in Rome on 29 October. The heads of state and government were unable to reach agreement, however, on who would be the new president of the European Commission. A Liberal candidate, Guy Verhofstadt, had worked hard to secure strong backing from Paris and Berlin; yet one clear consequence of a Union of 25 members was that France and Germany would no longer call the shots. Surprisingly, Verhofstadt had not secured the backing of his Liberal colleagues[207]. Moreover, a clear implication of the Constitutional Treaty, agreed if not yet ratified, was that political parties at EU level would assume a greater importance. Indeed, the EPP insisted that since it had emerged as the clear winner from the elections the Commission president should come from the ranks of its member parties. By the time I met Prodi and Bayrou again late the following week, to put the final touches to our alliance, it was clear to us that we would not have another member of our political family in the top Commission job.

The new ALDE group is formed

On 29 and 30 June 2004 the bureau members of the outgoing ELDR group convened. The remaining opposition to the creation of an alliance with the EDP, most of which centred on the change of name from ELDR to ALDE,

---

205   Not least in my own national delegation. At a meeting of the UK Liberal Democrat MEPs in London on the Tuesday evening I had listened to the monotonous lament of one who opposed the new alliance, one who opposed my re-election as leader and so on.

206   Poul Nyrup Rasmussen was Denmark's prime minister from January 1993 to November 2001. He was married to former ELDR MEP Lone Dybkjaer of Denmark's Radikale Venstre party.

207   Anders Fogh Rasmussen and Tone Rop both told me they would not support Guy. Anders Fogh at least also told Verhofstadt directly in advance of the Liberal prime ministers' pre-summit meeting.

was knocked firmly on the head. Talks ensued forthwith with MEPs Lapo Pistelli and Marielle de Sarnez, the co-leaders of the EDP MEPs, and a meeting of the national delegation leaders from both parties was called for the following week in Bath, the jewel of my constituency, where – assisted by generous glasses of Somerset Cider Brandy[208] – the Alliance of Liberals and Democrats for Europe was formally brought into being.

I had again explored with EU affairs minister Dick Roche the chance of bringing Ireland's Fianna Fail MEPs into our new group, but resistance in their ranks, especially from Brian Crowley MEP, and an unwillingness to force the matter on the part of Taoiseach Bertie Ahern defeated us and pushed the matter off the agenda for the duration of the parliament.[209] But with the entry in Bath of Lithuania's Darbo (Labour) party under the impressive Ona Jukneviciene MEP our ranks swelled from the 81 we knew we could count on to a total of 88 members[210]. Moreover, as I had anticipated, the creation of our new group was creating a dynamic which was already attracting others. I was able to overcome any residual opposition and persuade the two Italian Radical MEPs who had been elected, Marco Pannella and Emma Bonino, to join us, bringing our numbers to 90. We had begun to uncover the power latent in Europe's political centre. On Tuesday 13 July 2004, having led the predecessor ELDR group for two and a half years, I was elected to lead the new Alliance of Liberals and Democrats for Europe. It was the strongest third force the European Parliament had ever known.

German delegation leader Silvana Koch-Mehrin was elected as deputy leader of the group, a role she was to fulfil with verve and style while simultaneously leading the six male charges who had been elected with her.[211]

On 14 July 2004, at a press conference in Parliament, I launched the new ALDE group. The group should be measured by its ability to imprint Liberal and democratic values indelibly on the legislation of the European Union, I said. We published a ten point programme setting out our vision for Europe; it described a Union which would be economically stronger, more influential abroad, greener and more accountable and open to its citizens. We invited others to join us.

Among the MEPs in the new group was Poland's Bronislaw Geremek, who had been a leader of the Solidarity movement in Gdansk and later the foreign minister who took his country into NATO. A man of such stature was ideally qualified, many felt, to be the Liberals' candidate for the presidency of the European Parliament. He would be up against a colourless

---

208   I was already doing battle in Brussels with the Spanish over their attempts to outlaw the use of the name brandy for this product, despite its use in Somerset for over three hundred years. The issue remains unresolved.

209   Dick Roche and I were to enjoy the pleasure of the union being fulfilled five years later, when Taoiseach Brian Cowen insisted that his MEPs join us in the 2004-09 parliament. In this case the marriage was consummated in nearby Bristol, the capital city of my constituency.

210   The EPP/ED group had 268 members, the PES 200, the Greens/European Free Alliance 42 and the EUL 41. At more than twice the size of the smaller groups ALDE had formed a category of its own. And it would not be long before journalists started to use the expression 'the three big groups'.

211   Since Sylvana is tall, pale and blonde and her colleagues were generally not very tall, one wit was cruelly to dub the German delegation 'Snow White and the six dwarfs'.

Spanish Socialist who owed his position as candidate mainly to the d'Hondt system for the division of spoils. Though Josep Borell Fontelles was to win the election on 20 July (and in time he was to gain the respect and friendship of many, including your author), Geremek polled a remarkable 208 votes against him in a field of three candidates.[212] It was a first sign of the punch Liberals were to pack in the new parliament.

Parliament proceeded to elect its vice presidents, its committee and delegation chairs and its quaestors. Where the Liberals had previously secured no more than one vice president and one committee chair, our new found strength was to reward us with two and three respectively. We proceeded to secure the election of Luigi Cocilovo and Janusz Onyskiewicz as vice presidents of Parliament. Since our new German members were all freshmen to the European Parliament, for the two committee chairs we fielded Frenchmen: Jean-Louis Bourlanges for the committee on citizens' rights and freedoms, justice and home affairs and Philippe Morillon for the fisheries committee. Italian Paolo Costa, a former minister for public works and the incumbent mayor of Venice, was re-elected to chair the committee on transport and tourism[213]. All three were well-qualified candidates from a group with many neophytes among its members and in each case they were to expand Liberal influence in important policy areas. However the rogue intervention of Christian Democrat Astrid Lulling as an unofficial candidate for quaestor[214] robbed ALDE candidate Anneli Jaatteenmaki of a post which should rightly have been hers and led to a frank exchange of views between the leaders of the two groups.

Liberal action was also to impact on Council and Commission almost immediately. Parliament's group leaders had agreed on 16 June, the day before the final European Council under the Irish presidency, on a Liberal initiative to continue the previous parliament's legal action in taking the European Council and European Commission to the European Court of Justice over the transfer of airline passenger data to the US authorities.

Since the Madrid bombings, the Counter-Terrorism Task Force within Europol had been re-established and the heads of the security forces in the member states had decided to meet regularly. Moreover the European Council had appointed Dutch Liberal Gijs de Vries as the EU's anti-terrorism co-ordinator; he had called for the establishment of an intelligence capacity on all aspects of terrorism. But the Council saw fighting terrorism essentially through the lens of repressive policies; and under American pressure, European governments wished to co-operate with the US authorities as far as possible. Liberals reminded them that to do so would breach the EU's data protection laws. Moreover we argued (and convinced others in Parliament) that indeterminate 'trawling' of individuals' records was hard to justify and should be carried out only in extremis and with adequate

212   Borell won 388 votes to 208 for Geremek and 51 for GUE group leader Francis Wurtz, a French Communist.

213   Since there had been a change in the responsibilities of committees, this committee no longer dealt with regional policy.

214   The quaestors are the EP's equivalent of trade union shop stewards, elected to look after the interests of MEPs in all matters.

civil liberties safeguards in place. Since Johanna Boogerd had not sought re-election, the dossier was to be taken on by Sophie In't Veld, a new MEP and now the group's only representative of Boogerd's D66 party in the Netherlands. Parliament's obstinacy on the matter doubtless made the EU-USA summit in Dublin on 25 June no easier, particularly for an Irish EU presidency; but had the Americans asked their Congress to break US law in order to please a third country their response would have been no different. Parliament was behaving as a parliament should.

Googling 'Barroso'

The most important immediate item of business for the new Parliament after the election of our speaker was the approval of the European Council's nominee for the presidency of the new European Commission.

Consultations among the 25 member states about the next head of the Commission since June's European Council meeting had brought to the fore the hitherto little-known name of Jose Manuel Durao Barroso. Barroso had been prime minister of Portugal during three difficult years[215] and emerged as a consensus candidate. Liberal MEP Jules Maaten, ever with a quick sense of humour, was to quip to a BBC journalist that 'we had to google his name to find out who he was'. But Barroso presented himself well at a hearing in front of the ALDE MEPs on 14 July. He appeared to be acceptable to the Socialists[216] and was deemed able to command the support of a parliamentary majority when the political group leaders met the new president-in-office of the European Council (Netherlands' prime minister Jan-Peter Balkenende) in the Ridderzaal in The Hague the following day.

The majority of ALDE MEPs appeared disposed to support Barroso, at least *faute de mieux*, though with some it still rankled that Barroso had been the prime negotiator in the move of his party from the Liberal family to the EPP in 1996. Yet although the Socialists had just secured EPP support for the election of Borell, their leader Martin Schulz led them immediately in a vote to reject Barroso. This afforded me the opportunity of turning to EPP leader Poettering on the floor of the House and pointing out how little his deal with the left counted for. Barroso secured 413 votes, a majority, but 251 MEPs voted against him and 44 abstained. It was hardly a good start for EPP-PES relations, nor a ringing welcome for the EPP's new Commission president, and was to be a foretaste of more trouble to come.

Over lunch with their commissioners from the outgoing Commission on 21 July, leading Liberal legislators had discussed prospects for the party's representation in the successor Commission. Liberals led the government in four EU countries and participated as coalition partners in three others[217]. Though neither Romano Prodi nor Frits Bolkestein was to return, both

---

215   6 Oct 2002 to 5 July 2004; a total of 21 months spread over three calendar years.

216   Speaking in the House on 20 July, PES leader Martin Schulz said the Socialist group would take a neutral and unbiased approach to assessing Barroso's suitabilility to the task of Commission president. It may be that he was subsequently outvoted in his own group; in any case the PES divided on the issue.

217   Belgium, Denmark, Finland and Slovenia. Hungary, the Netherlands and Poland.

Kallas and Potocnik were and prospects for a strong Liberal representation in the Berlaymont looked better than ever.

The process of establishing the new European Commission proceeded apace, continuing after Parliament rose for the summer recess on 30 July. It was a process in which the EP's political groups were to play an unprecedented role.

ALDE had been the only political group to insist, as a condition of our support for Barroso's new Commission, on at least one third of the commissioners being women. Under pressure from Parliament, Barroso had acceded to our demand. London, Berlin and Paris were to offer little help, nominating Peter Mandelson, Gunter Verheugen and Jacques Barrot respectively. Rome and Madrid also looked set to nominate men. Having long campaigned for more equal gender balance, and with two excellent women candidates, Liberals saw their chance.

As July gave way to August I co-ordinated much of the telephone traffic regarding the number and the portfolios of Liberals likely to be in the European Commission. I spoke to the Liberal prime ministers and to almost all the Liberals who had been nominated for the Commission, starting with Denmark, whose agriculture minister Mariann Fischer-Boel was well qualified and with the Netherlands, where Liberal leader Jozias van Aartsen was a junior coalition partner and Neelie Kroes his candidate for the Commission. Other (male) candidates included Louis Michel, the former foreign minister of Belgium; Olli Rehn of Finland, a former MEP; and Markos Kyprianou of Cyprus. I insisted with Barroso that one of the Commission's vice presidents should come from the Liberal family.

Barroso appeared keen to have people of economic Liberal persuasion in the key economic portfolios. However he had limited freedom of manoeuvre with the heads of state or government in the largest member states, each of whom sought control of an important dossier. Peter Mandelson, though nominally a Socialist, was very much 'New Labour' and could be trusted in taking over the trade portfolio from France's Pascal Lamy. Gunter Verheugen, though a member of the SPD since the change of coalition in 1983, had previously been secretary general of Germany's Liberal Free Democratic Party; Liberals would raise no objection to his being assigned the industry portfolio. Jacques Barrot of France came from a centrist, some would say Liberal, background; but he was not ideally qualified for the competition portfolio sought by Paris, which allowed Liberals to be supportive of the desire of our Dutch VVD party to put Neelie Kroes in charge of competition, though Barroso initially sought to pass on to her the single market portfolio held by her predecessor Frits Bolkestein.

Barroso wanted to announce his Commission early. In the event he was to present his line up on 12 August 2004, before the start of the Athens Olympic Games the following day. It was well timed, catching observers on the hop and preventing any jockeying for position from continuing during the dog days of August. It had however one flaw.

Barroso had wanted to give the transport portfolio to Italy's nominee, the former MEP Rocco Buttiglione, and the justice and home affairs portfolio to France's Jacques Barrot. Barrot resisted, possibly for reasons which were to be exposed highly effectively by the United Kingdom Independence Party on 18 November. So the portfolios were switched – with near fatal consequences.

Throughout September, MEPs prepared for the hearings of the commissioners-designate. Seven of the 25 were from Liberal parties, with an eighth – Ingride Udre – from a party with whom Liberals had close relations. Over lunch with Jose Manuel Barroso on 23 September I was pleased to find that on some issues we saw eye to eye: in addition to the commissioners' hearings we shared views on Turkey, whose Prime Minister Erdogan was in Brussels that day to meet Parliament's political group leaders, having just secured approval in his parliament for the seventh and final package of reforms needed to qualify for the opening of EU accession talks.

Italy's commissioner-designate Rocco Buttiglione came to see me on 30 September 2004, ahead of the approval hearings. He was concerned that Liberals might object to his nomination for the justice and home affairs portfolio. I had known him as an unexceptional member of the EP's committee on justice and home affairs while I was its chairman. I told him I saw no reason why there should be problems. What I did not know was that the Socialists were preparing an attack on Buttiglione, determined to exact revenge on Silvio Berlusconi's nominee following Berlusconi's attack on Martin Schulz in July 2003 and opposed to having a man with conservative Catholic beliefs in such a sensitive role; and what I had not predicted was that some of my own colleagues would take up the same cudgels. There was in my view no reason why private belief should interfere with the exercise of a public function in representing the views of an institution of government. But I was unaware of Buttiglione's controversial record as minister of culture and tourism in Italy and quite unprepared for the martyr's role he was quite clearly preparing for himself.

Rocco Buttiglione's answers to questions at his hearing left MEPs in no doubt that – in the words of Liberal MEP Cecilia Malmstrom – he believed 'that refugees belong in camps, women belong in the kitchen and homosexuals belong in hell'. The first of these issues was highly topical. The newspapers had carried prominently reports that Italy, Germany and the UK sought the construction of camps in North Africa to hold refugees they did not want in Europe. Italy was shortly to deport refugees from the island of Lampedusa back to Libya, their last transit country. Buttiglione clearly supported this policy. Liberals were strongly opposed to such moves and by the end of the first week in October there were signs of a growing opposition among our MEPs to Buttiglione's nomination.

Other candidates were under fire too. Neelie Kroes had come under attack[218] from French Socialists opposed to having an economic Liberal in the competition portfolio and, since she lacked confidence in front of large audiences, had failed much to impress either her fellow Liberals or right-wing MEPs at her hearing. Some ALDE MEPs feared Kroes was vulnerable and did not want to risk losing a Liberal commissioner by taking part in a witch-hunt against EPP nominee Buttiglione; others wondered whether she

---

218   Kroes was attacked on the grounds that her many non-executive company directorships might provoke conflicts of interest in competition decisions she would be required to make.

was ideally suited to the job proposed for her, and a few of our new Democratic colleagues harboured doubts about having an economic Liberal in such a post. But Buttiglione and Kroes were not the only casualties of the approval hearings. Laslo Kovacs and Ingrida Udre had also failed to inspire.

On Monday 11 October the justice and home affairs committee voted by one vote on a socialist initiative to reject Rocco Buttiglione for that portfolio. The Liberals, who held the balance on the committee, were divided. The EPP immediately voted to reject Socialist commissioner-designate Laszlo Kovacs in a tit-for-tat move and three commissioners-designate were given only conditional approval by the pertinent parliamentary committees, including Neelie Kroes.

Barroso enquired of me if Liberals were going 'to cause trouble' over Buttiglione and appeared at one point[219] to threaten EPP retaliation against Neelie Kroes. I advised him that he should not ignore the parliamentary committee's vote. The following morning, at the meeting of the Liberal group, strong feelings were expressed against approval of Buttiglione as justice and home affairs commissioner. I shared this information during a private chat with Buttiglione before dining with justice and home affairs committee chair Jean-Louis Bourlanges that evening.

Bourlanges and I could only conclude that we were in a conundrum. Buttiglione appeared to be enjoying his new found notoriety. Berlusconi was making no move to assist Barroso, either by withdrawing Buttiglione or by agreeing that he be switched to another portfolio; but nor was Barroso taking action to damp down an increasingly inflammatory problem. Would the European Parliament reject the whole Commission if Buttiglione were not moved?

By the end of the week such a scenario could no longer be dismissed. The story was out and the weekend newspapers were full of speculation about the gathering political storm. A comment by Buttiglione disparaging single mothers ('not very good mothers') at a weekend conference, swooped upon by gaffe-hungry journalists, was to add fuel to the flames.

I had asked to see Barroso at the first available opportunity. Thus on Monday 18 October, at 11 pm, returning late from a meeting of the ELDR council in Berlin, I told him I could not guarantee the support of my group for his proposed Commission unless he acted quickly to resolve the problem. He would need either to remove Buttiglione from a sensitive area where his maladroit expression of his views had caused ructions or to seek a fresh nominee from the Italian government. I might possibly still muster 50-65% of my colleagues in support of some lesser move, such as moving responsibility for minority rights from the justice and home affairs portfolio to that of social affairs, but even that would probably need to be accompanied by the promise of a directive to promote and safeguard them better. Yet the new Commission president was highly reluctant to ask Berlusconi to withdraw his nominee because of pressure from Poettering.

No action appeared forthcoming; and though I reported my discussion with Barroso to my colleagues at the ALDE group meeting the following

---

219   Author's telephone conversation with Barroso on 12 October 2004.

afternoon there was no immediate demand for a debate. Just 18 hours later, however (spurred on, I imagine, by reports of fierce opposition in the meetings of the Socialist and Green groups), the radicals in the Liberal ranks were angrily demanding a discussion, which I accommodated at our Wednesday morning group meeting. By now the mood towards Buttiglione – and Barroso too – was turning ugly. In addition to the predominantly female[220] and occasionally illiberal voices opposing Buttiglione were added those of parliamentarians seeking to assert Parliament's authority over the Commission and even some who saw in the matter an opportunity to attack their group leader by accusing him of being in league with Barroso to secure the competition portfolio for Kroes.

Over breakfast on Wednesday 20 October I advised Italian permanent representative Rocco Cangielosi to have Buttiglione withdrawn. That afternoon I met Romano Prodi, Francesco Rutelli and Francois Bayrou and shared with them my deepening concern about a situation in which the immobility of the new Commission president was leading to a showdown.

During a string of interviews for radio and television over the following 24 hours I heard a BBC radio journalist report that 'the European Union is in utter chaos.' As so often with UK reporting of the EU it was a ridiculous overstatement; yet when Parliament's conference of presidents convened on the morning of 21 October for a discussion with Barroso, participants had to run the unfamiliar gauntlet of a crush of TV cameras outside the meeting room.

Barroso made proposals to the conference of presidents about the roles and responsibilities of the disputed commissioners-designate. To deal with concerns about Buttiglione he proposed the establishment of a group of commissioners responsible for fundamental rights, anti-discrimination and equal opportunities which he would chair himself. He also brought with him a letter of apology from Buttiglione about his offending remarks; but it was already a case of too little, too late. On behalf of the Liberal group I called for Buttiglione to resign, saying he could never enjoy the confidence of the House in these circumstances. In a press release we warned Barroso against 'bidding too low', guessing that his strategy was one of not making too many concessions too early and that he had more up his sleeve.

The conference of presidents met on a Thursday. Had Barroso taken decisive action in the previous two days and announced it then, his Commission would have been voted into office the following week. He might even just have saved the day had he taken further action over the weekend of 23-24 October. Instead, as MEPs gathered in Strasbourg on Monday 25 October an issue of portfolio allocation had become a tussle of will between institutions of government.

The European People's Party sought to defend Berlusconi and Buttiglione. The left was baying for blood. The voting intention of ALDE MEPs was difficult to predict, but moving fast in opposition to Buttiglione.

---

220 One of the women involved was subsequently to organise - cruelly but amusingly - a spoof opening of an area of Parliament, the 'Espace Buttiglione', and to use the occasion to praise the contribution of Rocco Buttiglione to European Liberal ideals.

Probably two-thirds of them were now prepared to vote against the whole Commission if Buttiglione stayed. Though I knew I could count on the support of at least three prime ministers in persuading their MEPs to support Barroso's Commission if necessary, I told Barroso I could now deliver with certainty no more than 50% in his favour.

As controversy surrounding him had grown, Buttiglione's role in regressive legislation on abortion in Italy and his move to change the draft EU constitution to exclude sexual orientation from anti-discrimination measures had come to the attention of MEPs[221], hardening attitudes against him. Surprisingly, he failed to draw the political consequences of this and resign, though by now it was clear that he was putting in jeopardy Barroso's position.

Barroso made a statement to the House on Tuesday morning. He pointed out that one EP committee[222] had backed Buttiglione and expressed his confidence that Buttiglione, as justice and home affairs commissioner, would abide by the provisions of the EU's Charter of Fundamental Rights. He offered to make civil rights one of the Commission's top priorities. He appealed to MEPs' 'sense of responsibility' in approving the team he proposed.

Barroso's speech, however, failed to convince Liberals. We took his proposals seriously, I assured him in reply, but were not seeking to be placated or patronised. His problem lay not with MEPs but with the Council of Ministers, the invisible elephant in the room, which (in failing to withdraw Buttiglione or agree to a switch of portfolio) had been unwilling to recognise Parliament's rights. 'The silence you hear is the sound of Europe's governments leaving you and your new Commission swinging in the wind', I concluded.

I invited Barroso to my group meeting that evening, to give him another chance to convince ALDE MEPs; but by the time he came it was clear to me he had already lost his battle. A show of hands afterwards revealed 53 colleagues favouring rejection of the whole Commission, 23 against and five abstentions. Among the nine absent colleagues I believe a clear majority would have voted to approve the Commission, but it would not have saved Barroso; and by this point even some of Barroso's well-wishers were no longer convinced he deserved saving.

Parliament was due to vote the investiture of the new college of commissioners at midday on Wednesday 27 October 2004. Hans-Gert Poettering, Martin Schulz and I met Barroso at 9.45 that morning and advised him to withdraw his proposed Commission. He did so in a statement to the House at lunchtime, just before the vote was due. The 24 heads of state and government who had put him in place had subsequently failed to give him their support. The unintended consequence of their action was that the EP had won the right *de facto* to veto individual nominees to the European

---

221 The presidential election campaign underway in the USA revealed a similar north American debate about religious issues, but with a markedly different balance of opinion. Democratic candidate John Kerry was under attack for having backed gay marriage; George Bush was set to win because a reported four million fundamentalist Christians would come out to vote on 2 November 2004.

222 Buttiglione had been heard by two committees. The social affairs committee had raised no objection to his appointment.

Commission while *de jure* it had only the 'nuclear button' option of rejecting the college in its entirety.

It appeared to Liberals that Barroso was trapped by his own reluctance to upset either Palazzo Chigi[223] or an EPP group whose leader advised him strongly against moving Buttiglione from the justice and home affairs portfolio. As a result, the anti-Buttiglione camp was the week's clear victor and Poettering, Barroso and Berlusconi its losers. The power of the Liberals, crucial to the outcome of the matter, was set in sharp relief. Though the ALDE group's internal cohesion had been tested[224] it nonetheless carried the day without a single vote being cast in Parliament.

Late on Friday 29 October the Italian government announced its withdrawal of the nomination of Rocco Buttiglione. They were subsequently to present that of their foreign minister, Franco Frattini, whose role during the difficult Italian presidency had earned him wide respect and whose investiture would cause no problems. Over the course of the parliamentary recess the following week Latvia's Ingride Udre was also withdrawn and replaced by a Liberal, Andris Piebalgs, who was given the energy portfolio while Laszlo Kovacs was moved to taxation. Barroso decided to give Jacques Barrot the transport portfolio and put Frattini at justice and home affairs. He called me to tell me of his plans and express the hope that his new Commission would fly.[225]

The European Council meeting of 4 and 5 November 2004 provided an opportunity for Council president Balkenende and Commission president Barroso to meet Parliament's political group leaders and agree informally the new line up. For Liberals it came with one sting in the tail: Barroso had made it a private condition of accepting Andris Piebalgs (a member of the Liberal Latvia's Way party) that he take part publicly in EPP rather than Liberal events, since otherwise the Liberals would be seen to have as many commissioners as the right. Under this line up the EPP would have nine commissioners to the Liberals' seven, with seven Socialists and two independents.

The college of commissioners was now scheduled to be approved by the House on Thursday 18 November. In the meantime most commissioners from the Liberal family had agreed to my proposal to take into their *cabinets* (private offices) senior members of staff of Parliament's Liberal group,[226] to

---

223 Palazzo Chigi is the seat of the Italian prime minister.

224 In a welcome change from the divisive debate among Liberal MEPs I was pleased to receive plaudits for my handling of events from the Liberal prime ministers and foreign ministers at the signing ceremony for the EU's Constitutional Treaty in Rome on Friday 29 October. Otto Graf Lambsdorff told me in an email I appeared to be the only Liberal MEP who was keeping his head on his shoulders.

225 Telephone conversation with Barroso on 3 November 2004. For two hours I had been out of range of mobile phone coverage and he had been unable to reach me since I was sailing, my favourite leisure activity. A similar situation arose in April 2001, when I clinched the final deal on access to documents with the Swedish permanent representative; he was lounging on a deck chair by a hotel pool in Egypt, I on the English Channel with a force 5 wind gusting about my ears.

226 Mia Asenius joined Olli Rehn's *cabinet*, Stina Soewarta that of Piebalgs; Philip Tod went to Kyprianou. Commission staffer and LibDem activist Lawrence Meredith joined Louis Michel. Mikolai Dowgliewicz went to Huebner and speechwriter Stephen Adams was poached by Peter Mandelson. Desiree Oen was later to join Commissioner Kallas.

act as liaison persons with Parliament. It was a costly exercise initially, depriving the group of a number of its most experienced and valuable staffers, but was to be worth its weight in gold in providing a network for information about developments in the administration.

Barroso had remade his Commission, which was duly voted into office[227]. But the matter did not come to an easy rest. Parliament insisted on the negotiation of a new EP-Commission framework agreement which would give it more say over the appointment and dismissal of individual commissioners. It passed a resolution critical of the way the Commission's formation had been handled. And the 12 United Kingdom Independence Party MEPs elected in June had a nasty surprise for the Commission president with the revelation that his new transport commissioner had a criminal conviction for embezzlement, in his role as party treasurer, albeit one erased from his record by a presidential pardon typical of the French political establishment. This caused an embarrassment for Barroso at press conferences on 19 and 22 November, a three-day flurry in the UK, Italian and Belgian press, an uncomfortable three days of hectic phone calls for political group leaders, but little attention or concern elsewhere. That neither Prodi nor Barroso had been made aware of the conviction when Barrot joined their Commissions was a serious matter, for it would have disqualified him from holding office in some member states; but after the trials and tribulations of getting the new Commission established there was precious little appetite to re-open matters. A letter of explanation from Barrot to the president of Parliament for the conference of presidents on 25 November 2004 effectively closed the case.

The French and Italian members of the ALDE group remained restive, however, about the alleged insistence of their leader with Barroso that Neelie Kroes keep the competition portfolio. Barroso had said in an unscripted and poorly structured reply to the debate on 17 September that the ALDE group had 'asked him insistently' to retain Neelie Kroes in her position as competition commissioner. The French and Italian MEPs, who felt their new group had been in any case too welcoming of the new line up and who intended the following day to abstain from the vote of investiture out of opposition to Neelie Kroes, went ballistic.[228] I had to insist on an exchange of letters with Barroso in which he effectively retracted his erroneous statement.

I had not asked Barroso directly to keep Neelie Kroes at competition. True, he had asked me my views about moving her – under pressure from Paris and from the left – and I had replied I thought she was well qualified for the job and that there was no need. He had also asked for my help in persuading the Netherlands' government to agree to moving her; I declined. I had no intention of helping him move probably the best qualified competi-

---

227   The EPP/ED group voted in favour as did most of the Socialists and Liberals. But the French Socialists voted against the proposed Commission and the French and Italian ALDE members abstained from voting.

228   I was both surprised and dismayed by the ferocity of the attacks on me by Lapo Pistelli MEP and Marielle de Sarnez MEP, leaders of ALDE's Italian and French delegations respectively. They seemed oblivious to the damage which could be wrought by splitting the group so soon after its creation on a line which divided Democrats from Liberals.

tion commissioner the EU had ever had; and certainly not to please injured French pride! But neither would I have fought hard to keep her there against Barroso's will. There was no need for me to do so. I had spoken to Dutch Liberal party leader Jozias van Aartsen and deputy prime minister (and minister of finance) Gerrit Zalm about the matter; even had the former been prepared to accept a swap with McCreevy's financial services portfolio, the latter would certainly have not.

The formation of the new Commission had dominated the Netherlands' EU Council presidency, but not to the exclusion of everything else. Prime Minister Balkenende had addressed Parliament on 21 July and spoken of his determination to see progress in the development of a common EU asylum and immigration policy and a common policy to combat illegal drugs. He was keen too to prepare a common EU position for the debate which had begun on reform of the United Nations. The Netherlands' presidency made useful progress for the EU in justice and home affairs: five years after the action programme adopted in Tampere in Finland, a new 'Hague programme' was agreed by heads of state and government at their meeting on 4-5 November 2004. Recognising the need for greater democratic involvement in policy making, especially in the development of police (Europol) and judicial (Eurojust) co-operation, the Council agreed to move to decisionmaking by qualified majority within its own ranks and co-decision with the European Parliament 'as soon as the Constitutional Treaty has entered into force'.

Balkenende's predecessor Wim Kok was due to report to the European Council on 5 November on economic competitiveness as a contribution to the mid-term review of the Lisbon strategy. He would tell them that: 'Much of the Lisbon strategy depends on the progress made in national capitals: no European procedure or method can change this simple truth. Governments, and especially their leaders, must not duck their crucial responsibilities'.

China arms embargo

One early issue on Parliament's agenda allowed me to get down to the business of public policy-making which I much preferred to inter-institutional battles. At the EU-China summit on 8 December 2004 it was expected that the People's Republic of China would again ask the EU to lift the embargo on arms sales imposed after the events of Tiananmen Square in 1989[229]. The European Council meeting in June had asked the foreign affairs ministers to continue their discussions about the arms embargo. Aware that there were moves afoot among some EU governments to lift the embargo, I had written an article for the *International Herald Tribune* of 4 August 2004 warning against it. What surprised Liberals was that no credible argument for lifting the embargo had emerged other than to please the PRC, which did not like being treated as an international pariah in the arms trade. Almost every other signal the EU had sent to China for the last ten years had been positive, recognising the value of China's economic engagement with the rest of

---

229 On this issue I was fortunate to be advised by former European Commission official Simon Nuttall and one of his successors.

the world. There seemed to be no attempt by member states to demand improvements in human rights or better relations with Taiwan in exchange for a lifting of the embargo, so why act? Moreover, China was increasing its defence budget by more than 10% each year. When I raised the matter over lunch with Javier Solana on 13 October he suggested arrogantly that I concentrate on pressing for an EU code of conduct on arms sales. To legitimise the wish of European arms dealers to sell arms to a Communist dictatorship?! And while the distinguishing feature of such codes of conduct was that they were honoured mainly in the breach?!

The discovery of a nuclear-capable Chinese submarine in the Taiwan Straits and its escorting away by the Japanese Navy helped the Liberal argument. Thus it was that Liberals secured a statement to Parliament from the Council of Ministers on 16 November 2004 and the adoption of another resolution opposing a lifting of the embargo the following day, repeating the success of our previous such initiative ten months earlier, in the previous parliament. A letter to each of the EU's Liberal prime ministers, to those of Bulgaria and Turkey and to our foreign ministers drew their attention to ALDE MEPs' concerns.

This did not deter some of the EU's national leaders, however. On 16 and 17 December 2004 the heads of state and government reaffirmed their will to work towards a lifting of the embargo and asked the incoming Luxembourg presidency to reach a decision on the matter. That it was thereafter quietly dropped was due to the publication by the Chinese government on 8 March 2005 of an anti-secession bill which would allow the State Council to take military action against Taiwan without reference to wider bodies; and to the success of American diplomacy and UK hesitation regarding resumption of arms sales.

Ankara, Bucharest, Kiev

Eyes also turned closer to the east as events in Ankara, Bucharest and Kiev became the focus of attention.

On 23 September 2004 Prime Minister Erdogan visited Brussels. His government had recently adopted the seventh and final package of reforms needed to qualify for the opening of EU accession talks, as agreed by the Council of Ministers in Helsinki in 1999. I had arranged to take Erdogan to visit Verhofstadt to discuss closer Liberal co-operation, but this had to be cancelled due to the Belgian prime minister's involvement in a car accident. However it reached our ears that Erdogan had declined an invitation to join an EPP event that day, and on behalf of the Liberals I exchanged pleasant words with him.

On 6 October the European Commission gave the green light to the opening of accession talks with Turkey. Romano Prodi and Gunter Verheugen came to Parliament in Brussels to make the announcement. ALDE MEPs generally welcomed the prospect of Turkey's accession to the EU, though one or two Dutch and some French MEPs were aware that their voters were less than fully persuaded of the case. The murder of film maker Theo van Gogh in the Netherlands the following month was further to inflame tensions between Christians and Muslims there. In France the tensions were already considerable: UDF leader Francois Bayrou was to create a rumpus

![ELD LDE for Eu]

ELD congress in Aix-en-Provence (4-6 September 1981) *Right to left*: Martin Bangemann, Simone Veil, Florus Wijsenbeek, Willy De Clercq, Henning Christophersen

Liberal group leaders 1979 - 1998

Martin Bangemann 1979-84

Simone Veil 1984-89

Valery Giscard d'Estaing 1989-91

Yves Galland 1992-94

Gijs de Vries 1994-98

EP president Pat Cox and Liberal leader Graham Watson welcome to Strasbourg Lord Steel of Ettrickbridge, presiding officer of the Scottish Parliament (September 2002)

ELDR leaders and ministers meeting in Brussels on 17 June 2004

The ALDE group in support of Bronislaw Geremek (standing centre with Graham Watson on his left) in his candidacy for the presidency of the European Parliament (July 2004)

Graham Watson (12) in the Strasbourg chamber with deputy leaders Silvana Koch-Mehrin (11) and (behind) Karin Riis-Joergensen (33) (January 2005)

Graham Watson with new partners Francois Bayrou (leader of French UDF), *left*, and Romano Prodi, *centre*, at the launch of the new ALDE group in Brussels (July 2004)

Left to right: Belgian prime minister Guy Verhofstadt, Commission president Romano Prodi, Turkish prime minister Recep Tayyip Erdogan and Liberal group leader Graham Watson at the ELDR leaders' summit in Brussels in spring 2004

March 2006: European Commission president Jose Manuel Barroso (*left*) and Graham Watson (*centre*) celebrate together their 50th birthdays (Graham is four hours older). At the microphone is EP president Josep Borrell Fontelles.

The Liberal family's European Commissioners in 2007 (*left to right*: Leonard Orban, Mariann Fischer Boel, Siim Kallas, Meglena Kuneva, parliamentary group leader Graham Watson, Danuta Huebner, Janez Potocnik, Neelie Kroes and Olli Rehn; missing is Louis Michel, on mission in Africa).

Graham Watson with Finnish prime minister Matti Vanhanen (*left*) at a meeting of the ALDE group in the Aland Islands at the start of Finland's EU presidency. Behind Graham is ALDE group general secretary Alexander Beels (June 2006)

Left to right: Graham Watson with Ovidiu Silaghi MEP, Commissioner Olli Rehn, Romanian prime minister Calin Popescu-Tariceanu and Bogdan Olteanu MP on the day Romania joined the EU (1st January 2007)

ALDE group staff (26th March 2007)

As seen by Nicola in *The Guardian* (UK), *top left*; Marco in *European Voice, centre right*; and Waldemar Post in *De Volkskrant* (Netherlands), *bottom left*.

in France's Assemble Nationale on 12 October, forcing Prime Minister Raffarin to concede a debate on Turkish EU accession[230] and setting in motion a chain reaction which was to lead to France deciding it would need to approve by referendum any Turkish accession to the EU. An ill-considered move to gain short term party advantage risked storing up long term trouble.

Former European commissioner Emma Bonino, now an Italian Liberal MEP, had invited me to speak at a conference she was organising on Turkish accession to the EU on 6 December 2004. I used the occasion to fly a kite about the dangers of 'aggressive secularism' causing problems for the integration of Muslims (just as it caused some Catholics to question whether they were being discriminated against because of their religious views). It was my answer to the attitude of some Liberal MEPs in the debate about Buttiglione. I was to develop the theme further at a conference and in a published essay in the New Year.

When the European Parliament debated Turkish accession Netherlands' secretary of state for EU affairs Atzo Nicolai of the VVD, speaking for the Council, praised the 'impressive progress' Turkey had made. Despite the strong objections of some, on 15 December 2004 Parliament voted by 407 votes to 262, with 29 abstentions,[231] to open accession talks. French MEPs in almost all political groups voted against, despite the adoption of an amendment calling on Turkey to recognise the Armenian genocide. German CDU MEPs teamed up with the far right to force a secret ballot, but the move backfired on them by drawing greater attention to the resounding Yes vote. Liberals had decided to up the ante by inviting Erdogan to their prime ministers' pre-summit lunch meeting in Brussels. Council was not to obtain from Turkey a formal recognition of the Republic of Cyprus, but a promise to sign the Ankara protocol[232] prior to the start of accession negotiations. And though Parliament's vote was advisory rather than legally binding, it helped the heads of state and government to conclude that once the six important pieces of legislation identified by the Commission were in force, accession negotiations could be opened; this was foreseen for 3 October 2005.

In Bucharest a general election and the first round of the presidential election were due on 28 November 2004; the government had chosen a date just four days after a meeting with the European Commission at which they expected to be given the green light for EU membership in January 2007.

---

230 Bayrou's action was to divide both major French parties, with longer-term ramifications for the development of the debate in France on Turkey's EU membership. I fear his interest was in sowing division irrespective of the consequences which might flow from it.

231 In a disgraceful abuse of procedure, German CDU MEPs teamed up with the far right to force a secret vote, hoping it would encourage more colleagues to vote against Turkey. The move, permissible under Parliament's rules at the request of one-fifth of the members, was traditionally used only for the appointment of individuals to certain posts. The rules committee was subsequently invited to redraft the rule.

232 The protocol allowed the Ankara agreement to be adapted to recognise Cyprus' membership of the EU and its signature was considered to be an important symbol of Turkey's goodwill in the process of reunification of the island.

Liberals protested to Commissioner Verheugen[233] that to make such an announcement would be to give the sitting Social Democrat prime minister and presidential candidate Adrian Nastase a potentially important electoral advantage over his centre-right Democratic Alliance (DA) rival and Bucharest mayor Traian Basescu.

On 26 November I travelled to Bucharest to meet DA presidential hopeful Basescu and prime ministerial candidate Calin Tariceanu. My plans to assist in their campaigning efforts earlier in the week had been thwarted by the difficulties over Jacques Barrot, but Liberals were convinced that Romania needed a change of government if it were to make progress towards joining the EU as foreseen in 2007; and I needed to inform myself how the campaign had gone and how the ALDE group should best react to the result.

Romania's election campaign had been marred by reports of double-counting and dubious voting practices; moreover, the publication of verbatim reports of cabinet meetings in which ministers talked openly of 'silencing' journalists and 'putting pressure on' the judiciary had sent a shiver around Brussels. However, despite widespread allegations of vote-rigging by the government, the first round of voting on 28 November 2004 gave a slim majority to Basescu. The second round of the presidential election, on Thursday 12 December, saw him clinch victory by a small margin in the presidential race but without a parliamentary majority for his Democratic Alliance, leaving Tariceanu with the unenviable task of forming a minority administration.

The main focus of Parliament's attention, however, was the situation in Kiev. It was partly this development which had taken Commissioner Barrot's little difficulty out of the news headlines. The week of 22 November had found candidate Viktor Yuschenko's supporters massed outside the city's Mariyinski Palace in protest against a rigged ballot in the second round of the election. The orange revolution was in full swing. The ALDE group, under the influence of excited Polish members – who, despite their advancing years, had rediscovered a youthful enthusiasm for revolution to throw off the yoke of Russian Communism – had led the calls for statements to Parliament by Council and Commission. Polish ALDE member Grazyna Staniszewska returned from an election monitoring visit, made with representatives of the EPP and PES groups, to report first hand to Parliament on widespread ballot rigging and intimidation of opposition supporters. The European Parliament's foreign affairs committee, which had quizzed EU High Representative Javier Solana on 24 November, demanded a re-run of the vote under international scrutiny. This issue dominated the agenda of the EU-Russia summit on 25 November 2004, pitting Russian leader Vladimir Putin against the West. And an ALDE proposal to the conference of presidents that we invite the Ukrainian parliament's speaker and their European affairs committee chairman to the debate we had hurriedly scheduled for 1 December, found general approval.

The EP debate and the resolution it adopted on 2 December sent a clear

---

233   Your author wrote a letter of protest and visited Verheugen to discuss the matter together with ALDE MEPs Chris Davies and Emma Nicholson on 17 November.

appeal to Ukraine to re-run the vote and to the Russians to stay out. The speaker of the Ukrainian parliament, Boris Tarasyuk, was cheered as he stood in Parliament's visitors' gallery by a sea of MEPs sporting orange scarves or breast-pocket handkerchiefs. At a press conference I hosted for Tarasyuk afterwards, Bronislaw Geremek MEP called for Ukraine to be allowed into the EU. While my view and that of many of my colleagues remained more cautious, few of us would have excluded the possibility of EU entry in due course if the country proved capable of sufficient reform.

Though the European Council later that month was simply to reiterate 'the paramount importance of free and fair elections', Parliament's attention paid off. By the weekend it had been agreed to hold a re-run of the second round of the presidential election, on 26 December 2004.

EPP-ALDE competition

Largely unseen by the general public is the struggle for dominance between the EU's political parties. Yet as 2004 gave way to 2005 the European People's Party was growing worried about the benefit Liberals had gained from enlargement of the EU. Not only were Liberals de facto equal in number to the EPP in the college of European commissioners; the realisation that the EPP had no significant member party in Bulgaria or Romania and would in all likelihood see Liberal representation in Council, Commission and Parliament grow further in 2007 led them to work harder to secure their dominant position. In January 2005, with an eye to the future, the EPP sought to 'sign up' Viktor Yuschenko's party in the Ukraine and the Law and Justice Party in Turkey. Their existing members, however, had not been adequately prepared for these newcomers and their proposal to grant affiliate membership status was rejected in favour of the less important status of observer. However Liberals were unable to prevent their making overtures to Traian Basescu of Romania which would eventually culminate in success[234]; or to prevent the AKP MPs on the Parliamentary Assembly of the Council of Europe moving over to join the EPP group.

Romania and Bulgaria, due to join the EU in 2007, were fertile territory for Liberals. We were in government in both and enjoying some popularity. Fearful of embarrassment, the EPP teamed up with the PES in May to try to deny to Romania and Bulgaria the right to send 'observer MEPs' to Parliament in the period between the green light being given and accession taking place, as had happened with previous accessions. The move backfired on them badly. They not only lost the argument in the conference of presidents but were seen publicly to have tried to do down the newcomers – and I became a momentary hero in Bulgaria in defence of their MEPs' rights.

234 Basescu's party had been a member of the Socialist International but had been upset when SI secretary general Luis Ayala ignored them in favour of the, former Communist, Socialist party of Prime Minister Nastase. Tariceanu sought to bring Basescu to the Liberal camp, an endeavour in which I assisted, but once in office Basescu was tempted by the overtures of the EPP, to which he succumbed.

Christianity and Islam

Our new development aid commissioner, Belgian Liberal Louis Michel, had impressed Liberals considerably as foreign minister. He was to impress us more favourably still as news of the Indian Ocean tsunami over the 2004-05 Christmas-New Year break was followed within hours by news that he was on his way out there to offer assistance[235]. 229,866 people had died and 1.69 million been made homeless in one of the greatest humanitarian catastrophes in many years. Though western aid invariably came with strings attached and was notoriously slow in delivery,[236] this commissioner took seriously his duty, pledging an immediate three million euros in aid and help with the organisation of a donor conference. Within ten days there were total EU pledges of 1.5 billion euros.

I imagine Louis Michel's determination to help was fuelled by a wider consideration, common to Liberals. Worst affected was Indonesia which, however poor, was emerging after years of dictatorship and civil war as a country in which there was a consensus for democracy. The largest Muslim nation in the world had chosen a path few other Muslim nations were yet prepared to follow: that of secular democratic development. Liberals were determined to assist them.

In Europe too we were preaching the need for tolerance and good relations between different faiths. Our ALDE group's 2005 calendar opened with a conference entitled 'Unity through Diversity', at which prominent Muslim scholars spoke. It examined different approaches towards integration, advised by the European Council for Refugees and Exiles and by the Federation of Islamic Organisations in Europe. A Eurobarometer poll had shown 80% of EU citizens to be at least somewhat 'ill at ease'[237] in multicultural societies. Islamist terror through Al Qaida remained a serious threat, as the EU's anti-terrorism co-ordinator Gijs de Vries was to remind Parliament's justice and home affairs committee on 18 January 2005. It is never easy to uphold Liberal defence of multiculturalism when prejudice fills the air, so Liberals were redoubling their efforts. In contrast to the new mood of intolerance in Europe and North Africa, fed by the invasion of Iraq and its evocation of Arab humiliation under the crusades, Indonesia seemed to Liberals to foster a liberal interpretation of Islam under democracy.

I expressed to participants at the seminar two areas of particular concern. The first was that as memories of the Asian tsunami faded, western policies would once again be reviled in the developing world for the self interest and double standards they too often betrayed. Support for tyrannies as a trade-off for cheap oil or military bases or co-operation in the 'war against terror' was not a strategy but a short-term and unsustainable use of force majeure

---

235   The failure of new High Representative Catherine Ashton to take similar action following the earthquake in Haiti five years later led to criticism by Liberals. Instead, she flew to Washington DC, exacerbating the criticism.

236   Of 1 billion US dollars pledged to the holy Iranian city of Bam after the earthquake there on 26 December 2003 less than 2% had been spent by January 2005.

237   The poll also showed 20% of Europeans prepared to be active in helping new arrivals to integrate and 40% either ambivalent or openly hostile towards immigrants.

by the powerful against the dispossessed, I said. The second was that the secular state which Liberals had fought so hard to achieve was in danger not only from intolerant faith but also from intolerant secularism. A profound debate was required on the role and rights of religions in a secular liberal democracy, not least since faith groups were antennae just as valuable as those of business, trade unions and other bodies of civil society in making representations to government. 'Those deemed not to hold the politically-correct views of the moment are too often vilified and expected to remain silent or stay out of public life', I stated; ' Such secularism, masquerading as pluralism, is no Liberal value'.

The Danish cartoons affair and the murder of Theo van Gogh in the Netherlands had been followed by a riot in Birmingham in the UK against a play by a Sikh author about rape and murder in a Sikh temple. Some Sikhs alleged that this was an insult to their faith. Religious intolerance was gaining ground. Christianity appeared to have forgotten the history of the seven hundred years of an enlightened Islamic caliphate in Cordoba under which impressive scientific and cultural progress had been made; Islam remembered only too well the repression of the Catholic inquisition which followed.

If there was one aspect of 'old Europe' that put the EU to shame, Liberals argued, it was the continent's failure to eradicate the prejudice and persecution which had contributed to more than 300 years of net emigration. Now that economic imperatives required the EU to encourage immigration, the EU found its citizens ill prepared, ill educated and reluctant to embrace new arrivals. Where Canada – governed by Liberals for most of the previous century – was the world's best integrated multicultural industrialised country, Europe was a laggard.

MEP Emma Bonino, who had taken an apartment in Cairo and was learning Arabic, was fomenting revolution among educated women in Arab societies. She organised them into mutual support networks. A 2002 report by Arab scholars for the UN Development Programme had shown lack of empowerment of women in Arab societies to be not only a problem of justice and equality but also a major cause of economic weakness. Female illiteracy in the region, at 42%, was twice that of men. Women's participation in the labour force was among the lowest in the world. Forced marriages and honour killings were commonplace, divorce very difficult. Under the cover of the debate sparked by this report, much could be done. The ALDE group encouraged Bonino by hosting visits to Brussels by Arab women and taking part in events she organised in the region. Addressing the Arab International Women's Forum in Cairo on 12 June 2005 on behalf of the ALDE group, I paid tribute to the courage of women who deserved to be role-models for their societies and stressed that change in the status of women was a form of modernisation rather than westernisation. Women had been elected to the Afghan parliament in free elections. Bahrain had appointed a woman to head a government department. Women had played an important role that year in the first democratic elections ever held in Palestine and in Iraq. In Oman, women had been given the right to vote and to stand as candidates in elections. This was, as UN assistant Secretary General Rima Khalaf Hunaidi had said: 'a new direction … Change driven by the Arab street, not change adopted from afar'.

In addition to a dialogue with Islam the ALDE group hosted meetings in January with the European Jewish Congress and the Catholic Bishops' Conference.[238] In speeches to a conference of France's UDF on 23 January 2005 and to the Liberal group on the Parliamentary Assembly of the Council of Europe the following day I highlighted the need for greater dialogue to promote understanding. As EU leaders gathered in Katowice on 27 January for the 60th anniversary commemoration of the liberation of prisoners from Auschwitz, the only political leader among us with direct experience of the horrors perpetrated was Simone Veil, a former leader of the European Parliament's Liberal group, who had been an inmate in the camp. On 3 February 2005, interviewed on a BBC Radio 4 programme entitled 'Religion and Politcs', I reminded their listeners that by 2050 European Union citizens would make up less than 10% of the world's population and argued that religious tolerance would be a key factor in our success, our security and perhaps our survival.

The new mood of intolerance affected not only those of minority faiths but ethnic minorities too. On 4 February 2005 I breakfasted with Hungarian philanthropist and Liberal supporter George Soros to learn about plans for the 'Decade of Roma inclusion[239]' which he was sponsoring. My Hungarian Liberal colleague Viktoria Mohacsi MEP, herself of Roma extraction, had drawn the attention of parliamentarians to the horrific discrimination suffered by Roma people in a number of EU member countries. There were believed to be up to eight million Roma people in the EU – a population almost equivalent to that of Sweden – who, like the Palestinians, were stateless and often unwelcome. In preparation for Romania's accession to the EU the ALDE group was to host a conference in Brussels in June 2006 with government ministers and officials to discuss the challenges faced by the two million Roma people within its borders. Deputy Prime Minister Marko Bela was to commit his government 'not only to equality before the law [for Roma people] but to equality of opportunity'.

Economic reform

The European Commission presented to Parliament on 26 January 2005 its five year plan, of which a major plank was a re-launch of the so-called Lisbon strategy or agenda. When the EU's heads of state and government had met in Lisbon in early 2000 they had committed themselves to giving the Union 'the most dynamic, competitive, knowledge-based economy in the world by 2010'. Five years on, progress could be noted in the scope of the 'four freeedoms': the freedom of movement for people, goods, services and capital. There had been legislation on recognition of professional qualifications, co-ordination of social security arrangements and a simplification

238   In my capacity as group leader I also took colleagues to meet Ambassador Ahani of Iran; and as a constituency MEP I met the Catholic Bishop of Clifton.

239   This had emerged from a conference held in Budapest in 2003. On 2 February 2005, in Sofia, eight prime ministers were to sign a declaration leading to the establishment of a Roma education fund and other initiatives. George Soros provided – and continues to provide – generous sponsorship.

of access to health care through the European Health Insurance Card[240]. Consumer protection had been extended and environmental legislation too. Meeting in Brussels in June 2004 the heads of state and government had congratulated themselves on progress achieved; but the more reflective among them also recognised that far too little had happened. Key pieces of legislation to complete the single market were still mired in wrangling[241]; of the legislation adopted, much had not yet been transposed into national law by the member states. It cost three times as much and took twice as long to get a patent in the EU as it did in the USA. If reluctance on the part of some member states was the major problem, the political climate in the European Parliament was hardly propitious either. The left either feared or chose to paint the Lisbon agenda as an attempt to introduce raw, US-style capitalism into Europe; the centre worried that it took insufficient account of environmental sustainability and the right was not united in the need to resist temptations to economic nationalism.

Nor could the Commission do much more than to exhort, coax and cajole the member states and MEPs along the path to Lisbon. On 1 January 2005, Luxembourg had assumed the presidency of the European Council. Prime Minister Juncker's main aim was to reach agreement on the financial perspectives (medium term budget) of the EU; the Netherlands' presidency had been able to secure only a commitment that the ceiling for own resources (the maximum amount the EU could spend) would remain at its current level of 1.24% of the EU's GNI *pro tem*. As a convinced federalist, Juncker was also to seek to advance the ratification of the EU's constitution, rendered more difficult by the fact that a number of member states had decided to stage referendums to seek public approval of it[242]. He regarded the Lisbon agenda as important but 'stuck in the sand' and summed up the dilemma of the EU's heads of state and government in pursuing a policy of economic liberalisation with the crisp words: 'We all know what we have to do. We just don't know how to win re-election afterwards'.

The essential building blocks of the Lisbon strategy were proving hard to put in place. Continued obstacles to cross-border mergers and takeovers, for example, deprived EU industry of the critical mass needed to compete effectively in global markets. A directive to remove these was under consideration by Parliament and Council but was not to come into effect until May 2006 and even then only in watered-down form.

In February 2005 Commissioner McCreevy did the rounds of senior parliamentarians to discuss the draft directive on the opening up of the market in services, the scalding potato which his predecessor Frits Bolkestein had tossed him. For the left, opposition to this was becoming totemic. Strangely,

---

240   Danish Liberal MEP Anne Jensen was Parliament's rapporteur for this dossier. Agreement was reached in December 2003 and the cards were available to citizens from July 2004.

241   For example the services directive, the REACH directive, mobility for researchers and the promotion of environmental technologies.

242   Parliament voted on 14 October 2004 to adopt a proposal by ALDE MEP Thierry Cornillet for member states to co-ordinate their referendums in the period 5-8 May 2005, the 60th anniversary of the end of the Second World War, in order to stimulate a Europe-wide campaign and avoid a disparate series of national debates.

since it had the world's third largest services economy, the opposition was led from France. French Socialist MEP Pervenche Beres, who had taken over the chair of Parliament's economic affairs committee from an equally ardent red-haired German firebrand, was ferociously opposed to the Commission's plans[243]. Against the wishes of most Liberals, the European Parliament called on Commissioner McCreevy to withdraw the Commission's proposed services directive. He refused. He rejected similarly a request to withdraw the directive providing for patenting of computer software, despite a considerable public lobby. Lacking the suavity of his predecessor Frits Bolkestein, however, he won his battles only at the cost of attrition.

The draft 'computer implemented inventions' directive regarding the patenting of computer software was perhaps the most controversial item of economic policy on Parliament's plate. The software industry wanted patents to protect its investments; the open-source software lobby argued that they would slow the development of new tools and services. Both sides exaggerated the potential impact of the Commission's proposal. Nonetheless there was a growing feeling among MEPs that the internet was still a domain of experimentation and would not benefit from strict regulation; and the open-source software lobby was one of the best ever organised. I had warned Barroso, in the debate on the mid-term review of the Lisbon strategy, that Liberals did not see a place for this proposal in the Union's efforts to encourage innovation. Rather, we feared, it could stifle innovation. Moreover, understanding the proposed measure required a level of technical knowledge beyond the easy comprehension of the layman. To many MEPs the issue seemed simple enough. The baddies were the big American multinationals, the goodies Europe's local computer geeks. As a result, Parliament voted to reject the measure on 6 July 2005 in a vote which reminded me of the fate of the bus and coach directive, a similarly complex and technical proposal, in 2001.

Flexible working hours were of great concern to the UK, where a Labour government appeared to have taken over the economic policies of its Tory predecessor lock, stock and barrel. Unsurprisingly, some Labour MEPs – perhaps under the illusion they were beyond the discipline of their London party headquarters[244] – were supporting the Commission's proposal to tighten legislation on the hours an employer could require their employees to work. So UK Liberal Democrats were treated to the spectacle of UK industry minister Gerry Sutcliffe (Labour) coming to lobby us against the actions of his own party's MEPs; he was to be the first of many such on that particular dossier.

There was much debate too about the permissibility of decisions by private companies to switch investment from one plant to another. Alfonso Andria was active for the ALDE group in contesting a decision by Thyssen-

---

243   Pervenche Beres was even to argue in a referendum campaign against the EU's draft Constitutional Treaty on the spurious grounds that it ushered in raw capitalist practices.

244   If so, they were wrong. Ian White, a first class MEP for South West England until 1999, had been 'deselected' by his party for his independence of mind and replaced by the much less sympathetic former North West MEP Glyn Ford.

Krupp to close its plant at Terni in Italy in an example of 'delocalisation' being used even by companies who had benefited from EU funding to establish the plants now being closed. In my own constituency the closure of a cellophane factory after its purchase by a government-subsidised American rival caused heated debate; my Labour opponent and I took the opportunity to debate the matter in Parliament with Commissioner Verheugen.

Major newspapers such as *Le Figaro* and *The Financial Times* were highly critical of Barroso's record during his first 100 days in office. The Lisbon agenda, so grandly launched during Portugal's EU presidency in 2000, was now proceeding at a snail's pace, they argued. Barroso and Juncker were having difficulty imposing on member states even the discipline the member states themselves had approved; Juncker, who was also the Luxembourg finance minister and chairman of the Ecofin Council, could only despair when France and Germany both formally broke the discipline of the EU's Growth and Stability Pact by planning public deficits exceeding 3% of GNI[245]. Had smaller states attempted this, many suspected, the rules would have been imposed upon them against their will. An election in Germany's populous North Rhine Westphalia and the referendum in France were both used as sticks to prevent the European Council meeting on 22-23 March 2005 from taking important decisions on economic policy. But Juncker succeeded in annexing to the presidency conclusions the Ecofin report 'Improving the implementation of the Stability and Growth Pact', thus backing up his case for the future.

Liberals saw the difficulties as stemming in part from ideological approaches. I used the occasion of a debate on the mid-term review of the Lisbon strategy to point out the weakness of Europe's right-wing parties, who had still not embraced what I called 'the central fact of globalisation: that the nation state and the free market are no longer compatible' and the left 'riven by dissent over the role of the state in managing the economy'. To improve the economic vitality and the social and environmental health of our society simultaneously, I said, the Lisbon strategy had to combine flexibility, fairness and farsightedness. In subsequent interviews I was sharply critical of France and Germany[246]. In the resolution adopted by Parliament to close the debate, Liberals successfully inserted an insistence that a reduction in government debts and deficits was 'fundamental' for the EU.

The spring 2005 European Council meeting chaired by Jean-Claude Juncker was more sober than had been the meetings of the previous year. Carrying out a mid-term review of the Lisbon strategy it declared: 'Five years after the launch of the Lisbon strategy, the results are mixed ... there is a high price to pay for delayed or incomplete reforms, as is borne out by the gulf between Europe's growth potential and that of its economic partners'. Investment in human capital, in communications networks and –

---

245   This was to have serious consequences during a euro crisis five years later, sparked by the indebtedness of eurozone member Greece.

246   For political cover, Barroso needed MEPs outflanking him on economic liberal standpoints, Liberals felt. Yet in April Barroso urged me to moderate the harshness of my attacks on the offending member states.

backed up by the EIF – in innovative companies was seen as crucial. And in order to promote growth and employment and to strengthen competitiveness, the internal market in services had to be fully operational 'while preserving the European social model'.

To speed up progress, the EU's leaders agreed henceforth to work on a three-year cycle of economic reform taking into account competitiveness, environmental sustainability and social cohesion. Ambitious national reform programmes would be co-ordinated at EU level. The first three-year review would come in 2008, ahead of their 2010 deadline. But by 2008 the economic outlook was to be very different indeed.

EU-US relations

The EU's heads of state and government were to meet George W. Bush when he visited the EU institutions in Brussels on 22 February 2005. Parliament, however, was sitting in Strasbourg. An invitation to Bush to address Parliament in Strasbourg was declined; and in a tit-for-tat move Parliament's group leaders declined an invitation to join the audience for a speech Bush would make in Brussels. Neither party gained from this spat. Bush made little attempt to recognise the legitimacy of the European Parliament or its growing equivalence to the US Senate. Many parliamentarians did little to hide their sentiments that the EU and the USA were drifting apart and that America's diplomacy lacked the finesse to which Europeans were accustomed[247].

For 40 years, Europe's and America's values had been essentially the same, because we had the same starting point, 1945. But Europe's starting point was now the tearing down of the Berlin Wall in 1989. For America, it was the 9-11 attack in 2001. Indeed, invited to launch a book on EU-US relations[248] in mid-February I had remarked on how rapidly our positions were diverging.

The growing disparity in the values governing the two continents had been apparent for some while. When Bush visited London in 2003 he had been confronted by thousands of angry protesters in the country he had described as 'our closest friend in the world'. A Eurobarometer poll that year suggested that a majority of Europeans ranked his administration alongside that of North Korea as a threat to international stability. The USA had disavowed the Kyoto Protocol, the UN Convention on the Rights of the Child and the Biological Weapons Convention. The death penalty, abolition of which was a *sine qua non* for membership of the EU, was being used more and more frequently in some US states. America decided against ratification of the Rome statute for an international criminal court (ICC), which had become operational in 2003, keeping company with Iran, Iraq and North

247 This extended from some Republican politicians resurrecting, at the time of the Iraq War, the earlier characterisation in the humorous TV show 'The Simpsons' of the French as 'cheese-eating surrender monkeys' to the hamfisted diplomacy of US Ambassador to the EU Rockwell Schnabel Jr, who had been a business associate of the Bush family rather than a career diplomat.

248 *Superstate: the new Europe and the challenge to America* by Stephen Haseler.

Korea; and it had tried to strangle the ICC at birth by reaching bilateral agreements with countries such as Israel in order to prevent its nationals being surrendered[249].

Moreover, a government which had come to office promising to outdo its predecessor in its commitment to free trade had passed protectionist legislation on agricultural products and steel which had surprised even the WTO.

It was perhaps unsurprising that when the US government debated extending across the EU the UK-USA agreement to share sensitive information on security matters, the idea was rejected. The United States saw the EU as weak and divided, considered some of its members unreliable partners and appeared to resent its lack of a clear chain of command. Indeed, photographs from a recent EU-USA summit in Washington DC had shown George Bush with three EU leaders, with Barroso positioned as junior to Juncker and not evidently senior to Solana. Kissinger's famous question[250] remained unanswered.

Bush's visit to the EU and to NATO was to smooth the path for better co-operation between the EU and NATO, however. In Bosnia and Herzegovina the EU had taken on first a police mission and then a military mission – ALTHEA – in succession to NATO. The European Defence Agency was now fully engaged in its first year of work, though the UK was to continue to quibble about its budget for some months. Plans for EU battle groups and for rapid response capability were advancing: now agreement was reached to set up a strategic partnership on crisis management between the EU and the US.

Some on the left sought to portray the Americans as wild-west style capitalists. The term Liberal was increasingly abused. The association of economic Liberalism with Britain and America, however, was based on either insufficient study or malicious interpretation of history. As Pierre Nemo was to show in a book published late in 2006[251], continental European thought is at least as important in the development of economic Liberalism as political thought further west. Nor is European Liberalism, in the dismissive phrase of Socialist thinker Bertrand Russell, 'essentially an anglo-dutch phenomenon'[252]. But as Mark Twain pointed out, a lie is half way around the world before the policeman has got his boots on.

The EU's constitutional ills

On 12 January 2005 the European Parliament voted to approve the Treaty establishing a Constitution for Europe. Scare stories about Polish plumbers and nurses and misplaced fears of EU enlargement were to thwart the

---

249 Eastern European countries such as Romania had also come under pressure from the USA to make such bilateral agreements. The matter was to be resolved in September 2002 when the Danish EU presidency blessed an agreement in the Council of Foreign Ministers to allow member states to exempt Americans from being tried before the ICC if they were sent by a country which was not a signatory to the Rome Convention.

250 'If I want to speak to Europe, who do I call?'

251 L'histoire du Liberalisme en Europe, University of Paris.

252 See Russell's History of Political Philosophy.

Luxembourg presidency's desire to see the EU constitution safely ratified by all member states, however. Lithuania had been the first country to ratify the treaty, moving quickly after the Rome signing ceremony to secure parliamentary approval in November 2004. Yet on 20 April 2004 Prime Minister Tony Blair had unexpectedly promised a referendum on the treaty, an idea which he had previously rejected. The matter was to be pushed off the UK agenda by the government's decision to go to the polls in a general election on 5 May 2005, but was not without consequence. Blair's offer of a referendum increased the pressure on President Chirac of France, who subsequently promised a referendum there. Denmark, Ireland, Luxembourg, the Netherlands, Portugal and Spain also planned to put approval of the constitution to a popular plebiscite.

The year 2005 opened in a mood of some enthusiasm among pro-Europeans, with Spain the first country to put the matter to a popular vote. Speaking at a rally in Barcelona on 17 February, just before the poll, I said: 'You are not really voting about a document of 264 pages. You are voting about an idea... If we want the European way to work, we need a European Union which works. And that is what this Constitution is all about.' Spain voted to approve the treaty on 20 February 2005, with 77% voting in favour, although with under half of the eligible voters casting a vote. Yet by mid-April it looked as if things could indeed go wrong in France, with opinion polls predicting a No vote. Unable to accept an invitation from former commissioner Michel Barnier to campaign with him in Haute Savoie, I decided nonetheless to take a team of supporters a week or so later to spend a week campaigning in France. I found to my surprise (though the areas in which I campaigned were all to deliver a narrow Yes) a country at least as insular as my own and without the excuse of being an island. The Yes campaign was let down from the very top, with the president painfully and publicly unaware of the details of the treaty he was asking his compatriots to vote for; despite the best efforts of convinced Europeans like Barnier and Bayrou, the No campaign had all the fire and fury.

The rest, as they say, is history. France – which ten years previously had approved the Maastricht Treaty by only the narrowest of margins – voted No on 29 May 2005 by 55% to 45% and the Netherlands followed suit three days later. A Yes vote in Luxembourg on 1 July 2005 was not going to be enough to save the treaty. The UK government announced with condescension and relief the death of the European constitution: it would no longer be put to a referendum in the the the UK 'since clearly it could not be ratified'.

Meeting soon after the European Parliament elections in 2004 the heads of state and government had lamented the low voter turnout. Five months later they had reiterated the need to strengthen awareness among citizens of the importance of the EU; they had considered televised debates on EU issues prior to European Council meetings and had even foreseen, in the process of ratification of the Constitutional Treaty, an opportunity to inform the public about European issues. But in many cases they had taken no action and where they had it was often a case of too little, too late.

Liberals, however, were not prepared to let five years of work since the Treaty of Nice go to waste. In Helsinki and Tallinn on 16 May 2005 Prime Ministers Vanhanen and Ansip outlined to me their views on how we should react in the event of a French No. Both countries would continue the ratification process and urge others to do likewise in the hope that a French rejection might yet be reversed. Most of my colleagues in the Liberal group shared this opinion. The Liberal commissioners[253] took the same view. I had sounded out the other senior Liberals too. Welcoming the formation of the ALDE group on the Committee of the Regions on 2 June 2005 I argued for a one-year extension of the deadline for ratification of the constitution followed by a referendum in every member state simultaneously. At supper with Poland's prime minister Marek Belka[254] on 31 May, with senior colleagues from my group who accompanied me to Warsaw, we ran through the options available to the EU: carry on ratifying the treaty, country by country; declare the Treaty dead; or freeze ratification until somebody came up with a good idea. It seemed most likely that the majority of national leaders would choose that latter course. For Liberals it was the minimum acceptable. In a letter to *The Financial Times* on 1 June 2005 I pointed out that the UK and other EU member states were legally obliged to undertake the ratification of the document their governments had signed on 29 October 2004.

In the EPP and PES camps, too, the federalist diehards dug their defences. As Parliament gathered in Strasbourg on 13 June 2005 both French president Jacques Chirac and German chancellor Gerhardt Schroeder called for the process of ratification to continue, whatever London may have said. Liberals argued that the forthcoming European Council meeting should do three things immediately to make the EU more open and democratic: allow public access to the ministerial meetings at which policy is made; give the European Parliament powers of co-decision with the Council of Ministers over all areas of EU policy, including the ratification of international treaties; and give the European Court of Justice full judicial oversight of policy making. All could be done on the basis of the existing EU treaties and would go a long way to foster public confidence in the way the EU worked, we believed. We did not spare our castigation of the French: on France-Europe Express, their major TV current affairs programme, I accused them of being a nation of *je m'en foutistes*. Yet as I led my leading spokespersons to London that Friday to listen to the UK government's unimaginative plans for their presidency of the EU I gained little sense from Tony Blair or his colleagues of any emotional understanding of the EU nor any desire to address citizens' concerns by making it more open and democratic in nature. Blair could have exploited the evident seizure of the Franco-German motor to show leadership, but his commitment to reforming Brussels appeared about as deep as his commitment to his declared aim of reforming the UK's undemocratic system of appointment to the House of Lords.

The appearance of the EU's heads of state and government at the European Council meeting of 17-18 June 2005 was described by one wit as akin to an edition of the American TV soap opera *Friends*. Each of the principal actors came in exactly on cue with a pre-scripted remark, to pre-

253   Meeting over a supper I hosted on 24 May.

254   Our Unia Wolnosci party in Poland had merged with the Social Democrats to form the new Democratic Party. This brought President Kwasniewski and Prime Minister Belka into our camp.

dictable audience reaction – and nothing happened[255]. Juncker had succeeded in reforming the Growth and Stability Pact; but his colleagues in Council had allowed him no other prize to take home[256].

Having failed to secure ratification of the Constitutional Treaty, Juncker was keen to reach agreement under his presidency on the future budget of the Union. But either luck was not on his side or the larger member states were not prepared to give little Luxembourg the benefit of such a trophy. Government leaders continued to argue about a tiny percentage of public expenditure which – if agreed – would contribute massively to Europe's competitiveness through a pooling of resources for investment in trans-European transport networks, industrial research and development and education and training. Yet France chose to celebrate the 190th anniversary of the Battle of Waterloo in traditional style. That way her leaders could avoid discussing the French referendum.[257]

The president of the Commission was still having a torrid time. The failure of the referenda in France and the Netherlands, though hardly his fault, had deeply damaged the European Union's credibility. Barroso's speeches in Parliament's debates with Juncker and Blair the week after the summit were long and lacklustre and he had difficulty making himself heard above the hubbub of MEPs awaiting the 'main acts' of Juncker on the Wednesday and Blair on the Thursday. Moreover, he had suffered the indignity of a motion of no confidence[258] tabled by the United Kingdom Independence Party MEPs elected the previous year, who were becoming adept at using Parliament's rules to embarrass the EU. By teaming up with their natural allies on the far right they had gained the 73 signatures necessary for a motion of censure which was debated (and overwhelmingly rejected) by Parliament on 25 May 2005.

But nor was the European Parliament covering itself in glory. Giuseppe Gargani, the Christian Democratic chairman of Parliament's legal affairs committee, had made common cause with German Christian Democrat Klaus-Heiner Lehne to frustrate the reform of MEPs' pay and expenses, the preparation of which had been one of the achievements of Pat Cox's presidency of the House. Luxembourg had used its Council presidency to assist Parliament in the matter, by brokering a consensus among member states in Council on the level of MEPs' pay. The Italian and German MEPs – who, as the highest paid, had the most to lose – were doing their best to scupper it.

---

255   The difference, she added caustically, was that *Friends* was taken off air when the audience tired of it.

256   Under the Luxembourg presidency, for the first time ever, the leaders of the political parties in the European Parliament were given access badges to the Justus Lipsius building in which the Council meeting was being held. Where previously I had gained access using a press pass, now I had access to the antechambers where I could talk to officials.

257   Marielle de Sarnez did the same in the ALDE group. She made a rare appearance at a meeting of the group's presidency on a Monday night in Strasbourg where, in order to prevent criticism of France's referendum vote, she launched a pre-emptive attack on the UK's EU rebate.

258   The case against him centred on a holiday he had accepted on the yacht of Greek shipping magnate Spiros Latsis, a friend of 20 years standing, and the allocation of EUR 10 million a few weeks later to one of the shipyards in the Latsis group. The allegations had previously been investigated by Parliament's conference of presidents and had been answered to its satisfaction in a letter of 22 April 2005.

On 2 June 2005 Cox's successor Borrell had therefore convened the conference of presidents to discuss Gargani's latest act. His intervention succeeded, however; on 23 June Parliament voted to accept the Council's offer (though it would not enter into force until the new parliament convened in 2009 and then only with a 'grandfather rights' clause to protect returning MEPs who wanted to cling on to their historic privileges).

UK presidency talks tough on terror

Since the advent of the repeated public criticism of 'Brussels' which had accompanied Margaret Thatcher's arrival in office in London in 1979, the UK had suffered from having the reputation of a renegade within the EU. UK presidencies of the Council were anticipated with curiosity at best and with trepidation at worst. Blair's first presidency had come just six months after his election to power and had been handled magisterially by Foreign Secretary Robin Cook. Second time around, seven and a half years later, Blair was among the longest-serving prime ministers in the EU and a known quantity (albeit, among Socialists, often distrusted). The speech he made to the House on 23 June 2005 showed a prime minister buoyed up by a third general election victory which would guarantee him at least ten years in office; a man at ease on the world stage and a politician who seemed open, combative, and fun to be with. For the UK's pro-Europeans it seemed a great moment – though only if, we said to ourselves, he was being sincere. 'One speech', I said in reply to his address to MEPs, 'will not suffice to set aside years of suspicion. You need to show that Britain is of Europe, not just with it'.

The EU's new president-in-office was to receive a garland on 6 July 2005, when the International Olympic Committee announced that London had beaten Paris and other cities in the competition to host the 2012 Olympic Games. But a brickbat followed within 24 hours as Al Qaida suicide bombers wreaked havoc with four bomb attacks in central London.

The EU had hoped that its relations with the Islamic world were improving. At the Sharm el-Sheikh summit on 8 February 2005 it had been agreed to put an end to the Palestinian Al Aqsa intifada raging since October 2000. The holding of the first session of the Euro-Mediterranean Parliamentary Assembly in Cairo on 12 March 2005, and plans to hold an extraordinary Euro-Med summit in Barcelona to mark the tenth anniversary of the Barcelona declaration, also appeared to hold out hope of a new dawn. Israel had withdrawn its troops from the Gaza Strip, the EU was assisting in the process of elections to the Palestinian Authority and Syria had withdrawn from the Lebanon in advance of elections there. But the occupation of Afghanistan and Iraq continued, and the news from Iraq, with echoes of the Abu Ghraib scandal[259] of the previous year, supplied ample material for the whipping up of anti-western sentiment.

The EU's response to terrorism was again to dominate the agenda. On 7 June the European Parliament approved a package of seven recommenda-

---

259   US soldiers had been found to have raped and tortured male and female prisoners in the notorious Abu Ghraib prison, in which Saddam Hussein had also tortured his enemies.

tions to the Council proposing the next steps to be taken in the action plan against terrorism, which was due for review at the European Council meeting later that month. Antoine Duquesne MEP had been responsible for three of them, all concerned with exchange of information between national authorities relating to terrorism or suspicion of terrorist intent. He sought a European register of criminal convictions and a co-ordinated approach to data collection and protection with central roles for Europol and Eurojust in the former.

The main legislative achievement to date was the European arrest warrant, presented by some as an anti-terrorist measure but which had other benefits too. On 18 June 2005 a warrant was to be issued in Wiltshire in my constituency for the arrest of Hugo Quintas, the Portuguese boyfriend and prime suspect in the murder of my constituent Hayley Richards. Quintas had fled the UK after the murder but was arrested by the Spanish police on the border with Portugal just three days after the warrant was issued. He was eventually to be tried and found guilty. This was significant to me since I had piloted through the European Parliament in 2001 the measure which created the European arrest warrant and had been heavily attacked by the UK Conservative and UKIP MEPs. What would these MEPs now say to the family of Hayley Richards? That they would prefer her murderer to remain at large?!

The European arrest warrant had been designed as a measure to help combat serious crime in general. It had survived a challenge in the German constitutional court in mid-July 2002; in the UK it was soon to be used to extradite one of those responsible for the London bombings, Husain Osman, from Rome. Astonishingly, it is still (at the time of writing) heavily contested by the Conservatives, the UK's self-styled 'party of law and order'.

On 7 September 2005 Parliament heard statements from Council and Commission on liberty and security in the light of the threat of terrorism. The president-in-office of the Council, UK home secretary Charles Clarke, challenged jurisprudence under the ECHR and appeared to condone torture in certain circumstances, telling the House 'the right to be protected from torture and ill-treatment must be considered side by side with the right to be protected from the death and destruction caused by indiscriminate terrorism'. Replying to his statement on behalf of the ALDE group I told him: 'Human rights are indivisible. The public may not like it, but suspected terrorists do have rights: to a fair trial, to be interrogated but not tortured by the police ... Suspending rights such as those would lead to summary justice, the justice of high noon which leads to the deaths of innocents like Jean-Charles de Menezes'[260].

I had first met Clarke in 1978 when he was chairman of the National Union of Students and a renowned bruiser from the International Marxist Group. He had greeted me at the end of May, in the EP to prepare his presidency, with the words: 'are Liberals ever going to be serious about tackling

---

260   Jean Charles de Menezes was a Brazilian citizen who had been shot dead in London by anti-terrorist police on 22 July 2005 after he was mis-identified as one of the fugitives involved in a failed bombing attempt the week after the London bombings of 7 July 2005. He had no link to terrorism.

terrorism or will your legalistic minds continue to frustrate government action?'[261] He now sought me out in his role as president-in-office of the Council to see how the European Parliament might help him in further measures to combat terrorism.

Liberals were as convinced as ever of the value of Thomas Paine's dictum: 'He who would make his own liberty secure must guard even his enemy from oppression; for if he violates this duty, he establishes a precedent that will reach to himself.'

Thus the European Parliament had rejected in June, on the advice of the rapporteur, German Liberal Alexander Alvaro, an initiative by four countries – the UK, France, Sweden and Ireland – for a framework decision giving governments greater powers to retain email and mobile phone communications data in the fight against terrorism. MEPs had doubts not only about the proportionality of the measures proposed to the dangers faced, but also about the legal basis chosen and the lack of a majority in Council for such a proposal.

Liberals agreed with the UK presidency of the EU that anti-terrorism measures needed to be implemented fully and rapidly. But then why were seven of the 24 legal instruments considered by the justice and home affairs ministers on 24 May 2005 still not implemented in all member states? Why were six unratified EU conventions on security still occupying ministerial time, when framework decisions could be more easily implemented and enforced? Why had Europol and Eurojust still not been given the capacity to operate? And why was the EU's anti-terrorism co-ordinator not allowed the co-operation he needed from national governments?

A framework decision on data protection to accompany measures on data retention would have made Liberals more open to the measures being proposed, I told Clarke. And in the debate on 7 September 2005 I had told him: 'the nub of our dilemma is that the state is the main protector of both our security and our liberty. If the EU is to provide security against supranational threats, it must guarantee liberty supranationally too'.

Clarke had called an emergency meeting of the justice and home affairs ministers after the London bombings and had secured a majority in favour of a Council initiative. I told Clarke that the European Parliament was sick of measures being adopted by national governments under the infamous 'third pillar'[262] of the treaties, which gave MEPs no formal say in the matters legislated for. I gave him my frank assessment that if he adopted a first pillar legal base he would get his measure through, even at first reading. I guessed that my group would oppose it: Liberals, even at the worst of times, are not minded to assist the state in spying on its citizens. But he would create enough good will by involving Parliament fully in the decision – and establish a precedent valuable to Parliament – to permit success[263].   Now

---

261   Liberals were to get their own back when a Liberal Democrat candidate ousted Charles Clarke from Parliament in the May 2010 UK general election.

262   Decisions in the 'third pillar'', a mechanism incorporated in the Maastricht Treaty, were agreements between member states outwith the formal framework of the EU's treaties.

263   I took the precaution of reiterating my view in conversation with his deputy, Baroness Ashton, who suffered less than her boss from the arrogance of office and who possessed a greater natural understanding of the value of consensus-building.

extremely keen to achieve a success in the fight against terror under the UK presidency, the home secretary who had sought to abolish trial by jury at home saw the advantage of a little charm, at least in his dealings with members of the European Parliament. He took up my suggestion and worked closely with MEPs to achieve his goal.

Events were to come to the aid of the Council. A terrorist bombing in Bali on 12 October 2005 by Islamic group Jemmah Islamiah and an inflammatory speech by Iran's President Ahmedinejad, threatening to 'wipe Israel off the map' had again drawn attention to the seriousness of the struggle against violent Islam.

The president-in-office was to succeed in his drive for agreement on data retention, though only after hollowing out his proposal to such an extent that each member state could decide for itself what measures to adopt; the German telecommunications lobby and the continued distaste of some other governments for the draconian measures the UK minister sought left Clarke with no other choice. I was briefly public enemy No.1 for my excellent and conscientious colleague Sarah Ludford, who spies conspiracy at every corner (even among her political friends), but I felt the game was worth the candle. The Council of Ministers had chosen to involve Parliament fully in the drafting of legislation in an area where previously it had declined to do so.

UK Conservatives retreat

Developments in the UK's Conservative Party were also to have an impact on EU politics, though less immediate. On 18 July 2005, shortly after the start of the UK presidency, former prime minister Edward Heath passed away. He was 89 years old and had remained a Commoner, refusing to be elevated to the House of Lords where he would be a less obvious thorn in the flesh to his successors. Heath was the prime minister who took the UK into the European Community; like Kohl, he had been deeply marked by experience of the Second World War. A convinced pro-European, his period as prime minister seemed to have coincided with the high water mark of pro-Europeanism, at least within the Conservative Party. He was to criticise constantly his successor as party leader, Margaret Thatcher – she who had the gall to be photographed sitting at the feet of that other great Conservative pro-European Harold Macmillan in order to win over the Tory moderates – for her revisionism.

The last prominent 'Heathite' in UK politics, Ken Clarke, had remained a force within the Conservative Party capable of restraining it from wilder acts of xenophobic irresponsibility. However in October 2005 Clarke pulled out of the race for the leadership of his party vacated by general election loser Michael Howard, leaving in the field two candidates – Liam Fox and David Cameron – both from the anti-EU camp. Before the UK presidency was out, in December 2005, Cameron was to win, but not before throwing a bone to the running dogs of euro-scepticism in the shape of a commitment to pull the UK Conservative MEPs out of the European Union's main right-wing grouping, the European People's Party. Though the pledge was not to be fulfilled until 2009, it was to have an important impact on developments in the European Parliament.

Social policy – referendum fallout

Following the concern which became evident during the French and Dutch referendum campaigns – namely, that the EU was rather better at helping its citizens seize the advantages of globalisation than at protecting them from its negative effects – social policy was accorded a greater priority at EU level. The Union had very few policy tools with which to influence social policy, but sought at the very least to encourage dialogue among member states and political families. In 2004 the European Parliament started a discussion on the social dimension of globalisation with reference to a report on this topic by the International Labour Organisation. The European Commission published its own report in June 2004. When Parliament finally adopted a resolution, in November 2005, it noted the importance of trade but called on the Council and the Commission to promote a social policy agenda to favour the development of an inclusive and cohesive society, with gender equality and an absence of other forms of discrimination. It called too for greater responsibility to be shown by employers, particularly transnational corporations.

Liberals were not on the back foot on these issues. On 28 February and 1 March 2004 ALDE invited representatives of Liberal parties in national parliaments to discuss 'social Europe'; since the Socialists were stoking the fires of debate we had felt it wise to line up the fire tenders in good time. Parliament had requested the scrapping of the opt-out from the working time directive. Other aspects of the Lisbon agenda were under attack. Addressing MEPs and the national MPs on 1 March 2004 I pointed out that while we talked of Lisbon in terms of competitiveness or dynamism, at heart it was about work. A more flexible labour market was needed to create opportunities for work where they had not previously existed. Delegates to the conference agreed that the open method of co-ordination and soft law were not working well as policy tools. There were still many disincentives to work. As Frits Bolkestein had opined, the Lisbon agenda tended more towards bark than bite. Verhofstadt had suggested two weeks previously, in a Paul Henri Spaak lecture, that the EU needed to move beyond the system of peer review to a more focused method of encouraging economic reform. There was too little sense of urgency about reform in the Council, Liberals felt. A flexible market need not mean junk labour, as the left claimed; it need not mean weak protection for workers against unfair treatment or unacceptable standards. But it meant that businesses and workers should be more responsive to each others' needs in a competitive global marketplace. 'Nobody wants a Europe that looks like Wal Mart', I assured delegates: 'Employment is a power relationship and we have to handle it with care'.

ALDE MEPs had supported measures designed to ensure the mutual recognition of professional qualifications so that Europeans could move and work more freely within the EU. In the same spirit we had backed the provision of social support to mobile workers. We had campaigned for stronger anti-discrimination measures to open our workplaces to all. And we had repeatedly called for an open approach to labour migration within the EU. The illiberal responses of too many on the left to fears of job stealing by immigrant labour and of too many on the right to fears of benefit tourism were not for Liberals.

The left was keen to protect and enhance what it called Europe's 'social model'. With 25 different states there were in fact 25 social models, though economist Andre Sapir, in a study commissioned by the European Commission, placed them into four broad categories of approach. But there was a tendency to believe that what all countries shared – 20 days annual paid leave or more, a guaranteed minimum wage, fairly generous unemployment and sickness insurance and old age pension provision – made the EU superior to the USA and Japan.

Thus it was that the social model was put on the agenda for the Union's summit in October 2005 at Hampton Court and that Commissioner Spidla did the rounds of the group leaders in Parliament early in September with an 'ideas paper' which would form the basis of the Commission's contribution to the debate. Liberals had few disagreements with the paper's emphasis on social security measures such as unemployment and health insurance, nor indeed with its exhortation of the importance of education.

However Liberals are free traders and when the Commission sought also – in the interests of social policy but under the guise of 'anti-dumping' duties – to put tariff barriers on footwear which was made outside the EU, I sprang to the defence of Clark's Shoes, a company from my constituency which had successfully outsourced its manufacturing to lower cost countries and upgraded its UK operations into the general retail field. Clark's is a well-known Quaker company with a good social conscience and employed no fewer people in the UK as a result. If southern European shoemakers had called for an investigation by the Commission into alleged dumping of footwear from China and Vietnam it was because they were being priced out of the market by the northern European shoemakers who had planned ahead, knowing import quotas were to be lifted, and re-located production. Similarly, Swedish Liberals took up the cudgels for the port of Vaxholm, which was in trouble with the Swedish labour unions for having engaged the Latvian company Laval to carry out construction work rather than a Swedish company whose bid price was higher. This should have been possible under the terms of the posted workers directive, adopted in 1996 to protect the rights of workers abroad; but Swedish law focused on collective rather than individual rights and the engagement of Laval was challenged in the courts. The Vaxholm case became a cause celebre for the EP's Socialist group, who tried to use it as a stick to beat Commissioner McCreevy. They insisted on summoning Barroso and McCreevy to Parliament to debate the issue on 25 October. They had chosen a weak case, however, on which to endeavour to make their point[264], and were roundly worsted in the debate. The matter was finally to be resolved by a ruling in the European Court of Justice in 2008.

---

264 Laval bid in a fair and open competition for the contract, fulfilling public procurement criteria. The company had a collective agreement with its workers, just as Swedish employers had with theirs. Moreover, when challenged by the unions over labour rates, Laval offered to raise its wages to the level agreed by the Swedish collective agreement. But that was not good enough for the union, which demanded that the rates should be the Stockholm average rather than the Swedish national average. Finally, in a breathtaking lack of worker solidarity, the union prevented work from going ahead, which led to the company withdrawing from the contract and filing for bankruptcy. Now Latvian workers had lost their jobs thanks to the Swedish trade unions, who put protecting Swedish jobs ahead of the common market principles their country had signed up to.

What surprised me about the wish of Socialist leader Martin Schulz to major on social legislation was that Socialist MEPs themselves were bitterly divided on these issues; rather than choosing to fight on grounds on which his opponents were divided, he was in effect highlighting the divisions in his own ranks. Thus when Prime Minister Blair addressed the European Parliament in advance of the Hampton Court European Council on 23 November 2005 and spoke of the need for social and economic reform, his appeal was greeted by stony silence from many on the Socialist benches while Liberals and some right-wingers applauded enthusiastically. The Hampton Court summit at the end of October was to be described by German radio station Deutsche Welle as 'Bizarre ... all show and no substance' as the real issues were swept under the rug of the absence of EU competences in social policy. The decision of the UK prime minister to make a major announcement at Hampton Court about the war in Iraq in response to a journalist's question, doubtless 'planted' by a spin doctor, showed that Blair's press advisers preferred participation in aspects of EU co-operation to be kept out of the front page headlines and broadcast news bulletins.

The employment ministers, meeting in Luxembourg early in June, had discussed how to combine flexible labour markets with security of employment to achieve a fabled 'flexicurity'. The Danish model which gave its name to 'flexicurity' ensured that people are re-trained to meet the changing needs of the economy, thus cutting mid-career unemployment. They agreed to leave employment guidelines for member states unchanged from the previous year, but they stressed the need for active labour market policies, credible lifelong learning programmes, modern social security systems and portable pensions. Most sought to avoid the UK route of putting more and more people on short term contracts with little long term security. It was Liberal-led Denmark which showed the way forward, taking their flexicurity model on a roadshow around EU capitals in autumn 2006.

Twenty-three member states were failing to respect EU laws on working time. Contrary to instructions from the ECJ they were not treating doctors' hours spent 'on-call' as working time. The Commission was in a quandary, knowing that it should instigate disciplinary proceedings but reluctant to do so on such a broad front. But meeting again in November, the 25 employment ministers were unable to make progress on a dossier which had divided the EU for many years.

Liberals insisted however that the EU's social policy should consist of more than simply rights at the workplace. On 5 September 2006 Maria Carlshamre MEP, herself a victim, spoke in favour of a phase three for the DAPHNE programme[265] to combat and prevent violence against women and children. And in November she was to lead calls for an EU action plan to combat human trafficking.

Commissioner Kyprianou was to please his fellow Liberals no end by publishing a consultation paper in September 2006 on access to health care

---

265 This EU funded programme had been initiated in 1997 following Belgium's infamous Dutroux affair. Daphne is the young woman in Greek mythology who was chased by the god Apollo and transformed into a laurel tree to prevent him raping her.

services. ALDE was to launch the following month a campaign for a patients' rights charter, allowing those waiting for health care in one member state to seek it in another where capacity might be greater; this was spearheaded by Antonia Parvanova, an observer MEP and a medical doctor by profession. EU citizens had enjoyed since 1971 the right to free primary medical care in any country of the EU in which they were living or visiting; when the health commissioner came on 7 November 2006 to speak to ALDE MEPs about his plan he agreed to our proposal for draft legislation formally to provide the right for medical patients to seek treatment across borders.

It cannot fairly be said that the EU cared little for its workers. Recognising the problems of youth unemployment a specific 'European Youth Pact' had been launched by the Luxembourg presidency. Moreover, was it not the EU which had championed equal pay legislation? Health and safety in the workplace had always been a matter of concern too. The optical radiation directive, published on 5 April 2006 and designed to protect those exposed at work to sources of optical radiation, caused a minor flurry in a country more famed for its rainfall when it hit the headlines of UK newspaper *The Sun*. The paper presented it as another piece of crazy legislation from Brussels which would prevent barmaids and waitresses from wearing low-cut dresses when serving in the open air in summertime and thus, it argued, reduce the level of tips they could expect from customers. But the thrust of the directive was deadly serious. My colleague Liz Lynne MEP managed to amend the document, leaving it up to member states to decide whether or not to include natural radiation, and thus protecting readers of *The Sun* from the planet after which it is named.

Employers frequently complained, however, about 'social' legislation adding to their costs. A favourite theme of some governments at European Council meetings had been 'better regulation'. So Barroso also announced (through a 'leak' to *The Financial Times*), that he would scrap some 70 pieces of legislation which he described as 'inane'. This kind of action gained him few friends in Parliament, however; while it is for the Commission to propose legislation it is for Council and Parliament to dispose and we had not asked the Commission to take such action.

While Socialists campaigned against the evils of the free market, Liberals were on the warpath over the issue of transparency in government. ALDE MEPs had raised with UK officials at the start of the presidency their wish to see the Council of Ministers legislate in public. Since nothing had happened, a group of mainly British colleagues had decided to ambush Tony Blair as he entered Parliament in Strasbourg in October through the diplomatic entrance. Bearing placards with the words 'Make EU laws in public' they were attacking the practice of the Council of Ministers of legislating in secret[266]. And while Blair himself probably had sympathy with their cause

---

266   Blair was to be met as he entered Parliament that day by a protest from Liberal MEPs holding placards decrying the lack of transparency in EU law-making. UK Permanent Representative John Gray, furious about this, tried to prevent his prime minister from attending a choir concert later that day by the Somerset Youth Choir from my constituency. Blair was sufficiently politically astute, however, to see the danger inherent in such advice and to maintain his commitment.

(I heard him turn to his chief official, UK permanent representative to Brussels John Gray, and ask 'why don't we open the meetings to public scrutiny?') his officials resisted it strongly. Liberals were however to succeed in extracting a pledge from the president of the European Commission to publish the membership lists of its many policy advisory groups.

Market opening directives

The EU's leaders were worried about the state of Europe's economy. It was characterised, the European Council noted, by intensified competition from abroad, an ageing population, higher energy prices and the need to safeguard energy security. Reducing unemployment and raising productivity remained key challenges for the EU, as identified in a report piloted through Parliament in June 2005 by Lithuanian Liberal Ona Jukneviciene[267]. While member states had drawn up national reform programmes, at EU level structural changes such as market opening were also needed.

The Commission had been embarrassed by revelations that mergers involving banks and energy companies in a number of EU member states had been blocked by their own governments. Legal proceedings were instigated against the offending parties. Italy's minister of economy and finance, Giulio Tremonti, had spoken of an economic patriotism akin to that immediately before the 1914-18 war. When Parliament debated the matter on 15 March 2006 I pointed out the irony that 'this so called patriotism – thinly disguised economic nationalism – will bring as few benefits to the citizens of France, Spain or Poland [the offending countries] as it does to the rest of Europe, for it is fair competition that drives the global market, raises quality and lowers prices'. The great success of the euro was that mergers and taleovers were proceeding apace; European industry was gearing up for the challenges of competing in a global economy.

Two market-related directives were to keep Parliament busy early in 2006. The first, the port services directive, was so strongly opposed by French and some other trade unions that Strasbourg saw its most violent protests yet as thousands of dockers descended on the European Parliament, smashing windows and putting 17 policemen into hospital. As I opened my group's meeting on 16 January we could hear the sound of missiles being hurled and tear gas cannisters being fired. It was a pointless protest, since the major political groups had already decided to reject the draft legislation, which was in any case poorly thought through; it was not one of the Commission's more inspired initiatives. But when the representative of my local trade union came to see me the following day I told him the protest had done their case more harm than good.

The other was the directive to open up the market in trade in services. That an undertaker from Belgium could not provide services across the

---

267 Jukneviciene was a prime architect of the European Globalisation Adjustment Fund, ensuring it met Liberal concerns that it should not distort competition. A 31 July 2009 report from the European Commission details the remarkable success of this fund in helping into new jobs those made redundant as a result of global competitive pressures.

border in France or a builder from Poland bid for work in Germany was a hindrance to economic growth; yet since the outcry from the left against Commissioner Bolkestein's first draft services directive the bureaucrats had run for cover and were leaving the legislation to Council and Parliament to frame. In Parliament, some forces within the EPP sought a deal with the Liberals for an ambitious market opening; others sought to cobble together a compromise with the Socialists. It seemed the latter were in the majority.

The main point of contention was the 'country of origin' principle under which a service provider whose qualifications were recognised in one EU country should not be impeded from offering services in other EU countries. Removing that principle from the draft directive, as sought by many on the left, would reduce the growth-creating impact of the directive by half. If we could create a single market in services to rival our single market in goods, however, it was estimated that we would raise GDP by nearly 2% and create up to two and a half million new jobs. 'This parliament must make a choice', I said in the debate on 14 February 2006: 'down the route of reform lies a dynamic, competitive Union which creates jobs, wealth and opportunity for its citizens. Down the path of protectionism lies short-term gain for some and long-term loss for all, especially our twenty million unemployed'.

At the end of January Commissioner McCreevy had sought me out to know the Liberals' position. I told him we wanted a purposeful directive and would not vote for a deal which made so many concessions to the left that it would be worthless. This was not what McCreevy wanted to hear: he told me he simply wanted a directive adopted with a sufficient majority in Parliament to have a chance of securing a majority in Council. My refusal to commit my troops clearly worried him so much that Barroso rang me, pleading for a wide consensus. By the time the college of commissioners discussed the matter in mid-February, however, the dice had already rolled[268]. Parliament was inching its way towards a solution and was due to vote on the matter after the Grand Coalition in Berlin, which was increasingly making its presence felt in the corridors of Brussels, had blessed a clumsy compromise between two mutually exclusive concepts of the market cooked up primarily by German MEPs. Liberals had secured little input into the legislation, partly because the MEPs we had designated to handle the matter did not give it the attention it deserved. By the time I realised this and stepped in to act, it was too late, although I was able to unite my colleagues in support of the final text, recognising that we could muster no majority for our amendments. For a second month running there was a massive public demonstration outside the European Parliament in Strasbourg, this time estimated at around 30,000 people. As Liberals perceived it, those in comfortable jobs were protecting their own privileges at the cost of denying

---

268   I took phone calls on 14 February from Commissioners Kallas and Kroes, both unhappy with the compromise which had been shaped in Parliament and Council. Danish PM Anders Fogh Rasmussen urged me to support the Berlin compromise. Barroso and McCreevy, eager to foster consensus, told me that my criticism of the first reading compromise was too harsh. They argued that it preserved more or less intact the 'country of origin' principle and was thus faithful to the Commission's original proposal. In my view much would depend on how the ECJ interpreted it. In any case, I had economic Liberal principles to defend to keep my troops happy.

work to the EU's (predominantly young) unemployed citizens. The services directive was approved at first reading in a vote on 14 February[269].

On 20 February 2006 the European Parliament's economic affairs committee held a supper in Parliament with ECB governor Jean-Claude Trichet as the guest of honour. To the evident discomfort of his fellow French citizen and committee chair Pervenche Beres (a Socialist MEP), Trichet proceeded to give a brilliant analysis of why the EU was failing economically and to berate MEPs for lacking the courage sufficiently to open the market in services.

Trichet also implicitly criticised the Commission, which had published at the end of January a report on the Lisbon competitiveness agenda, outlining the obstacles to progress, but which had failed to press for the policies needed to lift them. Earlier that day I had lunched with Commissioner Kallas, who had expressed concern about Barroso's way of dealing with these matters; while Prodi would have a debate in the college and draw conclusions afterwards, he told me, Barroso sought to strike a deal with the commissioner concerned and to force the subsequent agreement through the college of commisioners.

Innovation was needed too. The heads of state and government had asked former Finnish Liberal prime minister Esko Aho to draw up a report on technological innovation. The report, 'Creating an innovative Europe', laid the basis for the competitiveness and innovation programme adopted by the Council in June 2005. And to improve levels of education, the European Council in March 2006 was to commit itself to ensuring that by 2010, 85% of 22 year olds should have completed upper secondary level education.

A budget deal

The UK presidency's main achievement was to be securing agreement on the EU's 'financial perspectives' (pluri-annual budget, in this case 2007-12). Blair was prepared to envisage a reduction in the UK's annual rebate, which otherwise – as a perverse effect of the enlargement of the EU – would grow considerably at the expense of some of the EU's poorest countries. But at the same time he wanted to cut regional spending in the ten new member states by 10% and in the older member states by 41%, which would save the UK exchequer a substantial proportion of what it would forego in lost rebate. Moreover, he sought agreement on further reform of the CAP, though a deal he had signed three years earlier had only just entered into effect and was intended to last until 2008.

Though Blair was simply following the logic of his agreement with Chirac and Schroeder two years earlier[270] that the EU budget should be capped at

---

269 In the debate that day, PES leader Martin Schulz had said: 'Bolkestein is no more. That is the first piece of good news to come out of this debate'. I retorted: 'I can assure the House that Frits Bolkestein is alive and kicking and that is why Martin Schulz is looking so bruised'.

270 On 14 December 2003 President Chirac and five prime ministers - Blair, Schroeder, Balkenende, Persson and Schuessel - had signed a letter to Prodi calling for EU spending to be capped at 1% of the Union's gross national income.

1% of GDP, he came under attack from all sides. European Parliament president Borrell accepted unwisely from a leading adviser a suggestion that Parliament should take a stand as an institution: Commission president Barroso went dangerously off-message in a debate in Strasbourg, allowing the applause of MEPs for his attacks on the UK to goad him into the dangerous quicksands of unscripted remarks, and calling the UK's proposals 'dogmatic' and 'unacceptable'. Hapless British EU affairs minister Douglas Alexander was sent into the Strasbourg chamber on the morning of the day on which the official proposals were to be published, to defend his government's position while giving no hint of matters to come in the afternoon.

Speaking for the Liberals I castigated national leaders who 'simultaneously demanded of the Union policies that they are not prepared to finance'. This agreement on financial perspectives had been expected to pay the costs incumbent on a Union of 25. Yet what had the new member states found in their brave new world?, I asked. 'A French president who tells them to shut up, a German prime minister who denies them their own tax policies and a British presidency which moves the goalposts of solidarity.'[271]

Yet reporting to Parliament on 20 December from the EU Council meeting, Blair exuded confidence. He had secured a deal and knew that this brought a sense of relief to many. The UK newspapers were up in arms about Barroso's appeal for a 'euro tax' to provide a less divisive way of financing the EU. Blair had opened accession negotiations with Turkey and had seen EU candidate status granted to Macedonia. And, in an impressive performance, he rounded on the UKIP MEPs and gave them what for. Parliaments love theatre: MEPs were treated to a star performance and rose to the occasion. As the party group leaders set off to Vienna to meet the incoming Austrian presidency, nobody expected Prime Minister Schuessel to offer quite the same degree of excitement.

The European Parliament is, with the Council of Ministers, a joint arm of the EU budgetary authority. However, the treaties leave to the member states in Council the duty of determining the size of the budget. In June 2005 the European Parliament approved a report by a special committee established to look into the EU's budgetary needs from 2007 to 2013. German Christian Democrat rapporteur Reimer Boege had been much assisted in his work by Liberal MEP Anne Jensen. They had identified a need for 1.18% of GNI – some EUR 47 billion below the 1.24% of GNI sought by the European Commission.

However the restriction of the EU budget agreed under the UK presidency to just 1.045% of GNI for the period 2007-12 was, in the view of most MEPs, too mean to meet the policy demands placed on the EU by the member states who set it. It would have meant little money for R&D projects and cuts in programmes such as the Erasmus student exchange programme, which had boosted EU consciousness hugely through the

271 Chirac had infamously said at a press conference that some of the new member states 'would have been better advised to keep quiet' and Schroeder had expressed concern about corporate tax competition from the new member states.

financing of over one and a half million individual student exchanges. These were among the reasons why, on 18 January 2006, Parliament voted to reject the Council's budget. The rejection was mainly symbolic. It meant that the Council would have to come to Parliament and negotiate to find an agreement which would either provide more money or find creative accounting methods to allow for the proper funding of core policies.

Underlying the debate was a long-standing controversy about how the EU is paid for. This matter had been discussed for years and remained unresolved. Chancellor Schuessel of Austria plunged into it in January by suggesting a tax on capital transactions to fund the Union. The Commission was preparing other options.

The Council initially refused to put more money on the table. Parliament's budgets committee invited the head of the European Investment Bank, Philippe Maystadt, to explain how private money might be leveraged to permit the financing of trans-European transport networks or R&D projects; but while some of the shortfall might be made up, he described as 'a pipe dream' the belief that loans could be used to cover cuts in spending. I discussed the matter over supper with Barroso on 14 March and drew attention to the problem in a speech in Parliament the following day. By 10 April Parliament's budget team had managed to squeeze an extra EUR 4bn from the member states for the seven-year period – enough to make the cuts to the Erasmus programme less severe. Jan Mulder MEP also managed to persuade them finally to take full responsibility for the spending of EU funds in their countries through the provision of an annual 'statement of assurance' that spending had been audited in areas where the EU's Court of Auditors did not have the right to check their books. This paved the way to the Court of Auditors agreeing to sign off the EU's accounts, healing a matter which had been a longstanding sore.

Environment policy

Environment policy had again been a major area of work for Liberals in the European Parliament. Belgian MEP Frederique Ries had steered through the House legislation on eco-design and an action plan on environment and health; Holger Krahmer was in the process of guiding legislation on the recycling of motor cars. Jules Maaten was Parliament's champion of legislation to improve the standard of bathing water off Europe's beaches and Philippe Morillon on protecting fish stocks, especially those of sole. Anne Lapperouze was Parliament's rapporteur for European energy networks, essential to environmental policy.

The biggest single piece of legislation under consideration, however, was a directive about protecting consumers from harmful chemicals. From the time of the famous Seveso directive in 1982, after an accident at a chemical factory in northern Italy in July 1976 had left 447 people with skin lesions or chloracne, 15 children in hospital with inflammation of the skin and over 3000 animals dead, the EU had taken seriously public health as a part of environment policy. Following a campaign by civil society the Commission had agreed to legislate to control the growing use of untested chemicals and chemical compounds in everyday products, which some medical experts believed to be linked to the rise in cancer rates and other illnesses. Thus the

REACH (Registration, Evaluation and Authorisation of Chemical Substances) directive had been born and was under consideration in committee. While the rapporteur for the leading committee, the committee on the environment and public health, was Socialist MEP Guido Sacconi, Liberals had secured the leading role in consideration of the report in the industry committee, which I was pleased to entrust to Swedish MEP Lena Ek. Liberals were to play an important role in brokering the necessary compromises. Good teamwork by ALDE's leading spokespeople on the three committees concerned – environment (Chris Davies), industry (Lena Ek) and internal market (Alexander Lambsdorff) – meant that the group was able to reach a broad measure of agreement in the vote at first reading on 17 November 2005. Since others were divided, we won many of the votes.

Under the UK presidency there had been discussion about climate change and energy security. The European Union had been the key actor in the adoption of the UN's Framework Convention on Climate Change and its Kyoto protocol in 1997. It was seriously concerned about climate change and had resolved to act to mitigate it. While Japan and the USA were making little progress in meeting their climate change targets, the EU was: US emissions had grown by 13% above 1990 levels while the EU's had fallen by 5.5%. The European Commission – under constant pressure from the European Parliament – was working to cut the EU's carbon emissions further. Thus in December 2005 the European Parliament approved a measure presented by Commissioner Piebalgs to require member states, over a period of five years, to make energy savings of at least 9% through improving the efficiency of energy end use. The directive on energy end use efficiency and energy services, heavily lobbied against by the major energy companies but welcomed by Liberals, sought to encourage consumers to save energy by making them more aware of the amount of energy they were using. While Liberals had sought a target of 11% savings and to make the target binding, we supported the measure as – in the words of Fiona Hall MEP – 'a step in the right direction'. There was little in the treaties about the adoption of a common energy policy. On 7 December 2005 the Commission adopted a biomass action plan designed to increase the production of energy from forestry, agriculture and waste, prepared by agriculture commissioner Franz Fischler, an Austrian who was keen that progress should be made on biomass promotion under the Austrian presidency. Fischler foresaw 20 separate initiatives by the Commission to increase the amount of biomass used for energy production from 69 million tonnes in 2003 to 150 million by 2010, allowing the EU to cut energy imports by over 6% and bring up to 300,000 jobs to rural areas. Liberals welcomed Fischler's initiative.

The Middle East

Liberals were increasingly united about the rights and wrongs of the situation in the Middle East. Whereas previously Israel had been viewed as the victim of hostile Arab neighbours, now Israel was seen more and more as the aggressor and its policy of rapidly expanding settlements beyond its pre-June 1967 borders perceived as provocative. Under EU pressure, Palestine's government had conceded parliamentary elections in January 2006; these were supervised and monitored by EU observers. When Hamas beat Fatah at the polls it came as a surprise only to those who knew little of party politics in Palestine[272], where Fatah had become increasingly arrogant and uncaring and Hamas had acted as the champion of the downtrodden citizen.

Javier Solana had worked hard to make the EU a key player in setting Middle East policy in the 'quartet'. Yet MEPs were frustrated that the Americans still called most of the shots in the Middle East. We wanted a distinctive European approach, less uncritically supportive of Israel. Chris Patten, who had been external relations commissioner under Prodi, had frequently gained the approval of Parliament in arguing for a change of approach. When I suggested to Solana in a parliamentary debate early in February that MEPs wanted to see him rather more often in Parliament and rather less often on the TV screens I spoke for many colleagues, across the political spectrum[273]. It was perhaps not until early February 2006, when Muslims rioted and torched the Middle Eastern embassies of EU member states in protest against the publication, in Danish and other countries' newspapers, of cartoons they considered offensive, that the full extent of the challenge was appreciated. Agreeing with Sigmund Freud that the first person who hurled an insult rather than a rock was the founder of civilisation, and aware that Jews are regularly satirised and insulted in some Arab newspapers, I secured statements to Parliament from Commission and Council, to be followed by debate, on 15 February[274].

Parliament was due to be be addressed by Palestinian president and Fatah leader Mahmoud Abbas on 15 March 2006, but before he was able to speak Abbas had to return home in a hurry to deal with the Israeli siege of a prison in Jericho, which UK and US monitors had left, mysteriously, just before the attack and which in itself became the subject of a parliamentary debate.

Despite having urged and overseen the election in Palestine, the EU's foreign ministers had warned after the elections that they would cut off aid to Palestine unless Hamas renounced violence and recognised Israel's right to exist. Hamas failed to comply, though a ceasefire it had announced still held; the EU duly moved at the end of April to cut off aid to the Palestinian Authority, though pledging still to give humanitarian aid to international agencies working there. An EP delegation to Palestine reported that the decision was perceived by Palestinians as punishment for having elected Hamas into office; indeed, it was polarising opinion on all sides[275]; but most

---

272   Including many of the world's political and business leaders who were meeting at the self-styled World Economic Forum in Davos at the time.

273   Solana was to appoint on 29 January 2007 a personal representative responsible for relations with the European Parliament.

274   I was to choose not to lead for ALDE in the debate for two reasons. Denmark's prime minister, Anders Fogh Rasmussen, was keen that the matter should be played down as much as possible (telcon Mon 13 February 2006): and Nyrup Rasmussen was to lead for the PES rather than Schulz. ALDE deputy leader and Danish MEP Karin Riis-Joergensen therefore led for the Liberal group in the debate.

275   Chris Davies MEP, a Liberal member of the EP's delegation, had written an impassioned letter to *The Daily Telegraph* underlining the terrible plight of the Palestinians. Replying late at night to an email from a constituent who had been incensed by his 'anti-semitic' stance he let fly at her. She released his intemperate response to London's Jewish News, from where the broadsheet newspapers picked it up. In the resulting outcry Chris was obliged to resign from his post as leader of the UK Liberal Democrat delegation in the ALDE group. He was to be succeeded by Diana Wallis MEP.

Liberals were concerned that failure to work with an elected government simply gave the initiative to others, like Iran and the Gulf States, who stepped in to offer alternative financial support. Indeed, when Mahmoud Abbas, one of the authors of the Oslo agreements, finally addressed the European Parliament on 17 May 2005 his message was clear: an accommodation with Hamas had to be reached if progress towards peace was to be made.

On 2 May 2006 I met Leila Shahid, general delegate (ambassador) of the Palestinian Authority to the EU. She too urged that an exit strategy be found for Hamas, perhaps based on the plan put forward four years earlier by Prince Abdullah of Saudi Arabia under which all 23 Arab countries would collectively recognise the State of Israel. By late June, Hamas was to recognise – implicitly, at least – Israel's right to exist. But by mid-July the situation was to deteriorate badly with Israel's decision to start bombing the Lebanon in retaliation for Hizbollah rocket attacks on Haifa; within days it was to become all-out war.

The 34-day war in the Lebanon led to serious concerns about the country's sovereignty, unity and independence. 200,000 people were forced out of their homes and crucial infrastructure destroyed. Unexploded cluster bombs were still killing and injuring people, particularly children. There was particular concern about the incidents on the Blue Line on 28 May. Over lunch with Romano Prodi on 20 August 2006 in Castiglione della Pescaia[276] I discussed how best the EU could react to the crisis. Since Italy had closer commercial ties with the Lebanon than most EU countries, Prodi had assumed a co-ordinating role within the Council of Ministers.

On 25 August the foreign affairs ministers met in Lappeenranta, in Finland. They pledged 7000 troops to UNIFIL, to stabilise the situation in southern Lebanon, cut off the flow of arms to Hizbollah guerillas operating there and support the humanitarian effort. Javier Solana described it as the most important decision taken by the EU for many years. But Liberals worried that UNIFIL's mandate was unclear, that there was apparently no action aimed at lifting Israel's air and sea blockade of the Lebanon or its blockade of the Gaza Strip. Many agreed with Kofi Annan, who said it would not be through the barrel of a gun but as a result of dialogue and compromise that Hizbollah fighters would put down their weapons and negotiate a long-term solution.

On 6 September 2006 the House debated the situation. I was sharply critical of Solana's absence; he had sent Finnish foreign minister Erkki Tuomioja instead. When MEPs had asked about the rules of engagement they had been told by the Council that these were 'strictly a matter between the United Nations and the troop contributors'. As I pointed out in the debate, however, 'the European public at large believe that Europe has responded to the crisis. If things go wrong and we have large numbers of young men coming back home in body bags, people will want to know who in Europe is responsible'.

---

276   Prodi was now Italy's prime minister. The lunch was interrupted by phone calls from Solana, Erdogan and others.

Parliament adopted a resolution on 7 September 2006 which included Liberal calls for the establishment of a Euro-Mediterranean development bank as the best guarantor of lasting peace and human development and an enhanced role for the Euro-Mediterranean Parliamentary Assembly. We believed that peace in the region would depend, as in Europe, on building stable institutions. We also favoured a standing conference on security and co-operation in the Mediterranean and the establishment of two new universities, one to the north and one to the south of the basin, to promote shared understanding of each other's culture. Parliament also approved a proposal by the ALDE group to invite Lebanon's prime minister Fouad Siniora to address us, though when he came later in the month we were to find his address harsh and uncompromising and were to send him away with a flea in his ear[277].

The European Union was ready to host an international conference to support Lebanon as soon as it undertook the economic and political reforms agreed in UNSC resolutions 1559 and 1680. It was anticipated that the conference could be held in Paris in February 2007. But by the end of 2006 the situation had deteriorated further: both Israel and Syria continued to interfere and on 21 November 2006 industry minister Pierre Gemayel was assassinated, the fifth prominent anti-Syrian figure to be killed there in two years.

Not all the news from the Middle East was discouraging, however. When the Persian Gulf state of Qatar decided to enfranchise women, Liberals sought to use the news to draw attention to the case for similar political rights for women elsewhere in the region. Thus on International Women's Day on 8 March 2007 Liberal MEPs Emma Nicholson and Karin Riis chaired conferences on women in Iraq and in Turkey respectively. We believed that women would increasingly play an important role in development and sought to promote this. We agreed with John Kenneth Galbraith that the education and empowerment of women was the single most powerful factor in development.

Liberalism and globalisation

The divisions in the European Parliament on how to react to global pressures were the subject of a book I launched in January 2006 entitled *Liberal Democracy and Globalisation*, to which twenty of my colleagues had each contributed an essay. A previous attempt of mine to compile a coherent series of the views of leading Liberals about globalisation had been published in August of 2001; in view of the world-changing events of the following month it was almost immediately outdated. This collection showed Liberals united on one side of the new axis in politics: as 'drawbridge down' rather than 'drawbridge up' politicians. Since this axis divided the other major political families, Liberal unity had increasingly become a source of strength.

---

277 'Few of us here see the conflict in the way you have presented it to us today', I told him. I reminded him of Israel's right to exist, of Hizbollah's talk of armed conflict continuing after Israeli withdrawal and of the regular abuse of the Israeli people in the press across the Arab world.

The impact of the Al Qaida attacks on the USA had indeed changed the world and largely in a direction unwelcome to Liberals. Across the Atlantic, the optimism of the Clinton years had given way to the pessimism of George W. Bush's administration. 'Enemy combatants' were detained without trial at Guantanamo Bay in breach of international law; war had been waged on Afghanistan and Iraq; and brutal dictatorships around the world suddenly found themselves the friends of the West and were assisted in repression of their own people in the name of the fight against terror[278]. In the balancing of public security with civil liberties, Liberals were everywhere on the back foot, it seemed. In Canada, the Liberals were ousted by the Conservatives in January 2006 after being in power for the greater part of the previous century.

Liberals have traditionally been concerned to see the rule of law applied with due process. On 20 February 2006 the United Nations published a report on the prison camp at Guantanamo Bay. At the ALDE group's initiative, Parliament debated the issue the same day. MEPs resolved to call for the immediate closure of the camp and for trial of the 500 detainees in accordance with international law. It was by no means our first debate on the matter, or likely to have George Bush rushing to sign a closure order, but in politics it is important not to allow continuing injustices to be forgotten. Opposition to Guantanamo within the USA was also building and at the end of June the US Supreme Court would rule on the legality of trial by Military Tribunal. When three detainees committed suicide one weekend in June, after four years of incarceration in legal limbo, I used a speech in Parliament to urge Europe's leaders to put the issue at the top of their agenda for the EU-US summit on 21 June 2006.

In a similar vein, Liberals had pressed for and obtained the establishment of a special committee on the suspected use by the CIA of EU infrastructure for the transport and detention of prisoners bound for Guantanamo. This work had been started by a Liberal on the Parliamentary Assembly of the Council of Europe, the Swiss MP Dick Marty, whose pioneering research had uncovered much circumstantial evidence of the collusion of EU governments in the transit of suspects for the purposes of torture. The European Parliament's temporary committee on illegal rendition, established in January 2006, was to give the issue a greater salience than was possible in the relatively obscure Council of Europe assembly. When Parliament adopted the committee's final report in February 2007 it showed an embarrassing degree of complicity of some EU governments in the rendition of terrorist suspects. Yet despite heavy lobbying of MEPs by the governments named and shamed, criticism of these governments was in proportion to their apparent complicity. I noted in my diary at the time: 'It was Parliament at its best: measured, objective, determined to prevent similar practices in future'.

On 21 February the ALDE group hosted a networking breakfast for ministers from Liberal parties attending that day's meeting of the Justice and

---

278   Probably the most galling of such cases was that of Karim Asimov of Uzbekistan, whose outrages became the subject of a bestselling book by my former Young Liberal colleague and UK diplomat Craig Murray.

Home Affairs Council. I had established such networks across the spectrum of Council formations since the greater use of co-decision required better party political co-ordination between national government ministers and MEPs. The networks worked with varying degrees of success and only during the months when the Council met in Brussels rather than Luxembourg, but on this occasion five MEPs from Parliament's justice and home affairs committee met five ministers for breakfast at the Silken Hotel. That one of our MEPs, Antoine ('Tony') Duquesne, had recently served as Belgium's interior minister was of great assistance in our talks on immigration and other items on the Council's agenda and in facilitating the discussion of delicate issues such as illegal rendition. That we were to be robbed of Tony's immense powers of political analysis, his huge experience and his delightful political incisiveness barely a fortnight later, when he suffered a major stroke which was to leave him permanently incapacitated, is my major personal regret of the 2004-09 parliamentary mandate. No other former Belgian minister in Parliament possessed any of his charm or savoir-faire.

A long period of reflection

The Austrian presidency had started 2006 on something of a false note in announcing that it wished to revive the Constitutional Treaty. It had been widely felt that the 'period of reflection' should continue throughout 2006 and that the matter would be revisited under the German presidency of the EU in 2007. A distinctly lukewarm response from Chirac and a blunt No from the Netherlands' foreign minister sent Austria a clear message that as far as the two countries which had rejected the constitution were concerned, this was not on.

Liberals were divided over how and when to revisit the increasingly obvious need for constitutional reform. We kicked off the New Year with a conference entitled 'Communicating Europe', united in our belief that until national governments pulled their weight in explaining the benefits of the EU to their electorates there would be no chance of gaining public approval for treaty changes in all member states. Yet the December 2005 European Council had received an interim report from the UK and Austrian presidencies on national debates on the future of Europe underway in all member states which showed that little of substance was being done in this regard, other than in Liberal-led Belgium, Denmark, Estonia and Finland, where programmes of debates with citizens right down to village level were being delivered.

Actions on sorting out the mess left by the French and Dutch rejections of the EU's Constitutional Treaty were otherwise few and far between. Addressing the College of Europe in Bruges in October 2005 I gave a Liberal analysis of the problem. Where Monnet, Schuman, Adenauer and others had risen to the challenges of their times, I said, Europe's present leaders must rise to the challenges of ours. Leadership was needed by statesmen who defined a vision and prepared the path towards it – not by politicians who pored over opinion polls and preached popular prejudice back to their citizens. The Commission had given us a 'Plan D for dialogue', I noted; but we needed a 'Plan V for vision' and a 'Plan L for leadership'.

Liberal-led EU governments were showing such leadership. Liberal-led Belgium in February and Liberal-led Estonia in May 2006 brought to 14 and then 15 the number of countries which had ratified and many Liberals believed there might yet be life in the Constitutional Treaty. When Alexander Beels and I visited Prime Ministers Vanhanen and Ansip in Helsinki and Tallinn respectively on 6 March, both maintained their view that ratification of the treaty should proceed; although Vanhanen felt it unlikely that much progress could be made in 2006, he undertook at my suggestion to endeavour to see it ratified in Finland before the end of his country's presidency of the EU in the latter half of the year.

In the European Parliament too, Liberals were working on the involvement of citizens. Hannu Takkula MEP drafted a report entitled 'A Europe for Citizens 2007-13', in response to proposals by the Commission, which was adopted by the House on 25 October 2006. Irish MEP Marian Harkin succeeded, through a series of initiatives in the House, in having the role of the active citizen in society taken more seriously and having 2011 designated as the first European Year on Volunteering. They understood that by treating citizens merely as consumers, society was robbing itself of the civic freedom by which we control the aggregate outcomes of individual choices.

We were working on the promotion of women in the EU too. In 2005 the ELDR Party had elected a woman leader[279], Annemie Neyts MEP, and shortly thereafter appointed a woman, Federica Sabbati, as party general secretary.[280] Liberals had succeeded in increasing the number of women in the college of commissioners, thanks in large measure to pressure on Barroso, and two of them – Mariann Fischer Boel and Neelie Kroes – were among the stars of the Commission. Polish commissioner Danuta Huebner suggested she might also join the Liberal family; she had been appointed as a technocrat but showed sympathy for Liberal ideas. I had arranged for her to visit my constituency to meet Liberals in local government and at the invitation of ALDE MEPs Bronislaw Geremek and Janusz Onyskiewicz I met her in February.

The Austrian presidency made some progress in convincing national governments of the need to communicate better to their citizens the values and principles guiding the development of the EU. At the end of January it organised a conference in Salzburg under the title 'The Sound of Europe'; on 8 and 9 May the European Parliament and the Austrian Parliament co-hosted a joint parliamentary meeting on 'The Future of Europe'. The European Commission rolled out its 'Plan D' (for democracy, dialogue and debate), designed to bring the EU closer to its citizens by informing them better. Drawing on a paper from the Commission entitled 'A citizen's agenda for Europe', each member state government agreed to put effort into better explanation to citizens of decisions taken at EU level. Moreover the European Council adopted a policy of transparency 'aiming at stronger

279   I had been instrumental in this election, persuading the UK Liberal Democrat delegates and many others to switch their support from Netherlands' candidate Jozias van Aartsen to Annemie Neyts.

280   In 2008 the ELDR Party was to mark the progress of women within its ranks by publishing a calendar depicting leading Liberal women (in suitably conservative apparel and surroundings).

involvement of citizens in the work of the Union'; it extended the 'period of reflection' on the EU constitution but foresaw the adoption, on 27 March 2007 in Berlin, of a political declaration setting out the EU's values and ambitions. The Commission decided to make all new consultative papers and legislative proposals available immediately to national parliaments, inviting their comment, and to agree new rules on 'comitology'[281] with the European Parliament which would give MEPs the chance to inspect how legislation was working and the right to recall and review it.

German president Horst Koehler addressed Parliament on 14 March 2006. He pointed out that the German expression for a period of reflection, *Denkpause*, could mean both a pause *for* thought and a pause *in* thought and pleaded that it should be the former, calling for 'in-depth discussion in the member states about the purpose and substance of European integration'. The Constitutional Treaty, he said, contained much that is good and right and should not too readily be surrendered 'not least in view of the fact that 14 member states have already voted to approve it'. While the Party of European Socialists sought to use rejection of the treaty to argue for greater social protection, the European People's Party used it to argue against further expansion of the EU, for which they secured a parliamentary debate that week. Liberals believed that both liberalisation of the economy and openness to candidates for membership were important; we won an important battle in Strasbourg in April 2006 when the European Parliament called for free access to the labour markets of the EU15 for workers from the ten member states which had joined in 2004. However we felt the Union needed to communicate better to its citizens the benefits they received from use of the current treaty powers before asking again for their approval of new powers. I used the occasion of the ELDR's 30th anniversary celebrations in Stuttgart, the city in which the European Liberal Democrat Party had been founded in 1976[282], to argue for greater promotion of the EU's achievements. 'In the Stuttgart Declaration of 1976 we resolved to protect and promote people's rights and freedoms', I said. '30 years later we have a European charter of fundamental rights and a nascent human rights agency[283] … we resolved to create a European polity underpinning a free society. 30 years on we have a European Parliament whose powers are growing inexorably, a Council which meets regularly and a courageous Court of Justice. 30 years ago we promised a decent life to our citizens. Now the European single market is an engine for growth, prosperity and security. It is Liberal ideology which provides the tool-box for the breakdowns of the modern world.'

Liberals argued too for greater devolution of power to Europe's regions, many of which were nations which had lost out in the 17th century development of the nation state. We held a conference devoted to the topic in the Aland Islands of Finland in the presence of Prime Minister Vanhanen. The

---

281   The committee system which oversees the delegated acts implemented by the European Commission.

282   At the initiative of the Liberal group in the (then appointed) European Parliament.

283   The EUMC on Racism and Xenophobia in Vienna was due to be upgraded in March 2007 to an EU Agency for Fundamental Rights, though with fewer powers over national administrations than Liberals sought.

ALDE group contained many representatives of such regions: from Scotland, Catalonia and Sicily to name just three. There was a consensus of opinion that – within the framework of the European Union – American Liberal president Woodrow Wilson's doctrine of the self-determination of nations could unfold further without bloodshed. This expressed itself in our subsequent support for the greater recognition accorded to the Catalan and Irish Gaelic languages by the institutions of the EU.

In March 2006, as Jose Manuel Barroso celebrated his 50th birthday at a party in the European Parliament together with a political group leader (your author) who was four hours his senior, he might well have reflected ruefully that his Union was in the throes of a mid-life crisis. The conclusions of the March European Council, which had taken place on his birthday, were just so much blah-blah. They willed ends without providing means and used words about economic reform in directly inverse proportion to the amount of action. The Union was unable to make fast enough progress in economic reform, unable to secure the tools it needed for better administration of its affairs and unable to promote itself effectively – for want of legal powers – in the world at large. How much narrower were the opportunities open to Barroso from those which had presented themselves to Delors, almost exactly thirty years his senior? In Delors' day the drive for European integration had come from the statesmen within rather than from the pressures of the outside world on the new century's politicians who were uniting, if at all, mainly out of fear. In Delors' day the elasticity of public acceptance for the building of the EU had been so much greater.

To promote discussion of ways out of the constitutional crisis, Barroso gathered together his 24 fellow commissioners at the end of April 2006 for a full day's strategy discussion on the future of the EU. There had been a similar meeting the previous September. But this time he also took the initiative of inviting Parliament's group leaders on 2 May to the Berlaymont to report on the Commission's deliberations and to seek our views. We gathered around the large triangular table in the 13th floor meeting room normally reserved for the Wednesday morning meetings of the college of commissioners, to be told that the Commission would take no initiative at present on the future of the Constitutional Treaty; the member countries had to decide how they wanted to proceed, Barroso told us. I could imagine no previous president of the Commission relinquishing in such fashion the Commission's role as legal guardian of the EU treaties[284]. But, given that this was the case, the member states had to make their voices heard. I therefore proposed shortly thereafter that Parliament invite the heads of state and government of the member states to come and debate with us their ideas about the future of our Union. President Borrell took up my suggestion with alacrity, though it set a precedent, and thus we were to debate with Belgian prime minister Guy Verhofstadt on 31 May 2006, with Irish prime minister Bertie Ahern on 29 November 2006, with Italian prime minister Romano Prodi and Dutch prime minister Jan Peter Balkenende on 22 and 23 May

---

284   With the possible exception of Francois-Xavier Ortoli.

2007, French president Nicolas Sarkozy on 13 November 2007, Spanish prime minister Jose Luis Rodriguez Zapatero on 28 November 2007 and with Swedish prime minister Fredrik Reinfeldt on 19 February 2008. I had pressed for Chirac to come, but he no doubt did not wish to have to explain his failure in the French referendum.

Meanwhile the European Parliament chose 9 May 2006, Schuman Day, to host an inter-parliamentary meeting. The conference showed a remarkable degree of consensus, across national and party boundaries, that a 25 country union needed a constitution, and if it could not agree the one signed by its member states in November 2004 then it had better agree what changes were needed. Only the UK's Conservative representatives, led by MP David Heathcoat-Amory – and a few right-wing Czechs and Poles (with whom the Conservative MEPs were to team up in the subsequent European Parliament) – were opposed to the idea of a constitution for the EU.

Together with our leader in the Belgian Chamber of Representatives, Herman de Croo, I had co-hosted a supper at the Palais d'Egmont the previous evening (8 May 2006) for the 40 or so Liberal MPs who had made the journey to Brussels from their national capitals. We welcomed the Commission's launch of an online discussion on the EU's future, seeking the views of citizens across the Union. We also welcomed two decisions which presaged the new treaty. One was the agreement reached at the March 2006 European Council on energy security; as long as individual member states sought to do private energy deals with Russia there would be no security of supply from a country which practised a policy of divide and rule. The second was the Union's decision to send a military force to the Democratic Republic of Congo, another example of what could be gained by EU countries pooling their resources and seeking a common response to global challenges. Moreover, a review of the functioning of the European arrest warrant, published in mid-March 2006, had shown how we could win in the fight against crime by making extradition a matter of administrative rather than judicial co-operation. In short, we saw a European Union where the benefits of co-operation and the development of a common culture added to the freedom enjoyed by EU citizens and their governments' ability to defend their interests and promote their values.

All it needed was a proper legal base for the development of such co-operation. Why was it that national governments were communicating so little of this to their citizens?

The euro

The main recent success of the Union was proving to be the euro, a common currency in twelve member states. Already established as a reserve currency competing with the dollar, it had brought down the cost of doing business across frontiers considerably. Liberals were keen that other countries should join as soon as possible. We took up the cudgels for Lithuania's entry following a visit to Vilnius arranged in March 2006 by Ona Jukneviciene MEP, who had fixed meetings with the finance minister, the governor of the central bank and other government and central bank officials.

Lithuania's case for joining pivoted on an interesting legal conundrum.

Their inflation rate was slightly above the level stipulated in the convergence criteria contained within the Maastricht Treaty; but this was largely due to Russia's oil price hike. Giving Russia the power of veto over Baltic countries joining the eurozone seemed of dubious political wisdom. Moreover the inflation rate was calculated in relation to the average rate of inflation of the three countries with the lowest level of inflation in the European System of Central Banks[285] rather than simply those in the eurozone; if calculated in relation to the three eurozone members with the lowest levels of inflation, Lithuania met the criteria. Moreover its rate of economic growth, a healthy 8%, would be a boon to the eurozone economy.

The arguments which ALDE put forward through oral questions with debate were not to convince the Council of Ministers, however. In June 2006, on the basis of advice from the finance ministers and the Commission's recommendation of 16 May 2006, the European Council commended Lithuania for the convergence it had achieved and expressed its support for the stability-oriented policies of the Lithuanian government; but no invitation to join the euro was extended. Slovenia was to join in January 2007, but Lithuania would have to wait.

I recall an amusing story about our visit to Lithuania. The dinner which I hosted on Monday night for the visiting MEPs to meet leading members of our member parties there was held in an underground restaurant in the centre of town, a place of cellars and caverns by the name of *Zemaiciu*. We ate in a room laid out as if for a medieval banquet, with a throne-like arrangement for seating at the top table; three suckling pigs had been prepared for our degustation. Since neither the leader of the Darbo party nor the leader of the New Union graced us with their presence or that of their underlings, we ate only two of the pigs. Ona Jukneviciene recalled however that the governor of the Central Bank, whom we were due to visit the following day, had baulked at offering us lunch, on the grounds of our numbers and his limited budget. She instructed the restaurant to send the pig to the Bank. Unfortunately she failed to relay to the Bank the information that we would be bringing our own lunch; upon ascertaining the following morning that the roast pig they received had come from us and was intended for our consumption, the Bank's governor Reinoldijus Sarkinas was so embarrassed that he decided after all to feed us in his canteen. He had the pig put in front of us afterwards 'in case we were still hungry'.

Seven prime ministers

Two months previously, on 22 March 2006, the European Parliament had debated the role and power of EU-wide political parties. Since the adoption of a regulation on the financing of European political parties in 2003, ten parties had registered. Parliament now argued for a 'genuine' European party statute, the creation of political foundations at EU level and for EU political parties to be allowed to create limited financial reserves. Liberals

---

285   In this case, these countries were Poland, Sweden and Finland, only the last of which was a eurozone member.

argued too for the election of a percentage of MEPs on transnational lists 'to usher in a cross-border European political debate[286]'

I was working hard to consolidate the Alliance of Liberals and Democrats, with some success. The appearance of Poland's Marek Belka at the Liberal leaders' summit on 17 June 2005 had brought the number of prime ministers present to seven, our highest ever. With seven prime ministers, seven EU commissioners and 90 MEPs – and a king, no less – European Liberals, Democrats and Reformers were energising Europe like never before. On 3 February 2006 Romano Prodi had returned to Brussels to stage a rally for his supporters there in the Italian general election campaign. For the first time, Italian citizens living abroad would enjoy the right to elect their own representatives to the Italian parliament. The alliance supporting Prodi – Liberals, Greens and Socialists – remained firm, with Schulz, Cohn Bendit and I there to speak in his support. I had come from addressing 2,500 members of our French UDF party at a snow-blanketed rally in Lyon to launch Francois Bayrou's French presidency bid. The ties between Liberals and Democrats were proving strong and mutually beneficial, even if the French appeared keener on longer-term unification of our alliance than the Italians. I spoke again in Bologna later that month with Enrico Letta MEP, a candidate for ministerial office should his party triumph at the polls. And I was pleased to see at the thirtieth anniversary celebrations of the Liberal Youth Movement of the European Community, at whose founding I had participated, representatives of the youth movements of our French and Italian allies. Our alliance was developing in other assemblies too, as our new leader on the Committee of the Regions, former Rotterdam mayor Ivo Opstelten confirmed to me at a meeting in between flights at Zaventem airport on 23 February 2006.

ALDE's main Italian component was doing well in the election campaign. Invited to address a meeting of the Palombella Foundation on 22 February on the theme *Donna e laicita* (women and secularism) I had found the anti-Berlusconi camp full of optimism. And despite the European People's Party holding its annual conference in Rome a few days before the election, Romano Prodi was to clinch victory by a hair's breadth[287] in the election of 9-10 April 2006. The news a week later that our Hungarian member party SDS and its Socialist coalition partner had been returned to office was more icing on the Liberal cake.

Hitherto the European Liberal family had been only spasmodically organised. Unlike the EPP and the PES, sparse representation and the lack of central support for Liberals attending EU meetings had deprived us of a voice. One of the participants at the breakfast the ALDE group organised for justice and home affairs ministers had even remarked to the others present that 'I had no idea we were all Liberals!' The growth of Liberal political representation increased both the need for and the benefits of such co-ordination.

---

286   Speech by Jules Maaten MEP in Parliament, 22 March 2006.

287   Prodi's alliance polled 49.8% of the vote against 49.7% for Berlusconi, though in the lower House he was to win 348 seats against Berlusconi's 281. One painful consequence of Prodi's victory for me was to be the loss of valuable colleagues: MEPs Antonio di Pietro, Emma Bonino and Enrico Letta left Parliament to fill government posts in Italy.

But it had to be led from the top. So I sought out the one person who could put an official imprimatur on the process I had set in motion.

Simeon Saxe-Coburg-Gotha had been exiled from Bulgaria at the age of six after the Nazis had killed his father with a lethal dose of poisoned food and the Communists had given his mother just five days' notice to leave Bulgaria with the infant king and the rest of her family. As the train which carried them reached the border between Bulgaria and Greece in the early hours of the morning, it stopped. Simeon's mother feared they were to be taken off and shot. In fact, Simeon told us, a loyal train driver refused to be the person responsible for the exile of his country's royal family; their carriages had to wait until another steam engine could be brought from Athens to pull them. After some years in exile in Alexandria, King Simeon and his family were offered shelter by a cousin, the King of Spain; and it was in the Bulgarian monarch's royal palace in Madrid that I had first met him in 1986[288].

When the Iron Curtain fell, Simeon Saxe Coburg was free to return to Bulgaria. Barred from standing for election as president of the newly-democratic country, however, he ran for office as prime minister and won a handsome victory. His party, the National Movement Simeon II, had joined the European Liberal Democrat and Reform Party along with their coalition partners the Movement for Rights and Freedoms. I had been invited to meet Simeon on two or three occasions during his four years as prime minister[289] and had struck up a cordial relationship with him, empathising with his evident frustration with the boring details of administrative government[290]. What Simeon had which all other Liberal prime ministers lacked was the stamp of royalty; and despite our Liberal preference for republicanism I sensed that he was perceived by them as a person possessing a particular qualification.

I persuaded Simeon, who was no longer prime minister but remained a key partner in the three-party governing coalition, that we needed a weekend house party for our prime ministers and other leading members of our Liberal family. He kindly offered to host one at his hunting lodge in Borovets, in the mountains above Sofia. Thus it was that on the first weekend of September 2006 Prime Ministers Fogh Rasmussen of Denmark and Tariceanu of Romania, the presidents of the Liberal International and of the ELDR Party and ALDE parliamentary group and leading Liberal commissioners held their first weekend retreat to discuss in detail the EU strategy needed by the Liberal political family[291].

Later that month the Swedish Liberals and Centrists, both ELDR mem-

---

288   Simeon received for lunch UK Liberal Party leader David Steel, to whom I was principal assistant, and some of his colleagues from the House of Commons.

289   July 2001 to August 2005.

290   On the third occasion on which he complained to me of the frustrations of day-to-day administration I risked the observation, in Italian, that it was better than advertising vegetables preserved in oil on TV. Recognising immediately my reference to the activities of his Italian cousin, he broke into a broad and generous smile.

291   Prime minister Vanhanen of Finland was too busy with the Finnish EU presidency to attend; Prodi with the business of new office and his country's co-ordination of the allied effort in the war in Lebanon, and Ansip with other matters. Simeon married a Spanish aristocrat, Margarita Gomez-Acebo y Cejuela; I was to be amused by their sense of humour when I discovered on a coffee table in their living room a book entitled 'How to receive guests at home' ('Recibir en casa').

bers, were back in government for the first time in over twenty years in coalition with the Conservatives.

I used the occasion of the Finnish presidency and the extra demands placed on me by the growing strength of the Liberal family to expand my own staff[292]. I was beginning to make plans for the mid-term constituent session at which posts within our group came up for re-election; I would seek my colleagues' support to continue as leader and appeared to face no serious opposition, though I was already beginning to think that I would not seek to serve as leader of my group into the next Parliament.

In mid-June the Bureau of the ALDE group agreed the timetable I proposed to them for our end of year re-constitution. As the Liberal Democrat prime ministers convened for their meeting before the summit on 14 and 15 June I had even begun to entertain ideas of running in 2009 for the presidency of the European Parliament. I knew it was unlikely we would be able to elect another Liberal president so soon after Cox, but our new-found strength made a bid a more serious proposition. Moreover, if politics consists of a joust between ideas, our political family should not be without a lancer in the tournament.

My attention had been momentarily distracted from Brussels at the start of 2006 by developments in my party at home. Charles Kennedy resigned as leader of the UK Liberal Democrats in the early days of January, finally admitting he needed a cure for his addiction to alcohol and having suffered months of degrading treatment at the hands of his parliamentary colleagues[293]. The party's executive committee, on which I sat ex-officio but whose meetings I attended extremely rarely, was rumoured to favour a long drawn-out contest for the election of a successor, believing that the process might boost the party in the polls in a fashion similar to the success of the UK Conservatives' leadership contest the previous year. I felt this was a dangerously naive view and went to London early in January to try to persuade them otherwise. To my satisfaction they agreed that the new leader should be in place by time of the party's spring conference in March. I proceeded to campaign for the election of Sir Menzies Campbell MP[294] over his challenger and my former Brussels colleague Chris Huhne MP and was pleased to see him elected, though I knew from private sources that Menzies was unlikely to have the energy to hold the job for long and that the next contest would be between Chris Huhne and Nick Clegg, who was wisely biding his time.

---

292 In addition to Desiree Oen, the head of office who had served me so well, and her able No. 2 Edel Crosse, I moved to take on a political adviser and to create a private office or *cabinet* which would give me exclusive use of resources I previously shared with colleagues: a press officer, a speechwriter and an usher. Thus I was joined by Federica Terzi, Tsvetelina Nacheva, Christine Gilmore and Philippe Giblet. Though Christine Gilmore was later to be succeeded by Euan Roddin from the same stable and I was to take on Philip Drauz as the head of my office after the departure of Desiree to Commissioner Kallas' *cabinet*, this was the team which was to take me through until the end of the mandate.

293 Though most of the sniping at Charles Kennedy came from MPs at Westminster, including to my surprise one who owed her election to Parliament to his leadership, the foulest blow was to come from an MEP, who described his Westminster leader as 'a dead man walking'.

294 Though to my regret the ALDE group was subsequently to lose the services of Alison Suttie, an able policy advisor who had joined us at my initiative some years earlier, who returned to London to assist Sir Menzies Campbell in his new role as party leader.

This domestic development partially distracted me from a problem festering in ALDE's ranks.

Bulgaria and Romania

In April 2005 the European Parliament had given its assent to the entry of Bulgaria and Romania into the EU with substantial majorities in favour of both. Baroness Nicholson MEP had welcomed the progress made by Romania on children's rights, an issue about which she had been particularly insistent. For Bulgaria, reform of the judiciary and police services had been identified as an area where ongoing reform would be necessary.

Bulgaria had been to the polls in June 2005 and had elected a parliament in which the Socialists were now the largest party. They could not build a majority, however, without coalition partners. They chose the party which had led the previous government, King Simeon's National Movement, and the previous coalition partners the Movement for Rights and Freedoms of Ahmed Dogan. Liberals were keen for the two parties, both adherents to the Liberal family, to work together in government. But though relations between the two party leaders were good, the same could not be said of their generals. A certain condescension on the part of the ethnic Bulgarians towards the Bulgarian Turks did not help, and I was to spend some time that summer persuading the two to resolve their differences. Eventually they did; and in Bulgaria I was to find so many things which made me feel at home: tartan; a relative of the haggis and a relative of the bagpipes[295].

Colleagues from the Netherlands in particular were getting increasingly cold feet, however, about the entry of Romania, foreseen for January of the following year, despite the impressive reforms being carried out by the Liberal-led government there. A rearguard action by EPP MEPs to delay or prevent accession was winning some converts among Liberal backbenchers. In May the issue was due to come to a vote on the floor of the House. Thus in February 2006 I arranged for ALDE to send a delegation to Bucharest to meet ministers from the new centre-right government and to discuss progress in the country's programme of reform. Prime Minister Tariceanu fielded almost the entire team of his ministers, who offered us full access to information on their country's EU preparations. Reform was clearly progressing: the newspapers were dominated by reports of the first in a line of high-profile prosecutions for corruption – a case against former prime minister Adrian Nastase. Other EU member states were conducting a series of peer reviews of Romania's policies and administrative capacity which would inform the Commission's next progress report in May. The visit was soured by a maverick briefing from the EU's deputy representative there, a Dutchman who gave my colleagues and me a very downbeat assessment of the situation; it was so far removed from the line taken by enlargement commissioner Olli Rehn, who was to recommend to Parliament in May the entry

---

295 My visit in August of that year to the Estonian Centre Party's congress was to leave me feeling distinctly less comfortable. It was held in a fort in Rakvere where a large contingent of Scots mercenaries had been murdered in their sleep.

date of 1 January 2007, that I made a formal protest to the commissioner. Earlier that very week the government of the Netherlands had ratified the EU accession treaty for Romania; and though it had given rise to some political opposition, I was not prepared for Liberals in the EP to appear flaky on the issue when our sister party had recently taken over the reins of government in Bucharest and was working extremely hard to put back on track a process of reform which had stalled under its Socialist predecessor.

In September observer MEPs from Romania and Bulgaria joined the European Parliament. The ALDE group was strengthened substantially, our numbers rising to 103. At the end of September the European Commission again reported to Parliament on preparations in Bulgaria and Romania for EU entry. They maintained their recommendation that both countries join on 1 January 2007, though with some safeguards to encourage them both to pursue the process of reform. Parliament approved the reports, with the EPP divided but all ALDE MEPs present voting in favour of both Romania and Bulgaria. I had hosted a lunch for Prime Minister Tariceanu in Brussels on 21 September and discussed with him who he might nominate as the country's European commissioner. His initial proposal of Varujan Vosganian was to fail to gain support[296] and the more emollient Leonard Orban was to get the job. As Liberals gathered in Bucharest the following month for the ELDR congress we were aware of the powerful symbolism of meeting in a country shortly to consolidate its position after the long journey from Communism to membership of the free world.

The European Council on 14 and 15 December was to welcome the forthcoming accession of Bulgaria and Romania and to hold a deep discussion about enlargement, concluding that the EU would maintain its commitments to the countries in the enlargement process even if the pace of enlargement should take into account the capacity of the Union to absorb new members. It welcomed the launch of visa facilitation and readmission talks with the countries of the western Balkans and agreed to make available more scholarships for their students.

An uneventful Austrian presidency in the first half of 2006 saw the Union confirm its support for the accession of Bulgaria and Romania on 1 January 2007. But of its headline theme 'Europe listens', little more had been heard. And if one of the messages of the No voters of 2005 had been a rejection of rapid EU expansion, as some on the right argued, little listening was being done. One year on from the rejection of the Constitutional Treaty, Liberals were becoming impatient for a coherent response from the Council of Ministers. Speaking in the House in a debate with Council and Commission before the European Council of 15 and 16 June I opined: 'It is time to recognise that the sixteenth and final member state likely to ratify the Constitution in its current form is Finland. We must recognise that France, the Netherlands and the United Kingdom will never ratify the 2004 text. Denmark, Ireland and Sweden cannot ratify in current circumstances. The

---

296　Romanian president Traian Basescu did not support Vosganian and made this clear to Commission president Barroso. However a campaign was also run against Vosganian by the left, upset by remarks he had made about 'greater Romania' and his nomination had to be withdrawn.

Czech Republic and Poland choose not to ratify, and Portugal will find it almost impossible while committed to a referendum[297]'.

There were two possibilities: renegotiation or oblivion. The sooner the EU took steps to make structural and substantive improvements to that text and address public concern, the better.

PNR and SWIFT[298]

On 30 May 2006 Liberals celebrated a major victory when the European Court of Justice annulled the Council decision to send to the US government name recognition data of airline passengers. After the terrorist attacks of 11 September 2001 the US had insisted that any airline flying a passenger into or over the USA provide 36 different categories of information on them. EU airlines agreed, but broke the Union's data protection laws in so doing. The EP's civil liberties committee, which I then chaired, protested strongly and the European Commission and Council adopted measures to render the airlines' action legal. Liberals campaigned to have Parliament challenge these measures at the European Court of Justice, and despite the reluctance of Parliament's president at the time we forced it through. The judges at the ECJ did not comment on Parliament's assertion that the action threatened individual privacy. Nonetheless they ruled, as we asked them to, that the actions of Council and Commission exceeded the powers conferred on the EU by the treaties. The Court ordered that the practice be changed by 30 September 2006, giving the institutions just four months to comply.

This matter was not entirely over, however. Within six weeks of the judgement MEPs were to discover that SWIFT, the organisation which handled international bank transfers, was also transferring personal data to the US authorities in breach of EU data protection laws. This was to lead to a debate in Parliament on 6 July and further action, steered by Liberal MEP Jeanine Hennis, which was to see justice restored in 2010. When Parliament debated a proposed new transatlantic partnership agreement to strengthen EU-US ties on 1 June 2006 ALDE spokesperson Alexander Graf Lambsdorff said: 'Every partnership has its ups and downs, its strengths and weaknesses. The most important thing is that the basis is sound'. But this allowed the EU to insist that its data protection laws be respected, even in something as serious as the fight against terrorism, as Parliament did again on 6 September 2006.

Five years on from the 9-11 attacks, many more people had been killed in the 'war on terror' than in the attacks themselves. Few felt any safer as they went about their daily lives and political opinion was beginning to turn against those who championed the military response. To Liberals, the war needed to be more psychological than conventional. We saw terrorism as a tactic, not an enemy in itself. We needed to fight it, we felt, with all the intellectual, moral, judicial and where necessary military means at our disposal, without succumbing to an Orwellian type of society in the process. The collapse of the

---

297   This idea had first been crystallised by my colleague Andrew Duff MEP.

298   PNR stands for Passenger Name Recognition and SWIFT for The Society for Worldwide Interbank Financial Telecommunication.

Roman Empire had started with the undermining of its moral basis implicit in the Lex Gabinia of 68 BC, adopted in response to terrorist attacks on Rome. Liberals feared that a similar fate could befall the western civilisation of today.

In mid-June 2006 Parliament called for the closure of the Guantanamo Bay detention camp and on 5 July Parliament criticised the role of the CIA, which it believed to be 'directly responsible' for illegal activities in Europe.

Finland has it all

Finland's second EU presidency demonstrated a country now fully at ease in the Union and well prepared for the tasks it faced. Though Liberal prime minister Matti Vanhanen had to endure stinging personal attacks from a former partner[299] he presided with a degree of patience and stoicism which earned him wide admiration. Liberals in the European Parliament were pleased to see a former colleague, Astrid Thors of Vanhanen's coalition partner the Swedish People's Party of Finland, as EU affairs minister co-ordinating the presidency's business. She and her government colleagues were to deliver for Vanhanen a six-month stint universally perceived as a success.

The Finns used their presidency to endeavour to secure agreement on the use of the *passerelle* clause, a provision in the Amsterdam Treaty which allowed member states, acting by unanimity, to agree to move decision making in justice and home affairs matters to a basis of qualified majority voting in Council and co-decision with the European Parliament. I had proposed this to Matti Vanhanen, having learned from EU affairs minister Geoff Hoon that the UK government was reconsidering the matter; since the UK had been the publicly most reluctant member state this came as a pleasant surprise. On 28 June 2006 Commissioner Frattini launched a review of progress in justice and home affairs co-operation. He called on member states to recognise that progress would remain painfully slow if they insisted on taking decisions by unanimity. All member states had signed, though only 15 had yet ratified, a Constitutional Treaty which foresaw the introduction of majority voting in all but the most sensitive areas. The Finnish prime minister told Liberal Democrat MEPs meeting in the Aland Islands the same day that a move to majority voting in this area would be one of the priorities of his presidency. Finland had launched the Tampere agenda during its previous presidency in 1999, aiming at the creation of a common EU asylum and immigration policy. The lack of progress in the seven years since then had been due almost entirely to the need for unanimity in Council before decisions could be valid.

An example of where the *passerelle* was necessary was the European evidence warrant. Justice ministers agreed in the Council of Ministers in June to sign off a proposal from the European Commission for such a warrant scheme, which would allow the police in one country to seek assistance from the police in another in collecting and supplying evidence in serious criminal cases. Liberals welcomed such progress in police and judicial co-operation, but we objected strongly to governments being able to agree

---

299   Susan Kristiina Kuronen published in February 2007 Finland's first 'kiss and tell' tale entitled 'The Prime minister's bride', detailing their relationship. Vanhanen was to claim damages against the publisher.

these matters without reference to the European Parliament and, in some cases, with little if any reference to their national parliaments.

The Finns also showed a welcome commitment to transparency, broad-casting live on the internet inter alia the legislative proceedings of the Council of Finance Ministers. Some viewers were doubtless dumbfounded by their use of EU jargon, but those who persisted will have seen and heard 25 finance ministers at work. A total of 90 legislative decisions (86% of the total) were taken in public compared to only 17 the previous year. And ALDE launched a campaign 'Who makes my law?', pressing member states to publish correlation tables to show exactly which parts of national law came about as a result of decisions in Brussels. This would help identify 'gold plating' of legislation and make the process of transposition and implementation of EU law more transparent.

Human rights and development

In 2005, the G8 industrial nations committed at their Gleneagles summit to more than double official development assistance to Africa by 2010. An addi-tional $25 billion per annum was foreseen. The purpose of the commitment was to allow the achievement of the UN's Millennium Development Goals. In an heroic achievement, Commissioner Louis Michel had secured a total of EUR 78 million to mitigate the effects of a severe drought in the Horn of Africa and was also to secure, at a donors' conference in Brussels in June, pledges of $200 million to fund the operations of the African Union's mission in the Sudan through the summer and a further EUR 10 million of aid in July to pro-vide food for children in Niger. But Liberals believed that such aid, important as it was, would be mainly palliative; real progress in alleviating poverty and providing a stable economic basis to support democracy depended on the integration of developing countries into the world's trading system. On 6 June 2006 I had put this issue on the agenda of the Liberal networking supper for European commissioners. But by the end of July 2006 the Doha round of trade talks in Geneva had collapsed over failure to reach agreement about farming subsidies and lowering import tariffs; with President Bush's authority from Congress to negotiate due to expire in 2007 it looked increasingly unlikely there would be a global multilateral trade deal.

Accompanying poverty was the regular denial of basic human rights. In June 2006 Parliament obliged the European Commission to establish a finan-cial instrument for the promotion of human rights in third countries. This would replace the European Initiative for Democracy and Human Rights, which was due to expire at the year's end, and provide a budget of EUR 1.1 billion for work in the field over the period 2007-2013 out of a total external relations budget of some EUR 50 billion. It was a small but significant step in developing the 'soft power' of the EU and was the brainchild of a liberal Conservative MEP, Edward McMillan Scott[300], who had sought and obtained support from Liberals while unable to obtain it from all of his Conservative colleagues.

One of the casualties of the 'war on terror' had been respect for human

---

300 McMillan Scott was subsequently to join the UK Liberal Democrats and the ALDE group in the spring of 2010.

rights. The EU had failed to act effectively to help prevent genocide in Darfur. It agreed in March to send a military force to the former Belgian colony of the Democratic Republic of Congo to help ensure the smooth running of the first election campaign there in forty years; and it had succeeded in securing the extradition of Thomas Lubanga, a notorious militia leader from the Ituri region, to face charges of war crimes at the International Criminal Court. Parliament was to express concern in the coming months about Somalia, Mauritania, Sri Lanka, Zimbabwe, China and Russia.

Russia

The 15th EU-Russia summit, held on 10 May 2005, had seen progress made in the creation of the 'four common spaces' foreseen two years earlier in St Petersburg. On the economy, in the field of justice and home affairs, in external security and in research and education, plans for greater co-operation were laid. Russia had signed a border agreement with Estonia, though not yet with Latvia; it had agreed to evacuate its military bases in Georgia fully in 2008; and it had opened talks with the EU on human rights. On 26 May 2005 Cecilia Malmstrom MEP had secured the approval of the European Parliament for a report calling for further integration of Russia into the world economy and closer involvement of the country in European security, while voicing concern over human rights and the development of democracy. She identified the Yukos case as a fundamental test of Russia's respect for the rule of law, property rights, transparency and a fair and open market for investors.

Little more than a year later, however, Liberals were placed in some difficulty by the decision of Finnish president Tarja Halonen, a Socialist, to invite Russian president Vladimir Putin to join EU leaders for supper at a European Council meeting in Lahti. This stuck in the craw, particularly in view of the murder of journalist Anna Politkovskaya on 7 October 2006[301], the 21st journalist to suffer such a fate since Putin had taken office. True, the EU wanted – and was shortly to obtain – a new energy co-operation treaty; Russia's decision to cut off gas supplies to transit countries in January 2006 (to be followed by similar actions in 2007 and 2009) had sent a shiver through Brussels. But Liberals had requested at the start of the Finnish presidency that in the summits foreseen with the Asia and Russia 'you think not just of engagement, but of promotion of European values, of human rights and democracy, so essential to the development of our world[302]'; and despite the risk of offending Liberal prime minister Matti Vanhanen I led my group in securing the printing in Finnish newspaper *Helsingin Sanomat*[303] on the day of the summit of an open letter to the summit's chief guest about extrajudicial killings. I was pleased that Parliament's president

---

301   In a book published shortly before her death, Politkovskaya had written: 'Yes, stability has come to Russia. It is a monstrous stability under which nobody seeks justice in law courts ... Nobody in his or her right mind seeks protection from the institutions entrusted with maintaining law and order ... Lynch law is the order of the day. The president himself has set an example ... Putin considered Khodorkovsky to have slighted him personally, so he retaliated'.

302   My speech to the House on 5 July 2006.

303 The same letter was printed the previous day in Russian newspapers *Novaya Gazeta* and *Nevavisimaya Gazeta*.

Borrell and Prime Minister Vanhanen raised this latest murder case with President Putin. 'He was not a guest of honour and could not avoid awkward questions on the state of democracy in his country', said former Finnish prime minister and ALDE MEP Anneli Jaatteenmaki. At ALDE's initiative Parliament adopted a resolution calling for an independent investigation into the murder. Our action was praised over lunch on 18 October by former US Secretary of State Madeleine Albright, from a country which has traditionally been stronger than the EU in standing up to Russia and China.

Constitutional Treaty progress

June's European Council had made no decision on the future of the EU's constitution; they agreed to defer the matter. While I had attacked this as an evasion of responsibility I knew that Germany was pressing others to desist until the German presidency in the first half of 2007. Finland was to hold 'confessionals' with other member states, to seek their views on how to proceed. But no action was to be forthcoming.

In early September ALDE MEPs travelled to Berlin to meet German Liberals well in advance of 2007's German presidency of the EU. With 61 MPs our FDP friends were stronger than for many years; we entertained hopes that their success in re-entering governments at regional level in recent years would soon be reproduced at federal level. We were invited too to meet Chancellor Angela Merkel[304] and Interior Minister Wolfgang Schauble; their coalition was in difficulty and Merkel's popularity had plummeted, but their approach to the EU presidency was thorough and determined. Our discussions were somewhat interrupted by news of riots in Budapest where Prime Minister Gyurcsany had admitted[305] to having lied about the country's economic situation in order to be re-elected. The rioters burned cars and damaged other property and even briefly seized control of a television station. Germany, as the most powerful country in the EU, understood the need for a Union capable of integrating properly its new central and eastern European members; and the chancellor herself, coming from the German Democratic Republic, knew the stakes involved.

Nonetheless, as 2006 drew to a close the Union appeared to be developing a new sense of purpose. 300 national MPs descended on the European Parliament early in December for another inter-parliamentary meeting on the EU's future constitutional arrangements. As we were meeting, Finland became the 16th country to ratify the Constitutional Treaty. In my address to the conference on 5 December 2006 I told the assembled prime ministers: 'we in Europe's parliaments no longer urge but require the European Council to take the constitutional crisis seriously'. And, addressing an audi-

---

304 I was to discover on this occasion that she and I had been contemporaries at the University of Leipzig in 1977-78.

305 Ferenc Gyurcsany had made the remarks in a private meeting with party colleagues shortly after the election. They had however been recorded and were later leaked to the press. To my surprise, Europe's right-wing leaders, meeting in Brussels, were persuaded by the Hungarian opposition to call on Gyurcsany to resign.

ence in the ballroom at the UK's embassy in Paris, in one of a series of lectures entitled 'The EU at fifty', I spoke of the EU being a victim of its own success. Peace and stability were now taken for granted. Its leaders lacked the political courage, however, to make the case for supranational action to tackle new, supranational challenges. Since there was much discussion about the likely content of the forthcoming Berlin Declaration, I contributed my own 'Paris Declaration': 'The Union is about supranational solutions to common challenges. It is about recognising in our diversity a strength and not a weakness. It is about creating new ... links and solidarity between people, not just states ... About a concept of society shaped by solidarity.'

In typical Finnish style, Finland's presidency had been a success without fanfare. They had failed to get unanimous agreement to speed up policy making in justice and home affairs through the use of the *passerelle* clause in the Treaty of Amsterdam, but they had made progress on important energy, immigration and EU enlargement matters, including the extension of the Schengen information system to the new member states. Agreement had been found on both the liberalisation of the internal market in services and the registration, evaluation and authorisation of chemical products. They had seen the culture and media programmes adopted, and the 7th Framework Research programme. Reflecting the Liberalism of the host government, the presidency also made the connection between migration and development, recognising that if the EU did not take the products of poorer countries it would end up taking their impoverished people; and that remittance of income by migrant workers is the most effective form of development aid. And though my quoting a satirical Monty Python song about Finland did not go down well with one humourless government minister, its title 'Finland has it all' was not inappropriate.

ALDE developments

As the Liberal commissioners met MEPs for our networking supper in Brussels on 7 November 2006 we welcomed Commissioner Huebner for the first time; the following day I was to meet Commissioners-designate Orban and Kuneva, soon to be approved after parliamentary hearings. As I left on a whirlwind visit to deliver speeches in Marrakesh (at the Liberal International congress) and Ankara (2nd congress of the ruling AKP) it seemed that part of our mission had been fulfilled. Liberals were about to become the majority force in the European Commission.

In Bucharest on New Year's Eve, at the party[306] thrown for Romania's accession to the EU, Finnish enlargement commissioner Olli Rehn and I were to plan a second informal meeting of Liberal leaders in recognition of the fact that the Liberal family was increasingly influential. With a general election just three months away, Prime Minister Vanhanen could boast of a good

---

306   Relations between the prime minister and the president had reached such a low point that they each threw separate parties, the latter then trying unsuccessfully to 'poach' the foreign diplomatic guests of the former. In the early hours of the morning, having finally decided to join the international throng at the diplomatic club, Basescu was to exchange pointed words with me about what he considered to be an unjustified intervention into Romanian domestic issues. His behaviour was not unlike that of Silvio Berlusconi.

record in his stewardship of the EU. He was to win re-election in the New Year and a second term of office, though with a change of coalition partner.

But mid-term blues hit the ALDE group. Despite a painstakingly careful preparation of the mid-term constitutive session in the bureau of my group, including a two day retreat in Groot-Bijgarden outside Brussels, colleagues appeared unhappy with my leadership. Of 102 ALDE MEPs only 82 were present to vote in our group meeting on 29 November: of those, 58 voted to re-elect me and 24 against, though my only potential opponent, Lapo Pistelli, decided not to run. It is true that I was leading from the front. Not all colleagues shared my passionate defence of the Palestinians in the Middle East, for example, and I initiated a debate on Gaza just days before I was due for re-election. At least one colleague objected to my defence of Prime Minister Tariceanu of Romania in a row with his president[307]. I had gone out of my way to develop better relations with my UK Liberal Democrat colleagues, with four of them accepting invitations to come and speak in my constituency, yet some continued to undermine my efforts; and I had tried to have regular contact with other colleagues. And though any fair reading of the book of my speeches published at the year's close[308] would have shown a balanced approach to Liberalism, emphasising classical Liberalism and economic Liberalism at least as much as social Liberalism, my German colleagues were privately frustrated with what they perceived as my emphasis on the latter. I became aware that I was invited far more often to share platforms in France and Italy with our member parties there (on the 'democratic' side of our Alliance) than to events organised by the parties of a more economic Liberal hue. But most of our campaigns during the year had been on issues related to EU governance (comitology under the Austrians, transparency under the Finns, now our campaign for the publication by member states of correlation tables) rather than to economic reform.

In response to criticism that I took too little interest in policy-making I had established and chaired policy task forces on competition policy, limits to the EU, and defence policy. Over the course of the year I had made 27 speeches on the floor of the House, 47 in my constituency and at least 107 others, given 45 briefings or press conferences and at least 350 individual press interviews. As I was to note of our annual Christmas party, the biggest we had ever held, 'the group I lead is much nastier these days. Why? Because we are twice as big as when I took over and more than twice as powerful. And that is the nature of power'.

---

307   Nicolae Vlad Popa, an observer MEP, was to leave the PNL and the ALDE group, citing my intervention in Romanian politics – which had upset President Basescu – as the reason. I believe the real reasons were much wider.

308   *The Power of Speech*, Bagehot Publishing, December 2006

Chapter 5:   January 2007 – June 2009

During this period, the reforms envisaged in Europe's Constitutional Treaty were put back on track by a concerted effort of the German and Portuguese governments during their presidencies of the EU. After a new intergovernmental conference they were to emerge in the form of an amending treaty, the Treaty of Lisbon, which most national leaders wanted in place by 1 January 2009. However Ireland's voters subsequently rejected the treaty in a referendum and the presidents of Poland and the Czech Republic sought to avoid signing it, thus delaying its entry into force until after the 2009 European elections.

It was also a period marked by concern for the related issues of climate change and energy security. Preparation for the UNFCCC meeting in Copenhagen in December 2009 absorbed much of the attention of policy-makers. Russia's decision to cut off gas supplies to Belarus early in the New Year of 2007 again affected supply in the EU, as had the interruption in supply to the Ukraine a year previously, drawing attention to the EU's dangerous dependence on Russian oil and gas.

Most notably, western Europe was to enter its deepest economic depression since the Second World War. A stock market wobble in mid-2007 highlighted the instability of the market in financial paper and liquidity problems at UK building society Northern Rock were to lead to the first bank re-nationalisation[309]. By the autumn of 2008, following the collapse of American bank Lehman Brothers, contagion had spread across the financial sector and soon, inevitably, hit the real economy.

The presidency of the European Council and Councils of Ministers was held in 2007 by Germany and Portugal, in 2008 by Slovenia and France and in the first half of 2009 by the Czech Republic.

Liberals in expansive mood, People's Party divided

I chose the New Year to launch, together with Juergen Wickert of the Friedrich Naumann Foundation, an English edition of a book hitherto available only in Italian entitled 'The Art of Liberty'. A product of collaboration between Italian Liberal journalist Salvatore Carrubba and art critic Flavio Caroli, the book traces the development of Liberal ideas through their expression by fine artists over the centuries. Since liberty is an art that confers moral and spiritual dimensions to our lives and Liberalism a distinctive,

---

309 The problems became evident in the autumn of 2007. The bank was taken into public ownership in February 2008.

coherent set of supranational values which has contributed so much to the European Union, we saw it as a fitting prelude to the fiftieth anniversary of the EU's Treaty of Rome.

This event also provided a good atmosphere in which to give my colleagues a pep talk about our priorities for the remainder of the parliament. We had built the largest third force Parliament had ever known; with MEPs from the two new member states our number had passed the 100 mark for the first time ever. I reminded them of Europe's common historical and political culture and urged them now to seek to build a coalition capable of determining the next president of the European Parliament and the next president of the European Commission. We needed to identify and exploit the opportunities to divide the major political groups along the 'drawbridge' faultlines, I argued, and build a coalition of the coherent to take forward the EU's historic mission; and we needed to reach out more effectively beyond the Brussels bubble to engage and empower national politicians in the process of European construction. My remarks were greeted with enthusiastic applause. But to approve the building of a coalition is one matter, to agree on the choice of partner(s) is quite another, and by September – when I announced my own intention to run for the EP's presidency – my colleagues were to resist strongly the designation of any one specific target partner. Being elected on national party lists and with their thinking influenced in some measure by national political considerations, the more ephemeral demands of supranational democracy carried insufficient gravitational pull.

Parliament's year kicked off with a welcome from outgoing President Borrell for the MEPs from Bulgaria and Romania, who were now no longer observers but members with full voting rights, albeit appointed *pro tem* by their national parliaments until elections could be held. The Liberals and the Socialists were to see their ranks substantially enhanced by this enlargement, gaining 18 and 17 MEPs respectively.

The EPP, however, gained only 11. This added to the woes of a party in some turmoil, with insurrection among its troops. EPP leader Hans-Gert Poettering[310] was elected with a large majority, as expected, to the presidency of a House in which he was one of only five MEPs to have served continuously since 1979. But he was to leave turbulent waters in his wake.

For the first time anybody could remember, the succession to Poettering as leader of the EPP group was publicly contested. Three candidates – Othmar Karas of Austria, Antonio Tajani of Italy and Gunnar Hokmark of Sweden – were to challenge the Franco-German candidate[311] Joseph Daul, with their elimination in that order in three rounds of voting before Daul could secure election by a margin of just 19 votes. The Franco-German hegemony on Europe's right was under severe strain. The losers continued to

310 As one of the British journalists remarked, being not altogether flattering, Poettering was very much 'a European Parliament politician'. My relations with him had been businesslike rather than cordial, but he was unfailingly correct and hence I had greater respect for him than for other political group leaders.

311   Not only supported by the French and German delegations with the EPP, but also Franco-German in the sense that he comes from Alsace.

cause trouble, delaying by a fortnight the re-formation of Parliament's committees as they fought over the chairmanships.

Liberals secure UN backing for moratorium on death penalty

The ALDE group, by contrast, appeared united. Rumours that the Italian Democratic Party MEPs would join the Socialists after the 2009 election, about which I had received numerous entreaties, were firmly denied in June 2007 by the leader of their faction in Rome, Francesco Rutelli. And Francois Bayrou told me that were it to happen, his party would join the ELDR Party. Moreover the Liberal team appeared to have potential to grow still further. In May 2007 we welcomed a new Polish member, Marek Czarnecki, who joined our Polish Liberal delegation from another political group; and during a visit to Dublin that month I was again told by Irish EU affairs minister Dick Roche that Fianna Fail was set to join ELDR, though this had by now become a repetitive refrain.

Liberals chose a worldwide moratorium on the death penalty as a subject on which to campaign in 2007. The European Union had led the way in making abolition of the death penalty a criterion for membership. Now we sought to abolish it beyond our borders. It was a subject which united Liberals and on which our Italian Radical friends in the Transnational Radical Party had done a lot of good preparatory work[312].

On 9 October the previous year justice and home affairs committee chairman Jean-Marie Cavada and I had written a letter[313] to Solana in support of a move by the Italian and Spanish governments for a new EU initiative at the United Nations. ALDE had condemned the execution on 30 December 2006 of Saddam Hussein, film of which had gruesomely been posted on the internet. We now sponsored a resolution, adopted by Parliament in January, condemning the verdict of a Libyan court on 19 December 2006 which convicted and sentenced to death five Bulgarian nurses and a Palestinian doctor accused of having deliberately infected Libyan children with HIV. We were concerned too that the number of judicial executions worldwide had risen sharply in the years of the 'war on terror'.

Return of refugees from the EU to countries which practised the death penalty was also an issue. The danger faced by immigrants being returned to their home countries if there was a threat to their person was highlighted in August by the case of Pegah Emambakhsh, an Iranian lesbian woman who had fled to the UK and whose partner in Iran had been arrested and tor-

---

312   Italian MEP colleagues Marco Pannella and Marco Cappato were particularly active, leading a citizens' campaign on the issue for the Transnational Radical Party. Pannella was a veteran campaigner at home and abroad on this and other human rights issues and had been a force in the early parliamentary mandates, ever ready even to go on hunger strike for the cause he was promoting at the time. Marco Cappato was a disciple of Pannella's, a dashing, charming and energetic campaigner.

313   The letter was co-signed by Luisa Morgantini, chair of the EP's development aid committee and Helene Flautre, chair of the subcommittee on human rights.

tured. I was one of many who intervened with the UK home secretary to prevent her extradition back to Iran. After a long campaign she was finally to be granted asylum on 11 February 2009.

In Germany the case of Professor Devenderpal Singh Bhullar was also causing concern. Accused of planting a terrorist bomb on 11 September 1993, but protesting his innocence, this Khalistan Liberation Force member sought asylum in Germany. His request for asylum was turned down; he was deported to India where he admitted his guilt and was sentenced to death, but claimed subsequently that his admission had been extracted under duress. In the Supreme Court of India, hearing an appeal against the death sentence, the presiding judge on a three-judge bench proposed to acquit Singh Bhullar of the charge but was outvoted by his two colleagues.

The picture of executions was particularly galling in the People's Republic of China, where 470 were put to death in 2007. Yet in one corner of China there had been great progress. I was pleased to host in Strasbourg in July an exhibition celebrating the 20th anniversary of the lifting of martial law in Taiwan, with veteran democracy campaigner Peng Ming-ming as our guest of honour; the human rights situation in that country had improved much in the intervening years.

By 1988 over 50% of the UN's member states had abolished the death penalty. In 1993, when a proposal was made at the United Nations for a world-wide moratorium, 97 countries still favoured retention of the death penalty; by 2007, there were only 51. In December 2006, 93 countries had signed a political declaration calling for a universal moratorium.

I first persuaded the leaders of all the EP's political groups (except the far right, who declined my invitation) to sign a written declaration calling for a worldwide moratorium on judicial execution as a first step towards universal abolition. I convinced Parliament's President Poettering to raise the matter in a meeting with UN Secretary General Ban Ki-moon. Barroso assured me that he would support such a move; he put the matter on his agenda, for example, for discussions with Japan's prime minister. Colleagues and I then set out to lobby national leaders to arrange a co-ordinated action among EU countries at the UN General Assembly. We secured a Council statement to Parliament on the issue on 31 January and succeeded in gaining overwhelming support for a subsequent European Parliament resolution in favour of a universal moratorium[314].

On 27 September 2007 the European Parliament voted again, by 504 votes to 45, to ask the Council to present a resolution on the moratorium on the death penalty to the 62nd United Nations General Assembly in order to have it adopted before the end of the year. We also called for 10 October of each year to become the 'European Day against the Death Penalty'.

11 October 2007 was the fifth annual world day against the death penalty. The Portuguese presidency of the EU, thanks in large measure to Liberal campaigning, used it to proclaim the EU's commitment to work for abolition of the death penalty worldwide and to present a motion for a resolution at

---

314   There were 45 votes against and 31 abstentions.

the UN General Assembly for a worldwide moratorium on its use. MEPs observed a minute's silence in tribute to the victims of the death penalty and our president, drawing attention to the world's greatest offender, stated that we should use 2008's Olympic games in Beijing 'to break the wall of silence which China is hiding behind.'

On 15 November the third committee of the UN General Assembly voted (by 99 votes to 52, with 33 abstentions) in favour of a motion calling for a global moratorium on capital punishment. And on 18 December 2007 the General Assembly itself approved the call (by 104 votes to 52, with 29 abstentions) [315]. We knew that the resolution would be honoured partly in the breach, but the force of global public opinion is not to be underestimated.

Climate change and energy security

In January 2007 the European Commission published a white paper on energy policy in the light of climate change, building on its green paper of March 2006. It called for an EU target to produce 20% of all electricity from renewable energy sources by 2020. Specific reports on coal, biofuels and nuclear power were envisaged, as was a report on competition in the energy and gas markets. The proposals were the product of a strategic energy review.

They were much needed. As Russia's refusal to supply gas to Belarus took its grip, supply to the EU was again affected. Hungary scurried for reserves of gas and some EU citizens shivered in the cold.

The EU's energy ministers met in mid-February to review progress in inter-connectivity in energy supply and in liberalisation of the market. Inter-connectivity was already surprisingly high in some instances; the opening of a canal bridge to allow a ship to pass in November 2006 had required the temporary severing of an electricity connection which resulted in a loss of power to over ten million homes in eight different countries! But the networks for electricity distribution were generally poor compared to those for oil and gas, putting the development of renewable energy sources – particularly dependent on transmission capacity – at a disadvantage to fossil fuels.

The Competitiveness Council, however, meeting at the end of February, had warned that the fight against climate change should be pursued 'without harming the competitiveness of the EU economy'. The March 2007 European Council adopted an energy policy for Europe and welcomed the Commission's proposal to appoint co-ordinators for critical priority projects[316]. Solar power in Spain and wind power in the North Sea were also increasingly looked to for alternative sources of energy, but dependence on

---

315   A year later, on 20 December 2008, the General Assembly passed another resolution; the number of countries in favour went up to 106, those opposing down to 46 (34 abstained). The Italian Radicals' 'Hands off Cain' movement continues to grow in strength.

316   For the Nabucco project to bring oil and gas from the Caspian Sea, by-passing Russia, Netherlands' Liberal Jozias van Aartsen was to be appointed.

oil and gas would remain heavy and nuclear energy was seen by many as the main alternative. Although the heads of state and government re-committed themselves to fighting climate change, they did not set binding targets to cut energy use in government buildings or car fleets. As the writer Mark Twain observed, we can change the world or ourselves, but the latter is more difficult. Their lack of firm action was somewhat exposed by 14 major EU retail businesses including Carrefour and Marks and Spencer, who announced the same week that by 2020 they would cut energy consumption on their premises by 20% and source 20% of their energy needs from renewable energy sources.

In preparation for the UNFCCC gathering in Bali in December 2007, the EU's heads of state and government had reiterated in March 2007 their intention to play a leading role in international climate protection. They wanted to see the architecture of the Kyoto protocol built upon and broadened and believed that developed countries should take the lead by committing to reducing collectively their emissions of greenhouse gases by 30% (from 1990 levels) by 2020, with a view to cutting emissions by 60%-80% by 2050. They foresaw extending the scope of the EU emissions trading scheme to include land use, forestry and surface transport.

Germany had announced that tackling climate change would be one of the priorities of its 2007 EU presidency. The big question remained, however, how to get the Americans and others on board. When Parliament debated the Commission's draft legislative package on climate change on 31 January 2007, I welcomed the willingness shown by China in Bali to reach a global agreement. Henrik Lax MEP, frustrated with the attitude of the big-oil-bankrolled US administration, called for a direct dialogue with the newly elected US Congress. The political balance in Congress had changed and a special committee on climate change had been established. The key to success in influencing countries like China and America, we argued, lay in EU solidarity expressed through a common position of our Union's member states.

ALDE MEPs Chris Davies, Lena Ek and Vittorio Prodi had all been prominent in Parliament's work on climate change. Yet progress on the details of policy was not to be easy. Environment Commissioner Stavros Dimas wanted to legislate to limit the CO_2 emissions from cars built in the EU to a maximum of 120g per kilometre. The Commission had been expected to agree his proposals on 23 January 2007. But a rearguard action led by Industry Commissioner Gunter Verheugen and backed by the German car industry succeeded in blocking agreement, and when the paper appeared a week later the emphasis was on reducing emissions by improving fuel quality. Japanese manufacturers had invested heavily in hybrid vehicles; French and Italian industry in more efficient petrol and diesel engines. But German industry had not. Liberals were reminded of Konrad Adenauer's dictum that God had placed limits on man's reason but not on his stupidity.

Chris Davies brought to the floor of the House in October 2007 a call for a strict limit of 125g/km on CO_2 emissions from cars. He was accused by some Green MEPs of having 'sold out' in compromising from his original proposal of 120 g/km; but the best is often the enemy of the good and, had he not been prepared to compromise, his report would not have secured the comfortable majority needed to send a strong signal to the Commission about what Parliament wanted. By the time of the European Council meeting in June 2008, Germany and France had announced their agreement to reducing CO_2 emissions from cars to 120g/km by 2012[317].

The EU was working with Norway on the development of technology for carbon capture and storage following a successful experiment in storing CO_2 in saline aquifers in the Sleipner oil field under the North Sea. Parliament's rapporteur for this measure was again my UK colleague Chris Davies, who sought to fit every new coal fired power station with carbon capture equipment by 2020 and to retro-fit all existing stations by 2030. Emissions from coal accounted for 24% of all CO_2 emissions in the EU; and though EU dependence on coal might decline, other countries' consumption would rise rapidly.

On 25 April 2007 Parliament voted to establish a temporary committee on climate change, with a mandate of one year. I decided to nominate as ALDE representatives Lena Ek and Fiona Hall, both of whom were proving effective parliamentarians.

Liberals were leading by example. In March 2007 I managed to have the remit of Parliament's working group on internal reform extended to include reducing Parliament's own carbon footprint. The House already had an eco-management and audit scheme, but I felt we needed to take practical steps to reduce our carbon footprint, which meant looking at our use inter alia of paper, heating, lighting and means of travel.

After a visit to the Tallberg Conference in June-July 2007 I decided to offset the carbon emissions from my travel during this second half of the parliament through a social investment. I discovered I was the only political group leader to do so. And when ALDE MEPs Lena Ek and Chris Davies returned in December from a delegation of MEPs to the Bali UNFCCC meeting they were discovered to have been the only ones to have offset their travel there.

The environment ministers were to discuss in June the question of emissions trading. The EU's emissions trading scheme covered only power stations, refineries and heavy industry. Liberals wanted to see it extended to the transport sector and particularly to aviation; though air transport contributed just 4% of CO_2 emissions, emissions from aircraft had risen by 87% since 1990. We had no wish to restrict citizens' mobility but wanted airlines to invest in cleaner technologies and modern, fuel-efficient fleets. Air travel across Europe had never been so cheap, but the real price would be paid by future generations if we did not curb emissions of greenhouse gases. Early in October Parliament's environment committee was to vote by a massive majority to amend the Commission's proposal, so as to include aviation in emissions trading from 2010; the Commission had proposed 2011 for flights within the EU and 2012 for flights beyond our borders. This was upheld at first reading on the floor of the House in a vote in mid-November 2007. As I was able to report to the Liberal International conference in Hamburg on 16 November, Liberals had succeeded in 'greening' Barroso; but much more

---

317 The matter would again be heavily contested by German MEPs, however, in September 2008. Chris Davies MEP had enjoyed publishing a survey just before Christmas of the exhaust emissions from the cars used by European commissioners themselves. Dimas was the only one who drove a hybrid car, a Toyota Prius, with emissions below the level he sought to set.

needed to be achieved and there was insufficient sense of urgency in Council or Commission.

Many were beginning to see in unusual weather patterns the onset of climate change. In my constituency, the Severn Estuary was hit by flooding so severe that we applied for assistance from the EU's solidarity fund. In early August the climate scientists warned that the polar ice at the North Pole was melting much faster than had been predicted; some dubbed it 'the big melt of 2007'. On 19 September the European Commission approved a budget of EUR 50 million to help in climate change mitigation in developing countries. A series of 'Live Earth'concerts around the world, co-ordinated by Al Gore, served to draw public attention to a growing challenge.

On 23 January 2008 Barroso came to Parliament to present the Commission's proposals (four legislative acts and two flanking measures) to combat climate change. I was astonished to find in the chamber that of the leaders of the three other mainstream political groups – EPP, PES and Green – not one was present. For Liberals, this was a major issue: for the others, apparently less so. I described it in the House as 'the most important act of Mr Barroso's Commission thus far'. It appeared to me that Barroso had understood the importance of the investment in new technologies which would flow from action taken to combat climate change in providing 'green growth'. Developing new technology to reduce emissions from cars and aeroplanes, investing in more energy-efficient machines and in renewable energy production changed the parameters within which growth was defined; but it was capable of restoring to European industry the competitive edge it had lost in recent years. While the single market progressed all too slowly – a consumer credit directive and a directive to open postal services to competition were finally agreed in January 2008 – innovation to tackle climate change could not wait.

Parliament debated an interim report from its temporary committee on climate change on 21 May 2008. I used the occasion – and the launch the same day of an ALDE on-line climate change awareness campaign 'The Changers' – to promote the idea of solar thermal electricity generation in the North African desert and its distribution through high voltage direct current cables to Europe and to argue that this should be one of the first projects of the new Union for the Mediterranean which the French presidency wished to establish. I was pleased that French environment minister Jean-Louis Borloo, a former French MEP, was to host a meeting later in the year with the companies and MEPs interested in pursuing this proposal, which he had written in to the communique adopted by the Union for the Mediterranean[318].

At the G8 meeting in July 2008, the EU announced its readiness to cut its CO2 emissions by 50% by 2050 compared to 1990 levels. The European Parliament had voted the previous week on the greenhouse gas emissions quota trading system. Despite heavy lobbying from the airline industry we

---

318 I was to spend more energy promoting this idea than perhaps any one idea would normally merit, including through the publication in January 2009 of a policy pamphlet, *Making the green energy switch at a time of crisis*, with contributions from MEPs from different parties.

voted to include aviation in the system with effect from 2012 and were hoping for an ambitious agreement by the Council of Ministers for Europe to put on the table in Copenhagen in December the following year.

On 24 September 2008 there was a major disagreement in the EPP group about the Commission's draft climate package. The difference was essentially over the position of the German automobile manufacturers, who were defended ferociously by German MEPs. Similar tensions had surfaced in the Socialist ranks; the fragile agreement they had reached in their group meeting was to fall apart in committee on 25 September as the German lobby was defeated[319] in favour of an agreement close to the Commission's proposal.

Since I was leading from the front[320] on some of these issues I was pleased that generally we were successful on the environment committee, thanks to the efforts of our strong Liberal team. We dubbed 7 October 2008 'super Tuesday' after winning almost all our amendments to three major pieces of legislation in the EU's legislative package to fight climate change. We welcomed the agreement reached by ministers in October 2008 that the EIB was to make available EUR 450 million to promote renewable energy schemes and improvements in energy efficiency and their call for legislation to phase out over two years the sale of single filament light bulbs, to achieve a 75% cut in electricity usage for lighting. And as I took Energy Commissioner Andris Piebalgs around my constituency on 6 October to show him local plans for renewable energy development in the Severn Estuary, we were able to celebrate Liberal achievements in an atmosphere in which he could once again publicly be proud to be a Liberal.

The following month I stayed on in Strasbourg after the parliamentary session to address an inter-parliamentary meeting on energy and sustainable development, hosted by the European Parliament on 20 and 21 November 2008. I knew we needed the support of the parliaments of the member states for the ambitious package of measures to combat climate change which the 15-16 October European Council meeting had committed itself to agreeing before the end of the year. French environment minister Jean-Louis Borloo was working hard to narrow member states' differences over the Commission's proposals for cutting overall carbon emissions; Poland and Italy had expressed particular concerns at the European Council.

The contracting parties to the UN Climate Change Convention met in Poznan in Poland in December 2008. On 4 December, in a debate in the House to prepare the meeting, I said: 'It is irresponsible of Italy to claim that the Commission's proposal would push up power bills by 17.5%. Renewable energy generation will bring down bills and will save us not only money but lives ... a combination of industrial lobbying and national

319   Schulz and Daul were to leave a meeting of the conference of presidents that day, after flustered whispering between them and their secretaries general, as news of the committee vote came through. I guessed what was afoot. Initially I expected it to add to tensions within the EP's Grand Coalition; in fact it increased the desire of the Germans in both groups to continue their alliance into the following parliament.

320   For example, I intervened on one occasion by appearing at the environment committee at the time of the votes to persuade my colleagues to support a ban on dichloromethane when our shadow Holger Krahmer had signalled opposition to the proposal.

self-interest ... must not blight next week's historic opportunity.' Before Christmas, Parliament was to approve the Commission's proposals in toto. I was proud that Liberals had played such an important role in having them adopted.

Convinced as Barroso might now be of the opportunities for green growth, he had little in the way of resources to promote them. As 2009 opened, with the economic outlook still bad, the European Commission developed further its strategy to overcome recession by adopting a plan entitled 'Investing today for tomorrow's Europe', which proposed plough-ing EUR 3.5bn from the unspent margins of the 2008 budget into energy interconnection projects and EUR 1.5bn from 2009 into broadband internet access networks and climate change alleviation projects in rural areas. Attracting a further EUR 5bn in matching funds from member states, con-siderable investments would be possible, including perhaps some in the expensive technology needed for carbon capture and storage. By staking his prestige upon a budget which was not his to determine, however, Barroso was going out on a limb.

The EU was now taking very seriously the environmental challenge. Increasingly it was understood that investment in energy- and resource-saving technology was part of the answer to a return to growth. The end of January saw the establishment of the International Renewable Energy Agency (IRENA) at the initiative of Denmark, Spain and Germany. 75 coun-tries signed an agreement to give it a start up budget of EUR 25 million. But the member states were less than convinced that the necessary action should be initiated at EU level. When the 27 finance ministers met in Brussels on 10 February they applied the brakes to the Commission's EUR 5 billion recov-ery plan by refusing to allow spending of the EU budget up to its legally agreed maximum.

The following week the EU's energy ministers approved six infrastructure projects including an offshore wind generation network for the North Sea and an electricity interconnection between southern Europe and North Africa. But while they could will the ends they could not will the means. On 23 February the General Affairs and External Relations Council met to try to unblock Barroso's EUR 5 billion. Their heads of state and government were to agree at the extraordinary summit on 29 February to a EUR 20 billion reflation of the economy by member states and to envisage an extra EUR 11.5bn from the EU budget, but there was no commitment to the latter. Barroso was left dangling.[321].

Justice and home affairs

There was growing concern among Liberals at evidence of the complicity of EU governments in the practice of 'extraordinary rendition' of terrorist sus-pects for torture. The US president had admitted in September 2006, after repeated denials by the US and EU governments, that the CIA had indeed practised illegal kidnapping and detention. A parliamentary committee of

---

321   It was not until 6 May 2009 that Barroso's EUR 5bn was to be formally approved by the member states.

inquiry had delivered to Parliament in February 2007 its final report, which showed that over 1000 CIA-operated flights had used EU airspace between 2001 and 2005 and suggested that temporary secret detention facilities may have been located at US military bases in Europe. Speaking in the debate for the ALDE group on 14 February 2007 Ignasi Guardans castigated the EU member states for complicity in extraordinary rendition with the words: 'We are saying to them here, on behalf of millions of European citizens ... you cannot fight terrorism through a dirty war in our name'. Liberal MEPs have refused to let these allegations drop; action in Parliament continues to this day to seek justice for those detained wrongfully and treated badly.

In April 2007 five colleagues and I were given a gagging order in Singapore, where the authorities agreed to let us enter the country only on condition that we did not speak at a meeting of our sister party the Singapore Democratic Party. In authoritarian Singapore this was hardly a surprise, though we were pleased to have the opportunity to expose the lack of freedom there and the hypocrisy of the EU in its dealings with the country. At around the same time, however, Poland's right-wing government passed a 'lustration' (or monitoring) law under which they sought to revoke the parliamentary mandate of Bronislaw Geremek MEP because he refused to sign a statement declaring that he had never collaborated with the Communist-era security services. Geremek, one of the leaders of the Solidarity movement and a former government minister, had signed similar declarations on at least three previous occasions; but he objected to what was now effectively a witch-hunt against former Communists. In the European Union this was utterly unacceptable to Liberals. When I rose in our Strasbourg chamber to defend him on 25 April I was heartened to have almost the whole House cheering Bronislaw on, as I was the following month when Poland's constitutional court declared the offending provisions unconstitutional.

Ten years on from the signature of the Amsterdam Treaty, Germany was to use its EU presidency to make an ambitious push to drive forward Europe's agenda in justice and home affairs. They sought rapid progress in developing a comprehensive EU migration policy, foreseeing specific agreements with third countries on migration and a clampdown on the employment illegally of third-country nationals within the EU. Strengthening the capacity of FRONTEX through rapid border intervention teams and a coastal patrol network, swift action to establish the recently agreed visa information system and continuing efforts to strengthen police and judicial co-operation through the inter-connection of national criminal records systems, were all agreed at the European Council meeting on 21 and 22 June 2007.

It was not all plain sailing, however. The deep conservatism of Germany's interior minister Wolfgang Schauble did not find favour everywhere. Liberals had been the first to protest when he sought to have all EU member states sign the Treaty of Pruem, an agreement between just seven countries on sharing criminal intelligence data outwith the EU treaty framework, in other words exempt from EU data protection laws and immune from scrutiny by the European Parliament[322]. Schauble was to seek to develop the

---

322   Though Parliament was eventually to approve the treaty on 7 June 2007 after security guarantees.

approach of a 'directoire' of larger EU countries setting their own agenda; in May 2007 he invited Michael Chertoff, US secretary of homeland security, to discuss measures to combat terrorism with his European 'G7'. When Chertoff met Parliament's justice and home affairs committee there was a lively debate, the US Conservative doubtless returned home muttering that MEPs were a bunch of 'cheese eating surrender monkeys'[323].

Within the treaty framework, progress was easier. In early February the Commission proposed the use of criminal sanctions to combat environmental crime. Existing laws were being widely honoured in the breach. Sanctions were needed which would be effective, proportionate and dissuasive and Liberals would support them. Germany was also keen to see progress under its presidency on measures to secure the rights of defendants in criminal legal proceedings, an important accompaniment to the European arrest warrant mechanism; agreement on the Commission's proposals of April 2004 still evaded the EU. Here, despite a vigourous Liberal campaign, the lack of consensus among member states was to be the stumbling block when the proposal was discussed by ministers in June.

Following the return of Liberals to government in Latvia we had secured another interior minister, Ivars Godmanis, who had been prime minister of his country from 1990 to 1993 and was to become prime minister again by the end of 2007. Godmanis became the third[324] Liberal interior minister. Between them they were to be able to prevent the Council from taking positions too far removed from Liberalism.

The Liberal voice was also crucially important in immigration policy. Though Schauble was not the ogre which the left liked to paint him, he put pressure on Italian interior minister Giuliano Amato for repressive policies to deal with the arrival on Europe's shores of migrants from across the Mediterranean Sea. EU member states had no coherent policy for managing economic migration and the better weather of the summer months was expected to bring more boatloads of migrants. On 16 May 2007 the Commission published a communication on applying the EU's global approach to migration to the Union's eastern and southern borders. In early June the Commission further appealed to member states for more patrol boats and helicopters to help deal with the situation; as Commissioner Frattini pointed out at a press conference, less than half the equipment promised by member states had been made available. Four legal measures had been proposed by the Commission and were being debated by Council and Parliament: a directive on reception conditions, a directive on asylum-granting procedures, a directive on the conditions governing qualification for asylum and the draft Dublin II regulation[325]. As Italian Liberal and former interior minister Enzo Bianco was to point out, while most migrants were in search of labour opportunities, many among them were refugees from polit-

---

323   See footnote 247.

324   The other Liberal interior ministers were Christian David (Romania) and Patrick Dewael (Belgium).

325   This Council regulation of 18 February 2003 established the criteria and mechanisms for determining the member state responsible for examining an asylum application lodged in one of the EU member states by a third country national.

ical oppression or other forms of discrimination, some even fleeing for their lives. In 2006, 182,000 requests for asylum had been made. The draft directive on the rights of political refugees was to propose allowing them the status of long term residents, but this was opposed by right-wing MEPs.

The problem with a repressive approach, Liberals believed, was that it dealt with the symptoms but not the causes of the phenomenon of migration. Monitoring the flow of migrants, seeking to halt it or turning them back to the shores from whence they came was no substitute for a policy to deal with the poverty, oppression, environmental degradation and resulting despair which was causing so many to set off in search of a better life. I was to use a speech in a parliamentary debate in May 2007 on the plight of people in Darfur to plead for a Marshall Plan for Africa to be set up by the EU. Apart from the moral imperative of assisting those less fortunate, it would reduce the pressure for migration.

It was not until Portugal's presidency in the latter half of 2007 that the EU was to succeed in re-balancing the debate on migration. The second EU-Africa summit had identified migration as an area of mutual concern for which both sides would seek common solutions. On 19 November the justice and home affairs ministers adopted conclusions on the need for coherence between migration and development policies. The heads of state or government were subsequently to recognise the significant impact of migration on economic growth potential and employment growth and to welcome the Commission's proposals on the granting of work permits to highly skilled jobseekers. Not only were the remittances from migrant workers an important contribution to the development of poorer countries; their labour was essential to the wealthier countries.

In November 2007 the member states of the 2004 enlargement – with the exception of Cyprus – adhered to the Schengen Treaty, becoming members of the border-free area within the EU. But all was not well in Schengen. The European Confederation of Police, with the well-chosen acronym Eurocop, spoke out against the postponement until 2009 of the new-generation Schengen information system. Scheduled to be operational by March 2007, it was already a year delayed and due to be postponed by at least another year. Liberals recognised that the database would be a powerful tool in tracking the movements in and out of the EU of people-traffickers and others suspected of serious crimes. But while most of the delay was for technical reasons, some was political: Liberals were concerned that the large scale processing of data from frontier controls could lead to great intrusion into personal privacy. The EU's data protection supervisor shared this view.

The Slovenian presidency of 2008 was fortunate to inherit Jacques Barrot as JHA commissioner, albeit rather late in the day. Frattini had been struggling against powerful member states over whom the Slovenes could hope to have little influence. In mid-February the Commission agreed two communications on border control and studied a review of the development of the Frontex border control agency since its inception in 2005. They recommended tighter external border controls and much greater use of fingerprinting of those arriving and leaving. Liberals were not opposed to these in principle, but we would need to be satisfied that the measures were justified and proportionate to any threat, and that strict safeguards were in place to govern the retention and use of data gathered for border control purposes.

Parliament had grappled too with a draft directive governing return of illegal migrants. An agreement reached between Council and Parliament in April fell apart again early in May, with some member states refusing to accept the safeguards that MEPs insisted on. In Parliament, some of the Socialist MEPs also began to reconsider the deal.

Some member states simply sought repressive measures to deal with illegal migration, failing to recognise the importance of remittances of income to developing countries for which they brought ten times more money than official development aid. I had published in April 2008 a pamphlet written jointly with MEPs – fearing electoral populism – from other political groups entitled 'Making Migration Work for Europe' in which Jeanine Hennis and I set out the Liberal case. Jeanine was to do sterling work on the dossier. She was to broker an agreement between Parliament and Council in June 2008 on minimum standards for the treatment and repatriation of illegal migrants which was to improve detention conditions for thousands of people whose only 'crime' was to have sought a better life for themselves and their families. Designed to encourage the voluntary return of illegal immigrants, it nonetheless recognised that forcible return might be necessary and laid down minimum standards to be respected in this case. The agreement, approved by Parliament later that month, was to oblige nine member states which could previously detain illegal migrants indefinitely to limit detention to a maximum of six months (or 18 months in very exceptional circumstances) and to treat detainees fairly and humanely.

I was to experience at first hand the problems posed when I was called early one Saturday morning by a constituent living nearby who had come across a young Asian girl who appeared to be lost and to speak no English. Having a little knowledge of the language, I managed to ascertain that the girl was Chinese; she wanted to be taken to a railway station, though the nearest was some fifteen miles away. In a very small rural community such as the one I live in this was an unusual occurrence. The police eventually discovered that she had absconded from a hostel to which she had been sent by the immigration authorities at Bristol airport, having arrived on a flight from Amsterdam without the requisite papers. She was almost certainly a victim of child trafficking, probably bound for the sex trade in London.

The announcement by Malta in the summer of 2008 that the number of refugees arriving in boats in the first eight months of the year was double the number for the whole of the previous year, excluding at least 500 who had drowned in the attempt, gave further cause for thought. An Italian NGO published a calculation that over 12,500 had died trying to reach Europe's shores across the Mediterranean over the previous 20 years, and that the number making the attempt was rising continuously.

Nor was Europe proving willing to take refugees recommended by the United Nations for settlement. The UNHCR reported that there were 37 million refugees worldwide: in 2007 the USA had agreed to resettle 48,000, the EU only 4,000.

On 9-10 September 2008 the EP hosted an interparliamentary meeting on migration. MEPs and MPs were united in agreement that immigration should no longer be seen as a threat. With welfare systems endangered by an ageing European population and a shortage of workers in some sectors, migration – regulated at EU level – was widely perceived as the way ahead, though the need was stressed 'to link immigration and the law'. Gerard Deprez MEP warned: 'immigration without integration will cause us more problems than it will help to solve'.

Liberals were active on two other fronts in the field of justice and home affairs. The EU's requirement for visas for citizens of many poor, EU-oriented countries around our borders struck a discordant note against the messages of friendship we were sending out. Students, migrant workers and others – often among the poorest in society – were being disadvantaged and made to pay for the privilege of travel to the EU. The Liberal Youth Movement of the EU (LYMEC), under its president Roger Albinyana, launched a campaign for visa-free travel which MEPs were to take up in Parliament. As Henrik Lax MEP was to point out at a conference organised jointly by ALDE and LYMEC on this issue, 'thousands of legitimate short term visitors are deprived of experiencing European culture and educational facilities because of the obstacles in the way of obtaining a visa'. Procedural complexity, time delays, fees and security checks hardly suggested the welcoming, open society which Liberals sought to make the EU.

The Donnici case

Despite the development of a democratic culture in the EU, Liberals still sometimes had to resort to law for protection. Other than where a member sought arrest in order to gain publicity, as was twice the case with ALDE Cypriot MEP Marios Matsakis[326], it was my practice to defend my colleagues vigorously. Thus when the Corte di Cassazione (Supreme Court) in Italy found in favour of Beniamino Donnici MEP, a candidate from the list of our Italia dei Valori party who succeeded Antonio di Pietro in May 2007 but whose credentials to sit in the European Parliament were challenged, I leapt to his defence[327]. In a disgracefully partisan move by the other parties (primarily collaboration between former Communists and a right-wing Italian chairman of the legal affairs committee), the seat had been awarded to Achille Occhetto. It took us nineteen months, until 15 November 2007, to secure a judgement in the European Court of Justice to allow Donnici to take up his seat.

Liberals and transport

With Paolo Costa of Italy as chair of the transport committee and Dirk Sterckx of Belgium one of its most active members, Liberals lived up to their reputation as the key players in transport policy throughout the 2004-09 par-

---

326   Matsakis was hard to dislike and frequently amusing. Ever willing to tease the British, he liked to begin his speeches in ALDE group meetings with the words 'My British colonial masters ...' His behaviour, however, was sometimes indefensible. In April 2007, whilst on a parliamentary delegation visit to Akrotiri in Cyprus, he engineered his own arrest.

327   The other parties sought to award the seat instead to leftist dinosaur Achille Ochetto. Their bitterness towards Italia dei Valori leader Antonio di Pietro, whose 'clean hands' operation had put many of them in prison for corruption in the 1990s, was tangible. And despite an announcement by the president of the House in April 2007 that the Supreme Court had found in Donnici's favour and that he should rightfully take his seat, Parliament's legal affairs committee still sought to stall the matter.

liament[328]. While in the 1999-2004 parliament one committee had been responsible for regional policy, transport and tourism (which for the latter half of the parliament had been chaired by Italian Liberal Luciano Caveri), transport policy in the 2004-09 parliament had been given its own committee. Knowing the importance of transport policy, one of the areas of EU activity in which there was the most legislative activity and in which Liberals had traditionally played a leading role, we had fought to keep the chair; and Paolo Costa, a politician of considerable breadth, experience and cross-party appeal, had been the obvious choice.

Moreover, mobility was a key factor for the internal market. The effective free movement of goods, services and people required a safe, sustainable and reliable EU transport market. Liberals put the emphasis on five aspects of policy which we saw as key to a genuinely European transport policy: market opening, fair competition between operators, safety and security, passengers' rights and the financing of infrastructure development. These we sought to apply across the board to road, rail, sea and air transport.

On road transport, much of the necessary legislation was already in place. This had been the first sector to be studied at EU level in transport policy. There had been notable successes in opening markets for vehicle sales and freight cabotage and some in opening to international tender public procurement contracts for road building and maintenance. Vehicle safety had much improved. Much focus now was on the environmental aspects of road use, where surprising progress could be made. EU road pricing policies were said in June 2007 to have cut the number of lorries passing through the Alps by 16% over six years and to have increased by 66% the trans-alpine shipments by rail.

At the time of adoption of the second rail package in April 2004 the European Parliament had committed itself to a complete opening of national and international passenger rail transport by 2008. But the ghouls of neo-liberalism had since sown their terror. On 18 January 2007 the third liberalisation package was approved by MEPs at second reading, but only after it had been substantially watered down in Council and Parliament. Socialists including Luxembourg MEP Robert Goebbels and Belgian MEP Marc Tarabella branded it 'all-out Liberalism' and believed it would harm small businesses and lead to a loss of jobs. Others such as French far-right MEP Bruno Gollnisch pointed to the pitiful state of the railways in the UK as an example of what would happen on a wider scale were such measures adopted. But Liberal MEPs persisted and by June agreement had been reached in conciliation: the rail market would be opened up, there would be a European licence for train drivers and a directive on the rights of rail passengers. In September the measures were finally approved by Parliament.

---

328   Liberal MEPs Florus Wijsenbeek and Mechthild von Alemann had fought hard in earlier parliaments to have transport policy recognised as a community competence. In 1983 they persuaded Parliament to institute proceedings before the ECJ alleging the Council's failure to implement a Community transport policy as required by Article 74 of the treaty, and won. Sterckx was responsible inter alia for securing rights to compensation in the case of delay or cancellation and access for persons with limited mobility in rail travel.

International passenger transport had been liberalised; Liberals now sought to open up national markets too. Similarly, for shipping, we paid special attention to supervising state aid to public transport companies and to port authorities.

We sought to resolve the long-running debate about the transport of passengers or goods between two points in one member state by a company from another member state and tried, though unsuccessfully, to broker a compromise between the different political groups on the market access to port services directive, which was to be defeated in the House by a large majority on 18 January 2006. With regard to passengers' rights we sought equal basic rights for all passengers on all forms of transport and rights to compensation in the event of cancellations or delays to services. Liberals worked to ensure that receipts from transport infrastructure charging were reinvested in the transport network rather than alimenting the general budgets of member states. We worked hard to secure adequate funding for the Trans-European Network for Transport (TEN-T).

One aspect of transport policy which was regularly in the headlines was that of safety. In shipping in particular, Europe had suffered serious coastal pollution from the wrecks of ships such as the *Erika* (December 1999) and the *Prestige* (November 2002). Liberals had fought off Spanish right-wing attempts to prevent criticism of Spain's government over the *Prestige* accident; better to deal dispassionately with the causes of the accident to prevent recurrences, we reasoned, than seek to save the bacon of particular national government ministers. Lessons had been learned from a special committee of inquiry set up by Parliament in December 2003 to look at improving safety at sea.

These issues were brought home to me when the *Napoli* went aground in Lyme Bay in Devon, off the coast of my constituency, in a storm on 18 January 2007. Had she been an oil tanker, pollution might have been as serious as that from the *Torrey Canyon* in 1967; since she was a container ship the pollution from the incident was less serious. Nonetheless the events leading up to the accident raised important questions. I discussed these on 1 February with Commissioner Barrot and worked with Dirk Sterckx to set up in Parliament an expert hearing into the incident and with Devon County Council leader Brian Greenslade and local MP Richard Younger-Ross, both Liberals, for a thorough examination of the issues locally. We all worked hard to ensure co-ordination of the efforts to clean up the debris, crane off the containers and salvage the broken hull.

In March and April 2007 Parliament adopted its position at first reading on a package of seven reports designed to raise standards of maritime safety. The first looked at the duties of 'flag states' (where the ship was registered); the second at the question of civil liability. In late April Parliament voted to approve at first reading the other five measures in the package. But progress towards these objectives was to be frustrated by member states' transport ministers, who were to reject Parliament's proposals for over a year.

Parliament debated the first two proposals at second reading on 23 September 2008 and deplored the failure of member states to agree on the financial responsibility of ship-owners or the tasks of flag states, which Liberals regarded as essential components in reinforcing maritime safety. Issues of national sovereignty were blocking progress in the application of the Union's traditional approach in environment and consumer protection policy to water transport.

In October 2007 the Commission published proposals for an integrated maritime policy. With 90% of the EU's trans-oceanic trade and 40% of its internal trade conducted by sea; with 70,000 km of coastline and 40% of the world's merchant fleet; and with resources of oil, gas and fish and leisure opportunities provided by our seas, an integrated approach to the challenges of sustainable resource use, environmental protection and marine safety had become essential. Liberals welcomed the proposals for a maritime surveillance network, integrated coastal zone management and the setting up of an observation and data network to improve knowledge.

Farming

The Common Agricultural Policy was changing fast. Since the major 'Agenda 2000' review the EU had grown from 15 to 25 members. The 'decoupling' of payments from production, the boldest reform thus far, was intended to liberate farmers to produce what consumers wanted rather than according to subsidies on offer. Payments were increasingly to be linked to environmental objectives. Liberals had welcomed these changes. In Agriculture Commissioner Mariann Fischer-Boel we found a champion for further Liberal change.

In 2006 we had reformed the sugar sector, which had been largely unchanged for almost 40 years. Now we set about reforming wine production and the farming of fruit and vegetables with the aim of creating a single common market for the products covered by the CAP. In June 2007 the commissioner was to propose a mechanism to allow schools to distribute free fruit and vegetables to pupils who might not otherwise receive a balanced diet. And the following year the commissioner was to work with Donato Veraldi MEP to boost incentives for young farmers[329] to make the agro-food sector more dynamic.

Liberals were also concerned to improve provisions for the welfare of farm animals. Way back in the 18th century Liberal philosopher Jeremy Bentham had argued that ability to suffer, not the ability to reason, should be the benchmark against which humans decide how to treat other sentient creatures. The international dimension of animal welfare also concerned us, for we were not unaware of the burden placed on European farmers by having to meet higher standards than those prevailing elsewhere and we sought, through EU trade agreements, to improve standards beyond our borders.

The role of agriculture in renewable energy production and bio-technology was championed by Finnish Liberal MEP Kyosti Virrankoski, who argued that biomass, biogas and other biofuels could replace increasingly scarce oil reserves for heating, electricity production and traffic fuels, thus increasing income in rural areas. The commissioner visited my constituency

---

329   Veraldi's report was to be adopted by Parliament in June 2008.

in October 2005 and I showed her a bio-ethanol production scheme run by Somerset farmers and supported by Liberal-led Somerset County Council, whose fleet of vehicles used some of the fuel thus produced. [330]

In one area of agricultural reform, however, Liberal MEPs disagreed with the Commission's proposals. In the December 2005 budget deal the European Council agreed to a proposal from the Commission to allow member states the discretion to cut income support for farmers, the rates for which had been set two years previously, by up to 20% and to use the funds for wider rural development projects. Parliament disagreed and voted to reject the budget. Jan Mulder MEP argued that if an agricultural product in one member state could be produced with a 20% state subsidy while in another member state no such subsidy was on offer it would distort the internal market. In the subsequent annual budget Parliament voted to put 20% of the agricultural funds into reserve until the Commission could show that the so-called 'voluntary modulation' agreed on by the heads of state and government would not so distort the market. In February 2007 the European Parliament again voted to reject voluntary modulation; only 89 votes were cast in favour. Faced with the prospect of a 20% cut in rural development funding the member states relented and the Commission withdrew the proposal. The agriculture budget, hitherto seen by member states as their exclusive preserve, had been amended by Parliament even before the entry into force of the Lisbon Treaty which was to give MEPs formal powers in this area.

Transparency was also important to Liberals. If public money was to be spent to assist farmers, the public should know how much was being paid to whom. By October 2007 we had secured agreement to this from the member states, embodied in a regulation in 2008. From 30 April 2009 member states had to publish a record of CAP payments.[331]

Romania and Bulgaria: in but not settled

There was no doubt in my mind that the election of Liberal-led governments in Bulgaria and Romania had been key to the entry of these countries into the EU. Their leaders had worked hard and selflessly in the quest for reform of corrupt former Communist systems and in the drive to instil among their people a new sense of responsibility for their own destiny. But the process was not without its casualties.

Bulgaria was beset by difficulties within the governing coalition. I had to cancel a meeting of my group planned for Sofia early in March 2007 due to

---

330   I was also to introduce her to a local spirit, Somerset Cider Brandy, about the labelling of which she was later to be helpful to me beyond the call of duty in 2007 and 2008.

331   My constituents in the Westminster parliamentary constituency of Wells were therefore to be surprised to learn how much their famously anti-European MP claimed in subsidies for farmland he owned in Scotland, and were to unseat him at the subsequent general election. However this emphasis on openness was also to apply to MEPs. A request from a Maltese journalist to find out how much Malta's MEPs paid their assistants was initially turned down by the European Parliament's authorities. The EU ombudsman ordered Parliament to make the information available, resulting in a rule change in 2009.

disagreements between our members in the NMSS and those in the MRF, now both junior partners within a coalition under Socialist prime minister Sergei Stanishev, over the franchise for the elections to the European Parliament. I paid a private visit to Sofia nonetheless to see the leaders of both Liberal parties and the prime minister, whom I came to like very much. I was pleased also to welcome their commissioner, Meglena Kuneva, to Brussels; she and her counterpart Anca Boagiu of Romania had been in charge of the negotiations for their countries' entry and I had enjoyed the pleasure of describing them in Parliament as 'a pair of swans, appearing to glide effortlessly over the surface of the water but with their feet paddling away ten to the dozen underneath'. Meglena was to take the Commission's important consumer protection portfolio and was to join ALDE in a number of our campaigns.

Bulgaria held its elections for the European Parliament in May 2007. To assist in the Liberals' campaign ALDE again took up the case of the five Bulgarian nurses held to ransom by Libya on charges of having deliberately infected patients with HIV while working there as humanitarian assistants. It was a particularly nasty case. They had been held on death row for eight years and treated very harshly, including being subjected to prolonged physical torture. We decided again to draw attention to their plight by hosting a cross-party press conference in Parliament in Strasbourg on 19 April. Being now in the EU, we pointed out, Bulgaria had the right to expect the same level of solidarity in such a case as the UK had recently received for its naval prisoners in Iran, or France or Italy for journalists taken hostage in the wider Middle East. It was a campaign which showed Bulgarians both the advantages of the EU and the concern of Liberals for their people.

By mid-July Libya's High Judicial Council had commuted the death sentences into prison terms. After a long, exhausting and dramatic negotiation, this dark affair was coming to an end. The detainees were finally freed on 24 July 2007 after eight years in prison. On 10 October, which Parliament had declared the European Day against the Death Penalty, we brought the nurses to the European Parliament to have them formally welcomed by Speaker Poettering.

In May I visited Isperi and Stara Zagora to campaign for the election of MRF and NMSS MEPs respectively[332]. In the election later that month the MRF went on to top the poll with 26.3% of the national vote and elect four MEPs, while the NMSS performed disappointingly and elected only one, changing the balance from their previous representation by unelected 'observer' MEPs. At the NMSS conference the following month the party appeared to be disintegrating. Relations between the two parties were increasingly strained and I was to miss in the latter half of the year the sound advice and diplomatic skills of my Bulgarian press secretary Tsvetelina Nacheva, absent on maternity leave, who had guided me through the minefield of their sensitivities.

In April 2008 the Socialist-Liberal coalition government in Bulgaria was

332   In Isperi I was impressed to address an open air rally of almost 20,000 people in support of a list of candidates headed by the able Filiz Hyusmenova; I had previously spoken to rallies of that size only in Senegal and Cambodia. In Stara Zagora the NMSS commanded a much smaller but nonetheless inspired audience.

rocked by a scandal involving Interior Minister Rumen Petkov from the senior coalition partner the Socialist Party, against whom evidence of mafia connections was piling up in an investigation by the Agency for National Security. In a western European democracy the minister concerned would already have offered his resignation; Petkov refused to do this. I went to see Stanishev in the office which he had decorated so fashionably compared to his predecessor and urged him to sack the man, aware of the sensitivity of such a matter in a Union which had already put in place safeguard clauses to suspend EU funding for his country. Stanishev had established the Agency for National Security as a way of helping him fight the corruption so commonplace amongst the old guard in his own party, but insisted he had to let public pressure work its magic. Moreover, his opponent Boyko Borissov was not attacking the government over Petkov; some believed this was because Borissov himself might have been implicated in the scandal. The government thus survived a vote of no confidence over its handling of the Petkov affair. Stanishev was proven right, for Petkov subsequently resigned; but it gave onlookers a frightening glimpse into the difficulties his government faced.

The National Liberal Party (PNL) in Romania was functioning as a minority government with the leader of its former coalition ally, Traian Basescu, now in the president's palace and increasingly distant. Basescu had engineered the establishment of a rival 'Liberal Democratic Party' (PLD), steered by former PNL leader Theodor Stolojan, now one of Basescu's paid advisers. Just before the year's end they had attracted Georghe Flutar, the young and promising agriculture minister, from the PNL to their camp. Though I dismissed his defection with a joke at their annual conference[333] on 12 January 2007 I also warned my Romanian Liberal friends seriously: 'do not allow the arrogance of power to make you an exclusive sect'. It was a message aimed at the rising stars around Tariceanu, who were beginning to flex their muscles in a number of ways but not always in the spirit of pluralism.

Basescu had started to attack his prime minister openly, alleging later that month that Tariceanu had intervened improperly in government business in favour of his friend and former fellow businessman Dinu Patriciu. The smear was never found to have any substance, but it brought into the open the tensions between the two government camps. By 16 April 2007, when I took the national delegation leaders from my parliamentary group on a visit to Bucharest and Timisoara, Tariceanu had dismissed from his cabinet the ministers from Basescu's party and formed a new government[334] from members of his own party and the Hungarian minority party. We had barely left

---

333 Since his name means 'butterfly' I was able to accuse him of 'flitting' from one party to another.

334 This move was to deprive me of one of my deputy leaders, Adrian Cioroianu MEP, recalled home to become foreign minister; and another good MEP, Ovidiu Silaghi, who had become minister for small businesses. Increasingly, however, we were getting used to losing MEPs to national positions when their parties were in government at home. While we were in Bucharest news reached me that one of my Finnish colleagues, Paavo Vayrynen MEP, had been recalled to Helsinki to become minister for foreign trade and that a former MEP colleague, Astrid Thors, had been appointed EU affairs minister.

Romania before their parliament adopted by a large majority a motion sponsored primarily by the Socialists but finally supported by many PNL
deputies[335] to impeach President Basescu for overstepping his legal powers.
It was an ill-judged move, however. The president promptly called a snap
referendum to secure a vote of confidence and was to be returned on 19 May
2007 with the support of 74% of those voting, albeit on a low poll. The political confusion thus displayed allowed veteran German Christian Democrat
MEP Elmar Brok, still smarting from his ousting in January from the chair
of Parliament's foreign affairs committee, to put the cat among the pigeons
at EU level by calling for the Commission to invoke the safeguard clauses
provided for in the accession treaties and delay the benefits of accession to
Romania and Bulgaria.

Both countries were under pressure from the EU to tackle ongoing corruption, even among government ministers. Tariceanu's difficulty was that
the intelligence services capable of uncovering and reporting such corruption reported to the president rather than the prime minister; while
Agriculture Minister Traian Remes was forced to resign after having been
tarred by comments by the president, Tariceanu believed he may have been
innocent. He was to move in the autumn to allow the magistracy to appoint
people to a council to investigate ministerial corruption, to avoid the danger
of witch hunts, and report suspicions or allegations to him. Another German
EPP member, Markus Ferber, was to seize on this reform to accuse
Tariceanu of trying to cover up corruption.

Romania was to go the polls on 25 November to elect its 35 MEPs. On a
visit to Bucharest early in November to address student rallies I was
impressed by the PNL's campaign. Not only were they the party with by far
the most campaign placards, but their choice of independently respected
civil rights campaigner Renate Weber and financial expert Daniel Daianu to
head their lists was to give them a high profile. And with creative campaigners like Christian Busoi[336] and appealing personalities like Adina
Valean they were set to do well. While ALDE's allies in Dan Voiculescu's
Conservative Party, who had supplied us with two hard working observer
MEPs, were to lose their representation in Brussels, the PNL was to return
six members.

By the autumn it was looking as if Tariceanu might have to bring the
Socialists back into government; their leader Mircea Geoanna was under
such attack in his own party that he might otherwise be forced to try to bring
down the government. By Tariceanu's own admission, it was surprising he
had managed to survive so long in government since ejecting Basescu's ministers. But Tariceanu was reluctant to strike an agreement with a Socialist
party which he perceived as not yet ready to return to government. An
attempt I made together with PES leader Poul Nyrup Rasmussen to bring
Tariceanu and Geoanna together privately in Brussels (in March 2008) failed

---

335   Tariceanu, ever cautious, seriously doubted the wisdom of the move, seeing in it a Socialist attempt to reduce
to dust the ruling but already crumbling coalition.

336   Busoi had been elected as president of the Liberal Student Clubs of Romania in 2002 and had become a close
associate of Prime Minister Tariceanu. He was to impress me even before his election to the EP.

to engender close co-operation between them, though co-operation between me and Rasmussen led to my group helping elect Romanian Socialist MEP Adrian Severin to the chair of the EU-Ukraine parliamentary co-operation committee.

Liberal fortunes

The ALDE group in the European Parliament was working well. In Diana Wallis and Luigi Cocilovo we had two prominent vice presidents of Parliament who – together with our three committee chairs – allowed us to punch above our weight in the House. In the Commission, with the welcome addition of Leonard Orban and Meglena Kuneva, we were now the largest political family. In the General Affairs Council, with three foreign and two EU affairs ministers, our weight was increasingly felt. As 2007 opened we led the governments in Finland, Denmark, Estonia, Belgium, Italy and Romania; we were present as coalition partners in government in almost as many countries again. I found surprising reserves of energy for my campaign to create a governing coalition at EU level involving Liberals to replace the unnatural Grand Coalition which reigned. I undertook a tour of EU capitals which took me to Bucharest, Stockholm and Helsinki in January; Riga, Copenhagen and Dublin in February; Sofia, Madrid and Rome in March; Nicosia in May; Lisbon in June; Budapest in September; Valletta in October and Ljubljana in December: I was to visit the capitals of the other member states by the time the House rose for the EP elections in May 2009. Almost everywhere I was received by the prime minister, other senior ministers and opposition leaders. Liberals were in the ascendant.

The difficulty for me still lay, however, in choosing whether to seek a coalition with the right or the left. At the outset – and by ideological inclination – I favoured the latter. But my reason told me that Socialism was in crisis and that a centre-right coalition was the more likely to succeed. Though there were signs of Socialists modernising their economic thinking, it was not yet clear from their representatives in the European Parliament – particularly their leader Martin Schulz – that the commitment to reform had depth. Portugal's prime minister Jose Socrates set about promoting across the EU a culture of 'flexicurity' to reconcile the demands of competition with the need for security of employment, suggesting that Europe's Socialist parties, Portugal's included, were beginning to recognise that for economic policy, times had changed. Parliament secured a majority, which included some Socialist MEPs, at first reading in July to liberalise the EU's postal services and was to agree later in the year to further liberalise rail transport. The Commission's proposals to free up the energy market, published in the autumn, were also to find some support in Socialist ranks[337]. Yet the wobbles in the financial markets were to lead to Parliament's Socialist group reverting to their old certainties. In a parliamentary debate in September 2007 on the threat to jobs posed by the speculative activities of hedge funds, and in the economic and monetary affairs committee's grilling of the

---

337 For example from Eluned Morgan MEP.

European Central Bank, they paraded their old anti-market colours. Many MEPs, across the political spectrum, argued that we needed better to supervise lending and to control the activities of rating agencies, and within a year these matters were to dominate the EU's agenda. Yet no Liberal considered the fault to lie essentially in markets per se.

Moreover, try as I might, I found it difficult to strike up a good working relationship with Socialist group leader Martin Schulz, while EPP leader Joseph Daul, though not greatly charismatic, I found to be of even temper and generally good humour.

The ALDE family's members were divided: while the Germans saw the right as their natural allies, for the French it was the left. In France a refusal by presidential candidate Francois Bayrou to ally with Sarkozy was to cost him his chances in the second round of the presidential election. In the UK the main failure of Menzies Campbell's leadership (because, as *The Sun* put it, 'Ming' lacked 'zing') was inability to distance Liberal Democrats from new prime minister Gordon Brown, though any alliance with the Tories seemed unworkable. And in Italy, as in Poland, our allies were in the process of merging forces with the Socialists. A similar development had occurred in Austria. Austrian prime minister Alfred Gusenbauer had taken onto his party's electoral list a representative of Liberales Forum in a pact which would give the Forum representation in the Nationalrat and his election victory on 1 October 2006 had been so narrow that Liberal votes had in all likelihood secured him victory. While in Romania and Bulgaria the left seemed the natural allies and in Belgium the Liberals had run coalitions with the Socialists and the Greens, Denmark, Sweden and Finland appeared to favour alliances with the right. On 1 February 2007 I met Verhofstadt[338] to discuss my aim of creating a coalition at EU level to determine the next presidents of the Commission and the European Parliament. He told me he supported my initiative, with a preference for a centre-left agreement. The previous week in Helsinki Matti Vanhanen had given me his support, but for a centre-right deal.

In line with the wishes of my colleagues I had no choice but to cultivate good relations with both sides. Many in the Christian Democrats, particularly among the Spanish and the Italians, still resented the positions I had taken on issues relating to right-wing governments in their countries during (and since) my days as chair of the justice and home affairs committee and I needed to win them over; but many German and French Socialists saw me as too right-wing on economic issues. I started a programme of one-to-one meetings to get to know better potential friends in both camps; I was later to extend it to trying to win over likely enemies. I endeavoured to find issues on which I could work together with each of the two major parties in a more structured fashion[339] and started also to increase the attention paid to green issues in my speeches in the House.

---

338 Verhofstadt was to face defeat in the Belgian election of June 2007 but to remain in office as a caretaker prime minister until March of the following year pending the formation of a new, Christian Democrat led government.

339 For example, on 17 October 2007 I hosted a dinner with Commissioner Piebalgs on energy policy to which I invited MEPs from all three major groups.

Increasingly I found myself solicited by journalists: perhaps they were surprised to find a Brit who was strongly pro-European, a group leader who had succeeded in growing his own group and was now campaigning to reform Parliament as a whole, and an advocate for global awareness, ambitious for the Union in tackling the emerging global agenda.

Joseph Daul showed little sympathy for my approaches. Firmly in the camp of the Germans who wanted the Grand Coalition to continue, he remained friendly in our regular meetings but always non-committal. The dissidents within his camp were more than willing to talk, however. I was astonished on one occasion in May 2007, during a debate on EU-Russia relations, when Daul had left the chamber immediately after having made a very pedestrian speech and his benches were applauding loudly my intervention; Daul's rival Gunnar Hokmark, in a move which could have been symbolic, left his seat in the chamber and sat next to me in the seat of the leader he had failed by just 19 votes to unseat in January.

Schulz, by contrast, blew hot and cold. Inspired, he told me, by a conversation I had had with his general secretary, David Harley, at the end of 2006 he sought me out in January for a meeting. We met again in May to try to find common ground. Yet in meetings of his political group he would attack me constantly. He asked for my help on three issues, but offered little in return on matters which might have assisted me. Indeed I was to question in my own mind his good faith in the favours he had asked me, sensing that he sought my assistance simply to attack me in the event I was unable to provide it. Though we could work together on issues of parliamentary reform in the working group established under German Socialist MEP Dagmar Roth-Behrendt or Commission reform on Siim Kallas' drive to create a register of lobbyists, the growing closeness of our member parties in Italy and Poland sent jitters through a Socialist camp with increasingly shallow ideological roots; and in France and Britain, Liberals were rapidly recruiting voters who had previously voted with the left.

In Germany the Socialists were in trouble and the Liberal Free Democrats advancing inexorably in regional elections. Following Finland's election in March, Matti Vanhanen switched coalition partners, from Socialists to Conservatives. Appearing on French television the same month alongside Socialist presidential candidate Segolene Royal, I attacked her for her failure to advance any solutions to her country's economic woes; economics was not her strong suit. And I was to attack Schulz directly in the chamber, accusing him of speaking 'the language of the past'.

Perhaps I was perceived by both Daul and Schulz as a growing danger to the integrity of their own political groups. Social class and the choice between free market and social market economic policies, by which right and left were defined, were of declining importance; Europeans' attitudes to the challenges of globalisation more and more defined policy stances, dividing their groups.

I continued to seek new recruits to my group. In February in Riga I spoke to the Farmers and Greens party, which had traditionally been close to us. In Madrid in March I made an appeal for the establishment of a Castilian Liberal Party to reflect Spain's rich Liberal tradition and carve out new ground between the left and the right. Liberals from Catalonia and the Basque Country sat with us, but none from elsewhere in Spain. I spoke to individual MEPs from the Czech Republic, who might conceivably have joined us. I asked colleagues to befriend MEPs from the regionalist parties in the European Free Alliance[340], which sat (incongruously at times) with the Greens. In July 2007 I sought out Swedish MEP Anders Wijkman, elected on the list of the Christian Democrats, and in October I was to suggest to Malta's prime minister Lawrence Gonczi that it might serve his purpose to have one of his party's MEPs in the Liberal group, to give Malta a voice in all three major political groups.[341] But the two parties which could have fitted well into the ALDE ranks, Nea Demokratia of Greece and the PSD of Portugal, showed little interest in approaches from our side. In both cases their leading figures had been brought firmly into the European People's Party, where they were regularly feted.

When Europe's leading Liberals convened for lunch at the Lambermont Palace in advance of the European Council on 8 March 2007, Guy Verhofstadt had taken up my suggestion to invite French presidential candidate Francois Bayrou. Flushed with a remarkable degree of support in the opinion polls, Bayrou was radiant. *'Je ne le comprends pas. Ils m'aiment, ils m'aiment!'*[342] he exclaimed. I was to find myself in Bologna having supper with Prodi on 22 April 2007 when the results of the first round came through; together we had the pleasure of ringing Bayrou to congratulate him on a very creditable 18.7% of the poll, the highest third party vote in France in over a quarter of a century.

But before long I was to have my work cut out in Italy. Following the merger of Rutelli's troops with those of the Italian Socialists to form the new Democratic Party I had to work hard to keep their MEPs in our camp, knowing that some sought to move them to the Socialist group lock, stock and barrel. If I was to succeed in my endeavours throughout the parliament it may have been due in part to what one Italian newspaper dubbed 'the Watson factor', which in reality was little more than a regular presence in Rome and hard work on my part. It may also have owed something to the visit to Brussels of Democratic Party leader Walter Veltroni on 5 December 2007, when the PES group received him with brickbats and ALDE with bouquets.

By mid-year there was again much speculation in Slovakia that Vladimir Meciar's party would apply to join the ALDE. While Meciar himself had been a firebrand opponent of EU membership in the days prior to Slovakia's accession in 2004, his star had faded and the country's circumstances had changed. The new generation in his party sought to move it to a more centrist, pro-EU position and I had been in discussions with Irena Belohorska MEP and her party's general secretary about a possible move. Meciar him-

---

340   I had wooed the EFA at a seminar organised jointly with them prior to the 2004 elections, but to no avail. It nonetheless remained (and remains) my view that they share more common ground with Liberals than with the Greens.

341   I was also to suggest to the talented EU representative in Valletta, Julian Vassallo, that he stand for the European Parliament on a Liberal list. A small party in Malta which claimed to be the voice of Liberalism there was anything but.

342   'I don't understand it. They love me! They love me!'

self, who had suffered a heart attack, was thought to be fading fast. However an unexpected appearance at his party's conference in June saw him re-elected as its president, under which conditions any coming together would have been hugely controversial[343]. Unwilling to press my ELDR colleagues to accept MEPs from Meciar's party, I was nonetheless able to point them in the direction of our EDP allies. On 19 December 2007 the council of the European Democratic Party was to accept Meciar's HZDS party as an observer member. Although nothing was to happen in the 2004-09 parliament, their sole remaining MEP Sergei Kozlik was to join the Liberal group in July 2009.

Liberals were enjoying a string of successes in national capitals. In the Polish general election of October 2007 the Liberals returned to the Sejm for the first time in ten years, having polled 13% of the vote. In the first round of Slovenia's presidential election in the same month the Liberal candidate took 25% of the vote. And in Denmark a general election called for 13 November saw the Venstre party safely returned to office for a third term in government.

Angela Merkel and Germany

On 17 January 2007 German chancellor and president-in-office of the Council of Ministers Angela Merkel made her first appearance in Parliament's Strasbourg chamber. She presented the programme for the German presidency of the EU, entitled 'Europe succeeding together'. Of 27 heads of state and government she was the only woman. She was to be crucial to sorting out the mess left by the rejection of the Union's Constitutional Treaty in referenda in France and the Netherlands.

While France and Britain had traditionally applied the brakes to European integration at crucial moments, Italy could generally be relied on to help move it forward. So it was that Italy's President Giorgio Napolitano addressed the European Parliament in a formal sitting on 14 February 2007 and pledged his country to 'a single yet plural entity enriched by its diversity, aware of its common heritage of civilisation, and strong through combining co-operation among national governments with a new supranational dimension'. The Italians and the Germans were working together seriously to get the EU back on track. Combined, their forces were considerable.

Germany hosted in Berlin on 25 March, the fiftieth anniversary of the signing of the Treaty of Rome, a European summit meeting. There the heads of state and government adopted a 'Berlin Declaration' recalling how the member states had worked together in adversity and committing themselves to continue to resolve their differences peacefully while striving for common goals. In a covered courtyard in the centre of the history museum on Unter den Linden, in a room where a suicide bomber had been foiled in an attempt to assassinate Hitler, the presidents of the Commission,

---

343   Meciar was to announce from his party's conference platform that his party was 'in negotiations' with ALDE, which caused a flurry of press interest and was probably designed to prevent the Liberals in his party from achieving their goal; it was however untrue.

Parliament and Council addressed the heads of government and other assembled dignitaries. They were preceded by a speech from former Commission president Prodi, who quoted a Hungarian author's recipe for what was needed to build Europe, of which the final ingredient was 'a sprinkling of folly'.

Sentiment can be important on such occasions, even among heads of state and government. The mood music in Berlin persuaded all countries to pledge to try again before the end of the year to reach agreement at an intergovernmental conference on a revised Constitutional Treaty for the EU, to be ratified before the European elections of 2009.[344]

Among the 27 heads of state and government present there were five Liberals, including Estonia's prime minister Andrus Ansip, who had won reelection on 4 March 2007 in a victory which saw his party gain 12 seats in the 101-member parliament[345]. A fortnight later, Finland's prime minister Matti Vanhanen was also to be returned to office, with a good electoral showing for the Centre Party and their Liberal allies the Swedish People's Party.

Parliament had debated the Berlin Declaration ten days beforehand, though somewhat incongruously since no draft of the text was available, and the political group leaders were invited to Berlin to join the event. In a debate after the event, on 28 March 2007, I was able to praise Merkel with the words: 'Your celebration of the Union's success was both timely and appropriate. The Berlin Declaration will herald a new departure'[346].

The heads of state and government recognised that in order to persuade citizens of the merits of deeper EU collaboration they would need to allay popular fears. Thus at the March European Council they undertook to reinforce the European social model, agreeing that 'the common social objectives of member states should be better taken into account within the Lisbon agenda'; and they set out to reduce the administrative burden on business arising from EU legislation by 25% within five years. They sought to emphasise too the advantages of the EU to the consumer, such as the greater ease in transferring money from one country to another through the creation of the European payment area, the reduction in the cost of cross-border mobile telephony through the roaming regulation and the improvement of consumers' rights such as the new provisions covering compensation for delays in air travel. They described the EU as 'united in its resolve that only by working together can we represent our interests and goals in the world of tomorrow'.

It was truly Germany's Angela Merkel who was keeping the EU show on the road. Replying to her statement to Parliament on the June summit on 27 June 2007 I congratulated her on giving 'a green light for Europe and a

---

344   Because of problems in Ireland, Poland and the Czech Republic it was not finally ratified in all countries until October 2009, some four months after the election. It entered into force on 1 December 2009.

345   Ansip's Reform Party polled 28% of the vote and their ELDR sister party (but domestic rival) the Centre Party 26%. The two ELDR parties topped the poll.

346   I was however also critical of the EPP for a declaration it had issued which appeared to claim the credit for building the EU by reference to Monnet, de Gasperi and Kohl. 'Thatcher, Chirac, Berlusconi: they were all EPP leaders too, but you seem to have overlooked their contributions. The Union is not the product of one political party. It belongs to us all', I said.

grand legacy for your leadership'[347]. And Portuguese prime minister Jose Socrates told the House in July 2007 he would do everything in his power to secure agreement on a new treaty by October.

Gathering before the European Council meeting on 21-22 June 2007, Liberal leaders had agreed that the seemingly endless constitutional debate must be brought to a close. The key elements for us were to have the Charter of Fundamental Rights applying to all countries equally, to have a strength-ened formula for foreign policy co-ordination, more efficient and transpar-ent decision-making in the fight against terrorism and an enhanced role for national parliaments in EU decisions. The summit agreed the outlines of a mandate for the intergovernmental conference, but both the UK and Poland were being truculent and it was clear that EU integration would continue to be driven by developments in the outside world rather than by idealism from within. In the words of Andrew Duff MEP it showed 'the Council, forced to work by unanimity, at its worst'[348].

Gordon Brown and Great Britain

Gordon Brown assumed office at the end of June 2007, after a long battle with Tony Blair, in conditions he might not have chosen. His predecessor had called Britain's Brussels-based journalists to see him in London three weeks before his departure to complain that he felt trapped by their editors 'between isolation and treason'; he then departed with a schmaltzy and rather tasteless speech in his constituency about Britain being 'the greatest nation on earth.'[349] But Brown's debut was to depress the UK's pro-Europeans, returning Britain to the spirit of Waterloo; he was to boycott the first EU-Africa summit[350] in seven years in protest against the invitation extended to Robert Mugabe[351]; he would not agree the revised treaty text without satisfaction on issues defined by 'four red lines', thus portraying the Union as a threat to the UK rather than a benefit; and he deliberately turned up late at the ceremony arranged by the Portuguese government on 18 October 2007 for the 27 heads of state and government to sign the treaty[352]. His foreign secretary, David Miliband, there to represent the UK until the

347   Speech in the European Parliament, 27 June 2007

348   Though Andrew Duff would be a beneficiary of an agreement secured by president-in-office Merkel that the European Parliament would be allowed three representatives at the intergovernmental conference, in recognition of ALDE's growing prominence. I nominated him to represent our political family.

349   'This is a blessed nation. The world knows it. In our innermost thoughts, we know it. Britain is the greatest nation on earth'.

350   MEPs met African legislators regularly through the EU-ACP joint parliamentary assembly. But the African, Caribbean and Pacific legislators had boycotted this meeting in November 2002 in protest against the EP's refusal to admit two ministers from Mugabe's government.

351   Despite having arranged a state welcome for China's equally authoritarian president Hu Jintao.

352   Meanwhile a Eurobarometer public opinion survey in the UK in June found 43% in favour of a constitution for the EU and only 36% opposed. I argued that if the UK could no longer live with a treaty it had signed three years previously it would be more honest to seek an amicable divorce from its EU partners.

PM arrived, raised his glass to join a toast proposed by his hosts with the quip: 'This will probably cost me my job.'

One of Brown's 'red lines' had related to the Charter of Fundamental Rights. Apeing the approach of Margaret Thatcher and John Major to the EU's Social Charter, he had set up an Aunt Sally and refused to be moved until it was knocked down. By October it had been agreed that the UK, Ireland and Poland could opt out of the Charter of Fundamental Rights: the charter could not be used in the ECJ to challenge their current legislation or to introduce new rights for citizens. Many collective decisions in justice and home affairs and common foreign and security policy would also allow scope for opt-outs. This led some German MEPs to pose Europe's equivalent of Britain's 'West Lothian question', viz should UK MEPs have the right to vote on policy formation if their government did not intend to apply the policy? With these changes, however – and with the addition of an extra parliamentary seat for Italy – the European Council meeting of 19 October 2007 agreed to proceed to signature and ratification of the new treaty.

The Charter of Fundamental Rights, while not to be an integral part of the treaty, was solemnly proclaimed on 12 December and annexed to the text of the Treaty of Lisbon signed the following day. The Council called for a swift completion of national ratification processes to allow it to enter into force on 1 January 2009.

The informal meeting of the heads of state or government on 19 October 2007 had also looked again at the challenges facing the EU. By now, no member state government contested that these had changed fundamentally in the space of a decade. Whereas ten years previously most European Council members would have justified their country's membership of the EU primarily on the grounds of the peace and prosperity the Union had brought them, now they spoke of the need for EU solidarity in facing the pressures of wider, global developments such as climate change, migration and internationally organised crime. By December they had agreed to establish an independent reflection group of nine people, to be led by former Spanish prime minister Felipe Gonzalez, to study the longer term challenges for the EU and to report by June 2010 on their findings.

I sought to exploit Brown's obstructionism by demonstrating that there was a substantial UK political party fighting the European corner. Thus I procured for Barroso an invitation to address the UK's Liberal Democrat party conference in Brighton in September 2007, as our guest of honour. Speaking as the first serving Commission president ever to address the conference of a UK political party, he said: 'I am struck by how close my vision of Europe, as president of the Commission, is to that set out in your consultation paper'. It is unlikely that he could have said the same at a conference of the UK's Labour Party and inconceivable at a conference of the Conservatives with whom his EPP was officially allied.

In addition to scoring a 'first' and underlining the role of the Liberals as the UK's most constructively European party I had also been keen for Barroso to meet Sir Menzies Campbell, the new UK Liberal Democrat leader. I might as well not have bothered. Within a month Campbell had resigned and by December we had elected our most knowledgeable leader about EU matters ever, my former colleague Nick Clegg. Having worked in the Commission and served in the European Parliament, and with Dutch as his mother tongue, Nick had no need of any introduction to Brussels.[353]

Since the election of 12 UKIP MEPs, the UK's anti-Europeans were getting media attention out of all relation to their size. Partly it was through bad behaviour; their disruption of the solemn ceremony in Parliament in December 2007 for the signing of the Charter of Fundamental Rights of EU citizens was reminiscent of the behaviour of the UK's infamous football hooligans. But in part it was a more serious disruption of Parliament's procedures: their move in January 2008 to call for a roll-call vote on every vote held that week (a process which is normally reserved for only the tightest or most crucial votes) was to cost Parliament EUR 25,000 in the first week alone[354] and to slow considerably our voting procedures.

The European Parliament, like any other, has endured its fair share of histrionics from members wanting to draw attention to some cause or other or, often more accurately, to themselves. But with the rise of populist parties in Europe and the inevitable election of a number of MEPs from their ranks, parliamentary behaviour deteriorated. In February 2008 Parliament held a debate which (albeit gratingly self-congratulatory even to some of us who work for a federal Europe) led to the approval by Parliament, by a margin of four to one, of the Lisbon Treaty. In London and in Dublin the treaty's opponents were stealing the headlines. They now tried to do the same in Strasbourg by arriving in yellow sweatshirts dressed as chickens, accusing the majority of 'chickening out' of a referendum. Parliament's president was applauded when he said to the protesting MEPs: "If your parents could see you now they'd be ashamed of you!"

But some of the cases with which President Poettering had to deal were of an altogether more serious nature. In late January Conservative MEP Daniel Hannan, an anti-European polemicist dignified only by the management of *The Daily Telegraph*, compared a procedural vote in the House to a vote in the German Reichstag in 1933. In so doing he was seemingly effectively labelling the EP's German president as a Nazi. Poettering had put to a vote a ruling which would stop political groups abusing procedures to disrupt business, as UKIP MEPs had done at the previous session with their demand for a roll-call on every single vote and the right of reply on every item of business. Preventing deliberate wrecking tactics could not reasonably be compared to the anti-democratic practices of the National Socialists in Germany nor could the president of the European Parliament implicitly be painted as a Nazi. Hannan was duly expelled from his political group on 1 February 2008.

In March Britain's *Sunday Times* reported that UKIP MEP Nigel Farage had been using public money to employ his son as a researcher while the

---

353   The UK Liberal Democrat leadership race had centred on two former MEPs, the other being Chris Huhne. Having worked closely with both I had no hesitation in supporting Nick, a team player and potentially a good team leader.

354   Since each member's vote had to be recorded and registered and the result published in each EU language, the cost was estimated at EUR 300 per vote. UKIP were to agree that in future they would ask for roll call votes only on legislative votes; nonetheless they have continued the practice to date.

latter was also a full-time student at Exeter University; and that Conservative MEP Giles Chichester had paid his parliamentary staff allowance for many years straight into the accounts of his family's business. Chichester was forced to step down from his post as leader of the UK Conservative MEPs, but no other party sanction was brought against him and his party reselected him as their No.1 candidate in SW England at the following election. The same week, Parliament voted to lift the immunity from prosecution of Austrian MEP Hans-Peter Martin, who faced criminal charges of fraud against the taxpayer for abuse of his allowances. The European Parliament was obliged to begin to grapple – which it was to do far more effectively than the Westminster Parliament – with abuses of trust by its not always honourable members; as a result, three MEPs from the United Kingdom Independence Party were subsequently to serve prison sentences for fraud. Liberals recalled the need to introduce swiftly reforms to the system of payment of allowances and expenses to MEPs which, despite the efforts of Pat Cox three years previously, were not to be in place fully until July 2009.

On 1 January 2008 Slovenia became the first of the new member states to take on the rotating presidency of the Union while on the same day Cyprus and Malta joined the eurozone. This had the welcome effect of making the euro legal tender on British territory, albeit in a far-flung corner of the empire: the UK government decided it made sense to make the euro legal tender at British military bases on Cyprus; but they kept it very quiet.

Slovenia and Serbia

Though Slovenia was to be the first of the 'class of 2004' to assume the rotating presidency of the European Council, with Prime Minister Janez Jansa at the helm, the battle for media coverage in the EU in January 2008 was won hands down by President Sarkozy. His press conference, in which he laid out his plans for a French presidency of the EU due to start on 1 July, overshadowed news of January's meeting in Ljubljana of the college of commissioners[355] with the incoming Slovenian presidency. Sarkozy had entered the Slovenian fray with all the sensitivity of Napoleon 208 years before.

Slovenian prime minister Jansa nonetheless had an intelligent programme of his own to present, including further development of EU co-operation and a stabilisation and association agreement with Serbia. He came to Parliament in Strasbourg on 16 January 2008 to outline his plans. My speech writers had managed to find little in Slovene history which I could deploy intelligently in my reply to Jansa, so I dug out a book of poetry by Franz Preseren and scoured it for a suitable line or two. One of the by-products of having to speak on behalf of Liberals during seven and a half years at the helm was that I became well acquainted with Europe's national poets, from Franz Preseren to Fernando Pessoa.

Slovenia's presidency drew on the experience of Janez Potocnik. In the

---

355   Led by Vice President Wallstrom, since Barroso had a heavy cold.

autumn of 2006 Commissioner Potocnik, keen to put to best use the limited extra funding for research which Parliament had squeezed out of the Council of Ministers, had been confronted with a fierce lobby claiming to defend human rights by opposing research on embryonic human stem cells. The influence of a more conservative Pope was making itself felt in the European People's Party. The Liberal commissioner's opponents managed to force onto Parliament's agenda in June 2006 a vote on the matter, which dominated the news headlines in Italy, where the government was divided, and caused a flurry of diplomatic activity by the Vatican. Their move was to fail, but by a margin of only 45 votes. The EU did not seek to decide what research was legal and what was not; that was a matter for each member state, but if a country allowed research using stem cells, Liberals reasoned, it should be allowed to seek financial support for this from the EU. Potocnik now wanted to launch a campaign for a 'fifth freedom'. Economic success, Slovenia argued, required not only the free movement of people, goods, services and capital but also the free movement of knowledge. Thus it sought to emphasise the need to create greater mobility for researchers, greater freedom for universities and greater investment in people as the most important resource in a 'knowledge economy'. It sought to advance joint initiatives such as Galileo[356], the European Institute for Technology and the European Research Council and to give the EU the goal of making high speed internet available in all schools by 2010.

A competent EU presidency was not to help Prime Minister Jansa at the polls, however. When his countrymen went to cast their ballots in September 2008 they ejected his party from office. The Liberal Democrats of Slovenia – now divided into two parties since some members had left and formed a new party, ZARES – managed to win 15% of the votes between them[357]. They formed a coalition with the Socialists.

Slovenia, long the most developed part of the former Yugoslavia, had been fortunate largely to escape the immolation of the 1990s. Alone among the nations of Yugoslavia, Slovenes had joined the EU and the euro[358]. Their first presidency of the EU was to involve them, however, in helping some of their former compatriots.

The quest for a stabilisation and association agreement with Serbia was to

---

356 Central to economic competitiveness was investment in high-technology infrastructure. While America possessed a system for global positioning by satellite, Europe did not. The Galileo system, however, initiated in 2003, was designed to overcome this disadvantage. The challenge with Galileo was to find the substantial sums of money needed to develop it. Liberals were determined that Europe should have its own system. Thus it was under a Liberal initiative that agreement was reached in September 2007 that the system would be financed from the EU budget with a view to launching the 26 remaining satellites in the autumn of 2009 and having the system fully operational by the middle of 2013. EP budget rapporteur and ALDE MEP Kyosti Virrankoski was to develop a funding mechanism to allow almost EUR 300 million in unspent agricultural funds to be re-deployed to the Galileo project. The second satellite was launched in May 2008, carrying an atomic clock accurate to within less than a nano-second a day.

357 LDS polled 9.37% and ZARES 5.21%.

358 In May the EU was to celebrate the 10th anniversary of the decision to create the euro and the European Commission and ECB to recommend that Slovenia join on 1 January 2009, bringing the number of member countries to 16.

absorb much of the energies of Prime Minister Jansa and Commissioner Rehn. The consensus of opinion in the EU was that a guaranteed independence for Kosovo was the price Serbia would have to pay for closer relations. In January 2008 Tomislav Nikolic, leader of the Serbian Radical Party, beat the more moderate incumbent Boris Tadic in the first round of Serbia's presidential election, with a four point lead.

The EU's General Affairs and External Relations Council, worried about a lurch towards extremism, discussed Serbia on 28 January 2008. Three weeks later, on 17 February 2008, Kosovo declared independence from Serbia, leading to a riot in Belgrade. 18 of the 27 EU member states recognised it almost immediately, but in Belgrade and in Moscow the move was heavily contested, if not unexpected.

ALDE MEPs had discussed Serbia and Kosovo in depth in April 2006, at a seminar held jointly with our counterparts on the Parliamentary Assembly of the Council of Europe. Kosovo had been administered and protected by the UN since the war ended in 1999. Legally it formed part of Serbia; but most Liberals, still imbued with Woodrow Wilson's doctrine of the self-determination of peoples, believed its future lay in national self-determination within the context of EU membership. Indeed, we saw the promise of EU membership as the glue which held the western Balkan states to the path of reform and stabilisation.

In the autumn of 2006 the UN secretary general had commissioned a report about the future status of the province; it had proven impossible to reach a negotiated settlement between Kosovans and Serbs, yet Kosovo could not return to the status quo ante 1999. The UN therefore stressed the need for a settlement to guarantee a democratic, multi-ethnic Kosovo committed to the rule of law, and to the protection of minorities and of cultural and religious heritage. Finnish diplomat Martti Ahtisaari had proposed giving Kosovo the status of 'sovereignty supervised by the international community'; this had been backed by MEPs on 29 March 2007. The EU, convinced that the future of the western Balkans lay within the European Union, had expressed its willingness to take over responsibility for the security of Kosovo and to assist in its economic reconstruction.

Former Slovenian defence minister Jelko Kacin MEP was Parliament's rapporteur for relations with Serbia. In a report presented to the House on 27 June 2007 and approved on 25 October he praised Serbia for its peaceful handling of the separation of Montenegro, welcomed progress made in improving administrative capacity and inter-ethnic relations but pointed to 'grave systematic weaknesses' in the judicial system, including a problem of corruption. He called on the Serbian government to re-open the Truth and Reconciliation Commission established in 2001 and to continue to improve its co-operation with the ICTY. But he trod carefully on the question of Kosovo's independence, arguing that the final status of Kosovo should be treated separately from the integration of Serbia into western European governance structures.

I had put the matter on the agenda of our group meeting on 18 February in advance of a debate in Parliament on 20 February 2007. Opinion was divided, but the majority agreed with Kacin that the best solution would be de facto independence. On 23 February we were to lose the wise counsel of former Slovene prime minister and president, Janez Drnovsec, who died after a long illness[359].

Nonetheless we followed developments closely and in late March 2008 I led a four person delegation of colleagues to Pristina to meet the government and the international peacekeeping forces stationed there. We found a well-functioning multi-ethnic society being undermined by forces in Belgrade, who still held sway north of the Ibar river where they sought to radicalise the Kosovan Serb population.

For the EU to take on responsibility for the security of Kosovo would be a big challenge. If the chronic unemployment (officially 33% but really over 60%, the Minister of Labour told us), poverty (average per capita income just EUR 1000 per annum), electricity shortages and dearth of water were not problem enough, recent armed attacks by Serbs on customs points, railway lines, police forces and the judiciary were stretching substantially the resources and the mandate of the 300 or so UNMIK troops there. Kosovo was to become an early test of the EU's capacity to mount operations.

At the beginning of April 2008 the matter was discussed at the NATO summit in Bucharest. On 11 May Serbia went to the polls in round two of its general election. I was pleased to be able to congratulate Serbian Liberal leader Cedomir Jovanovic[360] on having won 13 seats, up from nine in the previous Parliament, thereby becoming key to the formation of a pro-EU government. Olli Rehn had called me in January, after the first round of elections, to urge me to speak to Jovanovic and persuade him to throw the weight of his party behind Tadic in round two. Janez Jansa and Olli Rehn now both called me on 13 May to urge me to intervene with Jovanovic to secure his support for a coalition with Tadic's Socialists. I had already invited Jovanovic to Brussels to address our group meeting on 15 May, but managed to catch him by telephone the day before. As I suspected, for his view had been similar in January, he was reluctant to put the Socialists into power, telling me Tadic had done the Liberals no favours during the election campaign and that the Socialists were unreformed and could not be relied on to lead the country towards the EU. Nonetheless he recognised that the alternative would be worse.

No party had gained enough votes in the general election to form a government on its own. However, Nikolic was to strike a deal with the Socialists' President Tadic on a technocrat, Mirko Cvetkovic, taking office as prime minister. The European Council in June noted the EU's success in signing a stabilisation and association agreement with Serbia, anticipating an acceleration of its progress towards joining the EU; as for Kosovo, the EU would now make

---

359   Nonetheless I had the good fortune to be advised by Brigadier Anthony Welch, a former UK army officer who had served the international community there and a fellow Liberal Democrat candidate in the European elections of 2004, whom I had invited to a Liberal conference on Kosovo the previous year and whose wise advice I appreciated.

360   Jovanovic was a slight but courageous man, not afraid to tell Serbs when he thought they were in the wrong. His home had twice been attacked by Nikolic's thugs and his car blown up.

preparations to appoint a special representative[361] there and a EULEX mission and would shortly take over security responsibilities from UNMIK. And when Jansa reported to Parliament on 24 June 2008 he told MEPs that the new government in Serbia would favour EU accession and that the EU would support the forthcoming donors' conference to raise money for reconstruction.

Among the states which failed to recognise Kosovo were divided societies like Cyprus who feared the repercussions of similar developments in domestic politics. Yet the EU's soft power was working the same wonders internally, in Cyprus, as externally in Kosovo. In March 2007 another wall dividing a city had been torn down without a drop of blood being spilt when the barriers in Nicosia's Ledra Street[362] which separated north from south were removed by the president of the internationally-unrecognised Turkish Republic of Northern Cyprus, Mehmet Ali Talat, and the (Greek Cypriot) president of the Republic of Cyprus, Demetris Christofias, allowing trade and normal shopping to resume. Karin Resetarits MEP, the Liberal member of the European Parliament's contact group for relations with Northern Cyprus, had reported to colleagues that good progress was being made.

In March 2008, MEPs voted to approve a new commissioner from Cyprus. Markos Kyprianou, who had played an active role in Liberal co-ordination meetings despite coming from a party which was not formally aligned with the ELDR, had been recalled to serve as foreign minister; he was succeeded by a member of his country's longstanding Liberal party, Androulla Vassiliou, wife of former president George Vassiliou. Mrs Vassiliou secured overwhelming support from MEPs to take on the health portfolio vacated by her predecessor.

Gaza

Throughout 2007, conditions in the Israeli-Palestine conflict had deteriorated. Gaza had been besieged since June. One and a half million people were trapped with hopelessly insufficient provision of water, electricity, fuel or sewage services. Many businesses were bankrupt and four people out of every five depended on UN assistance. The kidnapping in Gaza of a BBC journalist, Alan Johnston on 12 March 2007 and his detention for 113 days had become a matter of particular concern to MEPs. On 19 June 2007, after a rapid deterioration of the situation, Parliament held a special debate on Palestine with interventions by all the group leaders during which President Poettering spoke of 'the terrible situation and frightening developments over the past days in the Gaza Strip.' Over the coming months the matter was to dominate debate: Parliament adopted a resolution condemning the Hamas takeover of Gaza in July and another on 11 October on the humanitarian situation in Gaza. We were to hear from King Abdullah of Jordan in December 2007 and from High Representative Solana and Commissioner Ferrero-Waldner in January 2008 about the impact of the Israeli blockade lasting several weeks; in

---

361   Peter Feith was to be appointed on 4 February 2008.
362   The barriers had been in place longer than the Berlin Wall.

a resolution adopted three weeks later the House reiterated 'its deep concern at the humanitarian and political crisis'. On 10 March 2008, Parliament debated the situation again. The Annapolis agreement[363] had promised peace within ten months, yet on 1 March 2008 56 Gazans died and on 8 March eight Israelis died in an attack in Jerusalem. Though a truce was reached on 11 March 2008, the region remained a tinderbox.

The EU's policy was based on three assumptions: the impossibility of dialogue with Hamas; the need to treat Israel as a normal democracy, and Palestinian president Mahmoud Abbas being the voice of reasonable Palestinians. Many of my colleagues and I questioned these assumptions.

The Israeli authorities which collected tax receipts on behalf of the Palestinian Authority were refusing to release the monies collected. Liberals took this matter extremely seriously. Commissioner Louis Michel had worked hard to find and release EUR 229 million in aid to Palestine in March, which would help rebuild infrastructure, fund the activities of the UN Relief and Works Agency and allow the Palestinian Authority to pay key staff.

Parliament debated a motion critical of the number and the detention conditions of Palestinian prisoners in Israeli gaols in July. We were naturally concerned too about the case of Israeli corporal Gilad Shalit, who had been taken prisoner by Palestinian militants on 25 June 2006 and held hostage since: but there were an estimated 11,000 Palestinians being held by Israel. We decided not to vote on a motion for a resolution until September, however. In the meantime Israel decided to release on 25 August some 198 Palestinian prisoners, which Parliament recognised as a helpful gesture. Nonetheless, opinion among MEPs against Israel was hardening. And when ministers from the countries of the new Union for the Mediterranean met on 3-4 November 2008 their discussions were again overshadowed by the Israel-Palestine conflict. They were able to agree only that Barcelona should be the seat of the secretariat for the new body.

On 2 December 2008 Israeli foreign minister Tzipi Livni visited Parliament's foreign affairs committee. She told MEPs that the terrorist threat left Israel with no choice other than its current policies in the Gaza Strip. Louis Michel had attacked Israel's blockade of Gaza, pointing out that in the last month only one crossing point had been open, and only for four days, making it almost impossible for humanitarian aid to reach the Palestinians; he described it as 'collective punishment which is a violation of international humanitarian law'. On 6 December 2008 MEPs voted to postpone a plan to grant Israel new privileges in scientific co-operation with the EU. Annemie Neyts had argued strongly at an ALDE group meeting the previous day in favour of the upgrading of relations between the EU and Israel and had swung support in her favour in a sparsely attended meeting. To me, however, this was unacceptable: I intervened on the floor of the House to ensure that the Liberal votes made the difference.

---

363 The Annapolis conference on 27 November 2007 took place 30 years after Egypt's President Anwar el-Sadat had signed a peace agreement with Israel and 60 years after the UN had approved the Palestine partition plan. Bush was able to persuade Olmert and Abbas to sign a joint statement supporting a two-state solution, which had been rejected by the Arab League 60 years earlier.

The level of force used by the Israelis in their siege of Gaza in January 2009 shocked the world – over 1,000 Gazans lost their lives against just ten Israeli soldiers and three civilians – and was to lead a year later to condemnation of Israel by the UN for war crimes. The Israeli use of white phosphorus caused horrific injuries. The Czechs got their new six-month presidency off to a bad start by a statement which sympathised with Israel: Foreign Minister Karel Schwarzenberg was later to tell incredulous members of the EP's foreign affairs committee that 'Israel is listening to us'[364]. President Sarkozy visited the region 'to broker a ceasefire' totally independently of the presence there of an official EU delegation and the EU's calls for a ceasefire were utterly ignored by the Israelis who knew that US president George W. Bush, a lame duck president with fewer than three weeks left in office, would do nothing to stop them. A cynical Israeli pullout just before President Obama took office told more about the operation than anything else. On 21 January 2009 I spoke to Javier Solana and told him of the deep disappointment of me and my colleagues that he had not put more pressure on Israel. As we expected, the EU's role was to prove depressingly familiar: Humanitarian Affairs Commissioner Louis Michel was to visit at the end of January to assess the damage and make arrangements for Europe to pay EUR 40 million for rebuilding work.

When Parliament debated the role of the EU in the Middle East with Solana on 18 February 2009 he said that although the war in Gaza had ended, 'the humanitarian situation remained heartbreaking'. However the conditions for Europeans and Americans to work together for peace in the region were probably better than ever, he added, and it was clear that no single country could tackle resolution of the conflicts in the Middle East alone. In reply I pointed out that Hamas had emerged from the conflict 'stronger politically, intact militarily and holding out against recognition of Israel' and that the new government expected in Israel as a result of the election would be more hard-line than before and resistant to the idea of a Palestinian state. I called for a free and fair international investigation into alleged war crimes in the Gaza conflict[365]. 'If Israel is wrongly accused, its name should be cleared', I said, 'but if it has committed those crimes it must face up to its responsibilities'.

Parliament's President Poettering, who had long taken an interest in the Middle East and who co-chaired the Euro-Med Parliamentary Assembly, had declared 2008 a Year of Intercultural Dialogue and set about bringing to Parliament a series of guests, each invited to address the assembly. Liberals were angry when we discovered that all were religious figures and all were men and that while the representatives of the Christian church and of Judaism were chosen from Europe, the representative of Islam (the Grand Mufti) was brought from Damascus, as if to suggest that Islam was

---

364   At the same meeting an Israeli diplomat, seeking to justify Israel's invasion by showing MEPs images of human shields allegedly used by Hamas militants, was embarrassingly exposed by a sharp-eyed MEP who spotted the date '2004' revealingly displayed in the lower corner of the transparencies.

365   The Goldstone report for the UN was to provide this.

not a European religion while Christianity and Judaism were. On behalf of the Liberal group I insisted at the conference of presidents that we also invite Asma Jahangir, a Pakistani intellectual who was the UN's special rapporteur on freedom of religion and belief, who came to address Parliament in Strasbourg in June 2008. I knew that she would argue for intercultural dialogue to be understood in a wide sense, embracing religious and non-religious perspectives. I was also successfully to suggest Sir Jonathan Sacks, Britain's chief rabbi, whose books I found stimulating and who was to address the House on 19 November 2008.

Long recognised by Liberals, the value of cultural co-operation and intercultural dialogue was now increasingly being recognised by all Europe's leaders as an integral part of foreign policy. The European Council in June 2008 would underline 'the importance of cultural co-operation in addressing political processes and challenges ... and in fostering good neighbourly relations'.

Human rights

When Parliament adopted its annual report on human rights in the world, drawn up for 2007 by Marco Cappato MEP, it noted continued cause for concern, particularly in Russia and China. Liberals saw another opportunity to draw attention to human rights abuses. We were concerned that right-wing MEPs were being too soft on Russia and the left too willing to overlook abuses in China. While we needed good trading relations with these countries and co-operation in the management of global affairs, to integrate them fully into the structures of global governance while they retained authoritarian regimes gave them a legitimacy which put at risk much of the progress which had been made in respect for the rule of law, freedom, human rights and democracy. Thus Bronislaw Geremek and I unveiled in Brussels a 'counter' recording the number of days spent in prison by Russian businessman Mikhail Khodorkovsky, whose main offence had been to fund the Liberal party Yabloko. Every day for 20 days in the run-up to Russia's parliamentary elections our Khodorkovsky counter would show one more day spent unjustly in detention and the countdown in the number of days remaining before a presidential election in Russia in which no Liberal candidate had been allowed to run and to monitor which no international observers would be permitted.

To step up pressure on the Chinese government to show respect for human dignity in the run-up to the 2008 Olympic Games, I used a meeting of the EP's China delegation in January to give an earful to the representative of the Chinese embassy about the case of Hu Jia, a lawyer who was being persecuted for defending AIDS sufferers. Liberals were active in securing the adoption of a resolution on 17 January 2008 formally calling on the Chinese authorities for his release.[366] In April the Liberal group secured a parliamentary statement on

---

366   In October 2008 we were to secure for Hu Jia the 2008 Sakharov Prize.

Tibet and a resolution condemning China's repression there[367]. I was to regret that a diary clash prevented me from joining former French prime minister Jean-Pierre Raffarin on a visit to Beijing in March.

On 7 May Sarah Ludford MEP was to call for greater EU support for the International Criminal Court in implementing the indictment of two alleged perpertrators of human rights abuses in Darfur, one of whom was a serving minister in the Sudanese government. (Liberals had celebrated the previous autumn when Salih Mahmoud Osman, a Sudanese human rights lawyer, was voted the winner of the 2007 Sakharov Prize for freedom of thought[368]. For over 20 years this courageous man had provided free legal aid to the victims of human rights abuses in his country.) ALDE MEPs were concerned too about the situation in the Congo, where sexual violence was the worst in the world. In April 2008 I was pleased to be able to put Emma Nicholson MEP into the chair of a new contact group for relations with Iraq, where she could continue her human rights work on behalf of the long-suffering Iraqi peoples. And though it was to be only a partial victory, Liberals cheered when Morgan Tsvangirai's Movement for Democratic Change beat Robert Mugabe's party in elections in Zimbabwe and welcomed Tsvangirai to the Liberal International congress in Belfast, Northern Ireland in May 2008. Liberal MEPs Marios Matsakis and Frederique Ries were active in preparing a parliamentary resolution about the abuse of human rights in Egypt, whose opposition leader Ayman Nour was to visit Brussels at the invitation of me and Edward McMillan-Scott MEP in April 2009.

Liberals became increasingly concerned about the plight of the poor in developing countries. World food prices had spiralled and in April 2008 OECD figures revealed that for all the continuing talk of millennium development goals, overseas development aid from EU member states had fallen to just 0.38% of GDP. In May 2008 Parliament debated the matter and called for investment in agriculture, aquaculture, rural development and agribusinesses in developing countries. Although the EU remained the biggest aid donor overall it was still far from the promise at the Gleneagles summit in 2005 to increase aid to 0.56% by 2010 and 0.7% by 2015.

Louis Michel put the question of aid on the agenda of the college of commissioners and obtained their approval for a communication on speeding up progress towards the millennium development goals. Seeking to mobilise concern about the sharp rise in world food prices, he made a statement to Parliament on 22 April 2008[369].

---

367   Zhang Zhi-jun, a senior official from the international relations department of the Chinese Communist Party, was subsequently to try – in a remarkably intense departure from normal diplomatic behaviour – to gag me by threatening that nobody would receive me in the PRC if I did not stop attacking his country and supporting Taiwan's democratically elected president; he knew that I was planning once more to take a delegation of MEPs to China.

368   This prize was established largely as a result of work done by ELD group staff member Richard Moore. Moore was so widely held in high esteem that he was sometimes invited to give his opinion in committee meetings, which would be unthinkable nowadays.

369   In May he was to visit Burma to offer immediate assistance of EUR 17 million to the victims of the devastation caused by cyclone Nargis; Parliament congratulated him on his prompt action. He offered help too to the survivors of the earthquake in China's Sichuan province.

The meeting of the European Council on 19 and 20 June devoted time to examining the policy implications of high food and oil prices. It welcomed the Commission's intention closely to monitor commodity market prices and to elaborate a proposal for a new fund to support agriculture in developing countries. The UN had also set up a high level task force on the matter, recognising that high food prices put at risk the millenium development goals. Europe's national leaders said: '2008 should mark a turning point in the collective efforts to eradicate poverty ... to ensure that by 2015 all the MDGs will be achieved worldwide.' Before the end of the year, Louis Michel had persuaded his fellow commissioners to establish a budget facility of one billion euros to allow a rapid response mechanism for soaring food prices in developing countries. This was adopted by Parliament on 4 December 2008.

Liberals prepare for the election

I had decided to use the New Year 2008 to start to draw public attention to my bid for election in July the following year for the presidency of the European Parliament. I had consulted widely among colleagues and staff and had put on paper a series of campaign ideas. I was shortly to record my first weekly videoblog, setting out my pitch.

I was to discover reserves of energy I had not known I possessed. At home I was about to chair the first meeting of the campaign in my constituency to re-elect me to the European Parliament; in Parliament I was organising my campaign for a run at the presidency. An active campaign was essential for each, but the latter occupied more of my attention. The European Policy Centre's 2008 New Year debate between the major political group leaders provided me with a platform to set out my stall. While Daul, Schulz and I agreed that public confidence in the EU must be improved, our recipes for achieving this differed. I wanted 'less introspection, more action'; I argued that there was too much red tape and that markets had to be made to work to boost public confidence in the EU. Schulz called for a more 'social and balanced' Europe. He argued that people felt the EU was threatening everything the trade unions and social partners had achieved over 40 years, that the Commission focused on economic strategies only and that the Union had to be more active in achieving social justice. Though better than Daul, Schulz was, however, not a convincing public speaker in front of audiences of this nature; dry and serious, he lacked the ability to make his public laugh or to leaven his points with anecdote and simile.

The ALDE group kicked off 2008 with a seminar on reform of the EU budget. We had argued in 2005-6 that the funds foreseen for multi-annual programmes were insufficient. Since the member states had agreed, despite massive pressure from Parliament, to increase them only very little we now argued for reform of the budget to prioritise better financial support for the Union's policy goals. The Commission had opened a consultation process the previous autumn designed to achieve this. Anne Jensen MEP led for Liberals in a discussion of the likely impact of the new treaty on the budget process and how the revenue-raising system might be reformed. Liberals were in no doubt that the horse-trading between member states over budget contributions had reached its natural limits. In future, a system of own-resources, directly raised, would be necessary.

I met Olli Rehn for lunch on 10 January 2008 to put the finishing touches to our plans for a second Liberal leaders' strategy weekend, which he had persuaded Matti Vanhanen to host in the north of Finland. The summit, on 6-7 April, welcomed Ivars Godmanis as Latvia's new prime minister and approved Anders Fogh Rasmussen as our candidate for president of the European Council, Olli Rehn for high representative and me for president of the European Parliament. It was the first time Liberals had organised any-thing of this nature in advance of a European election.

My bid for the presidency of Parliament in 2009, formally approved by my colleagues in January, and those of Anders Fogh Rasmussen and Olli Rehn for Council president and high representative respectively, showed Liberals better organised. With less than two years to run to the election or appointment to senior EU positions, eager candidates were setting out their stalls. Thus Commission president Jose Manuel Barroso wined and dined me at one of Strasbourg's better restaurants in mid-January and accepted with alacrity my suggestion that he come and address senior colleagues of mine in March; in the event he was well prepared, combative and impres-sive and I believe many left minded to give him a second term in office. Javier Solana, keen to continue as high representative, paid more attention than normal to MEPs, visiting Parliament to make statements on Iran and Gaza at the end of January. Anders Fogh Rasmussen, keen to become the first full-time president of the European Council, visited my parliamentary group in January to impress on Liberal MEPs his credentials as a candidate for the job. In February I hosted a lunch in Strasbourg for Simeon Saxe-Coburg-Gotha who, although over 70 years old, was fitter than many men of 40[370]. He was being touted by former Bulgarian foreign minister Solomon Passy as a candidate for Council president. A leading Brussels lobbyist was even to approach me in June seeking my support for Tony Blair's candidacy; he clearly had not researched my views on Blair or those of my party. At the Ruka strategy meeting we had appointed Vanhanen as the Liberal family's spokesperson on these issues and though finally we were to be unsuccess-ful across the board, with the continuation of the Grand Coalition, we were at once more disciplined than ever before. Even the president of the ELDR Party, to whom I chatted on the flight to Finland to try to overcome her feel-ings that she was being overshadowed[371], had to admit that our new strat-egy looked impressive to the political commentators.

---

370   Simeon had taken his fellow Liberal leaders for a long mountain hike the previous summer at their Borovets strategy weekend and had amazed us all by the speed and nimblebodiedness with which he walked.

371   The ELDR Party had moved into new headquaters on the Rue Montoyer and appeared – under Secretary General Federica Sabbati and a team of dedicated staff members – better organised than before. But it still failed too often to see the big picture in political terms.

Italy's government falls

In mid-April 2008 Silvio Berlusconi's Forza Italia won clear majorities in the House and the Senate and stormed into the Campidoglio in the city elections in Rome. Franco Frattini was recalled from Brussels to become foreign minister; MEP and Forza Italia delegation leader Antonio Tajani was nominated for the Commission and Parliament was awash with talk of a deal between Italian vice president Mario Mauro and Berlusconi's arch enemy Martin Schulz to share the presidency of the House in a Grand Coalition in the 2009-14 mandate. Liberals lost not only a prime minister, Romano Prodi, who had worked (as a cousin if not always as a brother) within our family; we also saw MEPs Lapo Pistelli, Alfonso Andria and Luciana Sbarbati depart for elected positions at home. But Barroso was wise enough not to put the untested Tajani into the challenging justice and home affairs brief in his college; instead, Barrot was moved to justice and home affairs and Tajani given transport. This led to a typically inane and offensive comment by Berlusconi himself, who quipped: 'It is better to be in charge of transport than in charge of homosexuals'. Liberal Italy winced at the crassness of their country's head of government.

The new Italian government was to face two early challenges for which it was ill equipped. The first was a crisis in waste management arising from a failure to implement properly management regulations put in place over a decade previously. Landfill waste disposal around Naples and elsewhere had fallen into the hands of organised crime. The European Commission was taking the country to the European Court of Justice. The second was a wave of physical attacks on immigrants, mainly but not exclusively from the Roma community. A populist election campaign had created a climate of impunity in which the mob (in Naples) and the police (in Rome) could enter migrant ghettoes with the aim of forcible eviction of the residents. Liberals called for urgent debate at EU level: when Parliament debated the matter on 20 May it transpired that while Spain and Hungary had made great strides in recent years to integrate such minority communities, drawing on EU funds voted specifically for that purpose, successive Italian governments had ignored the problem and were now reaping a harvest of bitterness and violence[372]. On 10 July 2008 Parliament called on the Italian authorities to stop fingerprinting Roma people, including children.

Ireland's No

In mid-February, Vaclav Klaus was re-elected president of the Czech Republic, by a margin of just one vote in a secret ballot in the Parliament. Klaus was a known opponent of the Lisbon Treaty and within 12 months was to move to delay its entry into force. But the real problem for Lisbon lay on the other edge of the Union. In March the process of ratification in the

---

372   In Naples, right-wing gangs set fire to people's lodgings and then denied access to the fire brigade; in Rome the police arrested 400 people and threatened them with summary expulsion.

UK's House of Commons was to be almost as messy as that for the ratification of Maastricht under Major, with Liberals at one point storming out of
the chamber in protest. Only in the House of Lords, under the able guidance
of Baroness Ashton, who led the government benches, was the process to be
smoother. Further west, in Ireland, an Atlantic storm was brewing.

The Irish poet Tom Paulin had written in his poem 'Juniper' of 'the
warped polities of ... trees caught in the Atlantic wind'. As Commission,
Parliament and Council representatives gathered in The Hague on 24 May
at the invitation of the European Movement to celebrate the 60th anniversary of the Congress of Europe there were worrying signs that Ireland, the
country of the meeting's host, Pat Cox, might again vote No to an EU treaty.
Much American money had poured into the coffers of the No campaign.

By midday on Friday 13 June 2008 it was clear that Ireland had voted to
reject the Lisbon Treaty, despite the best efforts of Cox and others. A hugely
well-resourced campaign against it by a movement called Libertas led by a
businessman called Declan Ganley and supported by some right-wing circles in the USA had outmanoeuvred the government, the major opposition
parties, the church and a whole host of organisations of civil society to persuade the Irish to reject it after a campaign of half truths and insinuation.
Voters had been told, for example, that voting for the treaty could mean that
Ireland would lose its European commissioner. In fact, not voting for it
would almost certainly have led to that since the prevailing Treaty of Nice
foresaw a reduction in the size of the college of commissioners. But the
public mood had become one of distrust of politicians and concern about the
impact on Ireland of the recent enlargement of the EU. For the Irish, to par-
aphrase their poet W B Yeats, romantic Europe was dead and gone; it was
with O'Leary, in the grave.

At the European Council meeting in Brussels on 19-20 June a tired-look-
ing Taoiseach, Brian Cowen, asked his EU partners for time to analyse the
vote and endeavour to save the treaty. After Ireland's rejection of the Nice
Treaty some years previously the question had been put to the people again
in a referendum eighteen months later and had secured approval second
time around. A similar period of reflection might be helpful in this case.

Cowen was to lay out to his colleagues at the October 2008 European
Council his plans to create a climate of opinion in which he could hold a
second referendum, approximately a year hence, in the hope of an affirma-
tive vote for the Lisbon Treaty. EU Affairs Minister Dick Roche was to
beaver away researching the reasons for Ireland's rejection and was to be
ubiquitous in explaining them to his fellow Europeans. Both argued that a
second referendum could be won if time could be granted to them.

Meanwhile the EU had to proceed on the basis of the treaties in force.
Liberals were divided over whether this meant electing the 2009 European
Parliament on the basis of the Treaty of Nice, although the number of seats
and their distribution between member states would be changed by
Lisbon's entry into force. All hoped however that the new Commission
might be established under Lisbon, if Ireland could vote by October of 2009,
although perhaps a little later than usual.

Thus the incoming French presidency of the EU took office with a significant problem on its hands. France had rejected the EU's treaty establishing
a constitution; now Ireland had rejected its successor. Yet the French presi-

dency was to show that the EU could work without a new treaty, for in August they were to mobilise EU solidarity to keep the Russian tanks out of Tbilisi; in September and October they did the same to keep the banks in business and in November and December to drill the EU's ranks behind a package of measures to fight climate change which the Union would take to the UN's Copenhagen conference in December 2009.

Geremek dies

A few days before the House rose for the 2008 summer recess a rain-drenched and busy stretch of road near Poznan in Poland was the scene of a tragic Liberal loss: Bronislaw Geremek MEP died when the car he was driving crossed the central reservation and ploughed into the path of an oncoming van[373]. Bronek had been generous in his four years in Parliament with his wise counsel and mischievous smile; his death brought messages of sympathy from far and wide, showing a man well-loved far beyond the Liberal circles to which he belonged. The Polish MEPs organised a small ecumenical church service in Brussels three days later. I cancelled a visit to the Far East the following week to attend the state funeral he was given in Poland, and in October the ALDE group organised a celebration of his life at the Grand Hall at the Free University in Brussels.

Bronislaw Geremek's death was not the only sad news for Liberals that summer. Lord Russell Johnston, a former leader of the Scottish Liberal Party, prominent Westminster parliamentarian, leader of the Liberal group on the Parliamentary Assembly of the Council of Europe and later president of that Assembly, died in early August. His death was apparently natural – he collapsed while walking down a street in Paris near his favourite hotel – but a few close friends also knew he was suffering from bone cancer and that the illness would have been terminal.

Russell and Bronek had campaigned for the same type of Liberalism – open to argument, understanding of human frailty but rooted in a strong sense of justice. I resolved, in their honour, to redouble my efforts for a more Liberal Europe.

Nicolas Sarkozy and France

In the week commencing 14 July 2008 no fewer than 20 French government ministers descended on the European Parliament in Brussels to talk to MEPs. Rarely, if ever, had the EP experienced anything like this charm offensive. Sarkozy had invited Parliament's president and its political group leaders to discussions over lunch at the Elysee on two occasions and Prime Minister Francois Fillon had invited us to the Matignon[374].

---

373   Geremek was succeeded in Parliament by Andrzej Wielowieyski, a charming man who had entertained me to lunch in Warsaw some years previously and who was to prove a conscientious MEP.

374   When the accounts were finally published, the presidency was revealed to have cost France's taxpayers EUR 171 million compared to EUR 57 million for the previous French presidency.

Moreover, as if to prove a point, Sarkozy had invited each of the major group leaders to meet him personally at the Elysee, with just two officials present; in my case on 10 April for a 45 minute discussion in which he surprised me by dwelling for a while on French politics and the position of Francois Bayrou, about whom he was not complimentary.[375]

Nicolas Sarkozy had assumed office as president of France in May 2007 after a ruthlessly effective campaign to win the nomination of the country's main right-wing party. At first he had appeared to be a president in a new mould: pro-American and an economic Liberal to boot. But his image as an economic Liberal was soon to be tarnished by his insistence on removing the words 'to create a free and competitive economy' from the text of the draft Lisbon Treaty; and again through his quest for special treatment for France, when he took the highly unusual step of turning up in person at a meeting of the EU's finance ministers which discussed the Growth and Stability Pact. When Sarkozy had come to address the European Parliament on 13 November 2007 he said that Europe should be a grand ideal and a grand promise, offering citizens hope of a better life. The institutional question had been settled, he said; only political questions remained. Yet when it came to details he was sometimes to prove as Gaullist as his predecessors.

I found Sarkozy a curious politician. Driven by an energy which doubtless owed something to his physical stature, something to his immigrant background and probably something to a natural pugnacity, he could be rash, ruthless and unpredictable. He was in every sense a man of action. Throughout our conversation he ate canapes, almost compulsively. I recalled that he had consumed chocolates in the same way on his visit to Strasbourg to meet the Parliament's conference of presidents on 13 November 2007; and yet he remained slim, partly through renouncing alcohol, partly through jogging every morning and mainly, I imagine, through the expenditure of many joules of nervous energy.

The French presidency was keen to make progress in EU legislation in a number of areas. Prime among these were fighting climate change, controlling immigration, developing common defence and security policies[376] and reforming the CAP. Sarkozy also spoke of his desire to have one major initiative in each month of his presidency beyond the legislative agenda. He cited bringing together health ministers and cancer research professionals; doing more to promote culture; uniting interior ministers and police chiefs to discuss security at sports matches. He may well have been unaware of the extent to which such initiatives were already underway. When I suggested to him that he use his presidency to promote citizens' rights, particularly the horizontal anti-discrimination directive which the Commission was soon to publish, he was unbriefed. But he was attentive, ambitious and keen.

---

375   I considered this approach unbecoming of a head of state. However Sarkozy knew that Francois Pauli, the deputy secretary general who accompanied me, had worked for the UDF in the French Senate and it may be that his words were intended to find their way back to Bayrou's camp.

376   In an early act of his presidency, Sarkozy had taken France back into the central military command structure of NATO after an absence of 42 years.

This was the Sarkozy who, in mid-July, was to tell Ireland it would simply have to vote again. And whose industry minister, Christine Lagarde, had made remarks about EU tax policy while visiting the Emerald Isle in March 2008, which had trodden on a sensitive area for Ireland and ran the risk of sowing further doubts in the minds of potential voters. But it was also the Sarkozy who was to impress even his Liberal critics by his handling of the Georgia crisis in August and the banking crisis in September.

Georgia

On 1 September the European Council met in extraordinary session for the first time since 2003 to discuss the situation in Georgia. The European Parliament had debated in May and voted in June a resolution expressing deep disapproval of Russia's announcement that it would establish official ties with the separatist authorities of South Ossetia and Abkhazia. On 7 August 2008, Russian tanks had rolled across the border into Georgia. Concerted action, orchestrated by Sarkozy, had achieved an agreement under which the Russians would withdraw. The heads of state and government now condemned Russia's military action and its unilateral decision to recognise the independence of Abkhazia and South Ossetia, predominantly Russian-speaking enclaves on Georgia's territory. They called for a peaceful solution to the conflict based on respect for the independence, sovereignty and territorial integrity of Georgia and the full implementation of the six-point agreement reached on 12 August, which meant full withdrawal of Russian forces. However, Russia drew an equivalence between the status of these two territories and that of Kosovo. Negotiations on the new EU-Russia partnership agreement, launched in July 2007, were to be suspended until the withdrawal of troops to positions held prior to 7 August 2008.

When the ALDE group discussed the conflict we found – as had the Council – that our members from the former Soviet bloc were more harshly disposed towards Russia than the 'western' Europeans. I had set out my views in an article published on the website of *The Guardian* on 18 August 2008, in which I argued that the EU could play the role of honest broker in Georgia more easily than the USA and that working in conjunction with the UN and the OSCE it should seek to engage the Russian bear rather than bait it, as some across the Atlantic[377] were doing. I was pleased to find that these views reflected the consensus of opinion among my colleagues, though I confess I had not troubled them in August to gauge their opinions.

By mid-October, in line with the agreements of 12 August and 8 September, Russian troops had withdrawn from the zones adjacent to South Ossetia and Abkhazia. Peace talks had been launched in Geneva. An EU-Russia summit was scheduled to take place in Nice on 14 November 2008.

An EU-Russia partnership agreement had expired at the end of 2007; talks on renewing it had started in July 2008 but were suspended following the

---

377   US Republican presidential candidate John McCain had suggested booting Russia out of the G8.

war in Georgia. The November summit agreed to reopen the talks. Following the summit, Polish Liberal MEP Janusz Onyskiewicz drew up on behalf of the House a report on EU-Russia relations which was adopted in April 2009 and recommended using the renewal of the EU's co-operation agreement with Russia to raise the human rights situation in the country, improve the security of gas supplies and seek assurances that Moscow would no longer use force against its neighbours. He called on Moscow in particular to introduce legislation to comply with its international commitments (as a member of the Council of Europe and the OSCE) on freedom of expression.

The crisis in Georgia had deepened the EU's resolve to adopt credible energy security and military policies. MEPs and Council were all too aware of how the EU's defence of Georgia had been based to a considerable extent on bluff and bluster. At the European Council meeting in October 2008 the heads of state and government agreed to pursue with determination the diversification of energy sources and to develop crisis mechanisms to deal with temporary disruptions to supplies. In November Parliament approved the orientation of the EU's space policy, essentially for civilian but potentially also for security purposes. In December the European Council decided to improve military capability: the EU should be capable of deploying 60,000 troops within 60 days for a major operation and of conducting simultaneously other operations supported by up to 10,000 troops for at least two years.

European security and defence policy was taking shape. Operations were still foreseen within the framework of the Petersberg tasks[378]. It was not anticipated that the EU should launch wars: indeed, we aimed to prevent them. But coherent action by member states was not always evident. In December MEPs voted to condemn the Council for its failure to draw up a stronger EU code of conduct on arms exports, as first called for by Parliament ten years previously and under active discussion since 2005. Moreover, Liberals had been active in securing parliamentary action to abolish the production of land mines and cluster munitions and to ban the use of depleted uranium.

Financial meltdown ...

In 2007 and 2008 the economy of the EU grew strongly. At the European Council meeting in March 2008 the national leaders could note with satisfaction that public deficits had been more than halved since 2005 and that public debt had declined to under 60% of gross income. While growth was expected to slow a little, six and a half million jobs had been created over two years, in significant part due to improvements in the functioning of the single market. Higher oil and commodity prices and ongoing turbulence in the financial markets were a matter of concern, but were not believed to be

---

378   See footnote 102.

insurmountable; greater transparency in the functioning of financial markets and improved supervision and regulation were sought. Moreover, the
EU had achieved an impressive level of co-ordinated economic governance
under its de facto finance minister Jean-Claude Juncker. The Lisbon reforms
needed to be continued and more done to unlock the business potential of
SMEs, but the policies were delivering the benefits long hoped-for. The economic and finance ministers were invited by the heads of state and government to seek further progress, particularly in financial supervision and, it
was added, on the management of cross-border financial crisis situations;
and it was foreseen – perhaps prophetically – that the European Council
would come back to these issues 'at the latest in Autumn 2008'[379].

Minds were soon to be focused, however, on clearer signs of a gathering
storm in the financial markets. Across the Atlantic, where Hillary Clinton
and Barack Obama were slugging it out in the Democratic primaries, the US
Federal Reserve had made its biggest cut in interest rates in over 50 years.
In Europe, MPs from 27 member state parliaments came to Brussels to
attend an inter-parliamentary meeting to discuss the impending crisis while
rogue trader Jerome Kerviel at France's Societe Generale was discovered (on
21 January 2008) to have lost EUR 5 billion in speculative trading. UK prime
minister Gordon Brown called a meeting on 29 January 2008 of the heads of
the larger EU member states, to which he subsequently deigned to invite the
president of the Commission 'to represent the other member states'. Billed
as 'the sub-prime summit' it lived up to its name in every sense, for it
achieved little other than a collective grinding of teeth about the problems
of sub-prime mortgage lending and the issuance of a communique calling
for more transparency in big-ticket financial transactions.

At supper in Brussels on 22 January 2008, seated next to guest speaker and
Italian finance minister Tommaso Padoa-Schioppa, I found his well-rea-
soned predictions of the contagion that could spread from the financial
sector to the real economy frightening. Liberals were even more worried for
his country, where Prodi's government had fallen on 24 January in part
because it had introduced the fiscal discipline necessary to deal with the
challenges he outlined.

At the World Economic Forum in Davos France's former finance minister
and recently appointed IMF managing director, Dominique Strauss-Kahn,
praised the USA for its fiscal stimulus and suggested by implication that the
EU should follow suit. The situation was not equally grave in all member
states, however, or a single policy response immediately obvious.

In mid February 2008 the European Parliament convened representatives
of the 27 national parliaments to discuss the state of the economy. Chaired
jointly by the president of Slovenia's national assembly and a vice president
of the European Parliament, it looked at responses to globalisation of the
economy, investment in people and labour markets and how to measure
success in the Lisbon competitiveness strategy. Some member states, like

---

379   March 2008 European Council meeting, presidency conclusions.

Latvia, were experiencing sharp falls in economic growth and sharp rises in inflation.

I visited Belgian finance minister and Walloon Liberal leader Didier Reynders at the end of February 2008 in his ministry's impressive palace in the Rue de la Loi, to discuss the gathering storm clouds in the world economy. Reynders was one of the longer serving finance ministers; he had led his party and his country's monetary policy with charm and verve and had been one of the sources of Verhofstadt's success. Reynders was deeply worried, and neither of us was hugely surprised at the collapse of US investment bank Bear Stearns a fortnight later. While in the first quarter of the year the EU's national leaders had been cautiously optimistic, by April 2008 the finance ministers were discussing reckless bank lending and a month later the impact of salary bonuses on the speculative activities of investment bankers; and German Liberal Otto Graf Lambsdorff had joined Delors and others in writing a warning note to the EU's Slovenian presidency about the perils of an imminent financial market collapse.

In July 2008, in Parliament's annual report on the ECB, MEPs had praised the ECB for its 'excellent work' in managing the financial troubles of 2007. Its excellence was soon to be tested further. By mid-September 2008 the storm was raging at its full fury. American financial institutions were in serious trouble, with repercussions for the EU. The UK government had stepped in to rescue Halifax Bank of Scotland, a major high street lender. The ECB was making regular and very large injections of liquidity into the financial markets to stabilise them; on 24 September, as Parliament held an emergency debate on supervision of the financial markets, it released EUR 27 billion; the previous week it had pumped onto the markets over EUR 100 bn in total. Speaking for ALDE in the debate my deputy Silvana Koch-Mehrin had said: 'it is not the market economy which is to blame for the crisis; that blame attaches to those who refuse to abide by frameworks or rules'. But she pointed out that ordinary families were hardest hit by the credit crunch and the collapse in the values of shares and savings. The following week three governments united to bail out Dexia, a Benelux bank, which followed Dutch-Belgian bank Fortis into difficulty. By the time the leaders of Germany, France, the UK and Italy met on 4 October 2008 some seven EU countries had taken independent measures to stabilise their banking systems. On 30 September – sobered perhaps by the rejection in the US Congress of President Bush's bank bailout plan – Barroso had called the main EP group leaders and asked for our support for a package of regulatory measures. Worried by the unilateral action of the Irish government in guaranteeing depositors' savings to prevent a run on their six largest banks, he was determined to avoid a situation in which the EU had 27 different and uncoordinated national responses. The following week saw 20% wiped off the value of shares in the biggest stock market crash since 1929. A $700 billion bank rescue package in the USA and a $400 billion dollar plan in the UK had not stopped the financial crisis spreading across the economy. In a debate on 8 October 2008 I said: 'It is at moments like this that our Union is defined. We need a collective response. We cannot sustain a situation in which member states surprise one another through unilateral decisions with multilateral consequences'.

Our heads of state and government met in G20 format in Washington DC on 14 November 2008. They succeeded in preventing a further crash in stock market values but the outlook was bleak. Prime Minister Gordon Brown, whom I met at Downing Street on 14 October[380], two days after an EU leaders' preparatory meeting, was being hailed by UK newspapers as 'the saviour of the free world' for his role in helping avert financial meltdown; but the real hero was the ECB. Monday 11 October 2008 had been the best day for Europe since the launch of the euro, with the common currency having finally proven its worth.

The European Council meeting of 15 and 16 October 2008 was dominated by discussion of the storm raging in the financial markets. The heads of state and government moved to set up a financial crisis cell to allow member states to provide early warning to each other of trouble brewing and to exchange information confidentially. But the Council also reaffirmed the need for discipline in economic policy. To restore growth and create jobs, continued structural reform would be necessary.

The Commission published proposals for action which stopped short of calling for a unified EU financial services authority (FSA); its temptation to Keynesian economics was also tempered by a German attachment to von Hayek. The ALDE group believed a single FSA to be necessary. Beyond regulation, I used the crisis to call for the investment of up to EUR 45 billion in a renewable energy super grid, putting people back to work and generating savings estimated at EUR 250 billion over 40 years.

On 7 November the French presidency convened a further extraordinary summit of heads of state and government to discuss the financial and economic crisis. But there was little to add: indeed, there was a distinct risk of too much summitry promoting too little symmetry. As I wrote in my blog that week: 'Our national leaders should recognise that in politics the prosaic is normally preferable to poetry; they should stop grandstanding and get on with the business of doing.'

Parliament debated the financial and economic crisis again on 18 November 2008. Speaking for the Liberal family, I said: '2008 must be the year in which we remind ourselves of Adam Smith's warning that unbridled free markets have their limits … Liberals are not going to waste time looking for the guy who failed to spot the iceberg: we will concentrate on getting people into lifeboats … put people back to work installing solar panels and wind generators on every house in Europe, fostering innovation and providing jobs simultaneously.' At the end of November the European Commission published a plan for economic recovery. It foresaw an increase in the capital of the European Investment Bank from EUR 165 bn to EUR 232 bn, to allow it to fund new job-creating infrastructure projects. It also foresaw an injection of EUR 200 bn into the real economy, EUR 170 bn coming from national budgets and EUR 30 bn from from EU resources. Though member states had different views about the extent of any public stimulus, when their finance ministers met on 2 December they agreed on the emergency measures

---

380   To brief him on my campaign for the presidency of the European Parliament.

required to restore the smooth operation of the financial system and bring back confidence to financial markets. It was agreed to provide balance of payments support to member states in need and to double to EUR 50 million the fund available for this: financial bail outs had been arranged for Latvia and Hungary, which had got into difficulty[381], and for Romania.

The European Council hoped that negotiations with the European Parliament could lead to the rapid adoption of draft directives on capital requirements for banks, solvency of insurance companies, undertakings for collective investment in transferable securities and protection of savers' deposits. The impact of the financial crisis on the real economy was being felt: the EU was about to enter the deepest peacetime economic recession since the 1920s.

Just as the scourge of terrorism had served to advance EU co-operation in justice and home affairs, so the financial and economic crisis served to promote closer co-ordination of monetary and economic policy. In October 2008 Jacques de Larosiere[382] was invited to chair a high level group on financial supervision to draw up proposals for EU rules on financial sector regulation and supervision. Since needs must, an area which had previously been the preserve of national regulators was to become a competence of the EU without any new treaty being signed. Agreement was reached on a draft capital requirements directive, a credit rating agencies regulation and the solvency II directive. De Larosiere's report, which recommended the creation of a European systemic risk council, chaired by the ECB, for macro-financial supervision, and three new authorities (for banks, securities and insurance firms), was discussed at the European Council meeting on 19 and 20 March 2009. While co-ordinated action leading to the injection of over EUR 400 bn into the EU economy had succeeded in preventing a financial meltdown, new rules were needed to prevent similar crises arising in future.

... and its economic fallout

Socialist group leader Martin Schulz had sought to gain maximum party political advantage from the crisis. In an open letter to the heads of state and government in March 2008 he had positioned himself as a scourge of capitalism, accusing Barroso of 'burying his head in the sand' over lack of social cohesion and blaming the EU's policy of economic liberalisation for what he called 'social breakdown'. But surveys of public attitudes showed that few in Europe supported his view that the market economy was to blame. I used a speech in Parliament and my weekly blog to mount a defence of global capitalism, pointing out how freer trade had in fact created jobs and increased wealth. I noted that whereas twenty years ago less than 5% of investment capital went to developing countries, today the figure was 38%; and that while in

---

381   In the former, Prime Minister Godmanis resigned on 20 February 2009 after just one year in office though the offending policies had not been of his making; in the latter, Ferenc Gyurcsany was forced out of office in March as a result of multiple failures of his administration (which the Liberals had left in protest against his inability to carry out necessary economic reforms) and succeeded by a government of technocrats led by Gordon Bajnai.

382   Former managing director of the International Monetary Fund.

1990 only a fifth of humankind lived in economically open societies, now it was nine out of every ten. Moreover, as the architects of the welfare state, Liberals needed to take no lessons from Socialists. Schulz insisted that competition from developing countries was holding down wages in the EU and structural change was putting older, unskilled workers out of jobs; I did not deny there was some truth in this, but would not have followed the logical conclusion of his thinking, which lay in tariff barriers or currency exchange controls – and neither, by 2008, would many Socialists.

Indeed, as the financial crisis had loomed, economic liberalisation had become a major concern of France's 2008 presidency. I had published in mid-July 2008 a pamphlet called 'The Lisbon Strategy: mode d'emploi' in which I argued for a more flexible economy since wealth creation is for Liberals a key prerequisite for social policy. Parliament voted the same week to 'unbundle' or open up to competition the market in gas, preventing gas producers or suppliers from owning the pipelines through which gas is supplied. On 18 June 2008, Parliament had also voted in a hotly contested vote – to ALDE's pleasant surprise – to support full 'ownership unbundling' in the electricity market, to overcome what Alexander Graf Lambsdorff MEP called 'the sweet poison of national protectionism'. This went even further than the original Commission proposal and challenged an agreement reached recently by the Council.

With ECB interest rates at a 7-year high, reflecting jitters about the market, the EU needed badly to make its economy more competitive. Among the challenges for the EU which I discussed over supper with Barroso in mid-July was the future of the working time directive, agreement on which appeared finally to have been reached in Council. I told him I feared the Socialists would oppose the agreement in Parliament, highlighting their opposition as a totem in the election campaign to come.

In fact we did not need to wait for the Socialists. Sarkozy's EPP government proved unhelpful on the working time directive. By October it had also become clear that Parliament's employment committee would reject the deal, which they duly did the following month. In December 2008 Parliament voted to amend the Council's text in such a way that it would be unacceptable to many member states. Revision of the working time directive was to prove beyond the reach of those representing Parliament and the Council of Ministers in the final attempt to reach agreement in a conciliation session[383]; the 1993 directive, allowing a controversial opt-out from a maximum working week of 48 hours, would remain in force. It was the first occasion since the entry into force of the Treaty of Amsterdam that the European Parliament and the Council of Ministers had failed to reach agreement in conciliation on a piece of legislation. We were back at the drawing board with a directive which had been under discussion for 17 years.

It was barely credible for the Socialists to paint the centre-right dominated

---

383   The Council had reached a common position on 9 June 2008 which allowed a continued right to opt out of a maximum 48 hour week, but in more narrowly defined circumstances; Parliament rejected this in its December 2008 session, by 421 votes to 273, though most Liberals voted in favour of it. The main area of disagreement was over 'on-call' time, particularly important in the health sector.

EU institutions as the agents of uncaring capitalism. At the start of July Commissioners Figel (education, training, culture and youth) and Spidla (employment, social affairs and equal opportunities) had come to Parliament to present the Commission's long-awaited package of social legislation[384]. Proposed co-ordination of social security systems, ensuring that citizens moving within the community would not lose their rights, had been dismissed as 'a slick public relations exercise' by French MEP Bernard Lehideux but welcomed by other ALDE members Ona Jukneviciene and Siiri Oviir. The package also contained a comprehensive draft directive against discrimination, as had been called for by Liberals in a report adopted by Parliament on 20 May 2008, where previously legislation had existed only to combat discrimination in the workplace; a draft directive which would give medical patients the right to seek treatment anywhere in the EU; and green and white papers on other aspects of social policy. In many ways it was more 'Liberal' than 'social'. Indeed, it had come about largely as a result of Liberal campaigning. We had made it clear to Barroso that comprehensive anti-discrimination legislation and the right for patients to seek medical treatment in any EU country were prime among our conditions for offering him our support to continue as Commission president after July 2009.

I had lobbied Sarkozy when I met him privately at the Elysee Palace to give priority to the comprehensive anti-discrimination directive; since the walls of his presidential palace's courtyard carry an engraving of the opening words of the Declaration of the Rights of Man it seemed appropriate to propose it to him.

But Sarkozy appeared to fear Liberalism more than Socialism. He gave me little support on the matter. And barely had the French EU presidency begun when he lambasted Commissioners McCreevy (single market) and Mandelson[385] (trade) for what he alleged was an adverse social impact of the Liberal economic policies they were pursuing. Since policy is set by Council and Parliament, shooting the messenger is a cheap trick; but the scoring of political points at home was to prove a feature of the Elysee during France's six months at the helm. Speaking on behalf of my colleagues I told Sarkozy, in my speech of welcome to him in the House on 10 July 2008, to build consensus on economic policy rather than shooting its messengers.[386]

The European People's Party MEPs, led by Frenchman Joseph Daul, had celebrated the start of the French presidency in early July at a group meeting in Strasbourg. The meeting underlined not only the importance attached by the UMP to their European links but also the importance of the city of Strasbourg as the EP's formal seat. Unfortunately for Daul, within a month (on 7 August 2008) the ceiling of the Strasbourg hemicycle collapsed. Fortunately for MEPs – since the building is used one week every month but not in August – it happened without injury or loss of life. It could easily have been otherwise and the

---

384   This was to be debated in Parliament again and at greater length on 2 September 2008.

385   In fact, Mandelson was to leave office during the French presidency, to return to the House of Lords as deputy prime minister; he was succeeded as trade commissioner by the competent and considerably more modest Baroness Ashton.

386   He had recently plunged into polemics with two European commissioners and the president of the ECB.

benches which were hit by falling masonry were predominantly on the EPP side of the House.

Since the extra cost of Parliament's three-site operation is substantial, the embarrassment to the French government during its presidency was painful, particularly since the damage was such that extensive repair work and safety tests would have to be carried out before Parliament could use the chamber again. Sarkozy could not possibly, needless to say, come to Parliament in Brussels, to grace our buildings there, so in September he sent his foreign minister, Bernard Kouchner, to report to us on the extraordinary summit to discuss the Russian invasion of Georgia. He then immediately invited Parliament's president and group leaders again to the Elysee Palace the following week for a private discussion of the conflict. By the time he came to address us again in late October the French government had made sure we were safely back in our Strasbourg buildings, albeit with barely concealed interior scaffolding which was to remain in place for well over a year.

Sarkozy's return, on 21 October, was triumphal. In a robust debate in the chamber he worsted PES group leader Martin Schulz[387]; after his press conference that afternoon his acolytes were briefing the press about how Sarkozy should remain in charge of the eurozone's economic affairs beyond the end of the French presidency. (Asked by a newswire journalist what I thought of this I suggested that he had taken too much to heart the observation of the poet Emerson that 'There is no such thing as history; only biography'.)

Continental Europe's main economies were destined to remain in recession until the summer of 2009; though Liberals were not in government in France or Germany the influence of Liberal ideas in securing the exit from recession was felt strongly. In the UK, which was to remain in recession for a further six months, Liberals found themselves in the curious position of calling for a de facto nationalisation of banks, a policy the likes of which had not been heard since the days of Lloyd George and John Maynard Keynes, but which fitted nonetheless into the broad approach to economic management favoured by Liberals and pursued to some extent by all EU member states.

Meanwhile the Party of European Socialists, meeting in Madrid, adopted a manifesto for the 2009 European elections which attacked the 'liberal conservative' policies of Barroso's Commission and held those policies partially responsible for the economic crisis. In Oporto two years previously they had backed some of the policies which they now criticised.

On 3 December 2008 Parliament heard statements from French EU affairs minister Jean-Pierre Jouyet and Commission president Barroso about the preparation of the European Council scheduled for 11 and 12 December. Decisive measures towards economic recovery were outlined. On 17 December Parliament's group leaders met Barroso to hear the details of his

---

387 Sarkozy took Schulz to task for a bombastic speech containing a catalogue of Socialist demands by saying: 'I do not see ... why you should seek conflicts with the presidency under the pretext that I am not of the same political persuasion as you... Do not saddle Europe with the responsibility for a social failing that is down to national political debate! Do not ask us, Mr Schulz, to resolve problems that you Germans have not been able to resolve. You Germans have rejected a minimum wage. We French want to keep our minimum wage. Social harmonisation [which Schulz had called for] would mean that we would have to reject our minimum wage because the Germans do not have one.'

plan and how it had been received by the European Council the previous week. The Council had adopted a European Economic Recovery Plan on the basis of the Commission's communication of 26 November, recognising that a reflation of its economy to the tune of 1.5% of EU GDP would be necessary. The ECB had also moved to cut interest rates to assist in economic recovery. EUR 30 bn was to be provided by the EIB, especially for SMEs, for renewable energy, clean transport and the automotive sector; spending under the structural funds was to be advanced and the Commission asked to recommend specific projects for support from the Community budget. Moreover state aid and public procurement rules were to be relaxed a little, temporarily.

Liberals were enjoying the opportunity to make faster progress in economic reform, though none of us would have wished the circumstances in which we did so. Three reports piloted through Parliament by my MEPs were approved: a regulatory measure governing investment funds by my German colleague Wolf Klinz created a truly barrier-free common market for investment funds; a directive on public procurement contracts in defence and security by another German Liberal, which harmonised procurement rules to make defence and security markets more open and more competitive; a report by Diana Wallis endorsed the common tax rules which would soon apply to cross-border mergers and transfer of assets between companies. And with the publication of a cross-party pamphlet on the potential for feeding renewable energies into a super smart high voltage direct current electricity super grid and a speech in the House in our debate on 2 February 2009 on the consequence of the recent gas crisis, I placed our group once again at the leading edge of a climate change mitigation strategy, which would assist economic recovery.

Liberal ideas were needed more than for many years. The economic recession was leading to protectionist instincts at the highest levels of national politics in countries which should have known better. In February 2009 UK prime minister Gordon Brown promised 'British jobs for British workers' during a dispute involving Italian construction workers in northern England. Simultaneously, President Sarkozy of France was publicly critical of French automobile manufacturers for investing in production facilities in the Czech Republic rather than investing in production at home. Interviewed on the BBC Radio Four lunchtime news programme I warned against such populism; the danger of a descent into the politics of the 1930s was all too evident, I said[388].

The European Parliament was all for upholding the law; we voted in mid-February to approve a proposal to penalise employers guilty of hiring illegal migrants[389]. Liberals argued that rogue employers commit a triple offence: they encourage traffickers of illegal migrants; they exploit vulnerable people with low pay and poor conditions, and they cheat legal workers and the tax system by undercutting the legitimate labour market.

---

388   The leaders of Business Europe, the ETUC and the Union for Small and Medium Sized Enterprises were all also to add their voices that week in warning of how the perils of protectionism could undermine the EU's single market, generator of 17 years of prosperity.

389   UK Liberal Democrats were dismayed but not surprised that the the UK's Labour government announced its intention to opt out of this legislation.

But we would oppose moves to fan the flames of prejudice by targeting those who migrated legally to seek employment opportunities elsewhere, knowing that if labour could not migrate to where jobs were to be found then investment would surely migrate to areas where labour was cheap and plentiful.

Parliament also approved new energy labelling standards and a further liberalisation of the gas and electricity markets, though for Liberals the latter fell short of the ideal. Where a year before the EU had capped the roaming charges[390] levied by mobile telephone service providers in cross-border calls, now we legislated to cap the price of cross-border text messaging. It was not often that Liberals would support price controls, but here was a case where the market was not working.

There was co-ordination of state aid policies too, to help struggling sectors of industry and agriculture (mainly car-makers and cow-milkers). The Commission published on 25 February 2009 a plan to help the automobile industry which allowed member states to introduce scrappage schemes as incentives for the purchase of new vehicles. The previous month they had agreed to reintroduce market intervention mechanisms and export refunds for butter, cheese and milk powder.

In short, the EU was showing itself capable of pursuing both economic- and social-Liberal remedies to economic recession. Resort to the laissez-faire or planned economy policies traditionally advocated on the right and the left was out of the question.

Budget discharge creates tensions

Jan Mulder, a senior member of Parliament's budgets committee, and Siim Kallas, the commissioner responsible for controlling the EU budget, were at loggerheads. Though relations between the two were never personally warm, the matters at stake were fought over not out of personal enmity or incompatibility of character. It has been said that where a person stands on any issue is influenced in large measure by where they sit. MEPs had long sought greater transparency in the Union's budget and more effective controls over spending. The Commission was naturally pleased to comply with Parliament's demands where possible: but in the vexed area of spending carried out by national governments in areas where the Commission's auditors had no legal power to carry out enquiries, there was little it could do. MEPs threatened to refuse to give discharge to the EU's accounts for 2007 unless the Commission were seen to take an initiative and hence, through co-ordination between the offices of MEP and commissioner in March 2008, the Commission agreed to demand annual 'compliance tables' from member states and to take legal action against them if they failed to file annual summaries showing how EU funds spent in their countries had been audited. After sustained pressure from Mulder, solic-

---

390   MEP Sarunas Birutis, who had become the leader of ALDE's Lithuanian delegation, was part of Parliament's negotiating team with Council to achieve this.

itor's letters were duly despatched to eight member states and Kallas undertook to provide Parliament with an assessment of the quality of the compliance
tables by member state and by policy area and to ensure the recovery of any
undue payments.

In terms of public perception, one of the challenges for Brussels was that
the European Court of Auditors had for many years refused to sign off the
EU's accounts. Few electors wanted to trust Barroso with more public
spending if he could not account effectively for the money he currently con-
trolled. This criticism was partially unfair, since 80% of EU funds were
spent in and by the member states themselves and it was in this area that
the auditors were dissatisfied. It had taken Commissioner Kallas, the
person in charge, some three years to put the Union's house in order. He
had been much assisted by MEPs, especially the Liberal MEPs who had
fought hard with the member states to have certificates of assurance.
Nonetheless, the announcement by the European Court of Auditors on 11
November 2008 that it had signed off[391] the EU's 2007 accounts came as a
welcome relief; they identified areas where improvements were still
needed, especially in agricultural spending, but their overall opinion was
an unqualified OK.

Beyond Brussels

Zimbabwe

While EU diplomacy was generally successful, it was put under strain in three
areas under the French presidency. French foreign minister Bernard Kouchner,
himself a former Radical MEP, had first to grapple with the situation in
Zimbabwe, where the opposition MDC candidate Morgan Tsvangirai had
pulled out of the second round of the presidential election at the end of June
after numerous cases of his supporters being raped, beaten and killed by
Mugabe's thugs. Parliament had debated the climate of terror sweeping
Zimbabwe in July 2008 and condemned the 27 June run-off election as illegiti-
mate, calling for fresh elections and tighter sanctions against members of
Mugabe's government. Addressing Parliament on 9 July, Commissioner Louis
Michel had described the election result as 'a victory that was wrongfully won,
and is very far from the spirit of democratic renaissance that animates Africa
today.' Fiona Hall MEP, speaking for ALDE, had called on the EU to offer
diplomatic support to those seeking an interim transitional government and
suggested that South Africa might not be ideally suited to broker negotiations
between Mugabe and Morgan Tsvangirai. At a meeting of the ALDEPAC network in Lome I was to call for Mugabe to be brought before the International
Criminal Court to face trial for crimes against humanity. In December 2008 the

391   The ECA found that the accounts in general gave a fair representation, in all material respects, of the EU's
financial position and results. The qualifications expressed in the previous year's report were no longer necessary,
the auditors said, 'due to the improvements that have taken place'. While the court still found errors in payments
made within member states, it gave an unqualified clean opinion on the Union's administration.

ALDE group co-hosted with the Liberal International a one-day conference in Brussels, with participants from many African parliaments, to discuss the situation in Zimbabwe where cholera had become a major problem and life expectancy for women had dropped to just 34 years.

China

Authoritarian rule in China also continued to pose problems. In July 2008 Parliament adopted another resolution criticising China for its human rights abuses. Though Sarkozy attended the opening ceremony of the Olympic Games in Beijing in August, risking some controversy at home, he agreed later to meet the Dalai Lama at a prize-giving ceremony for Polish Solidarity leader Lech Walesa. Parliament's 2008 Sakharov Prize was awarded in September to Chinese dissident, AIDS activist and human rights defender Hu Jia, the candidate of the Liberals and the Greens. At the end of November 2008 the PRC decided to cancel (at very short notice) the annual EU-PRC summit. The news reached me while I was leading a delegation of five colleagues to Taipei to meet new president Ma Ying-jeou and new opposition leader Tsai Ing-wen. The president, a Conservative, had defeated the Liberal incumbent seven months previously; but Taiwan remained a democracy, in stark contrast to the mainland.

My ALDE delegation to Taiwan and Japan went smoothly and without incident. The same could not be said of a delegation from Parliament's international trade committee, visiting Mumbai the same week, whose members found themselves in the Oberoi Trident hotel at the time of a terrorist attack organised from Pakistan. My colleague Ignasi Guardans MEP and ALDE staff member Barbara Melis were lucky to escape with their lives from an incident in which over 100 were killed and 287 injured.

Turkey

In view of majority public opinion in France opposing Turkish membership of the EU, Liberals worked hard to keep Turkey on the agenda. The ruling AKP, which had won re-election in July 2007 in an election in which democracy was the principal victor and had seen former foreign minister Abdullah Gul elected as president at the end of August 2007, had been threatened with closure for undermining the nation's legal tradition of secularism[392]; on 1 August 2008 Turkey's Constitutional Court decided by a one-vote margin not to ban the AKP. On 18 September 2008 I took a delegation from my group, including French members, to Ankara for discussions with government and opposition parties. We were received by the president, the prime minister, the speaker of parliament and leading figures from all parties. The tension between the democratically elected AKP and the Kemalist military

---

392 Intermittent bans on alcohol, a clampdown on pork production and an attempt to render adultery illegal were cited by Chief Prosecutor Abdurrahman Yalcinkaya as evidence of this. The Welfare Party, to which Erdogan and Gul previously belonged, was banned in 1997 on similar charges.

establishment was tangible; but the success of the AKPs programme of social investment in housing, sanitation, health and education was almost everywhere to be seen. As a result, the AKP's popularity remained high.

On 24 September, Patriarch Bartholomew I of Constantinople, the spiritual leader of the Greek Orthodox Church, addressed the European Parliament as part of our year of inter-cultural dialogue. I found the call of Morpheus more powerful than most of his address, but at one point I was awoken by his saying that the EU had to bring Turkey into the European project. I immediately started a round of applause, which spread and was to be the only spontaneous applause he received from the assembly.

The USA

Parliament grappled too with challenges in other areas of foreign policy. On 4 November 2008 the United States of America elected Barack Husain Obama to the presidency. Not only was Obama the first non-white president ever to hold the office, but his remarkable personal history again demonstrated the power of the ballot and the magic of democracy. Though the election was America's it was followed with riveted attention around the world. To a Europe increasingly distraught by the policies of George W. Bush's administration, Obama's election came as a welcome relief. It also threw into sharp relief the failure of the European Union's democracy to inspire.

In the European Parliament Liberals were active in the campaign to close the detention centre at Guantanamo Bay. The EU's foreign affairs ministers had welcomed the US announcement of the planned closure but had shown little enthusiasm for helping the Americans by taking some of the detainees. The ALDE civil liberties team took the view that, since many EU governments were complicit in extraordinary rendition which led to torture, we should be prepared to resettle detainees against whom there was insufficient evidence to ensure conviction yet who could not safely return home and did not wish to remain in America. I was able to welcome in the House on 3 February 2009, on behalf of the Liberal group, the assurance of the Council presidency that the US had now disowned the squalid practices that had tarnished its government over recent years and to urge member states to act by saying: 'We cannot forever balance the Council's assertion that it is for individual member states to decide, with the Council's stated desire for a co-ordinated European position. Europe has to speak with one voice and play its part in ending this affront to justice'.

Belarus

Belarus held parliamentary elections on 28 September 2008 which the OSCE observers, whose work was rendered almost impossible, condemned as undemocratic. The opposition failed to gain any of the 110 seats for which elections were held. Liberals and others organised a cross-party conference in Parliament attended by the leaders of the opposition parties from Belarus, the only European country still to execute its own citizens in peacetime, labouring under the authoritarian President Lukashenko. The Union decided to invite the country to be represented at its eastern neighbours' partnership summit on 7 May but not to receive Lukashenko himself.

Moldova

In April 2009 ALDE insisted on and secured a statement on Moldova, where the Communist government had falsified the election results and brutally suppressed a public protest by young people in Chisinau, and we invited the leaders of the three Liberal opposition parties to Strasbourg to listen to our debate from the public gallery. There, democracy was to triumph; and later that year I was delighted to meet one of them again as his country's new prime minister.

Russia

Underlying relations with Belarus and Moldova was continued tension with Russia. As 2009 opened, Russia had once again cut off energy supplies to the Ukraine in a clear warning signal to the EU[393].

Initially the European Commission dismissed the gas supply disruption by saying it was purely a commercial matter between Russia and the Ukraine, though with five EU countries hit and supplies to others reduced the Commission soon realised it had to seek to assist. Russia's Gazprom and Naftogaz of the Ukraine were summoned to Brussels to have their heads banged together and the pretence thus maintained that Gazprom operated independently of the Kremlin. And statements were prepared for parliamentary debates in Strasbourg in the middle of January, on both Russia and the Middle East[394].

Though relations with Russia remained difficult, as highlighted in a report to Parliament by Polish Liberal Janusz Onyskiewicz, in April our House was proud to dedicate its oval courtyard in Strasbourg to deceased Polish Liberal Bronislaw Geremek in memory of his work in liberating his fellow countrymen from subjection by their Russian Communist neighbours. It was clear to Liberals that it was still a work in progress.

Gibraltar

On 5 August 2004 I had paid a visit to Gibraltar. Since 1973 the people of Gibraltar had been part of the EU through their connection with the United Kingdom, of which it is a dependency, but they had not been able to elect their own representatives to the European Parliament. A judgment in the European Court of Justice had obliged the UK to enfranchise Gibraltar's citizens, however. It had been added to the UK's south west England con-

---

393   The EU's coherence in energy supply policy, until recently very poor, was improving. ALDE MEP Anne Lapperouze had been charged by Parliament with preparing its response to the Commission's proposed 'Second strategic energy review'. Her report, adopted on 5 February 2009, called for an ambitious and far sighted diversification plan. And Hague mayor and EU Nabucco coordinator Jozias van Aartsen chose Budapest, which had been under Russian pressure to back the South Stream Russian gas pipeline project, as the venue for a big conference on the Nabucco pipeline project which would bring gas from the Caspian Sea through Turkey to Europe, thus reducing dependence on Russian goodwill. It would take four years to build some 3,300 km of pipeline, but the recent problems with supply to the Ukraine had added impetus to the plans.

394   The main New Year news headlines had been about Israel's invasion of Gaza.

stituency and I was proud to be one of its seven MEPs. Despite a bad tempered campaign of obstruction from the Spanish government and a European Commission far too willing to avoid antagonising Madrid, the rights of the people of Gibraltar had won the day. Addressing the crowd at the 300th anniversary celebration of the current settlement of the Rock, I was able to inform them of the ELDR Party's resolution, adopted at its congress in Amsterdam in November 2003, which called on Spain to drop its proposed legal action against the UK's enfranchisement of Gibraltarians, and to say that having its rightful place in the new Europe of 2004 was 'the birthday present Gibraltar deserves'.

In mid-2006, just prior to the Finnish presidency, I had been able to secure a small victory for some of my constituents in Gibraltar. The Committee of Permanent Representatives (COREPER), the regular gathering in Brussels of member states' ambassadors, had approved in May a draft regulation to improve rights for airline passengers with disabilities; airports and airlines would in future be required to provide assistance to such passengers and airlines would not be allowed to deny boarding except in the case of very small aircraft where to allow the passenger aboard might compromise safety. However, this regulation – as with previous regulations relating to air travel – would not apply to Gibraltar (if it did, it would never be approved because of the dispute over the sovereignty of the Rock). This matter came to Parliament in June and I was to see my amendment to include Gibraltar in the legislation (by removing the Gibraltar exemption clause) successfully adopted by Parliament at first reading despite the efforts of Spanish right-wing MEPs to defeat it. I saw no reason why my disabled constituents in Gibraltar should be denied the rights other European citizens enjoyed simply because of a 300 year old dispute over territorial sovereignty; and I had made this clear to Spain's deputy prime minister, Maria Teresa Fernandez de la Vega, when she visited me on 13 June.

We had scored a further small victory in Gibraltar in mid-September 2006, when the European Court of Justice threw out a Spanish objection to the way in which the UK had enfranchised the citizens of the Rock for European elections.[395]

As 2008 wound towards its close I took 11 senior colleagues from the bureau of my group on a study visit to Gibraltar. A part of my constituency since 2004, the inhabitants of the Rock faced intriguing challenges arising from their strange constitutional status. Sovereignty over Gibraltar was held by the United Kingdom but contested by Spain. The UK had failed to resolve the issue when it had the chance, prior to Spain's entry into the EU, and had left the Gibraltarians in the precarious position of being EU citizens but outside the EU for some purposes. Though Gibraltar had enjoyed huge

---

395   Spain argued that Commonwealth citizens who were not citizens of the UK or Gibraltar should be denied the right to vote in elections to the European Parliament. Had the court upheld their argument the effect might have been to withdraw the franchise from one million Commonwealth citizens who enjoyed voting rights in the UK in European Parliament elections.

economic success in the years since it had been essentially a garrison town, the fruits of that success were unevenly distributed and discrimination of all kinds was rife, perpetrated sometimes by Spain or the UK but just as often by Gibraltar's own government.

I led my colleagues in highlighting one particular case of discrimination by playing a game of football against the Gibraltar football association. They thrashed us, of course, by four goals to one in a match of only fifteen minutes each way (our players, like me, were mostly over 50). But the TV cameras rolled as Gibraltar played against a multi-national team of MEPs. Despite two rulings in their favour in the Court of Arbitration for Sport, UEFA bowed to Spanish pressure to prevent Gibraltar from playing in international tournaments, although the Faroe Islands and San Marino were allowed to.

On 21 April 2008 I defended Gibraltar against an attack in the European Parliament by two MEPs from Spain's Partido Popular, who had tabled an oral question on the sinking of the ship the *New Flame* off Gibraltar the previous August. They sought to accuse the Gibraltar authorities of negligence in failing to prevent oil pollution from the wreck; in fact, co-operation between the Gibraltar and Spanish authorities had been excellent and no pollution other than a minor spill of engine oil had occurred as a result. Transport Commissioner Jacques Barrot agreed with me and the resolution adopted by Parliament was largely to reflect my intervention; but it could easily have been otherwise.

In the four years I had represented Gibraltar I had stood up for Gibraltar in the European Parliament more energetically than any other MEP representing the Rock. I had taken up concerns by many constituents there. Moreover, I had made sure my group was the first to visit and to request meetings with representatives of government and opposition. I was surprised, therefore, that Liberals were snubbed in a sarcastic speech by petulant Chief Minister Peter Caruana at the supper he hosted on our behalf. It was hardly the welcome we felt we deserved.

The Czech presidency

The Czech presidency which took office in January 2009 managed to offend sensitivities across the board. In his opening address to the European Parliament, Prime Minister MirekTopolanek described the EU's hard-won Lisbon Treaty as 'worse than the Treaty of Nice'. And in the Council of Ministers HQ his government had displayed a piece of modern art billed as 'the work of 27 European artists, one from each member state' (but which turned out to be the work purely of Czech artist David Cserny); claiming to 'demolish stereotypes by mocking them' it depicted Bulgaria as a toilet, Germany as a motorway bedecked with swastikas and the Netherlands as a lake with minarets poking up through the water. Other Europeans were (unsurprisingly) not amused and the Czechs had to make copious apologies.

Czech woes were to be little eased by the official visit to Parliament in February 2009 of President Vaclav Klaus. He had secretly recorded on audio tape the proceedings of a meeting in his palace in Prague with European Parliament group leaders just before Christmas 2008, and selected parts of an exchange in which he had goaded Cohn-Bendit and Schulz into criticism of him had subsequently been released to the press. He chose his address to the EP to air again his famously euro-sceptic views, providing a rare piece of political theatre which livened up what was often a tedious ritual. When, however, visitors in the public gallery protested volubly against the EU and displayed banners, it became clear to MEPs that either Vaclav Klaus or his soul-mates had brought their rent-a-mob supporters with them; any remaining respect quickly drained away as Klaus blamed his country's economic troubles on 'central control [of the economy] from Brussels'. While Green MEPs left the chamber and many of the rest of us sat in stony silence, the competent Czech EU affairs minister, Alexander Vondra, could only look on helplessly at the damage done by a speech on which he had not been consulted and which he had seen less than an hour before its delivery.

The Czech diplomats were to be spared some of their embarrassment by the EU's timetable, which provided for Parliament to rise at the beginning of May ahead of the European elections one month later. It also provided for a level of activity in inverse proportion to the results achieved. On 22 February the leaders of Germany, the UK, France, Italy, Spain, Netherlands and the Czech Republic met in Berlin to co-ordinate their positions on the economic depression ahead of the G20 economic summit. But since this had been organised by the Germans, the following Sunday the Czechs hosted in Brussels an extraordinary EU summit of 27 heads of state and government to discuss the whole thing again. While some Liberals believed that talking was important to reduce the risk of individual exit strategies which might involve protectionism, others were highly critical of a burgeoning of high-level meetings which inevitably absorbed the energies of those who would otherwise be translating their agreements into action.

While France had chosen to develop during its presidency co-operation with the countries of the Mediterranean basin, the Czech Republic sought to promote relations with the east through an Eastern Neighbourhood Partnership. The Commission had made proposals for action on 3 December 2008. On 7 May 2009 the Czech government hosted on behalf of the Union a summit with countries on the EU's eastern borders. Economic integration and approximation of laws would be sought to ease co-operation with Georgia, Armenia and Azerbaijan and with Belarus, Moldova and the Ukraine. EUR 600 million was to be made available over four years for the promotion of democracy and good governance, people to people exchange, energy security and economic convergence with the EU.

Approval of the Lisbon Treaty would bring the EU's foreign policy into the mainstream of policy making by putting the high representative for common foreign and security policy into the European Commission. The occupant could be expected to deal directly with Obama's Secretary of State Hillary Clinton. It would also create the post of full time president of the European Council, bringing the number of EU presidents from two to three. But in stark contrast to the USA, the candidates for the presidency of the Council would not run public election campaigns, setting out their qualifications and their ideas. The president would not be directly elected; rather, she or he would be chosen in the equivalent of a papal conclave by 27 heads of state and government, and possibly from among their number. The president of the Commission was more evidently Obama's opposite number, though again without having to run the gauntlet of direct election.

2009 presidential bid launched

As Parliament returned from its Christmas recess in January 2009 I wrote to every MEP (and, in May, to almost every candidate for Parliament) announcing my intention to run for the presidency of the European Parliament in July, if re-elected. I held a press conference to announce it to the media. The news will have surprised few, but the reactions to it were by and large warm. It was to be the first ever public campaign for the presidency of Parliament; previously these contests had taken place purely within the confines of the House. I saw no reason why these decisions should continue to be made behind closed doors. I had spoken individually to many MEPs over the previous year and made no secret of my plans. I believed Parliament needed to break the stale hegemony of the Grand Coalition. I argued that we needed an open debate about the role of Parliament and its president in promoting democracy, human rights and the fight against climate change. I made the case for greater public debate with EU institutions, which needed to be more citizen-focussed and citizen-friendly. I knew that few, even among my own colleagues, believed I stood a real chance of success; but also that many shared my frustrations, saw in me a credible Liberal candidate and would be prepared to work for a change if the June 2009 European election result was propitious.

Only once had the two major groups failed to persuade their troops to follow their official agreement: in 1987, at the mid-term of the parliament, when Sir Henry Plumb, a UK Conservative, had defeated the pre-selected Spanish Socialist to become the only UK president yet. I took the view that whether or not I succeeded I could nonetheless use the campaign to highlight issues of importance to the future of the House. And I had decided some two years previously – and informed Liberal colleagues well in advance – that I would not seek to lead my group into the next parliament, thus avoiding the risk that a failure to obtain a good score would damage the standing of the ALDE group.

My candidature for the presidency of the European Parliament was hardly going to set the heather alight. Indeed, the UK press and electronic media reported it hardly at all. In other EU countries it was reported, in some with a moderate prominence. But I knew it would afford me sufficient oxygen of publicity to campaign for changes to Parliament's sometime arcane procedures and for sorely needed reforms in some areas of EU policy.

I was helped by the fact that as Parliament moved towards elections, Liberal influence was on display. The directives for which Liberals had fought hard were put to votes in the House just before the end of the mandate. On 2 April we saw the successful passage at first reading of the anti-discrimination directive and later that month in Strasbourg the same for the patients' rights directive. Thanks to the good work of my colleague Sarah Ludford we voted to prevent children under the age of twelve being fingerprinted for visa or immigration purposes[396].

---

396   In a cruel twist of fate, this would not apply to children in Sarah's own constituency since the UK government announced its intention to opt out of the measure, wanting to fingerprint children as young as six.

In another sign of Liberal strength, Parliament was to reject in May the draft package of telecoms legislation after 18 months of work because of disagreement over the right of member state authorities to deny internet access to citizens. Public authorities should be allowed to cut users' internet access, we argued, only after strict judicial procedures during which the user had the chance to defend themselves. In line with the European Convention for the Protection of Human Rights and Fundamental Freedoms, restrictions should only be imposed if appropriate, proportional and necessary; and adequate procedural safeguards had to be in place to ensure this.[397]

At the European Commission, too, Competition Commissioner Neelie Kroes was again taking on US giant Microsoft, threatening Microsoft with legal action for tying Internet Explorer to its Windows software, thus breaching competition law. Humanitarian Aid Commissioner Louis Michel was active in securing support for the rebuilding of public infrastructure in the Gaza Strip.

All this was in stark contrast to the absence of initiatives from the Socialist or EPP camps. Within the PES the major delegations were in disarray: many of the Spaniards preferred an arrangement with the Liberals to another agreement with the EPP; disunity in the French Socialist ranks was put on public display in the acerbic farewell speech delivered by prominent leader Michel Rocard, who left Parliament early in the year; UK Labour MEPs chose a new leader by a margin of ten votes to nine; and the Italians were still deep in debate about the location of their troops in the next parliament. When Schulz declined to attend the European Policy Centre's New Year debate with other political group leaders in February, sending one of his deputies instead, tongues started to wag about his unwillingness to enter the political fray. When shortly thereafter former EP president and leading Spanish Socialist Josep Borrell publicly backed my bid for the presidency of the European Parliament, my position as a leading challenger was considerably strengthened. As Liberals in my own constituency, traditionally strong only in the rural areas, took control of Bristol City Council from Labour in February, I felt I was riding the top of a wave.

In the EPP camp there was little consensus and even less enthusiasm. Buzek stayed in the background; Mauro tried to move to the centre. When the EPP group presidency met on 19 February 2009 for an orientation debate with regard to renewal of Parliament and Commission after the elections we knew there would be some who would speak out in favour of an arrangement with the Liberals. Key to the decision would be the attitude of the German Christian Democrats – would they stick by their SPD coalition partners or switch their affections to us in the belief that the government to emerge from the German elections in September would be black-gold rather than black-red?[398]

Though in all likelihood the two big groups would again seek a deal on the presidency of Parliament, the mood in the Liberal camp was buoyant. And as

---

397   The member states backed down and the telecoms package was agreed in the autumn.

398   Black was the colour of the Christian Democrats, gold that of the Liberals, red that of the socialists.

I briefed Guy Verhofstadt early in March about developments in the EP and the conditions I would place on any leadership contest to succeed me, I left him in no doubt that my contest for the EP presidency was in earnest.

In addition to wooing EPP MEPs I spent some time cultivating their parties at national level too. In the space of the previous fourteen months I had visited most national capitals and met nine EPP prime ministers and two EPP opposition party leaders. I had also met five PES prime ministers. With Liberals in government in Sweden, the country which would hold the presidency at the crucial moment, I remained in regular contact with EU Affairs Minister Cecilia Malmstrom. I had also kept close links with Jose Manuel Barroso at the European Commission, who led a centre-right administration there and could be expected (though he strenuously denied it) to be influential in internal party debates about the 2009-14 arrangements. We could not predict the outcome of the European elections with any certainty, but it seemed highly likely that the EPP would again be by far the largest party and that the Socialists would lose even more ground. Indeed, I began to brief journalists about a power relationship between the three major groups which was in a ratio of 3-2-1 rather than the traditionally assumed 2-2-1.

The EPP was worried, however, about the impact of the likely loss from its ranks of the British Conservative MEPs, who sought to create a new Conservative group along with some Czechs and Poles. Although when this was formally announced in March it was met by some EPP MEPs with sighs of relief[399] – since the Tories had been difficult partners over recent years and some despaired of the UK's likely approach to the EU in the event of their return to government in London – most feared the loss of influence it would give their group in Parliament. The 27 British Conservatives formed an important component of the EPP's total strength and its leading position might be jeopardised by their loss.

These and other considerations combined to complicate the internal politics of the EPP group. The German Christian Democrats and their German Socialist counterparts clearly wished to form a coalition to divide the presidency of Parliament in the 2009-14 mandate[400], putting 'their man', former Polish prime minister Jerzy Buzek, in office first and ensuring the election of a German (albeit Socialist) candidate in the second half. But they had not yet convinced all other national delegations. Unable to choose between the Polish candidate favoured by the Germans and Mario Mauro, an Italian vice president of Parliament, promoted by other delegations – and unwilling to risk a divisive public contest at their spring conference in Warsaw – they decided to delay their choice of candidate for Parliament's presidency until after the European

---

399   UK Labour prime minister Gordon Brown, addressing Parliament on 24 March 2009 about the preparation of April's G20 summit with a positive, pro-EU message, was far more to their liking than Conservative leader David Cameron; though even some Christian Democrats flinched at his opposition to the proposed working time directive, abhorring the long-hours culture and lack of security in the workplace which characterised the UK's labour market.

400   Since Germany had secured substantially more MEPs than any other country in the Treaty of Nice, German MEPs were dominant in Parliament through force of numbers.

elections. By chance I saw the two gentlemen concerned at a leaving reception for Parliament's outgoing secretary general[401]; they were standing at the front of the gathering, three feet apart, listening to the speeches and I was unable to resist the temptation to stride over, shake each vigorously by the hand and plant myself between them in front of two or three hundred onlookers.

The surprise announcement after the spring European Council by President Sarkozy that he was re-thinking his backing for Barroso to continue as Commission president (despite having given him blank cheque support at an EPP meeting prior to the European Council in December) added to the sense of unease in the European People's Party about a Union which they dominated numerically but which still lacked the legal basis to act decisively, pending decisions by Ireland, Poland and the Czech Republic, and the political will to move forward together at times of crisis.

My campaign set out to show that the EU was a success, though it appeared not to know it. It was celebrating ten years since having locked together the currencies of the core member states to create the euro, without which the financial crisis would almost certainly have blown the Union to smithereens. Its 2004 and 2007 enlargements, according to a study published in February by Commissioner Almunia, had benefited the economies of previous and newly joining member states alike, creating 3 million new jobs, adding 1.7% to economic growth in the new member states and improving economic competitiveness all round. And it had shown itself capable of mounting no fewer than 17 military missions around the world, including a 17-nation police mission in Afghanistan to train local police officers in law enforcement methods which showed respect for human rights, the human resources of which ministers agreed in February to double, from 200 to 400. As new US Secretary of State Hillary Clinton paid her first visit to Brussels in March 2009 she was the first occupant of her post to find a Union so well established; the visit of Obama the following month would be able to open a new chapter in US-EU relations.

Liberals celebrated the Union's achievements in this regard. In March my colleague Istvan Szent-Ivanyi MEP and I co-hosted a cross-party event to demonstrate the positive contribution made by twelve new member countries to the EU's development. The others appeared beset by doubts.

As I took my leading spokespeople to Stockholm to meet the incoming EU presidency (a government in which two Liberal parties were represented) we were keen to know how Sweden intended to deal with the climate crisis and the constitutional crisis. On the latter I took issue at the Liberal leaders' summit prior to the March European Council: I was deeply concerned that Sweden was acting as if Lisbon would be in place, when there were in fact still three countries to complete the process of ratification; and Irish prime minister Brian Cowen, attending his first ever Liberal prime ministers'

---

401   Dane Harald Roemer. In another sign of German influence, Roemer had been elbowed aside by former EPP group general secretary Klaus Welle, head of Poettering's cabinet: and in a surprising breach of etiquette Poettering was to speak more of Welle's virtues than of Roemer's at the latter's farewell reception.

event, confirmed that there was no certainty in either the date or the outcome of his country's second referendum[402].

With European elections due on 4-7 June, the parliament was drawing to
a close. Liberal fortunes looked mixed: in central and eastern Europe our
prospects looked slim, while in western Europe they seemed as good as ever
and in some cases better. The manifesto the Liberals had adopted in
Stockholm the previous autumn was shorter than previous such documents
and to the point. At the ELDR election rally in Brussels on 15 April I was
able to tell delegates: 'Things look good for Liberal Democrats. We have a
strong story to tell. We are the Zeitgeist for change ... between a Left uncomfortable with the market economy and a Right that remains suspicious of the
freedoms our young Europeans take for granted.'

The European People's Party was paralysed over its choice of candidate
for the presidency of the European Parliament; and the Party of European
Socialists, while attacking the president of the European Commission, could
find no candidate to put up against him.

As Parliament rose it was far from clear who would become the first full
time president of the European Council, should the Lisbon Treaty enter into
force, or who would succeed Javier Solana as high representative for foreign
and security policy. It was clear, however, that Jose Manuel Barroso would
be the nominee of the European Council to be the next president of the
European Commission. It looked highly likely too that the EPP candidate
would win the presidency of the European Parliament; President Poettering
told me in the margins of the 21 March European Council meeting that a
majority in the EPP group supported an agreement with the Socialists
whereby the EPP candidate would be elected in the first half of the mandate
and the Socialist candidate in the second half. While this news came as no
surprise, I detected considerable support for me from individuals and even
some national delegations in both Socialist and EPP groups and was sure I
could cause others some embarrassment by continuing my campaign.

Two candidates had emerged as possible successors to me. Diana Wallis,
a vice president of the European Parliament, had built up a good reputation
in the ALDE group and in the House and appeared to enjoy considerable
support. But so too did Guy Verhofstadt, the leader of his party's list for the
European elections and – as a former prime minister – a strong candidate.
As the outgoing leader I did not intervene in the process of choosing
between them; I took the view that after seven and a half years of my leadership and 18 months of knowledge of my intention to stand down, colleagues returning to Parliament after the elections would be well placed to
make up their own minds and to advise the newcomers accordingly. It
would be up to me to hold the ring at the first meeting of the delegation
leaders of the new group, but thereafter my job would be accomplished.

402   Cowen was to announce on 8 July 2009 that the referendum would be held on 2 October of that year.

Epilogue

This book ends, appropriately I believe, at the 2009 elections to the European Parliament. Though I oversaw the re-formation of the ALDE group after the elections and the procedure for the election of my successor as leader of the group, I did so essentially in a caretaker capacity.

The new group's bureau formally approved me as the Liberal candidate for the presidency of Parliament at its meeting in Bristol in June 2009. However the ALDE group found its numbers slightly reduced after the election. We could command a majority neither with the EPP nor with the Socialists without needing to add a third party to our coalition.

My subsequent decision not to pursue my challenge for the post was based upon the political situation in which we found ourselves as Parliament's political groups re-formed. For the first time ever, the EPP and PES groups together accounted for less than 62% of the membership of the House: the logic of the elephants' marriage that is convenient for securing an absolute majority of votes in co-decision procedures was greater than ever. Indeed, the numbers were such that my bid would have been credible only if it included an appeal to parts of the euro-sceptic right wing; my colleagues and I rightly preferred an alliance of the pro-EU forces in a parliament in which the political forces are more splintered than before.

Moreover, the Germans in both major groups were determined to unite and were more than a little keen to humiliate the new FDP MEPs for the aggressive and sometimes populist tone of their election campaigning.

I felt I had in any case made my point about the reforms Parliament needed, some of which have been taken up by President Jerzy Buzek.

Some have asked me why I stepped down from the leadership of the ALDE group. There is no one answer: my decision combined many considerations. I had enjoyed ten years in leading roles, first as chairman of a large committee and then as leader of my group. I had built and consolidated a stronger centre force than the European Parliament had ever previously known. I felt the moment had come to hand on the baton to a successor who could take it forward to new peaks of achievement. None of my predecessors had led the Liberal group for more than five years. When my colleagues re-elected me at the end of 2006 after five years as leader to serve a third two-and-a-half year term I decided that it was unlikely I would wish to serve more than seven and a half years in total. I enjoyed the buzz from high adrenalin levels but less so the way that being a centre of attention sometimes affected my own behaviour. My view remained settled thereafter and nothing has led me to regret my decision since.

Could I have stayed on to try my hand at the mid-term of the new parliament? Yes. At the time of my decision, in 2006, there was no obvious successor to me. But I sensed that I was too ideologically Liberal to secure the support of a broad range of MEPs to take on the Parliament's presidency. And I did not find the absence of a successor a convincing reason to remain in post as leader of my group. Had I stayed and succeeded, another five years would have rolled by. I believe the secret to a long life lies in knowing when it is time to go.

During my first 15 years in the European Parliament I had three major frustrations. The first was that the Parliament I joined in 1994 was used by political parties mainly as a rest home for those who had served careers in national politics or as a first step on the ladder for those who sought them.

My second was that in those 15 years an inordinate amount of time and energy was spent by MEPs, myself included, in achieving a treaty basis for the EU which would allow it to cope with the major supranational challenges it faces.

The image of the drawbridge serves to illustrate my third frustration (see Preface). That a significant number of MEPs on the left or the right still believed it desirable – until recently, at least – to have a 'drawbridge up' Europe strikes me as astonishing testimony to the difficulty of conquering ignorance.

All three frustrations have been substantially alleviated.

The 1994 Parliament was marked by an influx of younger politicians seeking to make a political career in the EU rather than in national politics, the 1999 and 2004 Parliaments even more so. Increasingly, Brussels has attracted a new breed of continental politician: young, polyglot, ambitious, inter-culturally sensitive; more diverse in gender and even (though to a pitifully small degree) racial origin.

With the Lisbon Treaty the EU has overcome the dissatisfaction with Maastricht, the disappointment with Amsterdam, the bathos of the Nice Treaty and the rout of the Treaty establishing a European Constitution. The EU can now get down to business on behalf of Europeans.

As I enter my fourth term in Parliament I see fewer who maintain that isolationism is a credible policy response for Europe. I look forward with hope to a future in which the European Parliament can play a more important role in a more outward-looking EU.

I hope still to contribute to the task of building Liberal strength across the continent of Europe and beyond. I believe there is much to play for. The European People's Party is an inherently unstable coalition, the European Socialists a party in terminal decline. The opportunity for a stronger centre is immense. If the parties which joined forces with the ELDR to form the Alliance have remained in the new European Democratic Party it is of course partly from choice; but it is also in part because the ELDR Party has not sought to embrace them in a spirit of pluralism which might have allowed the creation of a new ALDE political party. That course remains an option. Francois Bayrou's remark to me in June 2007 that his party would one day join the ELDR Party reflects, I believe, a recognition that the UDF strand of political thought in France belongs firmly in the European Liberal family, however vilified has become the epithet 'Liberal' in France.

Looking back at the events covered in this book from a distance of some nine months since their end I am struck already by how the origins of subsequent developments can be traced to what was achieved during the period covered and by how perspective changes with every new day. Inevitably, given more time, I could have written a more fully considered and comprehensive account. But writing about politics, as involvement in politics, is the art of the possible. I hope to have made a useful contribution to understanding of the period covered and of the unique and valuable contribution of Liberals and Liberalism to it.

Brussels and Langport, March 2010.

INDEX